MEDIAEVAL GREECE

MEDIAEVAL GREECE

Nicolas Cheetham

Yale University Press
New Haven and London
1981

Set in Monophoto Times by Thomson Press (India) Ltd., New Delhi.
**Printed in the United States of America by
Vail-Ballou Press, Binghamton, N.Y.**

Published in Great Britain, Europe, Africa, and
Asia (except Japan) by Yale University Press,
Ltd., London. Distributed in Australia and
New Zealand by Book & Film Services, Artarmon,
N.S.W., Australia; and in Japan by Harper & Row,
Publishers, Tokyo Office.

Library of Congress Cataloging in Publication Data

Cheetham, Nicolas, Sir, 1910-
  Mediaeval Greece
  Bibliography: p.
  Includes index.
    1. Greece, Medieval—History. I. Title.
DF552.C48   949.5   80-13559
ISBN 0-300-02421-5

LIST OF CONTENTS

MAPS

INTRODUCTION

'I shall not pursue the obscure and various dynasties that rose or fell on the continent or in the isles.'

Edward Gibbon

'The hurried traveller in quest of the antique will hardly pause to note these interesting survivals.'

Rennell Rodd

UNTIL FAIRLY RECENT times Greek history meant the history of classical Greece from its Homeric dawn down to the death of Alexander the Great. The Mycenaean legacy was either undiscovered or misunderstood. The Hellenistic era, with its fabulous record of expansion to the Oxus and the Ganges, was studied by scholars but found too complicated and indigestible by the general reader. The Roman period was deplored as one of exhaustion and decadence. The Byzantine centuries, the province of brilliant specialists from the seventeenth century onwards, were long viewed by the uninterested through Gibbonian spectacles. So indeed was the Frankish interlude, concerning which the great historian uttered his supremely dismissive judgement.

When Greece shook off the unmentionable—and largely unstudied— Turkish domination Philhellenism came into its own. Patronized by Byron, its liberation assured by Codrington, rewarded by Gladstone with the gift of the Ionian islands, Greece basked in Victorian favour. Nevertheless its inhabitants were regarded with vague suspicion in academic circles, especially as their connexion with antiquity was not thought quite genuine. They were, in Robert Byron's words, 'discounted as the unmoral refuse of mediaeval Slav migrations, sullying the land of their birth with the fury of their politics and the malformation of their small brown bodies'. As late as 1924, when my father was appointed British Minister at Athens, the classical master at my school commiserated with me, with a curl of his clerical lip, on the prospect of my having to consort on my holidays with what he called 'those nasty little Slavs'.

So much for the Greeks of the Middle Ages and of now. As for the Franks, that most fervent Philhellene and pro-Byzantine writer, Patrick

Leigh Fermor, confesses that he has 'always instinctively hated Frankish ruins in the Greek world'. He is not attracted by 'the distant echoes of horns and Burgundian hounds along the ravines of Achaia'.[1] For my part I respectfully disagree. I like Frankish battlements in the landscape and the Burgundian horns and hounds are just as fascinating for me as those of the old soldier Xenophon, who hunted along the same ravines, and as those of any intervening Byzantine huntsman. My own sympathies are with the eminent late Victorian Rennell Rodd, poet, diplomatist and chronicler, for whom the story of Greece in the Middle Ages is 'a thrilling chapter of romance, unrivalled in the interest of its setting'.[2]

We have now, I hope, all learned to consider Greek history as a whole and not as a string of disconnected periods. Thus the Mycenaean merges into the Classical, the Classical into the Byzantine, the Byzantine into the Frankish and so on, without any loss of continuity. My excuse for embarking on the present study of the age when Greece was ruled by princes from the West is primarily that no work of this kind has been published in English since Rodd's *The Princes of Achaia and the Chronicles of Morea* (1907) and William Miller's admirable but minutely detailed *The Latins in the Levant* (1908). Since then, although a vast amount of scholarship has been devoted to the feudal age, little of this erudition has filtered down to the general educated public. For most people the Greek Middle Ages are a blank. This book seeks to fill the gap and present the main features of the story without entangling the reader in a too fearsome labyrinth of names, dates and events. To a certain extent the very strangeness of the subject invites exactly that risk, and I can only apologise if the reader feels stuck like an armoured Frankish knight in the marshes of the Kephissos. I have thought it necessary to begin with two chapters giving a broad sketch of what happened in Greece during the eight hundred obscure years preceding the advent of the Franks. Without it many of the succeeding episodes would seem to have no meaning.

My second concern has been to throw light wherever possible on the human and cultural relationship that developed between the Greeks and their conquerors. Any encounter between peoples with deeply rooted and obstinately conflicting traditions is bound to be an enthralling subject of study. In this particular case, when the two groups confronting one another were both European and shared so largely in the same heritage, it is instructive, if depressing, to observe how hard it was for them to achieve any significant degree of understanding and cultural fusion, even when they faced the same menace from the alien Orient.

I- GREECE & THE AEGEAN

SERBIA

Nikopolis

Tirnovo

BULGARIA

Varna

BLACK SEA

Sofia (Serdica)

Philippopolis

Klokotnitza

Adrianople

Skoplje (Scupi)

MACEDONIA

Didymoteichos

THRACE

Constantinople

Dyrrhachium (Durazzo)

Ochrida

Pelagonia

Edessa

Christoupolis

Rodosto

SEA OF MARMORA

Kastoria

Thessalonica

THASOS

SAMOTHRACE

Gallipoli

Berat

Athos Mountain

YMBROS

Lampsacus

Cyzicus

Brusa

Valona

THESSALY

LEMNOS

Butrinto

Joannina

Kassandreia

ASIA

CORFU

EPIROS

Larissa

LESBOS

Arta

AEGEAN SEA

Pergamon

MINOR

LEVKAS

Neopatras

EUBOEA

CHIOS

Phocaea

Magnesia

CEPHALONIA

BOEOTIA ATTICA

Thebes

Smyrna

Nymphaion

Patras

Athens

ANDROS

SAMOS

Ephesos

Andravida

ACHAIA

Corinth

KEOS

TENOS

IKARIA

Philadelphia

ZANTE

MOREA

Nauplia

SYRA

MYKONOS

Chonae

IONIAN SEA

KYTHNOS

SERIPHOS

PAROS

NAXOS

KOS

Bodrum

MESSENIA

LAKONIA

Mistra

SIPHNOS

AMORGOS

Modon

Monemvasia

MELOS

Ios

ASTYPALAIA

RHODES

Coron

SANTORIN

ANAPHI

KYTHERA

KARPATHOS

Canea

Rethimnon

Candia

KASOS

White Mountains

Mt Ida

Seteia

CRETE

| 0 | 50 | 100 miles |
| 0 | 50 | 100 | 150 km |

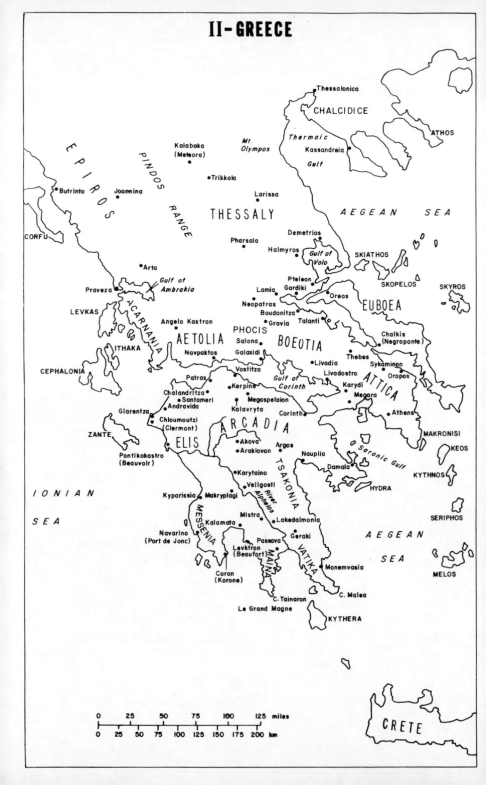

II-GREECE

CHAPTER ONE

The Death of Ancient Hellas

Classical Twilight

IN THE YEAR A.D. 400 the greater part of the country we now call Greece was contained within the third-class province of Achaia, a territory belonging to the eastern half of the Roman Empire. The latter's ruler, the Emperor Arcadius, held court at Constantinople. His brother, Honorius, ruled the Western half from Rome or Milan, but was soon to take refuge from his troubles behind the marshes of Ravenna. Their father, Theodosius the Great, had been dead for five years. He had been a Spaniard of enormous ability and fiery spirit. Unfortunately for the Empire as a whole he failed to pass on his talents or his temperament to the sons between whom he divided his vast dominions.

The governor, or proconsul, of Achaia was not a very important official. In the complicated administrative structure of the Empire his province formally ranked as part of the 'diocese' of Macedonia, which was governed by a higher dignitary known as a *vicarius*. The latter was in turn subordinate to a much greater hierarch, the praetorian prefect of Illyricum, who was in effect the civil governor-general of the Balkans. But although Achaia fell within the geographical area of the Illyrian prefecture, it was for administrative purposes treated as independent of both diocese and prefecture, and its proconsul was directly responsible to the Emperor and his ministers at Constantinople.

Certainly this illogical and rather un-Roman arrangement derived from the legendary and historical glamour with which the name of Achaia was still invested in the fading Roman world of the fifth century. There may also have been reasons of state for keeping the Greek-speaking and maritime Achaia separate from the continental and mainly Latin-speaking Illyricum. More potent, however, was the influence of tradition and its link with the Hellenic past in preserving for this poor and unimportant province a special position in the eastern half of the Empire.

Although, as a result of the triumph of Christianity in the preceding century, Hellenism was becoming suspect as synonymous with an unfashionable if not treasonable adherence to paganism, eastern Rome was at the same time profoundly conscious of the Hellenic sources of its

1

culture and ready to treat the survivals of Hellenism in the little Greek homeland with toleration and respect. For the governing class, steeped in classical literature and pagan reminiscence, Achaia meant the land of Homer's Achaians, the land of Achilles and Agamemnon. To the more historically minded it might recall the Achaian League of Greek cities which in the gloomy period after the death of Alexander the Great had struggled to maintain Greek independence against Macedon and ultimately Rome. The original district of Achaia, after which the Roman government had named the province, was strictly speaking confined to the narrow plain along the north coast of the Peloponnese, but the vitality of the name was so emotive and persistent that when the French conquerors took possession of the Peloponnese in the high Middle Ages they found it natural to give their feudal overlord the title of Prince of Achaia. While the Prince might himself not have understood it, a connexion, tenuous but tenacious, existed between his barons and the chiefs whom Agamemnon had led to Troy.

Achaia, then, was a backwater, and moreover one in which nothing had stirred for four hundred years, since the time of Augustus. History, in the sense of great events and radical changes, had passed it by. The people had remained attached to its ancient beliefs and habits, and spoke the same Greek language with little modification. The country had basked from century to century in a mellow pastoral calm, frequented only, so far as the outside world was concerned, by tourists and antiquarians, and by students attending the schools of philosophy and rhetoric at Athens which flourished without a break throughout the Roman domination. Christianity was penetrating slowly and super-ficially into the rural recesses and had by no means supplanted the doctrines of the schools. It is true that Theodosius had recently put an end to such hoary institutions of the ancient world as the Olympic Games, which had been held every four years since 776 B.C., and the few surviving oracles, but he sensibly forbore from upsetting the University.

Nevertheless, all over the Mediterranean world, the temples of the old gods were being forcibly closed by the authorities or simply deserted by their worshippers, and Greece offered no exception. In the course of the fifth century, though we do not know exactly when, the Parthenon at Athens, the temple of the Virgin Goddess Athena, was converted into the shrine of the Virgin Mother of God, while St George moved into the temple of Hephaestus (the so-called 'Theseion'). As an official religion paganism was abolished, but peasants and shepherds continued ob-stinately to observe their own local cults, while the Athenian professors, who were also given to celebrating on the sly the almost forgotten rites of ancient religions, taught Neoplatonism undisturbed by government or Church. Proclus, the last great pagan philosopher, who died in 485, was allowed to propound to generations of pupils what J.B. Bury, in his *History of the Later Roman Empire*, described as 'a thoroughly articulated system that bears a distinct resemblance in its method to Hegel's logic'.[1] It was left to the Emperor Justinian to dissolve the schools and confiscate their endowments. This occurred in 529, when the seven remaining academics were expelled from Athens. In their indignation, and in the hope of meeting a sympathetic reception outside the Roman Empire, they made their way to the court of Persia, only to return in equal disillusionment after a few years' stay.

Four centuries of gradual though not ungraceful decay are indeed a long span of time when measured by the dynamic standards to which Europe has become accustomed since the Renaissance. But in Hellas, the very heart of the ancient world, the processes of internal change were so slow as to be almost imperceptible by contemporaries, while we, for our part, are struck by the extraordinarily static conditions which prevailed throughout the period. Not only was Hellas poor, depopulated and secluded from the main course of history, but it failed to produce anything like a normal quota of eminent men. It is as if the country was deserted by the spirit of endeavour. We look in vain for Emperors, statesmen or soldiers, poets or artists born in Greece proper. Although the Greek-speaking world as a whole continued to be a reservoir of talent, this almost invariably originated in Asia Minor, Syria or Egypt, and not in the impoverished homeland of the race. It was not that Rome, even in the days of her decline, had ceased to offer opportunities to her citizens from every corner of the empire, but as time went by these were increasingly grasped either by quick-witted orientals or, at the other extreme, by the rougher products of the frontier provinces.

The root cause of national exhaustion in Greece was the lack of sufficient population to sustain a proper level of political, social and economic vitality. In high Classical times the country had been thickly, indeed too thickly, peopled. It teemed with walled townlets contending fiercely with each other for the possession of precious agricultural land: the same olive groves and strips of cornland changed hands interminably in bloody conflicts and the needs of the larger cities, and particularly of Athens, had to be satisfied by imports of wheat from the South Russian steppes. The process of depopulation began when the conquests of Alexander the Great opened up the whole of the Middle East to Greek enterprise. In the wake of the Macedonian armies Greek colonists poured into the derelict Persian Empire, not only reinforcing the Greek communities which had already been established in Asia Minor for half a millennium but spreading out as far as the Persian Gulf and the Oxus, while in the second century B.C. the Greek kings of Bactria invaded North India and planted outposts of Hellenism in the Punjab.

This massive emigration drained away the most energetic elements among the population. Nor was it counter-balanced by a corresponding immigration of non-Hellenes, who might have filled the gaps and stimulated the energies of the Greeks who remained at home. Meanwhile the country suffered grievously in the wars waged by the Roman Republic on its soil against Macedon and the Asiatic dynast Mithridates, as well as in the Roman civil wars. Any Greek city or league of cities taking the wrong side in these conflicts was mercilessly punished; thus Corinth was destroyed by Mummius and Athens plundered by Sulla. When peace and security had at last been restored by Augustus, it was too late to bring about a real revival.

Nevertheless some Roman rulers worked hard to repair the damage. Julius Caesar refounded Corinth with Roman colonists and Augustus did the same for Patras and for Nikopolis in Epiros. Subsequent emperors lavished immunities and benefactions on the Greeks and liked to be seen patronizing them. When Nero paid his well-advertised visit to Greece in A.D. 67 he appeared at the Olympic and other principal festivals and performed in the artistic events before packed audiences, predictably with brilliant success. He made an abortive attempt to cut a canal through the Isthmus of Corinth and crowned his tour with a resounding but meaningless proclamation of 'Freedom for Greece'. The Greeks, who had heard that sort of thing before from republican generals, were not impressed, but Nero's gestures and buffooneries did them no harm, and may conceivably have gained them some advantage.

A more serious imperial visitor was Hadrian, who spent the winter of A.D. 125–6 at Athens. Although the city had never lost its attraction for students and sightseers, the Emperor, the most ardent of Philhellenes, was distressed by its shabbiness. He decided that it must be cleaned up, its monuments renovated and its revenues increased. He launched a grand programme of public works and started to build a whole new quarter centring on the enormous temple of Olympian Zeus. This had been founded as long ago as the sixth century B.C. by the Athenian tyrant Peisistratus. Re-planned and greatly enlarged in the second century by another Philhellene, King Antiochus IV of Syria, it had never been finished. Hadrian completed it, and further embellished both the old city and the new Athens of his own creation with numerous buildings on the same imposing scale. Other cities, especially in the Peloponnese, were similarly rehabilitated and adorned with new temples, theatres, market places, gymnasia, aqueducts and public baths. Three years later he spent another winter at Athens, supervising the progress of the work. In order to flatter Greek self-esteem he set up a Panhellenic Council with himself as president, but, like Nero's declaration of freedom, this amounted to a ceremonial gesture devoid of political significance.

The Emperor's munificence gave a lead to private benefactors. Prominent among them was Herodes Atticus, an Athenian from Marathon and one of the few non-Asiatic Greeks of his age to rise above mediocrity. Vastly rich, he was also a distinguished man of letters and a generous patron. His endowments included a great concert hall on the slopes of the Athenian Acropolis, the ruins of which still serve its original purpose, and the reconstruction in Pentelic marble of the Panathenaic stadium. But all Hellas benefited from the outburst of public-spirited spending and refurbishing which characterized the Antonine age throughout the Empire.

Behind this brave facade, however, the picture of gentle stagnation had not changed. There was no widespread economic or demographic recovery, although material conditions had much improved since the days of Augustus. The persistent depopulation is frequently commented on and deplored by writers of the first and second centuries A.D. Plutarch of Chaeronea, the last great Greek-born writer of classical times, who held office in the Roman administration, asserts that the entire country was hardly capable of putting three thousand infantry into the field. That might have been a rhetorical exaggeration; but Plutarch's remarks about the sadly deserted state of his native Boeotia are fully borne out by the evidence of his Asiatic Greek contemporary Dio Chrysostom, 'the Golden Mouthed', a picturesque character who after gaining a high reputation as orator and philosopher was expelled from Rome for political indiscretions and spent his time wandering through Greece and Asia until he was forgiven. He tells of abandoned cities where sheep grazed and corn grew among tumbledown colonnades and crumbling public edifices. And his impressionistic account is in turn corroborated by the assiduous traveller Pausanias (yet another Asiatic), who compiled his invaluable guide-book, the *Description of Greece*, during the reigns of Hadrian's successors Antoninus Pius and Marcus Aurelius.

While Pausanias was primarily interested in antiquities rather than in day-to-day matters, what he says about the condition of Greece is revealing enough. He duly lists the empty or decaying cities, such as Megalopolis in Arkadia and Panopeus in Phokis, the ruined shrines, the grass-grown market places and the stretches of abandoned countryside, for the land was largely worked not by free smallholders but by slave-gangs on great estates belonging to capitalists of the type of Herodes Atticus. But while the glimpses which he affords of the life and ways of the people inevitably suggest a rundown culture and economy, they by no means add up to a picture of unrelieved gloom. On the contrary, they tend to prove that the long afterglow of Hellenic civilization diffused an uncanny delight and the slow, sleepy rhythm of provincial life an irresistible charm.

It is important not to overemphasize the somnolence and apathy. By contrast with scenes of desolation Pausanias also mentions lively little cities with fine buildings and civic amenities. Corinth and Patras were bustling commercial centres. As for Athens, Delphi and Olympia, they were huge museums of art and architecture. Although the Romans had stripped Greece of thousands of bronze and marble statues, thousands more remained for the tourists to admire, and the more persevering among them could still discover the most breathtaking antiquities in scores of smaller places. The cultured and nostalgic travellers for whom Pausanias wrote, if they could put up with bad roads and uncomfortable inns (like travellers in Greece fifty years ago), might look forward to an unexampled feast of artistic beauty and historical associations.

An additional attraction was that time in many places seemed to stand still. Visitors from overseas Greece and other parts of the Roman Empire could, if they wished, consult ancient oracles and seek initiation into the Eleusinian mysteries. It was fascinating for them to browse among the trophies of the Persian wars and the marvellous works of art surviving from the Periclean age. It was equally intriguing to watch the citizens of the small provincial towns minutely observing the ways of their ancestors, electing the same magistrates, clinging to out-of-date constitutional forms carefully preserved within the limited authority allowed them by Rome, and celebrating ceremonies of which the exact significance had long become obscured. An exaggerated sense of tradition gave rise to absurdities and enormities, two examples of which are worth citing. The first, from Tacitus, describes how the Spartans and their neighbours the Messenians were still nursing, and submitting to Roman arbitration, a quarrel about boundaries which had originally driven them to war in the eighth century B.C. In the second Plutarch rather casually mentions that he himself had witnessed Spartan boys being whipped to death at the altar of the goddess Artemis Orthia in a religious ceremony which may have started as a fertility rite in the dark ages but had degenerated into a cruel and meaningless test of endurance and an exciting spectacle for curious onlookers.[2]

Further, for those with an antiquarian bent, there was displayed an astonishing wealth of relics from a remoter past, from the world of Homer and an even earlier, primitive era which had left a weird legacy of queer rituals and fossilized folklore. A rich collection of these survivals is listed in Sir James Frazer's introduction to his commentary on Pausanias, such as

> the thirty square stones revered as gods at Pharae . . . the pyramidal stone which represented Apollo at Megara; the ancient wooden image of Zeus with three eyes on the acropolis of Argos; the old idol of Demeter as a woman with a horse's head holding a dove in one hand and a dolphin in the other . . . holy men staggering along narrow paths under the burden of uprooted trees . . . husbandmen sticking gold leaf on a bronze goat in the marketplace to protect their vines from blight . . . the priest making rain by dipping an oak branch in the spring on the holy mountain . . . the great bonfire on the top of Mount Cithaeron where the many images of oak wood, arrayed as brides, are being consumed in the flames, after having been dragged in lumbering, creaking waggons to the top of the mountain, each image with a bridesmaid standing by its side[3]

In the Augustan and Antonine periods life was neither disagreeable nor dangerous for the majority of Greeks, and their freedom from war and political discord amply compensated them for the lack of excitement. The Roman shield, represented by the legions on the Danube, protected them from barbarian incursions. But even before Pausanias had finished writing his *Description*, an ominous incident disturbed the atmosphere of absolute security which Hellas had so long enjoyed. By some chance a raiding band from an obscure Germanic tribe called the Costobocs (it would be hard to invent a name more suggestive of crude barbarism) slipped through the barrier, made its way downward through the Balkans without being intercepted and appeared unexpectedly just south of the pass of Thermopylae. Once it had eluded the legions there was no local militia to protect the provincials, but fortunately, as Pausanias records, Mnesibulus, a private citizen of Elatea, raised a force on his own initiative and, at the cost of his own life, succeeded in crushing the barbarians.[4]

At the time this disturbance was an exceptional phenomenon, but the Germanic peoples, whether in migratory hordes or small war bands bent on plunder, were always hovering and probing, and in the next century they flooded across the frontiers. So far as Greece was concerned, it was the Goths who put an end to its long immunity from external threats. By 240 they were already raiding, and their attacks came from the sea, for while maintaining pressure on the Danube they also managed to outflank the Roman defence line. They were able to do this because their migrations had brought them gradually from their original homeland in south Sweden as far as the Ukraine and they had settled in strength on the Black Sea. They soon adapted themselves to seafaring and did not take long to discover that there were plenty of rich and undefended cities to be sacked in Asia Minor, where they committed fearful ravages. Then, sailing through the Bosporus and Dardanelles, they descended on the coastal towns of the Aegean. After they had unsuccessfully besieged Thessalonica in 253, the Emperor Valerian hurriedly called on the Greeks to raise forces and repair their long-neglected city walls.[5]

Throughout the fifties and sixties, with the Empire grappling desperately not only with several barbarian nations in Europe, but with the Persians in Asia and frequent internal revolts as well, Gothic pirates frequently rampaged in the Aegean area. Pillage, not settlement, was their object, but it was pillage on the grand scale and Greece, though a poor province, was still worth looting. Their final and most destructive assault was made in 267, when Argos and Corinth were taken and plundered, as were Piraeus and Athens. In the latter case the barbarians broke through the city walls and caused widespread destruction. Excavation has revealed that although the Acropolis was unharmed, the region of the ancient Agora with all its monuments was burned and left in ruins, the debris of which were used for the hurried construction of a new inner wall around the Acropolis and a small adjoining area. As the Goths were retiring, the Mnesibulus episode of the preceding century apparently repeated itself. The Greek hero on the second occasion was an Athenian historian of some distinction named Dexippus, who subsequently published an account of the Romano-Gothic wars. Assembling a force of two thousand men, he effectively harassed the Goths until the imperial fleet came up and chased them away.[6]

In the years that followed the Gothic menace petered out as successive Emperors crushed their armies in the Balkans and the Aegean was swept clear of their piratical fleets. Hellas settled down to another century of humdrum peace. When Constantine the Great founded Constantinople in 324, the Greeks were forced to submit to a further levy on their artistic treasures for the embellishment of his new capital. They tended, however, to benefit from the short-lived revival of paganism under

Julian 'the Apostate' (360–3). This Emperor, who had previously studied at the university of Athens (where he had as his fellow pupil St Basil, the future father of the Church and founder of Eastern monasticism), encountered much sympathy in old Greece for his forlorn attempt to put the clock back. But after his death in battle against the Persians the slow but inexorable pressure in favour of Christianity was resumed. As has already been mentioned, Theodosius I (379–95), dealt sternly and unsentimentally with the obstinate pagan rearguard. He did not, however, uproot the schools of philosophy. Indeed professors and students abounded in the Athens of the fourth and fifth centuries, and shortly after 400 much rebuilding was carried out in the previously devastated Agora.[7]

So long as he lived Greece was kept safe from a formidable resurgence of the Gothic threat which was on the point of overwhelming the whole hinterland of Constantinople. Since the repulse of their first onrush of the third century, the Goths had evolved very rapidly under the influence of their continuous contacts, both hostile and friendly, with the Empire. Constantine again defeated them, with the result that for the next thirty-five years a more or less peaceful relationship was maintained on and over the frontiers and the Goths were increasingly exposed to the material and social lures of a superior civilization. Numbers of them, along with Germans from other tribes, served in the Roman army and were settled as colonists in Roman territory. Many of their officers, men of considerable culture as well as of talent, achieved high rank : they had polish, presence and charm. Outside the Empire the nation was divided into two groups, the West Goths (Visigoths) who occupied the country roughly corresponding to modern Romania, and the East Goths (Ostrogoths) who lived in South Russia and were united under a strong monarch named Hermanric. Moreover they had recently been converted to Christianity and possessed their own Church and bishops. They had chosen the Arian, as opposed to the Catholic, form of Christianity, but that was not considered strange at a time when Arians and Catholics were contending for supremacy within the Empire, and some Emperors preferred Arianism. In short, the Goths were no longer the unregenerate barbarians whose savagery had caused such horror in the previous century. Nevertheless they were a dour and harsh people, prone to violence when it suited them and always greedy for loot.

The famous Alaric, whose army of Visigoths was to loot Rome in 410, had been a Roman officer under Theodosius, and at the time of his best known exploit he was still technically a Roman general, no less than the *Magister Militum per Illyricum*, or Commander-in-Chief in the Balkans.

The chain of events which set him straying outside the bounds of his command began in the Russian steppes with the break-up of the Ostrogothic realm and the westward migration of both branches of the Gothic people under the onslaught of the ferocious nomadic Huns. In 376 the Visigoths asked the Roman government for permission to cross the Danube and take refuge in the province of Moesia (now northern Bulgaria), where they hoped to settle as allies of Rome under imperial suzerainty. After some hesitation over admitting so coherent and powerful a group, the Emperor Valens agreed to their request, but it was not long before Roman tactlessness and Gothic arrogance caused a breach. The Goths took up arms and Valens hurried to quell them, but in the ensuing battle near Adrianople the field army of the eastern part of the Empire was virtually wiped out and the Emperor himself was killed.

The catastrophe was thoroughly unexpected. By this time the dying ancient world had become inured to barbarian incursions, but experience had so far taught that despite temporary Roman setbacks the barbarians must invariably be defeated with immense slaughter. Nobody dreamed that the Empire was doomed to dismemberment and society to disintegration. Now, suddenly, the army of the East had vanished and the Goths were masters of whole provinces. At this moment of crisis Gratian, the Emperor in the West, raised the Spanish general Theodosius to be his fellow Augustus with the task of repairing the disaster as best he could. In the event Theodosius managed to fend off the Goths by an adroit mixture of military skill and diplomacy. Fortunately they were seeking security within the Empire rather than outright and extensive conquest and were disposed to come to terms. But the price which the Empire paid was the Germanization, and consequently the basic unreliability, of its army as more and more Germans took service in it, and at the end of the century its three leading commanders, Gainas, Stilicho and Alaric, were all Germans. In the wars of that chaotic period it was generally barbarians who were fighting other barbarians.

The chaos started after Theodosius's death in 395 and Greece was its first victim, with Alaric as its instrument. The Gothic leader, who had been serving under Theodosius in the West, had recently brought the contingents of his countrymen back to their homes in Moesia. For reasons which are obscure he proceeded to fall out with Rufinus, a native of Bordeaux who was Praetorian Prefect of the East and chief minister of the new Emperor, Arcadius. Presumably he thought that he and his Goths had not been suitably recompensed for their services. In any case he decided to blackmail the government by launching a campaign of terror and pillage of the kind at which the Goths were adept. He first advanced towards Constantinople, but on failing to obtain satisfaction marched through Macedonia and descended upon Greece, plundering all the way. On reaching Thessaly he was confronted with the Vandal Stilicho, the co-Emperor Honorius's Commander-in-Chief in Italy, but in the event no clash took place, as the two rival German generals temporarily composed their differences.

Greece therefore lay at Alaric's mercy. The proconsul of Achaia, Antiochus, offered no resistance, but the Goths were repulsed from the walls of Thebes. Athens, on the other hand, surrendered and was spared the worst, while Alaric was wined and dined in the city.[8] The legend propagated by Byzantine historians of the fifth century who still sympathized with paganism was that he was scared by a vision of Athena standing on the walls of the Acropolis, or alternatively impressed by the sight of Pheidias's great bronze statue of the goddess with shield and spear. More probably he judged that the citadel was too strong to be assaulted, and accepted a heavy bribe. But the temple of mysteries at Eleusis was destroyed before the Goths moved on to the Peloponnese.

We cannot be sure how much damage they inflicted; but when allowance has been made for the rhetorical exaggerations of contemporary writers, and for the fact that the Goths' main purpose was exaction and not destruction, it was certainly very considerable. But it is unlikely that they would have spent their time wrecking antique monuments for the sheer joy of it: we know that the temple of Zeus at Olympia was still standing in the reign of Theodosius II (408–50), when it was burnt out by accident.[9] There would have been no point in trying to demolish marble temples once they had yielded up their loot, and it is indeed remarkable that enough wealth remained in them to make them worth looting. It was earthquakes, rather than any human agency, that eventually overthrew the neglected, pillaged and sometimes fire-scarred shrines.

While the Goths were still gathering their booty, Stilicho intervened for the second time. He personally led an army into the Peloponnese and pinned down Alaric in the uplands of Arkadia. But instead of coming to grips with the Goths, he again preferred to parley and ended by allowing them to leave Greece unhindered with all their booty. The fifth-century historian Zosimus attributes his inaction to a bout of debauchery with prostitutes, a distraction hardly available, one would think, in the Arkadian mountains. Bury, however, convincingly suggests that what really emerged from the second confrontation between the two warlords was a political deal by which Alaric agreed to support Stilicho's aim to secure imperial rank for his son Eucherius. Whatever the nature of their arrangement, the price paid by the Roman government for the cessation of Alaric's ravages was his appointment as *Magister Militum per Illyricum*. A few years later he transferred his attentions to Italy and Greece was no more troubled by the Goths.[10]

Since the ancient culture of Hellas took so long to die, no conveniently exact date can be fixed by which it may be regarded as extinct. The Delphic oracle uttered its celebrated epitaph in the reign of Julian the Apostate when, in response to an enquiry from the Emperor, the Pythia or prophetess declared, 'Tell the King that the splendid hall has fallen to the ground. Apollo no longer has his dwelling, nor his prophetic laurel, nor his babbling spring; the water of inspiration has ceased to flow.' The answer may have reflected a genuine world-weariness and despair, or, as it has been cynically suggested, the priests may have been bribed by the Christians to damp down the Emperor's pagan enthusiasm. But the classical pulse was still beating, throughout the fifth century, and if it is absolutely necessary to name a date for its ceasing to beat, that of Justinian's closure of the University of Athens (529) would do as well as any. A sure sign of Christianity's advance during the period was the increase of church building in the Greek cities, as is attested not only by the discovery of fragmentary remains and foundations, but by the survival of a whole group of churches at Thessalonica with some of their contemporary mosaics.

Meanwhile, at Constantinople, the Emperor Theodosius II, grandson of the great soldier, chose to marry a girl from Athens, famous for her learning and beauty. She was Athenais, daughter of the pagan philosopher Leontius, and the event caused a sensation at the time. It was also symbolic, for Athenais was required, on becoming Empress, to renounce paganism and to assume the less pagan-sounding name of Eudocia, and her conversion was followed by the foundation of a new, Christian university at Constantinople designed expressly to eclipse the Athenian academy. Immensely proud of her Hellenic ancestry and culture, Eudocia dominated her easy-going husband for many years, but when she fell from favour as the result of an affair, or a suspected affair, with one of the Emperor's chief ministers, it was to Jerusalem, and not to the Athens of her youth, that she preferred to retire.[11]

Justinian's reign at last ended the era of slow decadence and transition and ushered in political and demographic changes of the most radical kind.

Slavs and Plagues

The term 'Dark Age', when applied to a period of history, has fallen deservedly into disrepute. There are few stretches of time on which no light whatever falls, and the darkness is seldom so opaque that when it is even momentarily illuminated the scene revealed is not found to be full of variety and movement. Nevertheless it must be confessed that so far as Greece is concerned the sixth, seventh and eighth centuries are indeed obscure. Facts and events are unusually elusive, and scarcity of evidence adds to the difficulties of interpretation. What is not in doubt is that, by contrast with the immobility of the preceding age, the period witnessed an abrupt break with the past. A sharp and brutal revolution altered the whole character of Hellas and profoundly influenced the whole course of its development in the Middle Ages. It also involved a steep decline of civilized life and an almost total rejection of former values.

The most striking change affected the ethnic composition of the people and resulted from the mass migration of Slavs into the Balkans which began in the sixth century.[12] There is surely no historical controversy more tedious than that which agitated scholars in Victorian times, and has not yet entirely died down, on the subject of the racial origin of the modern Greeks, and in particular the thesis propounded by the Tyrolese professor Fallmerayer that the Hellenic racial element in the Greek population had been virtually eliminated by the Slavonic. Fallmerayer's writings infuriated all those who preferred to believe that the Greek patriots who had recently so bravely won independence from the Turks were in the main descended from Hellenic ancestors, while assuaging the outraged feelings of others who professed to detect no resemblance between the traits, physical or moral, of contemporary Greeks and those of the heroes of antiquity. Today, when more objective attitudes prevail, such impassioned arguments sound somewhat absurd. They would also have appeared equally pointless to educated persons of the high Byzantine age who, though intensely proud of their Hellenic culture, tended to indifference toward their racial antecedents. They were quite accustomed to the situation in which the Empire had become, since late Roman times, an ethnic mixture on an enormous scale. Successive emperors, themselves of very diverse origins, had indulged for reasons of politics and defence in vast transfers of populations from one corner of their domain to the other. After a successful campaign, or even in peace time, tens of thousands of Slavs or nomads from the northern steppes might find themselves settled in Asia Minor, or corresponding numbers of Armenians in the southern Balkans. In such circumstances it made no sense to bother about racial purity. The only fact that mattered was that the mixture was held together by an apparently indissoluble cement compounded of Greek civilization, Roman law and the Christian religion.

These Byzantines were aware that the inhabitants of old Greece were, like those of the other provinces, a racial mixture. In fact there were probably fewer ingredients in the mix than elsewhere. At the beginning of the sixth century the sparse population of Greece was generally speaking still homogeneous, despite the new elements introduced over the years by Roman military colonies and by slave-gangs working large estates. It will be worthwhile to take a close look at the processes by which the Slav immigrants came to be progressively intermingled with the Greeks and an eventual fusion took place.

In the fifth century Slavonic tribes were occupying a wide and undetermined region in northern Europe extending from the Elbe eastwards to the Vistula and the Niemen and southwards to the Carpathians. Circumstances favoured the further expansion of this prolific race towards the south and south-east into a void created by the catastrophic irruption of the Huns into Europe in mid-century and the subsequent ebbing of the Hunnic flood after Attila's death. Under pressure from the Huns the various Germanic tribes established in the country north of the Roman Danube frontier began to move west, and the Slavs advanced to take their place. Those who did so were known as Slavinians and were the ancestors of the present Central European and Balkan Slavs. Another branch of the race drifted into South Russia and eventually emerged as the Ukrainians and Great Russians.

The Slavs were countrymen pure and simple; farmers, pastoralists, hunters, fishers and bee-keepers. Their religion was a polytheism vaguely subordinate to a supreme deity and based on respect for, and sympathy with, the forces of nature. They had no pretensions to an advanced culture and no consideration for the civilization of others. Not naturally aggressive, they were at the same time untiring and ruthless in satisfying their hunger for new lands. They had the strongest possible sense of community but little genius for political organization. The latter weakness frequently subjected them to temporary domination by more vigorous nomadic tribes of Hunnic and Turkic origin, who used them as their auxiliaries and instruments in their raids on the Empire.

Early in the fifth century the Slavinians already had their eye on the Balkan peninsula. The Empire's Illyrian provinces had been much more severely mauled than Greece by previous barbarian invasions, but like Greece they had preserved their indigenous population. This was made up of the tribes which had lived there since before the Roman conquest but had become to a large extent Latinized. That is not to say that the native languages had died out (their last surviving representative, Albanian, is still flourishing); but Latin was used as the *lingua franca* of administration and commerce. The great Justinian was a Latin-speaking Thracian from the area south of Nish in Serbia, which served as an important recruiting ground for the imperial army.[13] South of a line running from the Adriatic in northern Epiros through Macedonia to the Black Sea Latin gave way to Greek and tribal vestiges disappeared.

Slav raids started about 530 and soon became a destructive nuisance. The invaders were at first no menace to the walled towns, but they harried the countryside and reduced its taxable value before retiring with their plunder north of the Danube. But the scale and frequency of the attacks increased rapidly. So did the warlike efficiency of the attackers, especially when their operations were directed by the Kutrigurs, a persistent and ferocious horde of nomads. After a while they learned how to capture towns, while their penetrations of Roman territory lasted longer and were driven more deeply, as far as the Aegean coasts and the outskirts of Constantinople itself.

Against these encroachments the Roman government deployed an obstinate but less and less effective defence. For a time a Slav general named Chilbud, enlisted to fight against his compatriots, successfully held them in check.[14] But the Roman field army was too fully engaged in Justinian's ambitious and costly attempts to recover North Africa and Italy from the Vandals and Ostrogoths, and in campaigns against Persia, to be capable of simultaneously containing the Slav threat on a third front. The Emperor therefore resorted to an intricate system of fortification in depth, which is described in great detail by the historian Procopius in the book *On Edifices*. Line after line of castles and smaller forts were laid down to protect the Balkan cities, the productive areas and the approaches to Constantinople. Whether or not the plans were carried out in their entirety, an immense effort of building was involved. Although it held up the barbarians for decades, it did not in the end prevent a continuous infiltration, and infiltration was followed by settlement. The Slavs occupied the plains and river valleys, while the indigenous inhabitants sought refuge in the numerous mountain ranges.

In order to block the ways of access to Greece, Justinian's engineers constructed, according to Procopius, a string of fortresses across Macedonia, hinging on the impregnable bastion of Thessalonica.[15] To the south and west two further lines of defences guarded Thessaly and Epiros. Still further to the south, the pass of Thermopylae was refortified and garrisoned, the ramparts of Athens and Corinth were restored and, finally, hostile entry into the Peloponnese was barred by the repair of the ancient wall across the isthmus. But in spite of these elaborate precautions Kutrigurs and Slavs burst into northern Greece as early as 540, and in 559 they got as far as Thermopylae. This was one of the spearheads of a mass incursion which was triumphantly repelled by the veteran general Belisarius, conqueror of Vandals and Goths, and the Kutrigurs were so severely handled that they vanished from the scene altogether.

Unfortunately they were immediately replaced by an even more violent Turkic group from the inner steppes of Asia, the Avars. By the mid-sixties Bayan, their chieftain or Khagan, had driven the last remaining Germanic tribes, the Gepids and Lombards, out of Central Europe, and had built up a powerful Empire with its base on the Hungarian plain. Such hopes as the imperial government might have cherished of using the Avars to crush the Slavs were disappointed, for the Khagan, once he had awed the Slavs into accepting his overlordship, lost no time in employing them to weaken the Romans. Thenceforth the two peoples are found acting jointly or in collusion against the Empire. In general the strategy was to send swarms of Slavs to spread ruin behind the Roman lines while the Avars concentrated on reducing the Danube fortresses. And apart from the principal recorded invasions, we can be certain that minor raids and incursions never ceased.

> Then, in 581, according to the history of John of Ephesus, the Slavs overran the whole of Greece and the country of the Thessalonians and all Thrace, and captured the cities and took numerous forts, and devastated and burnt, and reduced the people to slavery, and made themselves masters of the whole country and settled it by main force and dwelt in it as though it had been their own without fear. And four years have now elapsed and still . . . they live at their ease in the land . . . and spread themselves far and wide, as far as God permits them . . . And even still [584] they encamp and dwell there.

Two years later they besieged Thessalonica, and in 587 they are for the first time specifically reported to have penetrated into the Peloponnese.[16]

The passage from John of Ephesus is often quoted as convincing evidence of the permanent settlement of Slavs in Hellas as well as in the Greek-speaking parts of Thrace and Macedonia. It does indeed sound more like a plain statement of fact than a piece of gloomy rhetoric, if only because it mentions the intruders' four-year sojourn in the territories in question. There should by that time have been every opportunity for a chronicler to confirm the bad news that had reached him. Without necessarily concluding that the Slavs had already found their way into every recess of the Greek countryside, it would be perverse to assume that the phrase 'the whole of Greece' does not mean what it says. But slavization was obviously by no means complete and most of the towns were intact. Moreover, in the course of the next decade, the Emperor Maurice (582–602) launched a determined counter-offensive which inflicted heavy damage on both Avars and Slavs and pursued them into their lairs on the north bank of the Danube. If it had been possible to sustain this military effort, the swamping of the Balkan peninsula by Slavs might conceivably have been arrested, but that was too much to hope for. The army, exhausted by endless campaigning against a hydra-like enemy, revolted and murdered Maurice and for many years the Empire was plunged into confusion. By the time that Heraclius (610–41) had restored internal order and Constantinople had repulsed, with unparalleled slaughter, the grand Avaro-Slav expedition of 626, the aim of which was to substitute the heathen Khagan for the Orthodox Emperor, the Slav deluge had rolled unchecked across the Balkans, effectively submerging Roman authority from the Danube to Cape Tainaron and extinguishing classical culture, or what was left of it, and the Christian religion.

When they passed out of Roman control the regions occupied by the Slavs slid straight into barbarism. The garrisons were massacred or withdrawn, and the complicated administrative and fiscal system of the Empire, with its carefully graded bureaucracy, simply disintegrated. So did the rule of law, guarantees for property and sophisticated commercial exchanges. The highways fell into disrepair and the superb posting network came to an end. The Church hierarchy suffered the same fate as the apparatus of the state. Just as there were no more provincials to be administered or taxed, there were no more faithful to be cared for, and many dioceses ceased to exist except on paper.

We cannot guess how large a proportion of the original population was killed off or driven out. In Greece persons of substance no doubt made good their escape to the coastal cities, to the islands and to Constantinople and Asia Minor. As for the peasants and shepherds, we may imagine that many pockets of Greek-speaking people survived, came to terms with the Slavs and eventually merged with them. There is also general agreement among scholars that there were some districts, notably the eastern Peloponnese and probably Attica and Euboea, where the Greeks held their ground and predominated. The fifteenth-century historian Phrantzes claimed that his birthplace, Monemvasia, the famous fortress city towering Gibraltar-like above the Peloponnesian coast and connected with the mainland by a narrow causeway, was founded during this period of insecurity and collapse.[17]

It is also impossible to list with any accuracy the towns which remained inhabited and with their civic and religious institutions functioning as before. Conspicuous among them was the great city of Thessalonica, one of the few which, besides throwing back all barbarian assaults, continued to grow and prosper.[18] Athens, Corinth, Patras and at least a score or two of smaller ports on the Aegean and Ionian littorals maintained their maritime links with each other and the imperial capital. Possibly Athens had not entirely forgotten its culture, for if it is true that Theodore of Tarsus, the future Archbishop of Canterbury, who was born in 602, studied there as a young man, it must have been at the blackest moment of all, about 620.[19] It is unsafe to speculate about towns in the interior such as Larissa, Thebes and Sparta, but while they may initially have been sacked and ruined, it is hardly likely that they would have stayed utterly deserted if there had been any Greeks at hand to creep back to them. The Slavs themselves showed no inclination to become town-dwellers. On the other hand they took readily to piracy by sea, using their *monoxyla* which seem to have resembled outsize war canoes, to raid the Aegean islands. But the imperial navy was strong enough to make these ventures unprofitable.

A further factor which contributed to the general desolation and further thinned the already scanty population on the eve of the Slav invasions was the great bubonic plague which broke out in 542. It ravaged the whole Levant and carried off countless numbers of people, paralysing public and private life for several years as it flared up in one quarter or another. To make things worse, earthquakes were distressingly frequent during the period; in 561, for instance, four thousand people were swallowed up in a convulsion at Patras.

Thus the Slav immigrants took possession of a magnificent but half-deserted country. To the eerie remnants of a vanished civilization which they found scattered over it they paid no attention at all, and proceeded to establish their own primitive villages. Together with their women, children and animals, they brought with them their loose tribal organization built round the family. Groups of kindred families formed the clan occupying a certain territory. This was known as the *Zupa* and the leadership was entrusted to the principal head of the family of *Zupan*. The Greeks called these communities *Sklaviniai*. Since the Slavs remained consistently intolerant of any wider authority they failed to coalesce into larger political units, and they were slow to produce native princes. Among the tribal groups which settled in Greece were the Velzites, the Melings and the Ezerites. All were fiercely independent of each other and of any formal or tributary relation to the Empire.

The Mediterranean environment was of course quite different from their frigid and misty homelands in the north. They had to adapt themselves to the climate and to learn how to cultivate the olive and the vine. For economic reasons alone it was impossible for them to live in a state of perpetual enmity with their Greek neighbours. Consequently unmitigated hostility soon gave way to an uneasy peace, a *modus vivendi* which facilitated mutually profitable trade and the initiation of the Slavs into the Mediterranean way of life. No organized effort seems to have been made from the Greek side to convert or assimilate them, for in the seventh century the Empire was far too busily engaged in fighting off the Arabs to attempt so ambitious a task.

Nevertheless, during a lull in the Arab attacks on Asia Minor, the Emperor Constans II (642–68) successfully beat back the Macedonian Slavs who were threatening Thessalonica, and he subsequently spent the winter of 662–3 at Athens. A strange man, grim, arrogant and self-willed, Constans was depressed by the relentless Arab advance but determined to keep the Empire alive. He estimated that his best chance of success lay in transferring the seat of government from vulnerable Constantinople back to Rome and in directing the defence of the whole empire from the middle instead of from the eastern Mediterranean. His choice of Athens as the place of assembly for his consequent expedition to the West suggests that the city and its port, Piraeus, were by no means derelict at the time. The Emperor's grand conception was finally foiled when he was stabbed to death in his bath at Syracuse six years later, but his view of Empire entitles him to be regarded as the last of the Roman Caesars, while the date of his death serves as a convenient point of departure for the Byzantine age.

Thessalonica was ineffectually besieged three times by Slavs between 675 and 678, and saved by the valour of its citizens and, according to tradition, by the intervention of its patron St Demetrios. Justinian II (685–95), the grandson of Constans, later undertook a major campaign against these enemies, of whom many thousands were captured and deported to Asia as colonists. The same monarch created a new *theme* (military district) in central Greece, under the name of Hellas and with its headquarters at Athens. Clearly the Byzantine government was fighting back and slowly gaining the upper hand; we hear of no more trouble caused by Slavs in that area. It may reasonably be supposed, given the lack of evidence, that the land was being repeopled: the Slavs were learning Greek ways and were in all probability being attracted to Christianity. Hellas, however, was still commonly regarded by foreigners as a Slav preserve, and the contemporary biography of St Willibald of Eichstadt, a German bishop but an Englishman by birth who travelled to the east in 723, places Monemvasia, known to us as a Greek foundation, in 'Slavinian' territory.[20]

The situation was complicated by a second great plague which raged through the eastern Mediterranean countries from 744 to 747 and fell with peculiar violence on Constantinople. When it abated, Constantine V (741–75) removed large numbers of Greeks from Hellas and the islands to repopulate the city. Apparently the old Greek population had sufficiently increased to make such a measure practicable. Its effect on the ethnic balance in Hellas is a matter of debate. The assumption that the gaps left by the departing Greeks were instantly filled by a fresh immigration of Slavs in the mid-eighth century rests largely on a statement by Constantine VII Porphyrogenitus (911–59), a literary Emperor writing two hundred years later, that 'the whole country' at that time was 'slavized and became barbarous'.[21] This sweeping assertion makes more sense if it is applied to the year 600, and another Greek account, composed at Monemvasia about 900, is surely nearer the mark in saying that the Peloponnese was ruled by Slavs for 218 years from 587 (during the reign of Maurice) until 805.

The significance of the latter date is that it correctly marks the end of Slav freedom from imperial control. From the last quarter of the eighth century onwards the Byzantine government pursued an energetic and well-thought-out plan of reconquest. It was no accident that the initial, and very effective, campaign was conducted in 782–3 by the eunuch Stavrakios, the Empress Irene's chief minister and general, for like Eudocia in the fifth century, Irene was an Athenian and deeply interested in promoting a Greek recovery in the country of her birth. Formerly married to Leo IV (775–80), the widowed Empress was at the time acting as regent for her son Constantine VI (780–97). Stavrakios made a thorough success of his mission: he not only defeated the Slav tribes living between Thessalonica and the southern Peloponnese but compelled them to acknowledge imperial supremacy and pay tribute.

A few years later Greece was involved in a murky series of Byzantine court intrigues and personal tragedies. Once she had experienced the joys of power the ambitious and unscrupulous Irene could not stomach the prospect of relegation to the background when her son came of age. She became increasingly estranged from Constantine and eventually had him deposed and blinded. Shortly afterwards she herself became the target of a conspiracy to which her late husband's five brothers were parties. Indeed the inept role which they had played in previous plots had already cost the eldest his eyes and the four others their tongues. This time Irene merely packed them off into exile at her native city, Athens, where she no doubt counted on their being kept out of mischief. In 799, however, she discovered that they were intriguing against her with the help of the *Zupan* of the Velzite Slavs, who in fact rose in revolt. This was duly suppressed, and the four tongueless princes had their eyes put out as well. Three years later Irene was deposed in her turn and her *Logothete*, or Minister of Finance, Nikephoros (802–11), was called to the throne.

The new Emperor was talented and vigorous, an excellent soldier as well as an adroit financier. He fought strenuously against Krum, King of the Bulgarians, a Turkic tribe which had imposed its ascendancy on most of the Balkan Slavs, but his success in the field was nullified by the last fatal battle in which he lost his life. As regards the Slavs of Greece his actions were decisive. In 805 they rose *en masse* and attempted to seize Patras, but the city held out and they were crushed by imperial troops.[22] The victory was followed by effective measures of repression, and the booty and captives were donated to the cathedral of St Andrew, the local counterpart of the Thessalonian Demetrios. A separate military district was set up for the Peloponnese and another for southern Epiros. In 850 we find Theoktistoss Bryennios, the commander in the Peloponnese, putting down yet another rebellion. Nevertheless, the particularly intractable Melings and Ezerites retained the right to govern themselves and elect their own chieftains, in return for a fixed annual payment to the Imperial treasury. The former lurked in the inaccessible fastnesses of Mount Taygetos, overlooking the valley of Sparta, while the Ezerites, 'people of the lake', seem to have occupied the swampy plain of Helos between Gytheion and Cape Malea. As late as 934 they were again refusing to pay their tribute, but were reduced to obedience by the imperial general Krinites.

As a complement to his military measures Nikephoros initiated a policy of re-colonization of a thoroughness which could only be achieved by a state with vast resources and a well-trained civil service. His successors carried it out with equal application for a century and more. The method adopted was to bring in peasant farmers from the *themes* of Asia Minor, where the free ownership of land was linked with an obligation to military service, and to establish them in the coastal plains and river valleys of Hellas, thus ensuring security for the towns and a continuous increase of Greek-speaking population at the expense of the Slavs, who were gradually pushed back into the more rugged and inhospitable regions of the interior. Those who stayed behind were easily assimilated.

This turn of the ethnic tide was accompanied by an inevitable blurring of the distinction between Greeks and Slavs, now that the latter were being transformed from tribesmen owing allegiance to nobody into Orthodox tax-paying subjects of the Emperor and were exposed to civilizing influences. Indeed the government had never ceased to regard them, as potentially good 'Romans'.[23] As early as the seventh century we hear of one Pervund, a troublesome Slav chieftain in the neighbourhood of Thessalonica, who spoke fluent Greek and affected Greek manners,[24] and in the eighth century, to quote Bury, Constantinople itself 'swarmed with numbers of wholly Graecized, half Graecized or utterly barbarous foreigners, especially Armenians and Slavonians'.[25] An enterprising Slav from Greece or further north could be sure of finding an outlet for his talents, a good example being a certain Niketas who actually became Patriarch, the head of the Orthodox Church, in 766 but was laughed at for his mispronunciation of Greek.[26] If this was the state of affairs in the capital, it must equally have prevailed at Thessalonica and Patras. In the tenth century, when the process of fusion had been carried a stage further, Constantine Porphyrogenitus, in support of his assertion that the whole of Greece had become slavized, mentions another Niketas, this time a rich landowner with a high social position at Constantinople, who made great play with his Peloponnesian origin but gave himself away by his strikingly Slavonic features.

Parallel with the recolonization, the Orthodox Church deployed an intense effort of conversion. The years 800–1000 were preeminently an age of monks, holy hermits and missionary saints, of whom the most outstanding were St Luke of Stiris and St Nikon. They both worked in the tenth century, the former in the region north of the Gulf of Corinth and the latter in the Peloponnese, where he evangelized, among other districts, the savage Maina. New dioceses were marked out and old ones revived, while the country was covered with newly built churches and chapels, many of them on the site of former pagan shrines. The religion of the Slavs yielded easily enough before this onslaught, but the conversion could not take full effect until Greek had ousted Slavonic as the dominant language of the people. Whereas the Greek missionaries to the Slav countries of Central Europe and the northern Balkans learned the language of their converts and translated the Bible and the liturgy into Slavonic, no such latitude was permitted in Greece, where religion and hellenization marched hand in hand.

The Slav type may be discerned today among the Greeks by those who look for it, but physical traits are an unreliable guide to origins. Socrates had a snub nose but that did not make him a Slav. Apart from the racial mixture the Slav legacy to Hellas was inconsiderable. In the high Middle Ages Slavonic may still have been spoken in the few restricted areas of the Peloponnese where the Slav communities clung to their tribal identity, but Slavonic elements in the mediaeval and modern Greek vocabulary are negligible, despite the numerous place names ending in -itsa and -ovo which betray a non-Hellenic origin (even if replaced on the official maps by Hellenic substitutes). The place name *Slavochorion*, too, significantly crops up. Otherwise Hellas retained remarkably few traces of the Slav presence. Only a fragmentary folklore peopled with vampires and watersprites lingered on to enrich, or at worst to confuse, remoter memories of nereids, centaurs and other creatures of classical fable.[27]

CHAPTER TWO

Hellas Re-Hellenized

THE IMPORTANCE WHICH the Byzantine government attached to the restoration of Hellenism in Greece in the ninth and tenth centuries was enhanced by the country's strategic position in the struggle between the Empire and the Arabs. Apart from continual campaigns in the frontier region (roughly corresponding to southern Turkey), this conflict took the form of a vast maritime war waged with varying fortunes around the shores of the whole eastern Mediterranean, from Sicily to Syria. Every year Saracen squadrons would set out to raid Byzantine territory from their home ports in Africa and Asia and from their base in captured Crete.[1] In the central Mediterranean the Arabs occupied Sicily, though its conquest took them fifty years to accomplish, encroached on the Byzantine provinces in south Italy and attacked the coastal cities of Dalmatia such as Ragusa (Dubrovnik) which acknowledged Byzantine suzerainty. In the Aegean, where their principal object was plunder and slaves as opposed to the acquisition of territory, they caused serious destruction and suffering, but without affecting the integrity of the Empire, and the fortified harbours and safe anchorages of Greece were an essential component of the Byzantine defences against piratical aggression. Monemvasia and Methone (Modon) gave especially useful warning of approaching corsairs.

Meanwhile the Byzantine forces returned blow for blow. They burned, for instance, Damietta in the Egyptian Delta and stormed Lattakieh in Syria. Very gradually they gained the upper hand. At first their attempts to regain Cyprus and Crete were failures, but in the 960s both fell to the brilliant general and Emperor Nikephoros Phokas, whose conquests finally disposed of the Arab menace.

For all their devastations the Saracens never obtained a foothold on the Greek mainland. Constantine Porphyrogenitus, the Emperor-historian, describes various episodes of the naval, or rather amphibious engagements which took place round the coasts in the time of his grandfather Basil I (867–86). On one occasion the Saracen emir of Tarsus in Cilicia crossed the Aegean with the intention of surprising the busy port of Chalkis in Euboea, but was routed and killed by the provincial troops of the theme of Hellas. On another we find the most resourceful of the ninth century Byzantine admirals, Niketas Oryphas, anchored at Cenchreae, the port of Corinth on the Saronic Gulf, and receiving a report that a Saracen fleet was entering the Adriatic. What is interesting is that in order to chase the enemy he was able to have his whole fleet dragged for four miles across the isthmus to the Gulf of Corinth over the ancient slipway or tram road which had been built for that purpose in the Classical age and apparently restored by the Byzantine authorities.[2] His warships were mostly *dromons*, galleys with a full complement of up to three hundred men, including seventy marines, and essentially the same type of craft as was employed in the Mediterranean in the Middle Ages. They were propelled by two banks of oars, that is to say that the oarsmen sat not in superimposed tiers but two to a bench, the benches being slanted slightly forwards and the oars projecting through one rowlock port. There were also more manoeuvrable biremes known as *pamphyli*, the cruisers of the fleet, and smaller vessels with one bank of oars for scouting purposes. The ships were equipped with rams and, for the discharge of that mysterious chemical compound, Greek fire, tubes or catapults in the bows, while the marines carried hand grenades of the stuff which exploded on hitting the target.[3]

So swiftly did Oryphas transfer his fleet that he caught up with the Saracens and annihilated them. A second admiral, whose rowers went on shore at Methone and deserted, had them replaced by the commander of the Peloponnesian theme and went on to score an equally crushing victory over the infidels. These accounts imply a high degree of competence and flexibility in the imperial navy. Sometimes, however, it failed signally in its protective task, as in 904, when Thessalonica itself was taken and savagely sacked by the most pestilential corsair of all, Leo of Tripolis. This terrible shock to Byzantine pride rankled the more because the Saracen admiral was a renegade of Greek extraction like the Barbarossa brothers, natives of Lesbos, who as Turkish commanders were to sweep the Christian fleets from the seas in the mid-sixteenth century, before Don John of Austria redressed the balance at Lepanto.

Thessalonica had survived so many sieges in the past that its immunity was taken for granted. Consequently, although warnings of Leo's designs on the city had reached Constantinople, no adequate measures were taken to strengthen its garrison and fortifications. So, when Leo appeared before the harbour with fifty-four ships and over ten thousand men, the defences were unprepared and easily breached. John Kameniates, an official of the Archbishop's court, wrote an exact account of what ensued.[4] Many of the two hundred thousand inhabitants of the city were massacred on the spot and about one-tenth of the population, carefully chosen for their suitability as slaves, or as offering prospects of a high ransom, were embarked on the fleet, together with an immense quantity of spoil, which took ten days to collect and stow away. Leaving Thessalonica desolate, but not destroyed, Leo sailed away to Crete, where the prisoners were due to be sorted out for distribution among the Syrian and Egyptian slave markets. Kameniates and his family, who had bought their lives at the price of revealing to the Saracens where their money and valuables were hidden, were stuffed with eight hundred other captives into the holds of an Egyptian warship. On arrival in Crete they were transferred to another vessel which took them and various privileged prisoners, including two Byzantine generals, to Tarsus, where thy were to await their exchange for Saracens in Byzantine hands. As in the days of Charles V and Suleiman the Magnificent, ransoms and exchanges were a source of profitable business to middlemen who bought prisoners from the pirates and arranged their redemption in return for a fat fee. Thus those whose relatives were willing to pay were not destined, like the less fortunately placed, to spend the rest of their lives in slavery. The native Cretans, some of whom had become Moslems for the sake of convenience, excelled in such traffic.

The worst sufferers from the repeated Moslem razzias were the Greek islanders. The corsairs ravaged even those islands nestling in the secluded gulfs and inlets of the mainland, such as Aegina, from where the grandparents of St Luke of Stiris were forced to flee. As their place of refuge they wisely chose Kastoria in Macedonia, a town remote from the sea. There the saint was born, but on deciding to become a monk he took his vows at Athens and spent his life as hermit and preacher on the shores of the Gulf of Corinth, dodging further Saracen raids and one full-scale Bulgarian invasion.

In spite of the insecurity resulting from the maritime war, Greece displayed a steady increase in economic activity and material prosperity. The emperors now regarded it as a valuable asset. The early career of Basil I, the first of the Macedonian dynasty, illustrates the strength of imperial interest in the provinces of Hellas and the Peloponnese. Basil's origins were proletarian and until he became famous it was not doubted that he was anyone but the son of a Slav peasant from the neighbourhood of Adrianople. Only later was it thought necessary to fabricate for him the pedigree of an Armenian aristocrat, because the Byzantine world was at the time teeming with noble Armenians. With nothing to recommend him except his good looks and a sound knowledge of horses, he had entered the service of a magnate named Theophilitzes and accompanied him on an official mission to the

Peloponnese. There he fell ill, and as luck would have it was nursed back to health in the household of an extremely rich lady of Patras, the widow Danielis, who took a liking to him, won him the friendship of her son John and presented him with large sums of money. Thus fortified, Basil bought land of his own in Macedonia. He also began to cut a figure in the society of the capital; he soon became keeper of the imperial stables and boon companion of the unsteady Emperor Michael III (842–67). He received high favour at court and was encouraged to marry Michael's former mistress. From that moment nothing would satisfy him but the acquisition of the supreme power, to which the first step was the assassination of the Emperor's uncle and chief minister, the Caesar Bardas, of whom Michael was jealous. When Michael made Basil co-Emperor he immediately proceeded to intrigue against Michael and after a while had him murdered too.[5]

After this breathlessly lurid career the ex-stable boy settled down to enjoy the rewards of his crimes, but he disappointed those who expected moral retribution by turning out a popular and efficient ruler, devoted to extending the power and prestige of Byzantium. The dynasty which he founded lasted for two hundred years and carried the Empire to its zenith. Nor did he forget his friends in the Peloponnese. His old companion, John, was promoted to the senior official rank of *Protospatharios* and the widow was invited to visit Constantinople, where her arrival created an unusual sensation even in an environment so perfectly accustomed to the most extravagant displays. According to Constantine Porphyrogenitus, her retinue included four hundred young men, a hundred girls and a hundred eunuchs, all of whom passed into the Emperor's service, while Basil was also pleased to accept quantities of magnificent gold and silver plate and precious textiles. Among the latter was a set of splendid carpets destined for the Nea, the great new five-domed cross- in-square church, a vanished landmark of Byzantine architecture, which Basil was building as an act of expiation in memory of the patron he had betrayed and killed.[6]

In the end the widow outlived first her own son and then the Emperor. On the latter's death she paid a second visit to the capital in order to settle the whole of her vast wealth on his successor, Leo VI. When she herself died the commissioner who drew up the register of her estate was amazed by its size and variety. The landed property alone comprised eighty large farms and so many slaves were available that Leo freed three thousand of them for settlement on imperial lands in Italy.[7]

The widow Danielis was probably an exception. Few Greek landowners of the time could have attained so high a standard of opulence. It is

27

also surprising that while it was Byzantine policy to reclaim land by introducing soldier–colonists there should have been large tracts cultivated by slaves or serfs on capitalist lines, as they were under the early Roman emperors. What seems likely is that the growth of population had already resulted in a vigorous revival of agriculture and industry. Greece was no longer a land of sheep walks and ghost towns and there was plenty of capital forthcoming from Byzantium to develop its natural resources. In the words of Finlay, it enjoyed 'a monopoly of the finer kinds of oil, wine and fruit', while the plain of Thessaly was a rich grain-growing area, the preserve of magnates of the Empire and monastic foundations.[8] Although there has never been a period of Greek history when too many goats have not been nibbling away at the trees, the mountains were still well forested and provided timber for ship-building. Less is known about the growth of manufactures, but the textiles of Patras, to judge only by the widow's gifts to Basil I, must have been famous, and at some unknown date the silk industry was established in Greece. Its products were unrivalled in quality during the early Middle Ages, those from Boeotian Thebes being specially prized.

Prosperity fostered the rebirth of old towns and the building of new ones. Typical of the latter were Nikli and Veligosti in the central Peloponnese, where the advance of cultivation in previously empty wastes demanded the creation of new markets for agricultural produce. Further to the south the ancient Sparta had disappeared, but St Nikon, on his way to evangelize the Slavs of Taygetos and the even wilder Greeks of the Maina, who still practised a kind of paganism, found it replaced by a new, thriving town called, in equally classical style, Lakedaimonia. He observed, with suitable indignation, that it had already attracted a community of Jews, a sure sign of economic growth, as well as visiting Venetian traders. The progress of re-hellenization was safeguarded by the military prowess of the Macedonian dynasty (876–1056). Nevertheless there were times at which the protective shield was thrust aside. The powerful Bulgarian Kingdom, whenever it was ruled by an energetic monarch, posed a constant threat to the Greek lands. After the conversion of Bulgaria to Christianity in the ninth century Tsar Symeon (893–927), who had received a Greek education at Constantinople, conceived the grandiose plan of substituting himself for the Macedonians as sovereign of a Greco-Bulgarian empire. In pursuit of that aim he waged war with Byzantium from 913 to 924. But although he cut to pieces several Byzantine field armies, his forces were never strong enough to attempt an assault on Constantinople itself. Consequently the war ended in a stalemate and a treaty which left both sides exhausted. While peninsular Greece was not a major theatre of warfare during those years, Byzantine defeats exposed it to continual raids. Imperial authority lost its grip and conditions north of the Gulf of Corinth were chaotic. Even St Luke of Stiris found it more prudent to retire for ten years to Patras. However the Bulgarian incursions had no lasting effect.

After Symeon's death Bulgarian power declined and the country became a Byzantine satellite. Forty years later one brilliant campaign of John Zimiskes (969–76) sufficed to intimidate the Bulgarians and to drive the Russian prince Sviatoslav of Kiev back beyond the Danube. For the first time in nearly four hundred years the imperial frontier was advanced to the line of the river, where it had been drawn in the reign of Maurice.

Nevertheless the spirit of the Bulgarians, which combined the dour obstinacy of the Slav with the savage *élan* of the steppe-dweller, had not been entirely quelled. So long as the Balkans were not fully comprised within the Empire's boundaries, the Slav threat still overhung Constantinople and the Greek peninsula. In the last quarter of the tenth century a new ruler, Samuel, challenged Byzantium and proclaimed himself Tsar. Initially he acquired territory with alarming speed. In 997, having driven as fas as the Adriatic and Aegean and cut land communications between Greece and the capital, he by-passed Thessalonica, swept down through Thessaly and penetrated as far as the Peloponnese. He was already besieging Corinth when the approach of a Byzantine force under the general Nikephoros Ouranos caused him to retreat northwards, and on the river Spercheios, just north of Thermopylae, he was heavily defeated. In subsequent years, Basil II (976–1025) penned him in within a steadily shrinking area and, in 1014, finally annihilated his army at the battle of Kleidion. Fourteen thousand Bulgarian prisoners were blinded and sent back to the Tsar who, overcome with horror, suffered a stroke and died two days later.

Basil spent four years in organizing the administration of the conquered Slav lands, showing in peace a leniency as remarkable as his cruelty in war. It was not till 1018 that he came south for a solemn celebration of victories gained in forty years of arduous campaigning in Anatolia, Syria and the Balkans. And the ceremony was held not, as might have been expected, in Santa Sophia at Constantinople, but in the cathedral of Our Lady of Athens, the ancient Parthenon, a shrine of Hellenism which had stood virtually unharmed for over fourteen hundred years.

We can only guess why Basil, the grim old *Bulgaroktonos* (Slayer of the Bulgarians) should have made this choice. Not, presumably, because he was stirred by reminiscences of the glorious Hellenic past. Although he was the grandson of the cultured historian, Constantine VII, he did not share his grandfather's enthusiasm for antiquity. He was no literary classicist but a warrior monarch cast in a mediaeval mould, austere, brutal when reasons of state demanded ruthlessness, and single-minded in his devotion to the Empire's well-being and integrity. He was never married, and was not attracted by the formalities and refinements of the court. His early life had been embittered by civil war against the unruly magnates of Asia Minor and once he had broken them he took rigorous measures to prevent the further growth of huge landed estates at the expense of the peasant farmer. The magnates were heavily taxed and landowning by the Church and individual monasteries was restricted by law. Thus, while Basil was deservedly popular with the soldiers and the class from which the professional soldiery of Byzantium was drawn, he was coldly regarded by the aristocrats, the clergy and the courtiers of the capital, and this antipathy, which was mutual, possibly explains his decision to hold his triumph well away from the suspicious atmosphere of Constantinople.

The well-known eleventh century miniature on the frontispiece of Basil's own psalter, an item of Crusader's loot preserved in the library of St Mark in Venice, depicts him as conqueror of the Bulgarians. A stocky, bearded figure, he stands booted and kilted in the ceremonial uniform of an emperor of the Romans, wearing jewelled diadem and tunic of mail, holding a lance in his right hand and a sword in his left. So he may have appeared when he climbed the steep approach to the Acropolis in procession to the Parthenon.

In the Dark and Middle Ages the Acropolis reverted to its essential role as a fortress. To Goths, Slavs and Saracens it loomed so impregnable as to be hardly worth attacking. But its gateway was still the Propylaea, the Doric-columned masterpiece designed by Mnesicles in the fifth century B.C. Having passed through its porticoes, the classical traveller would have passed into a wide open space liberally sprinkled with small shrines and commemorative statues, but in the Byzantine age this was filled with contemporary buildings of an official or ecclesiastical character which may well have blocked the view of the west front of the Parthenon. However the temple–cathedral itself, so far as we can judge, had marvellously withstood the assaults of time. Certainly the interior had been much altered to conform with Christian requirements. The changes involved the building of an apse at the east end and the conversion of the former opisthodomos at the west end into the narthex.

At the same time the flat roof had been replaced by a vault and a gallery added for the use of women worshippers. But the grand sculptural compositions of Pheidias, the gods and heroes of the pediments and metopes and the frieze with its Panathenaic procession, were intact or at the worst negligibly touched by decay. Basil's visit added immensely to the cathedral's prestige, and he enriched its treasury with the spoils of the Bulgarian capital, Ochrida. By his orders the walls were covered with frescos. A golden dove, the symbol of the Holy Spirit, swung above the altar, while the apse was dominated by the figure of the Virgin of Athens, the Atheniotissa herself.

As Runciman has observed, the Emperor was 'a philistine who resented spending money on the arts'.[10] Nevertheless it is he who, at about the same time as his embellishment of the Parthenon, sponsored one of the finest existing ensembles of Byzantine mosaic decoration in the monastery church of Hosios Loukas (the evangelizing St Luke of Stiris), hidden in the secluded highlands of Phokis. Stylistically the mosaics reflect Basil's stern asceticism and the somewhat Cromwellian character of his piety. Fifty years earlier a monarch of the same stamp, Nikephoros Phokas, had commissioned St Athanasios the Athonite to build the Great Lavra, the first monastery on the Holy Mountain of Athos. Both these emperors were unbending opponents of monastic encroachments on good agricultural land, but that did not deter them from encouraging religious foundations in the remoter and rougher districts. Aided by such benefactions, churches and monasteries proliferated in Hellas. Even more forcefully than at Hosios Loukas, the mosaic cycle of the monastery at Daphni near Athens, and especially its awe-inspiring Christ Pantocrator, sums up the spirit of this age of exemplary and deeply rooted Orthodoxy.

In the event the province's Orthodoxy and loyalty were soon to be at a premium. Daphni was founded about 1070, and 1071 was a very bleak year for an empire crippled by social decay and neglect of its defences. An intellectual revival, remarkable for its interest in Platonism and for an upsurge of Hellenic feeling in the arts, cloaked the reality, which was that the state was threatened with total collapse. In that critical year the Norman adventurer Robert Guiscard took Bari, the sole remaining Byzantine possession in south Italy, while the Seljuk Turks destroyed the imperial army at the battle of Manzikert in Armenia. Very soon the cities of Asia Minor were standing isolated amid the flood of invaders and the Turkish emirs were riding their horses into the Aegean. The empire had lost at one stroke the source of its economic prosperity and its main recruiting ground.

But as so often happened, Byzantium survived and staged a recovery. After a succession of incapable emperors had been set aside, Alexios I Komnenos(1081–1118),a masterly strategist and statesman, set to work to restore the situation. With the Asiatic provinces in disarray or under Turkish occupation, he was obliged to base his effort on his European dominions, and for that reason alone 'the Western Question', in other words Byzantium's relationship with the Latin West, suddenly usurped the political horizon. In practical terms, what Alexios had to face was a very real Norman threat to Constantinople itself.

Robert Guiscard was fully aware of how vulnerable the Empire had become. Among the numerous mercenaries serving with the Byzantine army in the Manzikert campaign was a contingent of Norman and Frankish heavy cavalry, and it was the refusal of their commander, Roussel of Bailleul, to engage his force in the battle that made disaster certain. Subsequently Roussel tried to profit from the prevailing confusion and to carve out a principality for himself in Asia Minor, to the detriment of both Byzantines and Turks. Although he failed in his attempt, the Byzantines grasped that Normans were apt to be as unreliable as allies as they were dangerous as enemies, and no longer regarded them as suitable for hiring. Mercenaries returning from the East, however, spread the word that Constantinople was ripe for conquest by an expedition from the West, and their reports determined Guiscard to make the attempt. In the summer of 1081 he landed in Illyria and attacked the fortress of Dyrrhachium, the Byzantine strongpoint blocking the highway to the Bosporus.

Alexios, rightly judging that it was more important to save the Balkans than to embark immediately on the tremendous task of recovering the Asiatic provinces, marched to meet him with an army the backbone of which was the brigade of Anglo-Saxon exiles incorporated in his Varangian Guard, a force previously composed mainly of Norsemen and Russians of Norse descent. Naturally these Englishmen were burning to avenge the humiliation which they had suffered fifteen years before at Hastings and which had driven them from their country for ever. But in the short time available to him the adroit Alexios had also enlisted the help of a potent ally, the Venetian Republic, which viewed with alarm the prospect of a Norman state controlling the approaches to the Adriatic from both sides of the straits of Otranto. The Venetians also perceived that the Emperor's plight afforded them a splendid opportunity of extending their trade in the eastern Mediterranean. In return for the co-operation of their fleet with the Byzantine forces they obtain unlimited commercial rights throughout the Empire, together with exemption from customs duties and facilities for shipping and warehousing at Constantinople. Once they had fastened their grip on Levantine trade they never relaxed it, and what began as a privileged activity under Byzantine sovereignty was converted gradually into a colonial empire which was to outlast both Byzantium itself and the rest of the Frankish presence in the East.

At the start the campaign went badly for Alexios. He was severely defeated at Dyrrhachium, where once again the English were overwhelmed by the Norman onslaught. The fortress was lost and the Normans led by Guiscard and his son Bohemond of Tarentum pressed forward into Epiros, Macedonia and Thessaly. But Alexios prevented them from penetrating further and Dyrrhachium was eventually regained by the Venetians. After Guiscard's death in 1085 the Normans withdrew to Italy, leaving their threat to Greece and the Empire in abeyance until it was revived by a vaster convulsion in the shape of the First Crusade.

Greece was not in the event seriously affected by the passage of the Crusading armies which in 1096 and later years skirted its territory on the way to their assembly point, Constantinople. In the course of the eleventh century the Byzantines had become accustomed to welcome more or less orderly bands of pilgrims arriving by land or sea, and to speed them on their way to the Holy Land, but large bodies of aggressive and fully armed knights presented them with far more delicate problems. The normal route followed by the Western princes and their forces, if they did not pass from Hungary through the Balkans, was via Dyrrhachium and along the imperial road, the ancient Via Egnatia, to Thessalonica and the capital. That they did not turn aside into Greece and attempt to seize that attractive province was largely due to the Emperor's diplomatic skill and good management. Alexios and his local governors took the greatest pains to conciliate them, laid down stocks of provisions at regular points along their route and patiently endured their propensity for pillaging the countryside. Detachments of Byzantine troops hovered ready to intervene if their behaviour became too outrageous. Some of the Western contingents were better disciplined than others, but none could be relied upon not to make trouble. Luckily the technique developed by the Byzantine government for channelling them across the Bosporus and into Turkish-held Anatolia, where some of them won through but more succumbed, was generally effective and restrained them from inflicting serious damage.

Friction, however, could hardly be avoided. The Western Christians regarded the Byzantines as smooth and treacherous and were in turn classed by their reluctant hosts as yet another horde of barbarians not essentially differing from the others encountered by Byzantium over the centuries. Most of the Crusading leaders were susceptible to tact and flattery, but one yellow-haired giant, Bohemond, nourished a peculiarly virulent hatred of the Empire and a strong personal antipathy towards Alexios, whom he could not forgive for having frustrated the Norman bid to break through in northern Greece. Nevertheless, while the Crusaders were grouping their forces at Constantinople in 1096–7, the relations between the two men were outwardly amiable. It was only after the Crusaders had recaptured Antioch, a key city of the Empire before the Turks took it, and Bohemond had established himself there as its independent prince without paying any attention to the Emperor's remonstrances, that enmity again turned into open hostility. Once installed in his new domain, Bohemond found himself fighting Byzantines as well as Turks. The latter took him prisoner and held him for three years, after which he decided that since in his estimation Byzantium was the arch-enemy, his best course was to resume the attack in Europe which had been interrupted by his father's death twenty years before. Handing over the government of the principality to his nephew Tancred, he left Syria for the West.

Bohemond planned his campaign very carefully. First he visited the Pope, whom he had no difficulty in persuading that the schismatic Alexios had betrayed the cause of the Crusade. From Rome he went on to France, where he told the same tale to King Philip I and to his fellow-Norman King Henry I of England. Everywhere he met with sympathy and offers of help, although the Crusade which he advocated was openly and unashamedly directed against the Orthodox Christian Empire. King Philip gave him his daughter Constance in marriage and when he mustered his army in Apulia it was swelled by recruits from the whole of Western Europe. His enemy Alexios's daughter, the historian Anna Komnena, says that it included 'men from the island of Thule [England] who usually fought for the Romans'.[11] Unchallenged by the Byzantine flotillas, Bohemond brought his host across the Straits of Otranto and laid siege to Dyrrhachium.

Alexios had also assembled a large and polyglot force stiffened by Turks, Pechenegs from the steppe and Western soldiers of fortune. As soon as the Normans had landed his fleet cut their links with Apulia and they were promptly suffering from lack of food and military supplies. Bohemond could make no headway against the fortress and failed to drive off the relieving army. After a year's struggle he had no choice but to acknowledge defeat and ask for a parley. The Emperor's triumph was complete, but he used it with discretion and refrained from harming or outwardly humiliating Bohemond, but before sending him home he forced him to sign a treaty by which the Norman was permitted to continue as Prince of Antioch, but as Alexios's vassal and with a strictly limited domain. It can hardly have been expected that Tancred would respect the terms relating to Syria, which indeed remained a dead letter, but what impressed the world was that the heroic Bohemond had been totally discredited and his ambitions dissolved into nothing.

The Byzantines could hardly believe their good fortune in having at last overcome a man who epitomized for them the best and worst in the barbarian character, a champion worthy of the *Chanson de Roland* (not that any Byzantine had heard of that epic). Anna Komnena, who knew him well, was both fascinated and repelled by him. Exceptionally tall and

> perfectly proportioned . . . built in conformity with the canons of Polycleitus . . . he was a marvel for the eyes to behold, and his reputation was terrifying . . . . A certain charm hung about this man but was partly marred by a general air of the horrible. For in the whole of his body the entire man showed implacable and savage both in his size and glance . . . . His wit was manifold and crafty. In conversation he was well informed, and the answers he gave were quite irrefutable

In short, no more brilliant example could have been imagined of that genius for adaptation to high Mediterranean politics displayed by the Norman house of Hauteville, of which Robert Guiscard and Bohemond were by no means the only outstanding representatives.[12]

Bohemond's death, which occurred three years after his debacle at Dyrrhachium, did not end the feud between the Hautevilles and the Komnenoi. In fact the confrontation between the leaders of the two ruling families sharpened as the twelfth century progressed and it so happened that its effects were chiefly felt in Greece. The protagonists were the Byzantine Emperors John II (1118–43) and his son Manuel I (1143–80) and, on the Hauteville side, the formidable Roger, Robert Guiscard's nephew, at first Count and then King (1130–54) of Sicily. All three were endowed with such remarkable talents that the long-drawn clash between their interests and ambitions assumed an epic quality transcending that of the normal interplay of war and diplomacy.

Their conflict was staged at a time when Mediterranean civilization, despite the apparently radical cleavage between Christian and Moslem spheres, had achieved a peculiar brilliance and homogeneity, radiating from its four principal centres, Cordova, Palermo, Constantinople and Cairo. The capital of Moslem Spain contained its substratum of old

Christians, as did Cairo in the shape of the Coptic community. At Constantinople, where so many human currents flowed into the Bosporus, an atmosphere of wary tolerance prevailed towards the Moslems, if only because at any given time numbers of Orthodox Christians were living in Moslem dominated territory, just as there were Moslems in frontier districts living under Christian rule. Before the Crusades Byzantines and Arabs exchanged hard blows, but fanaticism was usually eschewed by both sides, and 'a Byzantine felt more at home in Cairo or Bagdad then he would feel at Paris or Goslar, or even at Rome'. For an Anna Komnena, Christian Greeks and Moslem Arabs were civilized people: Christian Franks and Moslem Turks were not; they were purely and simply barbarians.[13]

But if a Byzantine could feel at home in Cairo, how much more at his ease was he in Palermo, King Roger's capital, for Sicily, dramatically poised at the junction of the Moslem and Byzantine worlds with the Gothic North, exhibited so many familiar features of the culture in which he was bred. When Sicily fell into Arab hands in the course of the ninth century, it retained most of its Greek-speaking population and the Greek element was still strong when Roger's father and homonym, the 'Great Count', seized the island from the Moslems. Roger's own court and administration were largely staffed with Greeks sporting elaborate Byzantine titles, the local Orthodox Church was encouraged to maintain its independence from Rome and Greek artists and scholars from the East were made welcome. The best mosaicists from Constantinople were summoned to decorate the Palermitan churches and Roger's superb cathedral at Cefalu. The political need to preserve a proper balance between the Moslem and Greek communities, and the increasingly numerous immigrants from Italy and further north whom the Norman rulers were introducing into the island ensured an even greater degree of racial and religious tolerance than prevailed anywhere else in the Mediterranean. Palermo, though basically an Arab city, bid fair to become a second Byzantium. And as the ill-fated Constans had dimly realised in the seventh century, it was more centrally and favourably situated than Constantinople as the capital of a Mediterranean Empire.

So rapid a development of a rival and equally sophisticated monarch in the central Mediterranean could not fail to alarm the Komnenoi. Alexios had found it hard enough to get the better of Bohemond, who had attracted to his standard troops of knights and adventurers from the whole of Western Europe by virtue of his individual genius and glamour. But John and Manuel faced an organized state comprising not only the island of Sicily but the whole of southern Italy with its ancient cities and ample resources, for in the Middle Ages the *Mezzogiorno* was the opposite of an economic slum. Moreover that state was headed by an exceptionally intelligent and versatile autocrat. Roger, son of an Norman father and an Italian mother, was perfectly attuned to both northern and southern habits of mind, the master of several languages and steeped in the highest culture of his time. A subtle politician, he was served by an efficient and cosmopolitan bureaucracy, and the finances of his kingdom were sustained by internal good management and a flourishing foreign trade. On the military side Roger, no soldier himself, had no need to rely exclusively on the fickle and unruly Norman baronage. The forces which made him so redoubtable an opponent were both professional and amphibious in character. The powerful Sicilian navy ranged far and wide over the Mediterranean and had the capacity to concentrate overwhelming forces swiftly at any chosen point. The Greek coasts, so accessible from Sicily, were particularly vulnerable. It was also deeply galling to the Byzantine emperors that Roger's supremely brilliant admiral, George of Antioch, was a Greek hailing from the easternmost outpost of Norman expansion.

In his intellectual attainments Roger was superior to both the Komnenoi, though they, the heirs to an age-long tradition, would certainly have considered him a cultural parvenu. John, brother of the blue-stocking princess Anna, was eminently a man of action, and his energy and strength of will were combined with a singular frankness and integrity of character. His people called him *Kaloyannis*, John the Good, and he in fact resembled an ancient Roman at his best, Horace's *justum et tenacem propositi virum*. His ambition was to restore the boundaries and prestige of Byzantium to the height which they had reached under the Macedonian dynasty. That meant consolidation in the Balkans while the Emperor set himself to win back territory from the Turks in Anatolia and from the Western Crusaders in Syria. John crushed an incursion from the nomad Pechenegs, and his marriage to the Hungarian princess Piroska ensured that there would be no serious trouble on the Danube frontier between the Empire and the Hungarian Kingdom. It remained to neutralize the potential threat from Sicily to prosperous Greece, and to that end John encouraged and subsidized an expedition mounted by the German Emperor Lothair against Roger's Italian domains. Having thus placed his Western rival on the defensive, John penetrated deep into Syria, overawing both Moslems and Crusaders. In 1138 he made his triumphal entry into Antioch and received the homage of its prince, Bohemond's great-nephew.

Byzantine aims in the East were, however, still unfulfilled when John died five years later as the result of a hunting accident and was succeeded by his son Manuel. The dramatic duel between Sicily and Byzantium lasted until the extinction of the Komnenan dynasty in 1185. Its first act reached its climax in Roger's attack on Greece in the forties; the second covered Manuel's riposte against Apulia in the next decade, and the third was played out in a final Norman effort to conquer the whole European domain of Byzantium.[14]

Manuel's nature differed notably from his father's. Pleasure-loving, extravagant and open-handed, he probably inherited these characteristics from his Magyar ancestors. But in his devotion to the greatness of Byzantium he was a true Roman and yielded nothing to John or Alexios. He was a resourceful statesman and a courageous, if somewhat rash, soldier. Most of his political life was spent in dealing with Western princes and he understood their psychology better than any of his predecessors. Unlike them he really wanted to understand it. Both his wives—Bertha of Sulzbach, sister-in-law of the German Emperor Conrad of Hohenstaufen, and Mary of Antioch, yet another descendant of Bohemond—were Westerners. He enjoyed the company of Latins and Germans and was fascinated by the more flamboyant manifestations of knightly behaviour. He even staged tournaments at Constantinople and entered the lists himself, but as might have been foreseen the novel informality of his court and his tendency to lavish favour on Latins in his service irritated the more conservative of his subjects.

His Western sympathies were put to a severe test by the Second Crusade. The misunderstandings and clashes which had marked the passage of the Crusaders in his grandfather's time were repeated when the French and German armies marched through the Balkans on their way to Constantinople. Like Alexios, Manuel tried to minimise them. He was in his element while entertaining his august guests Conrad of Germany and Louis VII of France, who was accompanied by his wife Eleanor of Aquitaine, the future Queen of England and the embodiment of the chivalrous culture of Languedoc, but the good impression which he made on those potentates faded when the Crusaders met with the usual reverses at Turkish hands and inevitably blamed them on Byzantine treachery or tepidity. Such charges were not made by Conrad who, when he fell ill during the campaign was nursed back to health by Manuel and subsequently taken to the Holy Land by the imperial navy. Louis, however, persisted in his grudge and some of his entourage, possibly stimulated by Roger's agents, had already been advocating an alliance between the two kings against Byzantium. Fortunately Louis who, although stupid, possessed a highly developed sense of honour, would have nothing to do with such a proposal: whatever distrust he felt for Manuel he was equally wary of Roger, and had previously declined the latter's offer of ships to transport the French army direct to Palestine.

Manuel, for his part, seems to have suspected that Roger was planning some act of aggression, but he was taken by surprise when in the autumn of 1147, just as the Crusaders were preparing to cross into Asia, the Sicilian fleet suddenly swooped upon Greece.

The attack was not an invasion but a razzia on the grand scale, brilliantly executed by George of Antioch. He began by seizing the island of Corfu, a move which made sense strategically whether it was defensively designed to ward off a Byzantine attack on southern Italy or offensively to cover an eventual resumption of the Norman march on Constantinople. In any case it accorded with Roger's policy of securing vital points; Tripoli, for instance, had been taken from its Moslem ruler only the year before. It is, however, hard to believe that Roger felt any immediate apprehension about Byzantine projects for the reconquest of Apulia. Even if he had been exceptionally well informed of Manuel's ultimate intentions, he knew that the Emperor was at the time fully involved in coping with the Crusade, and that before the Crusade started his military operations had been directed exclusively against the Turks. But he also knew that Manuel had no forces to spare for the defence of Greece against George's armada, and that the expedition would give not only Byzantium but the Western rulers as well a fulminating reminder of the realities of Sicilian power.

Leaving a garrison at Corfu, the Antiochene cruised leisurely round the Peloponnese and into the Aegean as far north as Euboea, then back again into the Ionian and up the Gulf of Corinth, plundering all the way, until his fleet lay within easy reach of Thebes and Corinth, the two richest cities of southern Greece. The former was the administrative and commercial capital of the theme of Hellas and the residence of its governor, or *dux*, but its chief pride was its silk industry; the surrounding land was known as the *morokampos*, or plain of mulberries. Thebes supplied fine silks for the luxury markets of Constantinople and the rest of the Byzantine world, and its products were much prized in the West. It had successfully resisted barbarian assaults in the past, but the Sicilians caught it unprepared and it was coldly and expertly looted. The costly contents of its warehouses, together with numbers of the silk-workers themselves, were embarked and carried back to Palermo. Similar treatment was meted out to Corinth, which was hardly less

famous for its silk factories and as a centre of maritime trade. According to one contemporary Western writer, Otto of Freising, Athens was also raided, but since it possessed no commercial interest it is unlikely to have yielded much spoil. As for the treasures of the Parthenon, they were protected by the inexpugnable walls of the Acropolis.[15]
George's depredations caused no lasting damage to the prosperity of Greece. Benjamin of Tudela, a Spanish rabbi who travelled through the country in the 1160s, cataloguing the whereabouts and activities of the Jewish communities he came across, wrote that his co-religionists of Thebes were 'the most eminent manufacturers of silk and purple cloth in Greece'. This does not mean that the Jews had a monopoly in silk or in the treating of cloth with dyes supplied by the Aegean purple-fishers. The industries were characteristically Greek and survived well into the period of Frankish domination. But the raid was a heavy blow to Manuel's prestige and from that moment, whatever plans he may have originally conceived for attacking Roger's kingdom, it was absolutely certain that he would seek revenge for his humiliation. What was once a simple objective of policy, to be pursued or abandoned as circumstances dictated, became an affair of outraged honour.[16]

The preliminary task, the recapture of Corfu, was accomplished with Venetian aid in 1149. There followed a period of intense diplomatic manoeuvring while each side tried to strengthen its position and to enlist allies. Unfortunately for Manuel, Conrad of Germany, his most consistent supporter, died in 1152, and his nephew Frederick I (Barbarossa) had no wish to see a rival emperor from Constantinople disputing the ascendancy which he himself aspired to assert in Italy. He held that there was room for only one Roman sovereign in the world, and that he should be of German and not Greek race. Frederick therefore withheld his assistance from Byzantine designs. On the other hand King Roger, Manuel's inveterate enemy, died two years later and Manuel decided that the moment had come to launch his counterstroke.

As it turned out, the gamble did not succeed. Initially everything went well. The able Byzantine general Michael Palaeologos, aided by rebellious Norman vassals and the Greek-speaking inhabitants of Bari and other key cities, soon made himself master of the whole Adriatic side of Italy from Ancona to the Gulf of Taranto. But his triumph did not last long. He himself died in 1156 and his successor, John Dukas, was crushingly defeated in a combined land and sea battle at Brindisi by the new King of Sicily, William I 'The Bad'. Byzantine ambitions for the recovery of southern Italy were utterly and finally wrecked, and the Sicilian fleet celebrated the victory by again sailing into the Aegean and plundering the coasts of Euboea and Thessaly. Thereafter the two monarchs patched up a peace which lasted for the next twenty years.

Michael Palaeologos had made his name as governor of Macedonia, an almost viceregal position in the Empire of the Komnenoi. We have a picture of him, and of the booming, cosmopolitan city of Thessalonica where he resided, in a curious work of mediaeval Greek literature entitled *The Sufferings of Timarion*.[17] This takes the form of a dialogue of the dead, a genre imitated by Byzantine writers from the second-century satirist Lucian. Timarion, the chief protagonist, recounts to a friend his experiences and personal encounters in Hades, where he found himself relegated after a severe illness, but from where he obtained his release through a technical error on the part of the powers below. The book consists mostly of light-hearted satire directed against contemporary medicine, with side-swipes at Byzantine judicial procedures and professional pleaders, but it includes in its introduction a lively description of the great annual fair of St Demetrios the Martyr at Thessalonica, which lasted for the week preceding the saint's feast day.[18]

After a few days spent in hunting with his friends in the valley of the Axios (Vardar), Timarion surveys the vast and ordered array of tents outside the city walls in which traders from all over the Mediterranean world and beyond display their wares. Portuguese and Spaniards, Frenchmen from beyond the Alps, Italians, Greeks and Bulgarians all mingle there, together with more exotic merchants bringing oriental goods from Syria and Egypt and Russian furs from the Black Sea ports. The writer has a special word of admiration for the fine textiles of Boeotia and the Peloponnese, and for those imported by sea from Italy. The colour and bustle of a huge eastern bazaar combine with the more familiar noises and smells of a rural show at which the farmers of Greece and the Balkans exhibit their horses and mules, cattle, sheep and pigs.

Meanwhile the Archbishop officiates at three glittering all-night services at the cathedral of St Demetrios, and the festival culminates in the Governor's state procession to the martyr's shrine. At the head of his bodyguard, mounted on superb Arab horses, their harness shining with silver and gold, the *Dux* rides serenely through applauding throngs to play his part in the elaborate ceremonial. The author of *Timarion* risks overdoing himself in his fulsome panegyric, but it looks as if he had some pointed reason for extolling the virtues of this forbear of the last dynasty of Byzantium, who was praised by Otto of Freising as 'the noblest of the Greeks and a prince of royal blood'.[19]

So long as Byzantium retained control of the Balkans to the north,

Thessalonica was a lively centre of commerce and culture, rivalling even Constantinople. But as Manuel's long reign of thirty-seven years drew to an end his empire was showing unmistakable signs of exhaustion. Under a still magnificent facade the fabric was crumbling. Social and economic resources had not proved equal to the strain imposed on them by the ambitions and extravagance of the grandest of the Komnenoi, although it is doubtful whether the situation would have been substantially less serious if he himself had been less prodigal and aggressive. In the hostile world of the twelfth century mere self-defence cost Byzantium an inordinate effort. Excessive sums had to be spent on the army and on subventions to allies. Meanwhile the quality of government was deteriorating. Power had slipped from the hands of the civil hierarchy into those of a pampered military aristocracy. These nobles differed little in their status and mode of life from the wealthy feudatories in the West. Under the system of *pronoia* as it was called, the Byzantine barons or *pronoiars* held large estates granted to them by the Emperor in return for the obligation of military service. In theory such lands could not be alienated and reverted to the State on the death of the holder, nor did the *pronoiar* exercise jurisdiction over the serfs or *paroikoi*. In practice, however, the estates were apt to pass from father to son in the great military families, their revenues were collected and retained by the *pronoiars* and the lot of the *paroikoi* was hardly better than that of their Western counterparts.[20]

The economic situation steadily deteriorated under the Komnenoi. The spread of serfdom involved the decay of agriculture, while the disappearance of the soldier–farmer who had formerly been the mainstay of the Byzantine armies resulted in an expensive and dangerous dependence on mercenaries. The debasement by Alexios of the gold currency, the famous *nomisma* which had held its value for centuries, was a symptom of the age. At the same time the free population bore an increasingly heavy load of taxation and fiscal oppression evoked bitter social discontent. The commercial class, so essential an element in any Greek community, lost ground as its share of the Empire's foreign trade was encroached upon by the Venetians and other Italians. Economic decline was however a gradual process and in the second half of the twelfth century the prosperity of the Greek cities and countryside was high enough to tempt any aggressor.

Conditions in the Greek peninsula reflected the general trend: the weakening of the central authority and the rise of the territorial and military magnates. We know the names of some of the Hellenic feudal families which lorded over the Peloponnese and the themes north of the isthmus of Corinth. Some of them, for example the Branas and the Cantacuzenes of Messenia, and the Melissenoi, who held huge domains in both the Peloponnese and Thessaly, distinguished themselves on the wider Byzantine stage. Others make their appearance solely as local despots. Such were the Chamaretoi of Lakonia and the heads of the three patrician houses of Monemvasia, the Mamonas, Sophianoi and Eudaimonoyannis. In the north, the Epirote family of Petraleiphas was founded by a certain Petrus de Alpibus, or Peter of Aups in Provence. Among the lesser nobles the Voutsarades of Araklovon, a stronghold dominating the rugged district of Skorta in Arkadia, were to win renown by the tenacity of their resistance to the Franks.

All these local magnates, or *archons*, profited from the lack of control at the centre. They acted like petty tyrants, levying private armies, defying the imperial officials, quarrelling with each other, squeezing the rural population and blackmailing the towns. The most unscrupulous of them all was Leon Sgouros, archon of Nauplia, who extended his rule over Argos and Corinth and had by the end of the century established a virtually independent principality in the north-eastern Peloponnese. A stock mediaeval villain who held on to his gains by the most savage exercise of terror, he too was capable of heroic behaviour and proved it in the drama of the Frankish conquest.

A further symptom of growing anarchy was the revival of piracy, not that this endemic plague of the Greek seaboard had ever been entirely wiped out. Many of the sea-robbers were themselves Greek islanders, a race which when free from restraints has never drawn too fine a distinction between piracy and trading. Athens in particular suffered from the depredations of bands infesting the islands and promontories of the Saronic Gulf. But it was the Italian maritime republics that produced the worst corsairs, because they not only tolerated piracy but encouraged their citizens to engage in what was for them an extremely lucrative form of big business. Foremost among them were the Genoese who haunted the Ionian islands, and a leading freebooter from that city, Vetrano, finally possessed himself of Corfu. The neglected Byzantine navy afforded no protection at all, while the special tax levied for the purpose was diverted into the pockets of corrupt officials.

Nevertheless, it would be a mistake to paint too dark a picture. Greece was not cowering abjectly under the misrule of its archons and of the venal agents of an ineffective government. Violence and abuses abounded, but there was plenty of vitality left in the provincial towns and the country regions displayed a spirit of obstinate independence. In Thessaly, on the eve of the Frankish invasion, a local commander,

Michael Kamytzes, threw off the authority of Constantinople by putting himself at the head of the Vlachs. This shepherd people of the Pindus range, descendants of the pre-Slav inhabitants of the Balkans and speaking, as they still do, a language derived from Latin, had no use for feudalism or bureaucracy. So far as the Peloponnese is concerned, a similar recalcitrance characterized the Slavs of Taygetos, the Greeks of Maina and the hillmen of Arkadian Skorta, who are sometimes assumed to have been Slavs too. Definitely non-Slav but equally fond of their liberty were the Tzakonians of the eastern side of the peninsula. Their speech had, and 'retains', according to R.M. Dawkins, 'large elements from some ancient Laconian dialect',[21] in other words a marked affinity with the tongue the Spartans spoke. To the south of their territory the burghers and shipmasters of Monemvasia jealously guarded the privileges which the Emperor Maurice had granted them in the sixth century.

Athens found a resolute protector against the evils of the time in her archbishop, Michael of Chonae in Phrygia, who was appointed to the see in about 1175. His younger brother, Niketas, held high official posts under the Komnenoi and Angeloi and wrote the liveliest and most informative of the histories of the period. Michael was an excellent classical scholar and a pupil of the even more erudite Eustathios, who was Metropolitan of Thessalonica at the same time. He himself had served as secretary to the Patriarch of Constantinople, Theodosius Boradioktes, and his colleagues in the Greek episcopate included several eminent men. Of these the most notable were the theologian Euthymios of Neopatras, a busy town west of Lamia in the Spercheios valley, and Nicolas of Methone, who looked further back into Hellenic tradition and wrote a refutation of the Neoplatonic philosophy of Proclus. The contrast between such learned and polished prelates and the rough, arbitrary barons of the new Greek feudalism was indeed profound.

Michael was not a great writer but his surviving works, and especially his correspondence with friends in Constantinople and elsewhere, give a wonderfully exact impression of the troubled era through which Greece was living and of a brave and attractive personality struggling to defend the dignity of the Church, the interest of his flock and the traditions of Greek culture against a multitude of dangers. Steeped as he was in the classics, the new Archbishop was thrilled by his appointment to Athens. He loved his cathedral with its Periclean sculptures and Basilian treasures, his palace on the Acropolis where he installed his own classical library, the superb view from Mount Hymettus over sea and islands. Indeed his ecclesiastical authority extended over Euboea, Boeotia and the north littoral of the Corinthian Gulf as far west as Naupaktos. He eulogized the Parthenon as the 'wonderful brightshining temple and graceful palace, holy dwelling of the true Light that radiates from the Mother of God; . . . everything in this church is great; there is nothing mean in it, as in the ancient mysteries.'[22] But he was bitterly disappointed by the forlorn aspect and depressed condition of the city, and even more by the decay or disappearance of ancient sites and monuments, on which theme he composed a rather uninspired dirge in iambics. Twenty-five years earlier Edrisi, King Roger's Arab geographer, had praised Athens as a populous city, surrounded by gardens and fields.[23] Michael, however, found it poverty-stricken and depopulated, and if he was pleased by the number of charming little Byzantine churches dotted among the ruins of the past, and by the enchanting monasteries ensconced in the wooded slopes of the Attic mountains, he omitted to say so.

The Archbishop was equally shocked by the low standard of education and morality prevailing among the inhabitants. He complained that when he preached his inaugural sermon his hearers did not appear to understand a word he said. Although he thought that his address had been simple and unpretentious, he might as well have been talking in Persian or Scythian. Of course his sermon was nothing of the sort; as we read it, it is an elaborate oration packed with biblical and classical reminiscences and couched in high-flown antique language. It was well above the heads of the simple citizens, a fact of which Michael was entirely aware; but when writing to his sophisticated correspondents on the Bosporus he could not resist labouring the obvious antithesis between the intellectual glories of the ancient Athenians and the painful rusticity of their presumed descendants. 'O city of Athens', he intoned, 'mother of wisdom, to what level of ignorance hast thou shrunk?'[24] Moreover the Athenians were also deficient in spiritual qualities. Their attendance at divine worship was perfunctory and even the monks were slack and venal. Michael had as poor an opinion of contemporary monasticism as his tutor Eustathios, who unsparingly castigated its abuses.

But when it came to practical matters, the Metropolitan dismounted from his high horse. As befitting a true Greek he had an eye for economics, and it distressed him to observe that in contrast, for example, with Thebes or Corinth, Athens possessed no industries to speak of and a dry, ungrateful soil producing only olives and a wine tasting more of resin than of the grape. Clearly *retsina* was not appreciated in Phrygia and Constantinople. As for local craftsmanship, the level was so low that Michael could not get an adequate carriage built at Athens but had to order one through his suffragan bishop of Gardiki on the Gulf of Corinth. It was a relief for him to slip away to Chalkis in Euboea, where he was impressed by the prosperity of the island, the efficiency of its defences against pirates and the Orthodox devotion of its people.

Nevertheless he struggled on for thirty years to help those committed to his charge. He built houses and improved the lands belonging to the Church. He pressed the central administration for relief when the harvests failed and for the remission of oppressive taxes. Since the visit of Basil II Athens had officially enjoyed immunity from all fiscal obligations except the land tax, but the privilege was frequently abused by imperial officials and the Governor of the theme of Hellas. In the eleventh century the great statesman and Platonist Psellos had already intervened personally to protect the Athenians from the importunities of the treasury. Now the Archbishop took the same firm line, protesting repeatedly and successfully to the authorities at Constantinople against the high-handed actions of the Governor and the blackmailing attempts of the magnate Sgouros to extort money from the citizens for the ostensible purpose of defence against piracy. Michael, whose own nephew had been wounded by an arrow from a pirate galley, knew that any funds collected for ship-money would be promptly embezzled, and it was even more embarrassing for him to discover that one of his most exalted correspondents, Stryphnos the commander of the imperial fleet, who visited Athens with an expensive retinue, was selling naval equipment for his own profit.

Although the Archbishop never slackened in his efforts, they were largely frustrated by events, for his episcopate coincided with one of the most disastrous periods of Byzantine history. He had hardly reached Athens when, in 1176, Manuel's army was annihilated by the Seljuk Turks at Myriokephalon in Phrygia. It was a catastrophe on the scale of Manzikert in the preceding century, but fortunately the Turks preferred peace to following up their victory. Manuel's death in 1180 opened the way for the usurpation of his cousin Andronikos, whose attempt to bring about a radical reversal of policies, combined with his penchant for inhuman cruelties, plunged the Empire into nightmarish confusion. For many years Andronikos had been waiting in the wings, distrusted by the Emperor for his latent ambitions, scandalizing society by his disreputable love-life and restlessly frequenting the courts of minor Moslem and Russian princes. A strange blend of genius and unbridled ruthlessness, he recalls Peter the Great or a tyrant of Milan. To his contemporaries he seemed to possess all the talents and graces of the civilization to which he belonged along with the most sinister and barbaric vices. After Manuel's death the regency was assumed by his widow, Mary of Antioch, on behalf of her young son Alexios II. She and her lover, a nephew of the late Emperor and also named Alexios, made themselves extremely unpopular by the incompetence of their regime and their partiality for Latin adventurers and merchants. The prevailing discontent gave Andronikos the chance for which he had been waiting so long. When he raised a revolt in Asia Minor and advanced on the capital, the Constantinople mob rose in sympathy and slaughtered the detested Westerners. On taking over the government he indulged in a blood-bath of his own. First he murdered the Empress–mother and her adherents and had himself crowned co-Emperor. Then, in a style anticipating the excesses of the Ottoman Sultans, he had the boy Alexios II throttled and thrown into the Bosporus, and as a final outrage, the sexagenarian usurper married his girl-widow Agnes of France, daughter of King Louis VII.

Such a surfeit of villainies led Andronikos in two years' time to an equally lurid end. In the meantime, however, he enforced enlightened measures of reform which might well have succeeded had they been adopted at the proper moment by a more conventional ruler. He aimed to restore state authority, break the power of the military magnates, eliminate undesirable foreign influence, root out corruption in the bureaucracy and shield the humbler taxpayers against official abuses. His policy was essentially anti-aristocratic and anti-Latin. It was a programme of which Archbishop Michael of Athens would have thoroughly approved, and it was indeed greeted with acclaim by his historian brother, Niketas of Chonae, and his old tutor Eustathios, although they were at the same time horrified by the Emperor's atrocities. But in their writings they did not try to reconcile the contradictions of his character, to palliate his crimes or to denigrate his achievements, for Andronikos was both statesman and monster under the same skin. His cruelty stultified his statesmanship and soon alienated even those who sympathized with his aims. Opposition and conspiracy were remorselessly crushed amid an orgy of torture, blinding, burning and decapitation. Andronikos began to resemble Ivan the Terrible rather than Peter the Great; he was obsessed by a kind of fatalistic savagery.

Byzantium's internal plight was desperate enough, but it was the reaction in the West that finally ruined the state which Andronikos had set out to save. After the massacre at Constantinople, all the Western kingdoms and republics desired his downfall and in 1185 the Normans of Sicily moved to accomplish it. Whereas the purpose of King Roger's raid on Thebes and Corinth had been simply deterrent and punitive, his grandson William II 'The Good' was bent on the capture of Constantinople. With no need to fear that Byzantine diplomacy might successfully intrigue behind his back with Venice or the German Emperor, he launched an enormous expedition across the Adriatic. Eighty thousand men disembarked at Dyrrhachium, stormed the fortress and marched eastwards along the well-worn Via Egnatia. They were soon standing before the walls of Thessalonica, while a Sicilian fleet blocked the harbour.

It was symptomatic of the demoralization of the Komnenan Empire that no serious resistance was offered at Dyrrhachium and Thessalonica, where the local commanders were paralysed by lack of resources or their own ineptitude. The second city of the Empire was taken after a nine-day siege and subjected to an ordeal comparable with its sufferings at the hands of Leo of Tripoli. At least five thousand persons were butchered on the spot and the furious prejudice with which the soldiers were imbued against the Greek schismatics was expended on the wrecking and defilement of the Orthodox churches. But Eustathios the Archbishop, who witnessed these excesses and wrote an account of them, just as Leo Kameniates had done of the Saracen sack in 904, rose to the occasion and prevailed on the Norman commander, Baldwin, to restore order. When that was done the Normans pressed on towards their more exciting prey, Constantinople. They were not, however, destined to anticipate the outcome of the Fourth Crusade. The news of the fall of Thessalonica sparked off a revolution in the capital, where Andronikos had intensified his reign of terror. Its leader, Isaac Angelos, was proclaimed Emperor by the same mob as had elevated Andronikos, and which now preceded to put him to death after a long agony of insult and torture. The unexpected result of this grisly event was to reinvigorate Byzantine resistance to the invaders: Isaac's general Alexios Branas met them half-way to Constantinople and crushed them in two successive battles. Those who got away were despatched by the populace of Thessalonica.

Unfortunately this brilliant victory, worthy of the best traditions of Byzantium, was a flash in the pan. It failed to avert the catastrophe which the only too obvious decadence of the Empire had made inevitable. Under the feeble rule of the new Angelos dynasty the *pronoiars* regained power and the old abuses flourished unchecked.

Greece was again the prey of unruly magnates and rapacious officials. In northern Thrace the nobles of Greco-Bulgarian stock revolted and revived the Bulgarian monarchy which had been extinct since the Tsar Samuel. After 1195, when Issac Angelos was deposed and blinded by his elder brother Alexios, anarchy prevailed. It was clear that one more firm push would overturn the ramshackle Byzantine state, and the only question was which hand would deliver it. For a time it seemed that the conqueror would be Henry VI, the Hohenstaufen Emperor of Germany and the husband of Constance of Hauteville, heiress of the Sicilian Kingdom. The joint German–Sicilian expedition which he was planning could hardly have failed. But Henry died in 1197 and Byzantium was granted a short respite.

The immediate origins of the so-called Fourth Crusade and the processes of its diversion from Palestine to Constantinople are outside the scope of this book. Nevertheless certain facts concerning its leadership should be kept in mind because they have a bearing on the subsequent conquest of the Greek peninsula. The first is that the military commanders were not, as in the Second and Third Crusades, the great sovereigns of Western Europe, the kings of France and England or the German Emperor, but feudatories of high and middle rank, drawn from a wide region stretching from Flanders and the Rhineland through France to northern Italy. The most exalted of them were Baldwin, Count of Flanders and the Lombard Boniface of Montferrat, and all had a stronger incentive than the monarchs to win for themselves new realms and territories. Secondly, the venture could never have been attempted without Venetian ships and money, and lastly the motives of the attackers were entwined with dynastic intrigues and the family quarrels of the Angeloi.

The old Doge of Venice, Enrico Dandolo, nourished a personal grudge against Byzantium. His famous blindness was due to an injury received in a riot at Constantinople many years before, but his main reason for exploiting the Crusade was to guarantee once and for all the commercial supremacy of Venice in the Levant without the handicap of having to renegotiate with successive Emperors the privileges first extracted from Alexios I. The destruction of the Empire would enable Venice to exercise untrammelled rights throughout the former Byzantine sphere.

As for Boniface of Montferrat, his personal and political involvement in Levantine affairs was bewilderingly complex. His father and two of his brothers had already achieved careers of legendary brilliance in Palestine and another brother, Rainer, married to the eldest daughter of

Manuel I, had been one of the most eminent victims of Andronikos. He himself subsequently married the Hungarian widow of Isaac Angelos. Lastly, he was encouraged in his ambitions by his friend Philip of Swabia, brother of the late Hohenstaufen Emperor Henry VI and, as it conveniently turned out, the husband of Irene, daughter of Isaac Angelos. Even more convenient was the fact that in 1201 Isaac's son Alexios escaped from Constantinople and joined his sister and brother-in-law in Germany. After tortuous negotiations between the parties to the Crusade he was invited to join the expedition as a suitable puppet candidate for the Byzantine throne.

It is hard to judge whether this prince or his uncle Alexios III was the most worthless of the Angeloi. Dethroned by the Crusaders, the uncle managed to preserve his life and we shall meet him again, after the sack of Constantinople, as a wandering exile in Greece. The nephew, installed by the Crusaders in his place as Alexios IV, reigned abjectly for a few months before being stranged by his own indignant subjects. It was only after the Latin conquest that the name of Angelos was rescued from ignominy by kinsmen who headed the Greek reaction against the conquerors.

CHAPTER THREE

The Coming of the Franks

THE SEIZURE OF Constantinople by the Franks, which exposed Hellas to subjection by these invaders from the West, ranks among the most extraordinary exploits of an extraordinary epoch. As the turn of the century ushered in the high Middle Ages, the Mediterranean lands were increasingly swept by great events and dominated by great personalities. They were pervaded by great movements of mind and spirit and by a sustained sense of high adventure. It was the age of the Hohenstaufens and Pope Innocent the Third; of Philip Augustus and Richard Coeur de Lion; of Albigensians and Franciscans, and of the vast intellectual feats which culminated in the work of Bonaventura and Thomas Aquinas. But the real grandeur of the times was marred by human ruthlessness, greed and perfidy on an equally grand scale. The rape of Constantinople was a giant crime, the product of the prevailing atmosphere of distrust, violence and unsettling excitement. In 1204 the misunderstandings and enmities dividing Eastern from Western Christendom had reached their highest pitch and became virtually uncontrollable. The hysterical rage which seems to have possessed the Crusaders surpassed even the frenzy with which the populace of Constantinople had assailed the Latins in 1182.

'The accursed Latins', wrote Niketas of Chonae shortly after the fall of the city

> lust after our possessions and would like to destroy our race . . . Between us and them the widest gulf is fixed. We have not a single thought in common. They are stiff-necked, with a proud affection of an upright carriage, and love to sneer at the smoothness and modesty of our manners. But we look on their arrogance and boasting as a flux of the snivel which keeps their noses in the air, and we tread them down by the might of Christ, who gives to us the power to trample upon the adder and the scorpion.[1]

Such were the sentiments of the educated Byzantine. His outburst suggests that the mutual animosity between Greeks and Latins had reached the point of total estrangement, of blind exasperation leaving no room for understanding and compromise. If the Greek and Latin characters were basically incompatible, the omens for the foundation of Latin rule over the prostrate Byzantine Empire could not have been less propitious. In fact the prospects were not quite so unpromising, but the reasons for the crisis in the relations between the two halves of the Christian world were sufficiently serious and complex. Some had their roots in the remote past; other were of more recent origin. Some were political, others religious, and much of the antipathy was simply due to deep differences in temperament, habits and general outlook on life which had tended to become more acute over the years.

Political hostility was not the principal cause of odium. As far back as the ninth century the revival of the Western Roman Empire by Charlemagne caused alarm and resentment at Byzantium. So did the similar action of the Saxon Otto I the Great in 962, and the pretentions of subsequent German kings. That such barbarians should set themselves up as rivals to the only legitimate Emperors of the Romans was regarded at Constantinople as grotesque and theoretically intolerable. Nevertheless these Germans posed no serious military threat to the Byzantine Empire in its heyday, when it was engaged first in beating off Moslems and Slavs and then successfully counter-attacking. Occasionally Byzantine forces would collaborate with Westerners against the common Moslem enemy. It was the aggressive ambitions of the Norman Hautevilles in southern Italy and the Balkans, followed by the unexpected strain of the Crusades, that upset the balance of Byzantine foreign policy and introduced a new element of insecurity into the Empire's relations with the West. The Komnenan emperors, however, went out of their way to humour the Latin rulers with whom they were forced into contact. In the twelfth century dynastic intermarriage became frequent, and the manners of Western chivalry exercised a powerful attraction over the Byzantine military élite. On the popular level the Byzantines were used to Western pilgrims passing through their country to Palestine from the tenth century onward and received them kindly and hospitably. They only reacted in anger when robbed and maltreated by Crusading soldiers.

Religious differences were more profound and thus more liable to engender suspicion and dislike. It was too much to expect that, even after the great heresies of the fourth and fifth centuries had faded from the popular memory, uniformity of doctrine and practice would prevail between the Greek East and the Latin West. Jealous rivalry between the sees of Rome and Constantinople was equally unavoidable. Papacy and Patriarchate were bound to quarrel. Similarly, since there was so little contact, except at the highest level, between the Western and Eastern clergy, and none between their respective congregations, and since knowledge of Greek had dwindled in the West and that of Latin had virtually died out in the East, the liturgies in use diverged rapidly in form. Long before the twelfth century they had become mutually incomprehensible: Greeks and Latins found each other's rituals strange and irritating. The less sophisticated Latins also tended to assume that behind the incomprehensibility of the Greek rite there lurked an unsoundness on the very principles of the Faith.

Such suspicion was in fact unfounded and, to do them justice, was not encouraged by Latin theologians. Their Greek counterparts were perhaps more justifiably alarmed when they protested against the Latin introduction into the Creed of the Procession of the Holy Spirit from the Son as well as from the Father, as not authorized by the General Councils of the Church, and to the Latin use of unleavened bread in the Communion. These and other differences, however, failed to upset the common understanding that Christendom was still one. Research into the major controversies that flared up, especially in the ninth and eleventh centuries, between Rome and Constantinople, indicates no moment in the Middle Ages at which it can definitely be asserted that a formal and clear-cut schism had developed between the Churches. There was no clean break, only a growing disinclination to come and live together in union, despite political pressures to find formulas for agreement.

The most obvious stumbling-block to union was the question of papal supremacy. Constantinople had always been willing to admit the historical primacy of the Roman see but not its supremacy in the sense of the undisputed authority of the Pope in matters of doctrine and administration. But an even more important obstacle was the psychological gulf which, as Niketas insisted, yawned between Greeks and Latins in the quality of their religious feeling and of their views on the very meaning of life. The average literal and legal minded Latin was content to accept authority in spiritual matters without question and to leave theology to the theologians. As the Spanish saying puts it, 'doctores tiene la Santa iglesia Romana para resolver estos asuntos'. (The Holy Roman Church has doctors to resolve these matters.) But no Byzantine with the merest smattering of education was willing to leave religious speculation to the doctors alone. He himself revelled in the nuance and the symbol, sharpening his mind on Christian theology in the same way as the ancient Athenian found intellectual stimulation in philosophy. All that appeared reprehensible to the Westerners, whom the Byzantines struck as being glib, hedonistic, over-subtle and cynical;

treacherous, arrogant and maddeningly contemptuous of anything foreign. The Latins were unable to appreciate the substratum of seriousness, wide culture and genuine religious devotion which underlay the superficial slickness of the Greeks. Still less did they understand the pessimistic realism which characterized the attitude of the Byzantines towards mundane affairs, or their preference for the mystical and intellectual aspects of Christianity over the ethical. What they especially resented, and to some extent with reason, was the superiority with which the Byzantines affected to regard, in varying degrees, all outsiders, including the Frank, the Slav and the Oriental.[2]

The Lombard Liutprand of Cremona, who twice visited Constantinople as the ambassador of Otto the Great, wrote an account of his missions which is a unique description of Byzantium in the tenth century. It is also the classic expression of the sense of spleen and outrage which Byzantium was apt to arouse in Western breasts. Over two hundred years before the Latin Conquest, Liutprand gave vent to all the familiar griefs and grudges: the boasts and humiliations which he had endured from the Emperor and his ministers, the ostentatious luxury of the court, the impiety of public entertainments, the decadence of Byzantine manners, the horrors of the food and wine.[3] At a later period his counterpart, Anna Komnena, had in revenge plenty to say about the barbarous habits and uncouth brutality of the Latins with whom her father Alexios I had to deal, voicing the repulsion which the raw Westerners inspired in the cultivated élite of Constantinople, brought up in refined ease to study Homer and Euripides, Plato and the Church Fathers, among the masterpieces of antiquity with which the city still abounded.

Even this combination of factors, however, does not seem to account for the violent explosions of hatred which culminated in the events of 1204. For the Franks who were to occupy Hellas itself, the sole hope of establishing any kind of harmony with their Greek subjects lay in making the latters' existence more tolerable than it had been in the last phase of Byzantine rule. South of Thessalonica the country had been spared such devastation as had struck that city and the capital, and it had tired of the anarchy which had prevailed under the Angelos dynasty. Most of its inhabitants were ready to welcome any regime, Greek or Latin, which put an end to disorder and corruption. Nevertheless the auguries were hardly favourable when the Franks set out to broaden their conquest by dividing the imperial provinces between them.

Bargaining among the leaders of the expedition over the partition of the territorial spoil had reached an advanced stage even before the storming of the city on 12 April 1204. It had been formally agreed that whoever was chosen as Latin Emperor should take for himself a quarter of the territories available, while the remaining three-quarters should be split equally between the Venetian Republic and such Frankish nobles as were prepared to overrun the lands outside the area to be directly administered by the Emperor. All eventual holders of fiefs were to acknowledge the Emperor as their supreme lord, but the Venetians were significantly excluded from this obligation. After the city was taken the conquerors sat down again to fill in the details of the arrangement, and this task occupied the next six months. The two main problems were the selection of an emperor and the exact disposition of the relevant provinces.

Of the two rival candidates for the imperial title, Count Baldwin of Flanders and Boniface, Marquis of Montferrat, the latter was considerably the more suitable. As a bold commander in the field, the elected leader of the Frankish army and a knightly figure of flamboyant glamour, he had won the respect and affection of the soldiers. Moreover, he was a shrewd and opportunist statesman, a fit associate of the Hohenstaufens with whom he maintained a close connection. Again, as we have seen, he and his family were already deeply versed in war and intrigue in the East, and he was more cosmopolitan and sophisticated than most Westerners of his rank. Precisely for that reason he was unacceptable to the Doge Dandolo, and it was the Venetians, with their maritime supremacy and financial power, with their fixed aims and political flair, who were in a position to make their wishes prevail. They were determined to lay hands on, or at least to stake a claim to, every island, promontory, port and fortress in the Aegean and Ionian seas that they might at some time find useful in the task to which they were dedicated, the expansion and protection of their commercial hegemony. Clearly a strong Latin emperor would be as likely as a Greek ruler to obstruct their ambitions. Dandolo therefore insisted that the colourless Baldwin should be chosen instead of Boniface.

The Marquis of Montferrat was forced to submit to this decision. Not wishing to quarrel with the Venetians, he even made the best of it by selling Crete, which he did not yet possess, to the eager Republic. His dissensions with Baldwin, however, nearly led to open hostilities, which were only averted by Dandolo's intervention. After they were more or less reconciled, Boniface managed to secure for himself the mainland provinces of his preference.

In the course of wrangling about partition, the Frankish leaders had shown little enthusiasm for the task of conquering the provinces still held by the Byzantines in the north-west of Asia Minor. There Theodore Laskaris, son-in-law of Alexios III Angelos, had assumed the imperial title and crown, and was aiming to re-establish Byzantine power from his new capital at Nicaea. Still less did the Franks relish the prospect of a conflict with the formidable Turkish (Seljuk) Sultanate which lay beyond the Greek buffer state. Baldwin himself had no desire to prejudice his triumph by a risky struggle with the Seljuks, who had mauled so many crusading armies in the past, or with more distant Moslem powers, and Boniface, for his part, insisted on being compensated for his rejection as emperor by a solid allocation of lands in Europe. He was equally shy of Asiatic hazards.

In the end Boniface had his way and it was Baldwin who found himself facing Laskaris and the Seljuks. After winning a battle against the former, he was hastily recalled to Europe to counter a challenge from the Bulgarian Tsar Kalojan, who had invaded Thrace. But the Frankish army was disastrously defeated; Baldwin was taken prisoner and subsequently died in a Bulgarian dungeon. He was succeeded by his brother Henry, a more competent ruler, who just managed to keep the Latin Empire alive in the narrow enclave between Bulgaria and the Nicaean state.

Meanwhile Boniface was comfortably established in Macedonia as King of Thessalonica, a new realm for which he agreed to do homage to the Latin Emperor while, of course, retaining effective sovereignty and receiving a free hand to add to it the whole of continental Greece, with the exception of any outposts claimed by Venice. So, in the autumn of 1204, having arranged his relationship to the Empire wholly in his favour, he led his host of land-hungry Franks southwards from Thessalonica. They threaded their way unopposed through the narrow gorge of Tempe, between Mounts Olympus and Ossa, and entered the Thessalian plain.

The knights enlisted under Boniface's banner were drawn from a broad variety of Western lands. There were Frenchmen from Champagne and Burgundy, Flemings from Flanders and Artois, Germans from the Rhine and Italians from Lombardy, Boniface's own country. All were amazed by their good fortune and exhilarated by the promise of fat fiefs for the asking, for they rightly did not expect much resistance. Not for them the terrifying uncertainties of campaigning in Asia, the heat, the Seljuk arrows, or the hopelessly precarious existence of Crusaders in the Holy Land, a dwindling garrison hemmed in ever more closely by Turks and Saracens. They, on the contrary, for the cost of the not too arduous capture of Constantinople from which each man had received his share of the fabulous loot, were apparently gaining undisputed possession of a rich and beautiful country inhabited by docile and industrious Christians. Conveniently, too, those Christians happened to be schismatic and as such had no right, in their eyes, to be treated with any special indulgence. Few of the Franks would readily have admitted that their knightly honour had been seriously tainted by the barbarities perpetrated at Constantinople. Most of them felt that such excesses had been amply excused by the results of the adventure, the establishment of Latin dominion and of the Latin Catholic religion on the ruins of Orthodox Byzantium. The invasion of the Greek peninsula was by comparison a light-hearted and chivalrous cavalcade, and it was not marked by scenes of horror: no city in Hellas was to share the fate of Thessalonica and Constantinople. In Boniface's train came poets and troubadours such as Rambaud de Vaqueiras from Provence, who celebrated the new King's conquests in courtly verse.

More significantly, Boniface was initially accompanied on his march by many prominent Byzantines, who had realistically decided that their best chance of preserving their property and status intact in an Aegean world dominated by the Latins was to attach themselves, at least temporarily, to the King of Thessalonica. They were drawn to him by his Greek connections and admired the personally attractive and heroic qualities which made men forget how ruthless and calculating he could be. Outstanding among his Greek retinue were two members of the former imperial family of Angelos. One was Boniface's own stepson Manuel; the other Michael, was a cousin of Isaac II and the illegitimate son of a John Dukas who had at one time governed Epiros. Michael himself had been appointed to command the themes of both northern and southern Greece shortly before the fall of Constantinople, but had been unable to take up his post before the catastrophe occurred. He was now watching for an opportunity to assert himself.

In Thessaly Boniface met the first signs of organised opposition to his advance. This came from the powerful Peloponnesian archon Leon Sgouros, who alone of the numerous Greek landed magnates was prepared to challenge the invaders. Pushing forward from his triangle of virtually impregnable fortresses, the rock of Nauplia, the steep citadel of Argos and the towering Acrocorinth, he first tried to seize Athens, which its archbishop Michael of Chonae was administering after the collapse of Byzantine civil authority. But Michael, who had ample reasons for distrusting Sgouros, barricaded himself in the Acropolis and inspired the citizens to repulse the attack. The archon was more successful at Thebes, which he occupied without difficulty before hurrying northwards to Larissa in Thessaly. There he met one of the first victims of Frankish aggression, the ex-Emperor Alexios III on the run from Boniface's army. The stage seemed set for a battle, but in the event Sgouros hardly had time to marry Alexios' daughter, who in the course of her family's vicissitudes had already been wedded to three successive potentates, before he was forced to turn in his tracks and make an equally hurried retreat to the south. As for his new father-in-law he disappeared in the prevailing confusion. Eventually, he turned up in Asia Minor at the court of the Seljuk sultan, was captured in battle by Theodore Laskaris and was put out of harm's way as a monk at Nicaea.[4]

While Sgouros halted at the first defensible position, the pass of Thermopylae, Boniface was distributing fiefs in Thessaly, where the existing estates belonged to the imperial family and to rich Orthodox monasteries. A Lombard gentleman received Larissa, and proceeded to call himself Guglielmo de Larsa; he also got Halmyros, the principal port for the grain trade which made Thessaly so valuable a province. The adjoining country was allotted to the Rhinelander Berthold von Katzenellenbogen, 'whose name', William Miller observes, 'must have proved a stumbling-block to his Thessalian vassals'.[5] But as soon as the Franks resumed their march Sgouros abandoned Thermopylae too without a fight. Boniface's troubadour inevitably made fun of Greek cowardice: Sgouros' men, he claimed, must have had their hearts in their heels, in order to spur their horses to so swift a flight, while Archbishop Michael's brother, Niketas, wrote that the merest glimpse of the mailed Frankish cavalry drove them to panic retreat. It is true that Sgouros fell back by stages, evacuating all Greece north of the Acrocorinth, until he reached the security of the fortress. But, as later events were to prove, he by no means lacked personal courage. His decision to avoid battle rested on good military grounds, for he simply did not have the resources to stand up in open battle against a Western army in full panoply. We have no estimate of the strength of Boniface's army, either in mounted knights and men-at-arms or in crossbowmen or other essential components of a mediaeval fighting force, but it is obvious that it would have been suicidal for Sgouros to try to meet the Franks in the field with his lightly armed Greek retainers and partisans.

Boniface, following at a leisurely pace, paused to distribute fiefs north of the isthmus of Corinth. Of these the most strategically important were Boudonitza, commanding the pass of Thermopylae, and Salona, which blocked the approach from the north to the Corinthian Gulf. The first he entrusted to the Marquis Guido Pallavicini, a member of a brilliant but unruly Lombard family. A French nobleman, Thomas de

Stromoncourt, was invested with the second. This barony was destined to remain in the hands of the same family longer than any other in mediaeval Greece, and the imposing ruins of the castle which Thomas built on a western spur of Mount Parnassus, overlooking the town of Salona (now re-baptised with the classic name of Amphissa) are a superb reminder of the Frankish presence.

Pressing on through Boeotia, Boniface next entered Thebes, probably the most populous town in Greece at the time and, according to Niketas, was welcomed by its inhabitants. Having installed a garrison in the citadel, the ancient Kadmeia, under a Burgundian knight Guillaume de St Croix, he marched without delay to Athens. This time the Archbishop wisely offered no resistance, but his submission failed to deter the invaders from remorselessly stripping Our Lady of Athens, the Parthenon, of the accumulated treasures of eight centuries of Orthodox worship. Even Michael's library was scattered to the winds. No wonder that he left Athens in despair, knowing that his cathedral would be turned over to the Catholics. He found a refuge in the neighbouring island of Keos, from which he could watch the coast of Attica.

The King of Thessalonica was riding on the high tide of successful conquest. The Fleming Jacques d'Avesnes received on his behalf the surrender of the island of Euboea, Attica's neighbour, with its key harbour of Chalkis. He himself allotted Boeotia, Attica and the adjoining Megarid to one of his most valued adherents, Othon de la Roche. The recipient of this truly magnificent fief was a young Burgandian knight from La Roche sur Ognon, a river which runs into the Saone between Dijon and Besançon. As a French monk, Aubri des Trois Fontaines, recorded in his chronicle, 'Othon de la Roche, son of a nobleman Pons de la Roche in Burgundy, became by a miracle Duke of Athens and Thebes.'[6] He was so deeply impressed by Othon's luck that he anticipated by half a century the bestowal of a ducal title on the lord of Athens, who was originally known simply as Sire d'Athènes, or in Greek as *Megaskyr*. But he was already master of the two most famous cities of ancient Hellas.

Thus the whole eastern side of Greece north of the Corinthian gulf, between the Aegean sea and the Pindus mountains, acknowledged Boniface's rule. It was quite otherwise with the western side, with Acarnania, Aetolia and Epiros. At an early stage in the Frankish march to the south the bastard Michael Dukas realised that, if he acted promptly, he might snatch the western province from under the nose of the Latins and found his own independent principality. Moreover, if he were successful, it might serve as a base for future expansion at the expense of the still unsteadily established Latin Empire. He chose the right moment to claim his rights, for Epiros was in confusion and only too ready to welcome the son of its former Governor. With a few followers Michael swung across the Pindus range and seized Arta, the capital. This bold stroke made him master of the whole western seaboard from Naupaktos on the Gulf of Corinth northward to Dyrrhachium. Therefore, less than a year after the fall of Constantinople, Latin rule was already challenged by the Empire of Nicaea, under Theodore Laskaris, on the east and by Epiros, under Michael Dukas, on the west. And even further east a branch of the family of the Komnenoi had set up yet another empire at Trebizond.

The ambitious and energetic Michael found himself the ruler of a rugged country with a mixed and warlike population of mountaineers. In the south Greeks predominated, in the north Albanians, and there was also a considerable Vlach element. All three races were happy to acknowledge an Orthodox prince. He had no difficulty in raising an army, and enough Byzantine officials were at hand to staff his administration. Strategically his state was well situated, covering the western approaches to Greece from the Ionian and Adriatic seas, and provided with useful harbours in the land-locked Gulf of Ambracia. Michael strengthened his position by marrying into the Melissenoi, the family of great territorial magnates which contrived to hold on to its estates all over northern Greece in defiance of the Frankish conquest. His restless temperament drove him to seek further opportunities, the first of which presented itself in the Peloponnese.

It was there that the Franks encountered real opposition for the first time. Their initial attempts to break into Sgouros's triangle of fortresses failed signally, although Boniface mustered all his baronage for the attack. He himself was unable to take Nauplia, while Othon de la Roche and Jacques d'Avesnes suffered a bloody repulse from Acrocorinth. The stalemate which ensued was only dissolved by a diversion from the south. It happened that in the winter of 1204 a young nobleman from Champagne, Geoffroy de Villehardouin, had been driven by a storm into the harbour of Modon in the southern Peloponnese. He was in fact trying to sail from Palestine, where he had been on pilgrimage, to Constantinople, in the hope of joining the crusading army. He had heard of the capture of the city, and his eagerness to share in the prizes of the conquest was enhanced by the knowledge that his own uncle and namesake was one of the outstanding leaders in that venture. The elder Geoffroy, who held the title of Marshal of Champagne, had distinguished himself both as a warrior and in the political intrigues which preceded the assault on the Byzantine capital: what was more important for posterity, he related his experiences in the most valuable chronicle which we possess of the Fourth Crusade.

While weather-bound at Modon, Villehardouin and his followers passed the time in helping a local Greek archon to extend his lands to the detriment of his neighbours, an occupation which he no doubt found profitable, but which also opened his eyes to the possibilities of carving out a domain of his own in a peninsula from which all orderly central authority had vanished. But after a while his Greek patron died, leaving a son who distrusted Westerners and would have no more to do with him. At that moment, providentially, the news reached him that the Franks had entered the Peloponnese. Without hesitation he rode for six days westward through the highlands of Arkadia until he joined the King of Thessalonica before Nauplia.

Boniface naturally welcomed him, and as luck would again have it, he also encountered among the besiegers an old friend, Guillaume de Champlitte, Viscount of Dijon, known as 'Le Champenois' after his grandfather Hugues I, Count of Champagne. Geoffroy persuaded both the King and the Viscount that despite Sgouros' resistance the Peloponnese was as a whole an easy prey; he did homage to Champlitte as his feudal superior and Boniface allotted to them a hundred knights for the conquest of the territory. Champlitte gladly grasped the chance of making himself an even greater vassal of the King of Thessalonica than Othon de la Roche, lord of Attica and Boeotia, who in their native country had stood much lower than himself on the feudal ladder. Without losing any time he and Villehardouin left Boniface beleaguering Sgouros' castles and set out to reduce the rest of the peninsula.[7]

They marched along the Gulf of Corinth as far as Patras, which was easily taken, then wheeled south-west and south, parallel to the coast, until they reached the ports of Modon and Coron. Most of the archons of Elis and Messenia hurried to make their submission, in the hope that they would not lose their lands, and of the coastal strongholds only Arkadia (Kyparissia) put up more than a token resistance. 'A powerful tower from the time of the Hellenes', it was battered into surrender by the siege engines (*trébuchets*, or *tripoutseta* in the bastard Greek of the *Chronicle of the Morea*).[8] But the campaign was not merely a triumphal progress; it gave the Franks control of all the ports facing west, thus ensuring that their access to their countries of origin, and the inflow of much needed reinforcements, would not easily be interrupted. The importance of keeping open this window on the West prompted them to establish their centre of government at Andravida in Elis and to keep it there. Another natural advantage of Elis was that its plain was peculiarly well suited to the manoeuvres of heavy cavalry, and to the breeding of the horses with which Frankish military prowess was so closely linked.

These preliminary successes provoked little hostile reaction from the Peloponnesian Greeks. According to the *Chronicle of the Morea*, Champlitte went out of his way to assure the landowners that they would not forfeit their estates and privileges.[9] Nevertheless, having secured the coastal towns, he was obliged to fight a single decisive battle before further extending his power into the interior. The force opposed to him was composed chiefly of Greeks from Arkadia and Lakonia, together with a contingent of Slavonic Melings from the Taygetos massif. Furthermore, as soon as Michael of Epiros learned that a fight was imminent, he hastened across the Gulf of Corinth to join the challengers. But the battle, which took place at Koundoura in Messenia, resulted in the complete rout of the Greeks. It proved that local Greek forces, however bold, patriotic and superior in numbers, were incapable of outmatching the Franks. In a frontal clash on level ground the heavily mailed knights and men-at-arms on their huge war horses were irresistible, and more subtle tactics were required to defeat them. Michael, now styled Despot of Epiros (in Greek the title carries no disparaging implication) made good his escape to his own principality.

It was easy enough to win a pitched battle, but when the Franks began to penetrate into the core of the peninsula they were held up by one resolutely defended castle. The hero of this episode was one Doxapatres ('Glory be to the Father') Voutsaras, lord of Araklovon, the key to the mountain massif of Skorta west of the upper valley of the Alpheios river. His castle, says the Greek *Chronicle of the Morea*, was small but almost impregnable, perched on a rocky hill, and its lord was 'a great soldier' (*megas stratiotes*).[10] In view of the violently pro-Frankish bias of the *Chronicle*, that was indeed a tribute to the gallantry of Doxapatres. The *Chronicle* infers that the fortress succumbed promptly to the Franks, but the Aragonese version of the book which was written somewhat later, asserts that it in fact held out for five years, and that Doxapatres himself, portrayed as a warrior of Herculean strength, performed striking feats of valour. Evidently his prowess had enlivened the local folklore, including a legend that Champlitte had fallen in love with his daughter, and that she, in order to resist his advances, had consented to be flung to death from the castle tower.

Thus while Champlitte and Villehardouin were free to overrun the rest of the Peloponnese gradually and as their resources permitted, much remained to be done before it could be completely subdued. By the autumn of 1205, however, Champlitte felt strong enough to assume the resounding title of Prince of Achaia, with the full approval of the King of Thessalonica and at least the tacit concurrence of the Latin Emperor and the Pope. It is interesting that the archaic name for the peninsula was adopted in preference to that of Morea, a term of doubtful etymology which was used in common speech by both Greeks and Franks, while the classical 'Peloponnese' was employed by Byzantine officials and scholars.

Further Frankish progress in the Morea was delayed, quite apart from local resistance, by events in the north, where the victorious Bulgarian Tsar, having defeated and captured the Emperor Baldwin, was threatening to deprive Boniface of his Macedonian territories. The King was obliged to abandon his blockade of the citadels of Corinth and the Argolid in order to safeguard his own capital, as well as to keep closer control of his vassals in the north. In the tradition of his family, who were experts in dynastic marriages, he gave his daughter to the new Latin Emperor Henry of Flanders. He soon restored the situation and his prospects in 1207 seemed as brilliant as ever when he was suddenly killed in a petty Bulgarian ambush, leaving his small son, Demetrios, in charge of his principal Lombard vassal, the Count of Biandrate.

His death was a tragedy for the Latins in the East. Had he survived, he might conceivably have arrested the imminent decay of their fortunes. His natural eminence as soldier and stateman was heightened by his intimate understanding of the Levantine world and by his talent for conciliating his Greek subjects, which overrode such aversions as they felt for him as one of the principal assassins of the Orthodox Empire. It was no accident that he named his son after the Orthodox warrior St Demetrios, patron and guardian of Thessalonica against countless barbarian assaults.

The disappearance of this strong and able man, extravagantly praised by Rambaud de Vaqueiras as having surpassed the deeds of Alexander, Charlemagne and Roland, created a vacuum in northern Greece, and the predominantly Lombard nobles of the kingdom judged that the time had come to shake off their feudal allegiance to the Emperor Henry. They aimed to create an entirely independent realm embracing Macedonia, all northern Greece including Epiros, and the Morea, which the ambitious Count of Biandrate would govern in the name of the child King Demetrios. Prominent in the plot were the Lombard fief-holders in Thessaly, the Marquis of Boudonitza and three noblemen from Verona, Ravano and Giberto dei Carceri and Pegoraro dei Pegorari, between whom Boniface had divided the island of Euboea after the return of Jacques d'Avesnes, its conqueror, to Flanders. But the two greatest feudatories of Greece, the Prince of Achaia and the Sire d'Athènes, remained aloof.

Henry acted with all speed to crush the rebellion. Fortunately he possessed all Boniface's good qualities, but with an even wider sense of tact and moderation. Having captured Thessalonica and clapped Biandrate into prison, he made an imperial progress through Greece as far as Athens, rewarding the loyal and sparing the rebels when possible. To the Greeks he was affable, treating them, according to the Byzantine historian George Akropolites, like his own people. At Ravenika, near Lamia, he held the first of the *Parlements*, those assemblies of feudal grandees which were soon to become so colourful a feature of mediaeval Greece. There he received the homage of Villehardouin and de la Roche. The former's stature had recently grown, since he was acting as bailie or deputy of the Prince of Achaia in the absence of Champlitte, who had left for France, while the Lord of Athens was seeking the restoration of Thebes, temporarily occupied by the still recalcitrant Marquis of Boudonitza. Othon's petition was granted, and he escorted Henry with great pomp to Athens, the first imperial visitor to the city since Basil the Slayer of the Bulgarians. Just as in the days of Basil, a service of thanksgiving was celebrated for him in the Parthenon, but this time it was a Latin Mass said by a Latin archbishop.

After a short visit to Chalkis (or, as the Latins called it, Negroponte) Henry summoned a second parliament at Ravenika, the main purpose of which was to settle church affairs. While feudal relationships in mediaeval Greece are sometimes hard to grasp, ecclesiastical matters are more complex still, involving as they do the dominant Catholic Church, the schismatic but tolerated Orthodox establishment and the exigencies of the Roman Curia. The Franks had hardly occupied the country when bitter antipathies began to arise from the jealousy with which the baronage viewed the simultaneous arrival of a swarm of clerics and members of religious orders avidly demanding a more than ample share of the spoils won by the soldiers. Although they could not reasonably object to their own Church usurping the most valuable properties and possessions of its Orthodox predecessor, they were determined that the ecclesiastical domain should not be allowed to encroach on their own; nor should it be unduly increased by donations and bequests. It seemed to them particularly important that in an alien country, where Frankish fighting men were so scarce, fiefs should not pass from the laity to the clergy. This issue immediately became a source of dispute, and there were also continual quarrels about who should be liable to pay tithes to the Church, and whether the clergy should be required to pay taxes to the temporal powers. Pope Innocent III, for his part, was equally insistent that the position of the Church in the Levant should be no less privileged than in the West and that the hierarchy, headed by the Latin Patriarch of Constantinople, should be treated with proper deference and protected from high-handed interference by the barons. Both the latter and the bishops were well represented at Ravenika, where Henry tried to compose their differences by getting them to agree to a concordat. This document was subsequently approved by the Pope, but as we shall see later it remained a dead letter in the Morea, and was regarded with scant respect further north.

On the political side, Henry was gratified by receiving the homage of Michael Dukas, though he must have realized that the Despot's gesture was purely formal and opportunist. It was, however, accompanied by the offer of his daughter's hand for the Emperor's brother. Yet at the same time Michael was again actively opposing Henry's vassal Villehardouin in the Morea. The three besieged fortresses were still untaken when, in 1208, Leon Sgouros, maddened by inaction and despair at being confined for three years in Acrocorinth, committed spectacular suicide by galloping his charger over the edge of the unscalable precipice on which the castle was perched.[11] His last act was typical of this strange, wild man, a curiously non-Greek figure with his uncontrollable rages and hatred of all conciliation and compromise. He was a natural *frondeur* who before the conquest regarded the Byzantine officials, his fellow archons and the prelates of the Orthodox Church with equal loathing and disdain. His treacheries were only matched by his cruelties. He put out the eyes of his guest, the Archbishop of Corinth, before hurling him to his death from the citadel of Nauplia, and requited the efforts of Archbishop Michael to tame him by kidnapping his young nephew, forcing him to serve as a page and then murdering him for having broken a drinking cup. Frustrated in his lust for power by the Frankish conquest, he held on stubbornly until convinced that he had reached a dead end. The Despot, on the other hand, had not given up hope of regaining the Morea for the Greeks. On hearing of Sgouros's death he arranged for his brother Theodore, a man even more daring and ambitious than himself, to slip into Acrocorinth and take over its defence.

In the year after these events Villehardouin replaced Champlitte as the leader of Moreot Franks. The newly styled Prince of Achaia had no intention of renouncing his family's rights in the principality, but on learning that his elder brother had died in Burgundy without an heir, he decided to return home and claim his inherited lands. In the meantime he appointed his nephew Hugues to act as bailie of Achaia, although the reality of power rested with Villehardouin. Moreover the situation developed rapidly in the latter's favour, as Champlitte died on the journey and the nephew shortly afterwards. So Villehardouin became the titular as well as the effective bailie.

It was the habit of all contemporary Frankish writers to denounce the Greeks for trickery and deceit. But the comedy which followed showed that for sheer deviousness the chivalrous Villehardouin could outdo any Byzantine. Perhaps that was one of the reasons why he was so popular with his Greek subjects. Apart from appointing his nephew as bailie, Guillaume de Champlitte had attempted further to protect his family's interests by agreeing with Villehardouin that any new Champlitte heir to the principality must arrive in the Morea and validate his claim within the period of one year and a day. If he failed to so do, his claim would be regarded as having lapsed. Once Hugues was dead, Villehardouin might reasonably have expected that his own supremacy would no longer be disputed by a Champlitte, but to his surprise he learned that another young kinsman of the late Prince, Robert, had left France and was on the way to make good his title.

Villehardouin resolved to thwart him by all means in his power short of violence. First he made use of the good standing which he then enjoyed with the Doge to have the claimant detained in Venice for as long as possible, under the pretence of doing him honour, before he sailed for the Morea, and to have his arrival further delayed by denying him a direct passage. On finally reaching his destination, Robert was kept moving from town to town and castle to castle in pursuit of Villehardouin, who always kept one step in front of him. The cumulative effect of this obstruction was that when Robert at last caught up with the elusive bailie at his camp near Lakedaimonia and found a parliament convoked there to judge his claim, the notables pronounced that the stipulated period had expired two weeks earlier and that this claim must therefore be rejected. Faced with the united opposition of the barons, he had no choice but to return to France.

By this piece of sharp dealing Villehardouin safeguarded not only his own position but the future of the principality itself. As the barons, whom he was in process of installing in their new fiefs, were well aware, the survival of Frankish Achaia depended on his own experience and prestige, and he could never have taken second place to a callow cadet straight from Burgundy. There was now nothing to prevent his acceptance by the Pope and the Latin Emperor as Prince of Achaia and from 1210 he was duly recognized as such.[12]

As Champlitte's right-hand man, as bailie and as Prince, Villehardouin spent the years from 1205 to 1214 in prodigiously sustained activity. Shortly after the battle of Koundoura he was already discussing with the native archons the division of Moreot lands between the invaders and themselves. In that settlement he was negotiating from strength, for the archons, despite Champlitte's assurances, were in no position to resist inroads on their possessions, but he was less sure of himself when he approached the more delicate task of dealing with Venetian claims to coastal territory as set out in the original partition agreement. These were both vague and sweeping. If the Venetians had wished to take advantage of all the concessions envisaged by the treaty, they would have demanded Patras and all the choice coastal districts. They had indeed already seized Modon and Coron, pushing out the Frankish garrisons. But Villehardouin had the diplomatic sense to avoid a clash. He abandoned any pretensions to the two ports and agreed to pay homage to the Doge for other regions allocated to Venice by the partition agreement. He was rightly confident that the Republic would rest content with this formality and would take care not to occupy more territory than it could digest, especially as he promised the fullest trading privileges to Venetian merchants in the whole of the Morea.

Geoffroy's successes in the diplomatic field did not prevent him from proceeding concurrently with the extension of his conquest and the organization of the peninsula on feudal lines. As the French *Chronicle of the Morea* says, 'Monseignor Geoffroy ordina sa gent et commenca a chevaucier par le pays et de conquester sur les Grex.'[13] One campaign sufficed to reduce the prosperous market towns of the central Peloponnese, Nikli, Veligosti and Lakedaimonia. There remained the three Greek strongholds in the north-east, the fortress rock of Monemvasia in the south-east, the domain of the mysterious Tzakones[14] between Nauplia and Monemvasia and the Slavonic tribes of Taygetos. Calculating that the Tzakones and the Slavs would be gradually tamed as soon as the Frankish fief-holders could be established in castles built to overawe and isolate them, Villehardouin concentrated his attack on the main fortified places. He was as before aided by the lord of Athens, while the Venetians provided ships for the capture of Nauplia. In 1210 Acrocorinth at last gave in, but Theodore Dukas managed to escape to the almost equally inexpugnable Argos. Soon afterwards Nauplia surrendered on condition that the Greeks might retain one of its twin castles. Finally, in 1212, Argos too gave up the struggle. Again Theodore emerged unharmed from an obstinate defence and was allowed to return to Epiros. Villehardouin rewarded Othon de la Roche for his assistance with the fiefs of Argos and Nauplia, which made him a great vassal of Achaia as well as Megaskyr of Athens. As for Monemvasia, it was considered too strong to be either assaulted or reduced by attrition, and it remained for the time being the only unsubdued city in the Morea.

The organization of the feudal state was Villehardouin's finest achievement and absorbed the greater part of his remarkable fund of energy. Before Champlitte's departure he had obtained the Prince's approval for the assignment of fiefs according to a plan drawn up by a small commission which included Frankish barons, Greek archons and Latin clerics. Armed with these proposals he presented them to a full parliament of Frankish notables at Andravida or, as the Franks called it, Andreville. The commission's report was however more than a mere register of fiefs; it laid down in detail the feudal framework within which the Morea would be governed for the duration of Frankish rule.[15]

The main pillars of this structure were twelve great baronies, exclusive of the fiefs granted to de la Roche. The functions which the holders of these fiefs were required to carry out were political and judicial as well as military. With their castles and armed retainers they were the mainstay of Frankish power, but they also acted as the political advisers to the prince in council and as judges of the high court. The roll of baronies recorded by the *Chronicle of the Morea* reads like an extract from an ideal romance of chivalry, but before listing the fief-holders it will be useful to say something about the Chronicle itself, not only because it is the most important source for the early history of the principality of Achaia but also because it is a curious example of the kind of literature which is produced as a result of a meeting or clash of diverse cultures. The book has come down to us in four versions, the Greek, the French, the Italian and the Aragonese, corresponding to the four main national elements in the history of feudal Greece. Of these the Greek and the French, both discovered about 150 years ago by the French scholar Buchon, are the most interesting. The Italian text is only a resumé, compiled at a later date, of the Greek; the Aragonese, which was completed in 1393 and covers the period 1197-1377, uses the Greek version and outside sources as well. Scholars disagree as to whether the Greek version preceded the French or vice versa, and some think that they both derive from a vanished original.[16] In their present form they are thought to date from about 1341. The former takes the story as far as 1292, the latter up to 1304. All four versions are anonymous and were obviously composed for the purpose of recalling to the fourteenth-century Frankish barons, whose memory of past events had grown hazy, the feats of the conquerors and their immediate descendants. The three versions in the Romance languages are in prose. The French text is headed, in a strain of romanticism, 'Livre de la conquete de Constant-inople at de l'empire de Romanie, et dou pays de la princee de la Moree, qui fut trove en un livre qui fut jadis del noble baron Messire Bartholomee Guys, le grand connestable; lequel livre il avait en son chastel d'Estives [Thebes].'[7] (Book of the conquest of Constantinople and of the Empire of Romania, and of the country of the principality of the Morea, which was found in a book once belonging to the noble baron Sir Bartholomew Guys, the grand constable; which book he had in his castle of Thebes.) The Aragonese is entitled, with a similarly chivalrous ring, 'Libro de los fechos et conquistas del principado de la Morea.' (Book of the feats and conquests of the principality of the Morea.)

One of the joys of the French version is the ease with which it can be read, despite its eccentricities of spelling, and its stately and aristocratic style is most attractive. The Greek text, on the other hand, running in one manuscript to over nine thousand lines, is written in the fifteen-syllable so-called 'political' verse which in the Middle Ages had become the normal medium for such Byzantine writers as preferred to use the spoken or demotic language for chronicles, satires and romances in place of the idiom based on classical models which was employed by the literati. The writer expresses himself with complete fluency in the popular Greek speech of the day, plentifully interlarded with words of French or Italian origin. It is however doubtful whether he was in fact a Greek, for his sympathies are outspokenly Western and Catholic and his attitude towards the Greeks is uniformly scornful and hostile. Indeed he seems to go out of his way to ignore their virtues and exaggerate their defects, while lavishing praise on their Latin rulers. If not a Frank himself—but of course a bilingual Frank—he was probably a *gasmoulos*, or offspring of a Frankish father and a Greek mother, and as such a member of a class which naturally grew more numerous with the prolongation of Latin rule. If so he did not follow the tendency of children of such unions to adopt the mother's Orthodox faith, a choice which gradually merged their descendants with the native race. His familiarity with feudal matters suggests that he was employed at the Prince's court or in the state chancellery.

The list of the twelve baronies given by the *Chronicle of the Morea* purports to have been taken from the original register, the '*registre dou seignor*', drawn up for the Prince by the commission in 1209. Other evidence, however, indicates that it in fact describes the distribution of fiefs which prevailed some twenty years later: it is known, for instance, that some of the barons mentioned did not arrive in Achaia until after 1209, and that some of the fiefs listed were unconquered at that date. Although certain names are still in debate and there are puzzling divergencies between the various versions of the *Chronicle*, a sufficiently clear picture emerges.[18]

The Prince reserved very extensive domains for himself. They included Kalamata and Kyparissia, both key ports on the western seaboard; lands in Elis adjacent to his capital, Andravida; and as soon as they were conquered, Corinth and its surrounding district and Lakedaimonia with the valley of the Eurotas. The approach to the Gulf of Corinth was guarded by the Provençal Arnoul Aleman at Patras, and to the south of that city the family of Dramelay or Tremolay held Chalandritza. Immediately to the east Othon de Tournay or Durnay took Kalavryta and Hugues de Charpigny Vostitza (the present Aigion). The central highlands were dominated by Gautier de Rosières at Akova and Renaud de Briel at Karytaina, while Veligosti and Nikli were entrusted respectively to Hugues de Mons and Guillaume de Morlay. A baron named Luc was installed at Gritzena behind Kalamata. There remained the still unsubdued regions of Tzakonia and the far south, comprising the Taygetos range and the Maina. After they had submitted to Frankish rule they were watched by Guy de Nivelet from Geraki and by Jean de Nully from Passava, a name derived from the war-cry 'passe-avant'. That completed the mediaeval tapestry of high feudatories.

The number of knight's fees attached to the baronies reflected the military importance of the latter in the first half of the thirteenth century. The most sensitive area was certainly Arkadia, where the mountaineers of Skorta above the upper Alpheios valley were always inclined to rebellion and the remaining Greek landowners were less docile than elsewhere. Thus twenty-four knight's fees were allotted to Akova and twenty-two to Karytaina, as against a maximum of twelve in any other of the chief baronies. But there were also plenty of knights holding separate fiefs, and additional fees were attached to the Latin archbishopric of Patras and to his suffragan bishoprics. The military establishment was completed by the Templars, the Hospitallers (knights of St John) and the Teutonic knights, the three Orders which, as elsewhere in the Levant, provided a powerful reinforcement for the secular chivalry.

It is impossible to estimate with any accuracy how many knights, esquires and lesser fighting men were initially available to man the defences of Achaia, or what size of field army the Prince could count on for a campaign. In theory the principality was permanently on a war footing. Every vassal was required to spend four months of the year, if necessary, in the field and four months in garrison, while in an emergency he was liable to be called upon at any time.[19] The lack of manpower was to become acute in future years, but for the moment an eager stream of recruits was arriving to join Villehardouin's banner. No sooner was it generally known how successful he had been than aspirants to fiefs flowed in from France, from insecure holdings in Palestine and Syria and even from the Latin Emperor's domain around Constantinople, which was exposed to as serious a threat from the Bulgarians as the Holy Land from the Moslems. By comparison with those regions Greece, and especially Achaia, seemed to offer security, dignity and affluence. But the largest number of early immigrants came from France itself.

Nevertheless, the new owners of Greece did not feel safe until they had built an elaborate network of castles. According to the *Livre de la Conqueste*, 'li baron dou pays et li autre gentilhomme si commencerent a faire fortresses et habitacions, quy chastel, quy maisons sur sa terre, at changier leurs sournoms et prendre les noms des fortresses qu'ils faisoient'. (The barons of the country and the other gentlemen thus began to build fortresses and dwellings, some castles and some houses, on their lands, and to change their surnames and take the names of the fortresses which they were building.) The remains of a hundred and fifty of these strongholds have been counted in the Peloponnese alone, where at every turn the traveller is confronted by *palaiokastra* or, as Baedeker used to say, 'Frankish towers'. That was nothing unusual in the history of Greece. Indeed no country is more thickly studded with the wrecks of ancient fortifications, ranging as they do from Mycenaean citadels to the bastions of Venice. So far as the Franks were concerned, this prodigious building effort was in the main concentrated in the early years of the thirteenth century, and the rate of construction was detrimental to the solidity of the work. Despite the number of ruins still to be seen in wildly picturesque sites, the castles have not stood up well to the test of time and the batterings of Turkish cannon.[20]

The pattern of Latin domination is clear enough. We know the names of the chief feudatories and can trace their domains on the map. But we have little idea of the manner in which the surviving Greek magnates fitted into the feudal picture. The sources tell us that Villehardouin's tact and moderation reconciled them to Frankish rule, that they were consulted over the distribution of fiefs and that some of them actually participated in Geoffroy's campaigns against Sgouros and Theodore of

Epiros. We do not, however, know how many were involved and who they were nor, what is more important, what proportion of the available lands they succeeded in retaining, nor to what extent they were permitted to fortify their residences and keep armed retainers, nor how much influence they were able to exercise in the government of the principality. All we are sure of is that they enjoyed a status as vassals roughly similar to that of Latin knights, that as such they remained an element to be reckoned with in Moreot life and that no sensible Prince could afford to ignore them. Geoffroy certainly never committed such a mistake. He realised that so long as the Franks were on top they would be wise to make reasonable concessions to the conquered majority, and especially to its upper class. The *Chronicle of the Morea* makes this plain enough, and the policy can be best summarised in a phrase from the Venetian archives to the effect that Westerners should not demand from their Greek subjects anything more than had been demanded of them in the time of the Byzantine Emperors: 'nihil ab aliquo amplius exigentes quam quod facere consueverant temporibus Graecorum imperatorum.'[21] (Not demanding from anyone anything more than they had been accustomed to demand in the time of the Greek emperors.)

This admirable maxim did not apply to the Orthodox Church. The Franks did not seek to interfere with their subjects' freedom of worship, but the Orthodox hierarchy was rudely displaced. Metropolitans and bishops, except for the very few who were ready to accept papal supremacy, were evicted from their sees, and unless they sought refuge in the Nicaean state or in some monastery, were obliged to supervise their flocks while deprived of the former revenues and appurtenances of their office. The new Latin hierarchy which supplanted them in the Morea consisted of the two archbishoprics (Patras and Corinth) and a varying number of suffragan bishoprics. In addition, the leading ecclesiastics who had received knight's fees were invited to join chief barons in the high court of Achaia. Since the total number of Latins to be ministered to was very small, the establishment of Latin clergy was inevitably overweighted at the top. There was little for simple priests to do in the way of pastoral duties, the cathedrals were full of idle canons and the bishops themselves tended to become absorbed in bickerings with the laity and in the defence of their benefices. In time various Orders of Western monks and friars moved into Greece, but they too were operating in a vacuum because the overwhelmingly Orthodox population had no desire for their services. Orthodox monastic life, on the other hand, was less disturbed by the conquest, while the village priests, firmly rooted in rural life and secure in the devotion of the Greek people to the

Orthodox faith, went their way as before. As has already been mentioned, Villehardouin's relations with the Latin clergy were not cordial. He despised them for their lack of quality, narrow-mindedness and greed, discouraged both Latins and Greeks from paying them tithes and squashed their claims to spiritual authority over the native community. His barons treated them with equal lack of respect, seizing their property and disregarding their privileges. While admitting that the Greek East had been conquered for the greater glory of the Catholic religion, the conquerors refused to tolerate the pretensions and short-comings of its agents, toward whom they themselves behaved in an unscrupulous and arbitrary manner.

The Pope's frequent protests went unheeded and relations between the Holy See and the Prince became so bad that the latter, together with his neighbour the Megaskyr of Athens, was excommunicated no less than three times between 1210 and 1223. So far as Villehardouin was concerned, the most substantial cause of the rift was the reluctance of the Catholic hierarchy and the military Orders to share with the Prince's government the effort and cost of the principality's defence. The Prince retaliated by appropriating the Church's revenues for the construction of the great castle of Chloumoutzi, or Clermont, near Andravida. But in 1223, after the completion of the castle, a settlement was reached between Geoffroy and the new Pope, Honorius III, covering both disputes about property and privilege and the question of ecclesiastical co-operation in military matters. One curious provision throws light on the position of Greek village priests enjoying exemption from taxes and service. These were limited to two priests per village of 25 to 70 households, to four per village of 71 to 125 households and to six per village of more than 125 households, any number in excess of the limits being subject to the normal obligations of the laity. Evidently the spiritual needs of the Orthodox peasantry were fully catered for under the Latin regime.[22]

Below the barons and the lower vassals there came into being a category of freemen of Latin origin. These consisted in the first place of soldiers, men-at-arms, sergeants and the like, and we may also envisage a small and floating population of craftsmen and seamen. The Prince's court attracted lawyers and clerks (although some of these would have been in holy orders). As conditions became more peaceful, commercial opportunities created a class of Latin citizens or burgesses in the towns, who eventually became important enough to require the setting up of an inferior court of justice. All these people, however, were in a tiny minority in the midst of the Greek population.

Far the greater part of the latter were serfs (*paroikoi*), bound to the soil in much the same way as the peasants of Western Europe. As we have seen, the *pronoia* of the later Byzantine era was hardly to be distinguished from the Western feudal system.[23] Thus the condition of the serf was in many respects pitiable. His lord could give him away at will to another lord, or take away his goods and give them to another serf. He was not allowed to marry without his lord's permission, nor could he be freed except by order of the Prince's court, or if the serf was a woman, by marriage to a freeman. If a Frank killed a Greek serf 'by mistake' all the Frank had to do was to provide his lord with another serf. Nevertheless, serfdom was not all-embracing. The Morea would not have been Greece if it had not contained freemen engaged in trade, both internal and maritime, and the evidence suggests that there was also a category of free farmers working the poorer lands. In spite of local war and administrative disruption, the whole of Greece was still a flourishing and productive area when it fell into Frankish hands, and although we do not hear much in the knightly chronicles of the time about economic life in Hellas, it was just that which made its acquisition so valuable to the Westerners, and especially to the Venetians. Their records at least make this point entirely clear.

At the apex of the feudal pyramid stood the Prince, Geoffroy de Villehardouin. Since the death of Boniface there was no question of his professing allegiance to the Kingdom of Thessalonica and although he owed homage to the Latin Emperor, he counted in practice as a sovereign ruler. His power, however, was exercised within a framework of institutions which matured very quickly. So did the body of law, custom and precedent which grew up in the course of the century. This was not codified, under the title of the 'Assizes of Romania', until the fourteenth century, at about the same time as the compilation of the *Chronicle of the Morea*, and the earliest surviving text is the official edition published by the Republic of Venice two centuries later, but it is clear that from a very early date the Prince felt bound to respect the rights of the feudatories, the Frankish settlers and the population as a whole, which came to be known as the *usages*. In future, on acceding to the principality, each ruler had to swear on the gospels to observe them.

The Prince presided over the high court of Achaia, which consisted of the twelve peers and seven episcopal peers. As so constituted, it dealt with questions of feudal inheritance and disputes involving the peers themselves: it alone possessed the right to inflict the death penalty on a feudatory. In addition, each lay peer exercised jurisdiction within his own territory. The remainder of the nobility was divided into two classes, the lieges and the vassals of *simple homage*, who included numerous Greeks, and in cases affecting those categories the court was expanded into a court of lieges. A lower court, presided over by the Prince's representative, judged the affairs of burgesses and simple freemen. In general, feudal practice ensured that the Prince's obligations towards the peers and other feudatories tended to balance his sovereign rights. As William Miller observes, he was not an autocrat but *primus inter pares*, and the extent of his authority depended on the strength of his personality. If a liege brought a complaint against the Prince to the high court, he was expected to relinquish his presidency and defend his case from the floor.[24]

The Prince in council was assisted by his peers, spiritual and temporal, and by the members of his own court and central administration. The latter inevitably assumed a semi-Byzantine tinge and some of the high officers, such as the *Logothete* or Chancellor, sported Byzantine titles. The Chamberlain or Protovestiary had charge of the register of fiefs, and before the end of the century we find this office filled by a Greek. The finances of the principality were administered by the Treasurer under the tax system also deriving from Byzantium, but which in Frankish hands became notably less onerous and corrupt than it had been under the later Komnenoi and Angeloi: in theory at least, no taxes might be imposed except by consent of the feudatories and all free subjects. On the military side the most important dignitaries were the Marshal, whose office became hereditary in the family of de Nully, and the Inspector or Purveyor of Fortresses. The Prince himself bore the honorific title of Seneschal of Romania.

As previously mentioned, the seat of government was at Andravida, close to the port of Glarentza and to the strong castles of Clermont and Beauvoir (to which the Greeks gave the less imposing name of Pontikokastro, or 'Mouse-Castle'). Geoffroy, however, preferred to reside at Kalamata or at Lakedaimonia, the town which the Byzantines had built, adjacent to the ruins of ancient Sparta, in the deep, lush valley of the Eurotas, with the jagged outline of Taygetos soaring above. The Franks, who had a cheerful genius for corrupting Greek names, called it 'La Crémonie'. There was something Spartan about the soldierly character of Frankish Achaia, and in the tight discipline which bound the feudatories to the performance of their military duties and forbade them to quit or dispose of their fiefs without the Prince's leave. The rules of their service were based on the fact that, like their predecessors the Spartiates, they were isolated in a sea of potential enemies. At the same time Spartan austerity was quite foreign to their way of life. While preserving their discipline intact, they extracted the fullest enjoyment from their power and affluence, behaving as if their good fortune was destined to last. Indeed, if he looked around him, the Prince could see little reason for disquiet. His immediate neighbour, the Sire d'Athenes, was friendly and attached to him by feudal ties. The Aegean coasts and islands belonged to the Venetian Republic, with which he was on excellent terms, or to private Venetian adventurers. He need not worry overmuch if the Kingdom of Thessalonica, or the Latin Empire itself, was ready to crumble, and he felt himself quite capable of dealing with any aggression by the Despot of Epiros.

Nevertheless Achaia, like all the states founded by the Crusaders in the East, was a rash experiment, the endurance of which depended on the strength of character and adaptability of successive generations of leaders. Some of these states, like the Empire of Romania and the Kingdom of Jerusalem, could not last long because they were built on insecure foundations and subjected to unbearable pressures. On the other hand the Latin Kingdom of Cyprus, with a social and racial structure closely resembling that of Achaia, survived for two and a half centuries under the same (Lusignan) dynasty before passing for another century into the hands of Venice. So far as durability was concerned the chief Latin principalities of Greece, Achaia and Athens, take an intermediate place. But none of the Latin states of the Levant, whether long or short-lived, ever approached the level of integration and harmony in government, religion or culture which had already been attained in the Norman Kingdom of Sicily. There the racial situation was far more complex, since the population included Norman and Italian Catholics, native Sicilian Catholics, Greek Sicilians still adhering to the Orthodox faith and numerous Moslems. Sicilian society was not so much a fusion of those elements as a peculiar coexistence between them. For reasons which will become apparent as the thirteenth century and fourteenth century unfold, so fruitful a relationship was never established in Greece between Latin Catholics and Greek Orthodox, and Western mediaeval society never struck lasting roots in Greek soil.

Like most Frenchmen overseas, the conquerors of Achaia and their descendants remained obstinately French, refusing to identify themselves more than was absolutely necessary with their new environment. If their compatriots in Syria were commonly and often justly reproached for allowing themselves to be seduced by oriental manners to an extent considered shocking to the West, the Moreot barons could hardly be accused of letting themselves become over-Hellenized. Indeed they were at all times but faintly tinged with hellenism in any form, and the finer aspects of civilization in the Byzantine world, where the educated could recite by heart whole books of Homer, interested them not at all. Priding themselves that better French was spoken at the court of Andravida than at that of Paris, they were content with their own culture, that of the troubadours and the *Chansons de Geste*, which when transplanted to the luminous landscapes of Arkadia and the Argolid coloured Greek life and popular literature with its own heroic and romantic qualities without absorbing any Greek features in return. Fortunately for them the three Villehardouins who followed one another as Princes of Achaia, although strictly non-Mediterranean in their family origins, were more subtly attuned to Levantine ways. From the beginning Achaia owed everything to its rulers, to their diplomatic flair, their competence in war, their brilliant style and panache and, above all, their inborn ability to understand and handle the two communities in their charge.

CHAPTER FOUR

Athens and Sparta

THE LORDSHIP OF Athens and Thebes conferred by the King of Thessalonica on Othon de la Roche did not compare in size or wealth with the Achaia of the Villehardouins. Nevertheless it was a valuable territory, compact, easily governable and well buttressed by its neighbours against external aggression. Besides Attica and Boeotia, it comprised the Megarid to the south and, to the west and north-west, the districts of Phokis and Lokris. On that side its boundaries were protected by the lordship of Salona and the marquisate of Boudonitza, both strongly fortified fiefs of the Thessalonican kingdom. Due north lay Euboea, held by the three Lombard barons or triarchs who shared the island between them. At the time of the Lombard rebellion against the Emperor Henry they hastened to offer it to Venice. The Republic, which had already staked a claim to Euboea under the partition treaty, readily agreed to accept the triarchs as its vassals and in due course installed a bailie of its own in the chief town, Chalkis or Negroponte.[1] The Venetian presence provided Athens with another useful buffer. Moreover Othon was on the best of terms with Geoffroy de Villehardouin and held from him, as the reward for his assistance in the campaigns against Sgouros and Theodore of Epiros, the rich fiefs of Argos and Nauplia. With such allies he had little cause to fear any resurgence of Greek power at the expense of the Kingdom of Thessalonica.

Othon's twin capitals, Athens and Thebes, were served respectively by the ports of Piraeus and of Livadostro on the Gulf of Corinth. A third important harbour, Talanti, faced the Euboean shore. Thebes, lapped by the fertile Boeotian plain, was the more populous city and the centre of industry and commerce, still famous for its silks and brocades. Its Jewish merchants were soon to be joined by a colony of Genoese, who were granted the same privileges and exemptions as the Venetians enjoyed in Achaia. In comparison with bustling Thebes, Athens had little to offer its Megaskyr but the beauty and security of its Acropolis. The other vestiges of antiquity that had fascinated the learned Archbishop Michael held little attraction for the Franks, who in the words of his brother Niketas, lacked 'every Grace and every Muse'.[2] But Pope Innocent III, when appointing the first Latin Archbishop, Bérard, to the see, did not fail to remind the new incumbent of its exceptional significance. 'The renewal of God's grace', he wrote, 'does not permit the ancient glory of the city of Athens to fade away. The citadel of the famed Pallas has become the humble dwelling of the glorious Mother of God.'[3] The feudal pattern of Othon's domain was not exactly similar to that of Achaia. With one notable exception we hear of no great Frankish family holding a substantial fief in Attica or Boeotia. Othon's original Burgundian followers were not persons of much consequence and he was under no particular obligation to them. As for the Greek archontie element, it was also less important than in the Morea.[4] He was therefore free to keep most of the territory for himself or to grant lands to the host of his own relatives who had accompanied him or hurried from Burgundy to profit from the spoils. Foremost among them was his nephew Guy, who received a half share in the lordship of Thebes. A second nephew, Guillaume, went on to the Peloponnese and eventually obtained the fief of Veligosti. His sister Sibylla, wife of Jacques de Cicons, arrived with her son Othon. Finally his niece Bonne, destined for a great future by her betrothal to Demetrios, heir to the Kingdom of Thessalonica, was married, after the expulsion and premature death of that prince, to Bela de St Omer, and invested with the other half of the Theban domain. Bela was a member of a noble family from Flanders which had sent three brothers to the First Crusade, one of whom became Prince of Galilee and another co-founder of the Order of the Knights Templar. His father Jacques and his uncle Nicolas had already been established by King Boniface in the key fief of Gravia on Othon's north-western border. Although the St Omers were great nobles and the de la Roches did not by origin belong to the same category, the marriage connexion through Bonne, coupled with the curious arrangement for the division of Thebes, ensured that the two families avoided rivalry and worked harmoniously together.

The Church of Rome laid a heavy hand on the former Orthodox establishments. Both Athens and Thebes received their Latin arch-bishops and the Pope was particularly concerned to enhance the prestige of the former see. He placed it under the special protection of St Peter, sent a cardinal-legate to instal its canons and allotted to it no less than eleven suffragan bishoprics, several of them outside Othon's secular jurisdiction. As the Latin clerics moved in, their Greek predecessors were evicted and their lands and revenues expropriated. Even the little monasteries of Attica, nestling in the folds of Hymettus, Pentelikon and Parnes, were turned over to the newcomers. As for the great Byzantine foundations, the monastery of the Blessed Luke of Stiris was occupied by the Order of the Holy Sepulchre and that of Daphni by Cistercians from the Abbey of Bellevaux in Burgundy, where the de la Roche ancestors were buried. Adjoining the church at Daphni the French monks built a Gothic cloister, the remains of which still stand, and the scratches made by the lances of Othon's men-at-arms are visible on the mosaics of the dome. But despite the shower of papal favours, donations and privileges, the Megaskyr's attitude towards the Latin Church, like Villehardouin's, was quite cynical and equivocal. At one moment he was imploring Innocent to appoint a priest to serve every settlement of twelve or more Latins throughout his territory, at another he was grabbing church property and revenues with a cheerful inconsequence which involved him, as it did the Prince of Achaia, in temporary excommunication.

The letters written by Michael of Chonae from his place of exile throw some light on conditions at Athens during the early years of Burgundian rule. Before settling for good in the island of Keos, Michael visited Thessalonica, apparently in the hope of winning from the royal and papal authorities there some alleviation for himself and for the Orthodox faithful in his former diocese of the harsh consequences of the conquest. When his mission failed he first went to Euboea, where he owned property, but he found the Lombard occupation of the island as distasteful as the Burgundian in Attica. Eventually he sought refuge in the monastery of St John the Baptist at Keos, where he remained undisturbed until his death in about 1220. The Venetian adventurers who seized the island left him in peace, and he was well placed both to observe what was going on at Athens, that 'lost Eden' on the western horizon, and to carry on a long and busy correspondence with friends in those parts of the Byzantine world which had retained their independence. Among these were the heads of the Greek Church in Nicaea and Epiros, through whom he kept in touch with the two potentates Theodore Laskaris and Michael Dukas. Afflicted as he was by the loss of his see and of his library, by the tragic fate of the Empire and by the plight of Orthodoxy, he set to work with typical Greek resilience to adapt himself to adversity and make the best of a sad old age. At least he was not entirely cut off from his former connexions; channels of communication were not closed and he remained in contact with Athens. He still felt bound by a duty towards its people. Therefore he refused invitations to the courts of Nicaea and Arta, as well as a proposal to make him Archbishop of Naxos in the Cyclades. Although he wrote 'I am like a weak old bird on a string, trying in vain to fly away home', he chose to stay where he was, reading and writing in his cell.[5]

At Athens, as he noticed with mixed relief and irritation, the Greeks were finding Frankish rule mild and tolerable. Prosperous citizens who had prudently fled from the invaders began to go back and were not harmed. They included his friend Demetrios Makrembolites, who sent him presents of food and wine from the mainland, and even his own nephew, another Niketas, with whom he was not unnaturally furious. But he himself could not resist slipping back for one secret visit, from which he returned swiftly so as not to provide 'a bite for the teeth of the Italians', as he called the Franks.[6] When the Abbot of the Kaisariani monastery on Hymettus consulted him as to whether he should accept the authority of the Frenchman Bérard in order to avoid expulsion, he broadmindedly advised him to do so, with the result that Kaisariani remained uninterruptedly in Greek hands. But most Orthodox church-men preferred to lose their sees than submit to Rome. The Bishop of Chalkis was one of the few who did submit, while the Archbishop of Neopatras, who began by cutting his hair, shaving his beard and celebrating the Latin rite, felt violently ashamed of himself, let his hair grow again and escaped to join Sgouros at Corinth.

Michael of Chonae lived long enough to witness the early stages of a Greek revival in the north, led by the Despots of Epiros, Michael and Theodore Dukas. We have seen how the former, while struggling to maintain a foothold in the Peloponnese, recognised the Emperor Henry as his sovereign at the Parliament of Ravenika. But no sooner had Henry left Greece than the Despot shifted his nominal allegiance to Venice, presumably as a reinsurance against the other Frankish states with which he was at variance. In fact he had already worked out a plan of aggression. To compensate for his loss of Argos and Nauplia, he first attacked the lord of Salona, Thomas de Stromoncourt, who was killed in the fighting, and annexed his port of Galaxidi. Then, in flagrant disregard of his engagements to the Venetians, he snatched from them their most recent and valuable acquisition, Corfu, without incurring any retaliation. Soon afterwards, in 1214, he was murdered, but his successor Theodore pursued a similar policy and achieved more spectacular triumphs. On the death of the Emperor Henry in 1216 his brother-in-law, Peter of Courtenay, was called from France to the throne of Constantinople. He landed at Durazzo and set out for his capital, but as he marched through the Albanian mountains he was trapped in an ambush laid by Theodore. His army was destroyed and he himself was never heard of again. Elated by this success, the Despot hastened to exploit it by invading Thessaly and Macedonia, thus severing the land link between Thessalonica and the Franks in the south.

Finally he entered Thessalonica itself and put an end to the Lombard Kingdom.

This turn of fortune upset the balance of power in the area. It also aroused new and acute dynastic rivalries. Clearly the Latin Empire was not destined to last much longer, menaced as it was by three contending and ambitious powers, the Greek successor state at Nicaea, the Bulgarian Tsardom on the north and the expanding Despotat on the west. Its only hope of a respite lay in the hostility between the contenders. To the fury of John Vatatzes, now ruler of Nicaea (1222–1254), the Despot had himself crowned at Thessalonica and assumed all the imperial trappings of Byzantium. Meanwhile the Latin realm, which Robert of Courtenay inherited from his vanished father, was confined to the environs of Constantinople.

The extinction of the Lombard Kingdom, while hardly comforting to the Franks in Greece, did not necessarily presage disaster for them. If united, the chivalry of Achaia and Athens, of Euboea and the buffer baronies on the fringe of Thessaly, was fully capable of repulsing an onslaught from Epiros. The Despot, for his part, would have been rash to challenge the Franks beyond his southern borders while preoccupied with his cherished prize, Constantinople. It is unlikely, therefore, that the Prince of Achaia and the Sire d'Athènes were unduly disturbed. Indeed Geoffroy de Villehardouin advertised his championship of the tottering Latin Empire by marrying his son, also called Geoffroy, to Agnes of Courtenay, Peter's daughter. The girl and her mother had been on their way to Constantinople by sea when Peter met with catastrophe, and when they put into a Peloponnesian port Geoffroy did his best to console them. His own wife, Elizabeth, had joined him in the Morea not long after his transformation from a simple knight into a prince. She brought the younger Geoffroy with her but her second son, Guillaume, was born in Greece and grew up bilingual; his roots were in Hellas rather than in France. Othon de la Roche, after twenty years at Athens, was less acclimatized than the Villehardouins. Whether his decision was prompted by plain homesickness or by an uneasy feeling that the Despot's progress had made his position less secure, he left Greece in 1225 and took his wife, Isabelle de Ray, and his two sons back to Franche-Comté, leaving his nephew Guy as the fortunate heir to his peaceful and increasingly prosperous domain.

The death of Geoffroy I de Villehardouin cannot be exactly dated. It probably occurred about 1228, by which time the threat from Epiros was on the point of receding.[7] In 1230 Theodore made the mistake of going to war with the Bulgarian Tsar, John Asen II, and was thoroughly defeated and taken prisoner at the battle of Klokotnitza on the river Maritza. At first he was well treated, but when the Tsar discovered that he was still spinning political intrigues in captivity he had him blinded. Nevertheless this misfortune did not end his career of hair-raising adventures. Luckily for him, the Tsar fell in love with his beautiful daughter, and she agreed to marry him on condition that he set her father at liberty. The blind Despot's first exploit was to recover his capital, which had been seized in his absence by his brother Manuel. His partisans managed to smuggle him into the city and the usurper was expelled. This done he resumed his rule, but since it was not considered fitting that a sightless man should occupy the throne, Theodore had his son John crowned Emperor while he himself continued to govern. But his bid to re-establish the Byzantine Empire under an Epirote dynasty had failed. Though a bold gambler, Theodore was no match, either in material resources or political astuteness, for the rival Greek sovereign, John Vatatzes of Nicaea.

A patient and methodical statesman, Vatatzes worked effectively to frustrate the ambitions of the Dukas family and to prepare for his own reconquest on Constantinople. At the same time he had to move carefully in order not to alarm the Bulgarian Tsar. He encouraged Manuel, Theodore's brother, to take possession of Thessaly while he himself, by sending troops from Asia Minor into Macedonia, reduced Thessalonica to the condition of a puppet state. The Tsar died in 1241, but the final occupation of the city and annexation of Macedonia by the Nicaean state were delayed for another five years while Vatatzes was anxiously watching his frontier in Asia Minor. These were the years when the Mongols, the heirs to Jenghiz Khan, were thrusting their destructive forays into Europe and the Near East and Nicaea's neighbour, the Seljuk Sultanate, suffered grievously from their devastations. But Nicaea escaped the storm, and Vatatzes was able to return and complete his work in Macedonia, where he installed Andronikos Palaeologos as Viceroy. It will be remembered that one of the latter's forebears, Michael, had been governor of the province when *Timarion* was written; and his own son, another Michael, was destined to reconquer Constantinople from the Latins.

Theodore and his sons were set aside, but the blind adventurer was allotted a minute domain of his own where, it was hoped, he would vegetate tranquilly until his death. As we shall see, however, he had not yet shot his final bolt.

These complicated struggles of Greek against Greek did not lead to the restoration of Frankish power in the north. This would have been an effort beyond the means of the rulers of Achaia and Athens, even if they had wished to attempt it. Nor was John Vatatzes strong enough to absorb all the dominions of the Dukas family. In 1236 Michael, a bastard son of Michael I, made himself master of Epiros and five years later, on the death of his uncle Manuel, he took over Thessaly as well. Thus the persistence of Greek disunion, while favouring the survival of the Frankish states, gave them no opportunity to win back lost territory.

In such conditions Geoffroy II of Achaia and Guy I of Athens enjoyed a long period of peace and quiet. Although the former's personality seems to have made curiously little impact on the imagination of later chroniclers, there can be do doubt that his reign was a minor golden age in the principality. The Peloponnese had not enjoyed such well-being and orderly government since the days of the Macedonian dynasty of Byzantium. Its new prince was not bellicose by nature: not only did he avoid strife with Epiros but he also abstained from attacking Monemvasia, which remained the sole Greek enclave in the Morea, and even from enforcing a strict control over the Tzakones and the Melings. On the other hand he considered it a point of honour and duty to defend to the best of his ability the decrepit Latin Empire, now no more than an outpost in a hostile world. Besides generously subsidizing its finances, he saved it from collapse when it was attacked in 1236 by the combined forces of John Vatatzes and the Tsar. Constantinople would certainly have been taken if Geoffroy had not personally led his fleet, manned by the knights of Achaia and presumably by Greek seamen, into the Golden Horn and routed the Nicaean squadron. This victory earned the Latin Emperor a respite of twenty-five years.[8]

It also conferred enormous prestige on the Prince. Of the Latin states in the east Achaia conceded the first place only to the Kingdom of Cyprus. The principality was a strong military power, constantly reinforced by young noblemen from France seeking their fortune overseas, and a flourishing centre of commerce. If his reign was uneventful, it was also extremely beneficial to his subjects of both races, and one must attribute to his tact and good sense the singular lack of friction which characterized his relations with the Greeks, with his own barons, with the Church and with neighbouring states.

Geoffroy maintained a magnificent court: eighty knights with golden spurs accompanied him on his progresses from Kalamata to Andravida, from Corinth to Lakedaimonia.[9] Ramon Muntaner, the fourteenth-century Catalan chronicler, claimed that the noblest chivalry in the world was to be found in the Morea, and that the French spoken there was as pure as that of Paris.[10] So far as the reigns of the three

Villehardouins were concerned he was not far wrong. Throughout Geoffroy II's peaceful tenure of the principality the French nobles may well have experienced a *douceur de vivre* which was unknown in the West, except in Provence and the Kingdom of Sicily, combined with a sense of security also rare in western and northern Europe and certainly absent in the shrunken remnant of the Crusaders' territories in Syria, where elegance and luxury could hardly compensate for the ever-present threat of extinction. They were also safe from the arbitrary behaviour of emperors and kings, for, as has already been stressed, the Prince was strictly *primus inter pares*, and could never have imposed on his feudatories the type of autocracy that prevailed in the Hohenstaufen dominions.

Provided that their castles were strong and their Greek neighbours and underlings contented, the French had nothing to fear. Although ready to take up arms in accordance with their feudal obligations, they had little opportunity to use them during the reign of Geoffroy II. We can imagine them living a comfortable rural existence, not untouched by Byzantine refinements and leaving ample scope for hunting, tournaments and listening to troubadours. No doubt the management of their estates was usually entrusted to Greek or half-breed stewards.

Such lands, especially in Messenia, Elis and the Argolid and along the shore of the Gulf of Corinth, were rich and profitable. Despite the scarcity of recorded facts, we may reasonably assume that the economy of the Morea (and indeed of Frankish Greece as a whole) was in a flourishing condition during the first half of the thirteenth century and was not seriously damaged by the sporadic warfare which broke out when Byzantium later regained a foothold. The plains and valleys of the Peloponnese were fertile and planted with a wide variety of valuable crops and trees. They provided in plenty wines, olive oil, fruits of many kinds, wheat, honey and wax; cochineal for dyeing, flax for the linen industry and, above all, the mulberry trees which produced the prized silks of the peninsula. The forests, still extensive in the Middle Ages, were full of game and their oak groves supplied acorns for vast herds of pigs. Sheep and (unfortunately for the forests) goats abounded in the mountain pastures, while horses and cattle were bred on a more limited scale.

So far as internal trade was concerned, agricultural products were marketed at the fairs which, as in the mediaeval West, were regularly held in the country towns. But in all normal years there was a surplus for export, and especially of wines, currants, wheat, silk and cochineal. The salt pans of the Argolid were also exploited. While the Morea was ideally placed, from a geographical point of view, to take advantage of the transit traffic between East and West as well as exporting its own products in both directions, its Frankish rulers, if not insensible of such advantage, were unskilled in the ways of commerce. The Venetians, on the other hand, exploited to the full the privileged position which they had in fact begun to build up under the Komnenan emperors and which, in spite of occasional setbacks, they continued to reinforce. Some ports, such as Modon and Coron, they already possessed in full sovereignty, and in the others, such as Glarentza and Patras, they soon gained a major share in the carrying trade. They maintained offices in all the ports from which their agents sallied forth to buy at the fairs and to sell, in return, textiles from the West and the manufactures which Greece could not produce.[11] The local goods which they purchased were marketed in the Moslem East as well as in the Christian West. Subject to intermittent piracy, always the scourge of the Levant, there was easy commercial intercourse throughout the Mediterranean and as far as the Black Sea. The Venetians themselves, and particularly those operating from Crete, had no scruples about engaging in that most lucrative form of piracy, the slave trade, and many unfortunate Moreots ended their lives as drudges of Western as well as Eastern masters.

For his exploits in the defence of Constantinople the Latin Emperor rewarded Geoffroy with the feudal overlordship of Euboea and the Cyclades. Although effective suzerainty over the former was already exercised by Venice, and the Aegean archipelago was subject to an independent Venetian duke, Mario Sanudo, his honorific titles were an indication of the deep respect with which he was regarded throughout the Levant. Achaia was the mainstay of Latin rule, the brilliant vindication of the founding of a New France on Hellenic soil.

Geoffroy had no children by his wife Agnes of Courtenay. Consequently he was succeeded on his death in 1246 by his Greek-born brother Guillaume. The new Prince differed sharply in character from his predecessor. He maintained the same splendid state, but his own style verged on the flamboyant. Ambitious and headstrong by nature, he was never the man to let well alone. His political projects, conceived on a grand scale, were apt to fail because he over-estimated his strength and took too many risks. Unlike his brother he enjoyed warfare and was always eager to throw his superb cavalry into a campaign. He kept eight hundred knights permanently under arms and longed to use them. On the other hand he was too rash to be a good commander in the field. He loved excitement and his reign of thirty years was one long story of strife and struggle. His courage, affability and courtliness aroused the admiration of all and evoked loyalty and affection in his subjects. Although he had more Frankish than Greek traits he was equally at ease in both milieux and possessed a perfect mastery of the Greek language. Guillaume's first concern was to reduce Monemvasia, the outlying bastion of Byzantium. For that purpose he assembled an imposing company of allies and vassals, including contingents from Athens, Euboea and the Cyclades, while a Venetian squadron cut off access to the city from the sea. All the same the siege lasted a full three years. It was impossible to take the rock by storm, and only the prospect of starvation eventually drove the garrison to negotiate a surrender. The Prince granted generous terms to the three ruling archons, who were given estates in the peninsula of Cape Malea and excused from feudal obligations.[12] When the campaign was over he decided to strengthen his authority over the Melings and Mainotes of the southern Peloponnese by building three new fortresses. These were le Grand Magne on the west side of the Maina peninsula, Leutron or Beaufort half-way between le Grand Magne and Kalamata and Mistra on the eastern foothills of Taygetos.[13] Together with Geraki and Passava, they formed a chain of strong-points, effectively clamping down on dissidence in these regions. The year 1249 marked the apogee of Villehardouin power. It was also the occasion for Guillaume to make a striking appearance on a wider stage. With twenty-four ships and four hundred knights, and accompanied by an exalted guest, Duke Hugh of Burgundy, he sailed to Cyprus in order to join the grand expedition which King Louis IX of France was mounting against Egypt. Although he had never set foot in France, the Prince felt, or at least affected to feel, a romantic devotion to the country of his ancestors. In the ultimate resort Louis, not the Latin Emperor, was his sovereign and to respond to the King's appeal for help in his cherished Crusade was a gesture which Guillaume could not afford to forego. The Moreot chivalry made a dazzling impression and proved its worth when Guillaume agreed to detach a hundred knights for the defence of Rhodes, which the Genoese had recently seized from the Greeks of Nicaea. This was a cause which was more likely to appeal to him than the royal venture in Egypt. To a ruler as intimately concerned as he was with Levantine politics the King's aim must have seemed misdirected and doomed to failure, while any opportunity of embarrassing John Vatatzes was bound to be welcome. Thus when the moment came to invade Egypt, Guillaume and his knights contented themselves with a token presence and by the time that disaster overtook the Crusaders in the Nile Delta, with the King a prisoner of the Sultan, they had already sailed home to the Peloponnese. Their departure was not an action which even so saintly a monarch as Louis could readily forgive, but it was not until ten years later that he found a chance to administer a snub to the Prince of Achaia. It must also have rankled that Guillaume, while still in Cyprus, had extracted from the King permission to strike a gold coinage identical with the French *tournois*. In this way Achaia gained its own currency, minted at the castle of Chloumoutzi, and was no longer dependent on the Byzantine *nomisma* or *hyperpyron*.

After a few years of inactivity Guillaume's restless temperament involved him in war with his Frankish neighbours and erstwhile friends. The quarrel originated in the intricacies of the feudal arrangements prevailing in the area. The Prince, who saw straight and clear in matters that concerned his rivalry with Nicaean emperors, was preoccupied to the extent of obsession by questions of precedence and prestige, even when this insistence on his rights resulted in warfare between Latins, the defection of his own chief vassals and lasting injury to his own real interests.

The discord began in Euboea. In 1255 Guillaume found himself a widower for the second time. His first wife, the daughter of one Narjot de Toucy, had died before he succeeded to the principality. His second, Carintana delle Carceri, was the heiress to one of the Euboean triarchies. On her death he claimed that triarchy for himself; he also sought to assert the suzerainty of the Prince of Achaia over the whole island which Geoffroy II had obtained after his naval victory at Constantinople but which had never been regarded as having any practical import. The remaining triarchs were alarmed by Guillaume's pretensions. So were the Venetians at Chalkis (Negroponte). It was risky enough to become embroiled with the Republic, and worse still the remaining Latin rulers on the Greek mainland drew together in a coalition hostile to Achaia. Ubertino Pallavicini of Boudonitza, Thomas II de Stromoncourt of Salona and even Guy of Athens, formerly Geoffroy II's firm friend as well as his vassal in respect of Argos and Nauplia, declared against Guillaume. Guillaume de la Roche, Seigneur of Veligosti in Arkadia, sided with his brother Guy against his feudal superior.

In its first phase the fighting took the form of a struggle for Negroponte. With the aid of his partisans in Euboea Guillaume captured the city and held it for a year, but on the arrival of reinforcements from Venice he was dislodged and suffered a sharp reverse. Meanwhile Guy made a diversion towards Corinth and when the Prince led a counter-attack into Attica he narrowly escaped being taken prisoner. While both sides were regrouping for a decisive confrontation Guillaume was faced by another serious defection. This time the offender was the greatest of the twelve chief barons of Achaia, Geoffroy de Briel, lord of Karytaina and warden of the highlands of Skorta. This magnate, the most renowned knight in Frankish Greece, had duly followed his suzerain to the war, but when this shifted from Euboea to become a direct clash between Guillaume and Guy, Geoffroy could not avoid a conflict of loyalties. His duty as a feudatory inclined him to the Prince, who was also his uncle, since his mother was Guillaume's sister. On the other hand he himself was married to Guy's daughter, and it was her influence that swung him to his father-in-law's side.

In 1258 Guillaume assembled the feudal levy of the Morea at Nikli and led it over the isthmus of Corinth. The northern barons, under the Megaskyr's command, awaited their opponents at Karydi, 'the place of walnuts', half-way between Megara and Thebes and perhaps the only level site in the region suitable for a battle between two armies each composed of heavily armoured cavalry. Helms lowered and pennants streaming, their shields displaying blazons derived from lands in the West which most of them had never seen, the knights of Athens and the knights of Sparta charged down on each other. The battle resembled a huge tournament, but it was fiercely contested and many warriors fell on both sides. It ended in a clear victory for Achaia. Guy was obliged to make a precipitate retreat and shut himself up in Thebes.

From that moment hostilities between Franks came to an abrupt end. Now that he had triumphed on the battlefield the Prince was sensible enough not to allow the destructive feud to prolong itself, and the original cause of the rift, Guillaume's inopportune claims in Euboea, was for the moment ignored. He made no serious attempt to regain Negroponte and establish his authority over the triarchies. He did, however, insist that Guy of Athens and Geoffroy de Briel should be judged by the high court of Achaia for their presumption in taking up arms against their feudal superior. A stickler for such decencies, he was probably more interested in formally humiliating them than in the severity of whatever punishment the court might inflict.[14]

The court was summoned to meet at Nikli, in the presence of a full parliament of feudatories and with appropriately elaborate ceremonial. Confident that no harm would come to him, Guy arrived with an impressive retinue of knights, but Geoffroy, whose offence was much more blatant, abased himself before the Prince with a rope around his neck. Whatever verdicts Guillaume was waiting for, and one suspects that for obvious political reasons he did not envisage radical penalties, the prelates and chief barons composing the court declared that they were not competent to give a ruling in the case of the Sire d'Athenes. They proposed, and the Prince was obliged to agree, that it be referred to the King of France. As for the lord of Karytaina, it was arranged that he should make a theatrical submission and beg for mercy, and that Guillaume, after a show of reluctance to grant it, should restore Geoffroy de Briel to his fief, on condition that he should hold it for life only and not transmit it to his heirs. When these stately formalities had been concluded, honour was deemed to have been satisfied and the assembly dissolved into banquets and jousting.[15]

The Megaskyr, however, believed that his appearance before King Louis might be turned to his own advantage, and therefore undertook the long journey to Paris. On the way he stopped for a while in Burgundy, where he showed himself off to his relatives and managed to borrow a large sum of money from the Duke. His reception by the King fully justified his hopes.[16] Louis had no reason to gratify Guillaume at Guy's expense. Not only did he satisfy himself, after consulting a parliament convoked for the purpose, that Guy's offence was venial, but he also ruled that he was entitled to some compensation for his arduous journey to the royal court. When Guy suggested that this should take the form of his adopting the style of Duke of Athens, the King found no difficulty in agreeing. There was indeed nothing strange in Guy soliciting or receiving such a title. Dukedoms were common enough in the West. It was also plainly unsuitable he should continue as a mere Sire, Dominus or even Megas Kyrios. So he became the peer of the Dukes of Burgundy and Brittany. Later in the fourteenth century, the Byzantine writer Nikephoros Gregoras invented a fanciful origin for the title, pretending that none other than the Emperor Constantine the Great had decreed that whoever governed Athens should thenceforth be known as its Duke or Grand Duke. Such an attribution was no less fictitious than a more famous Donation of Constantine, but it was true enough that the governor and military commander of the Byzantine theme of Hellas had been called Dux before 1204 and the title thus had a familiar ring for Guy's Greek subjects. More significantly, it was to strike the imagination of Western poets. When Dante and Boccaccio, Chaucer and Shakespeare, wrote about Theseus, the legendary hero of Greek myth, they all envisaged him as the mediaeval Duca d'Atene, 'a duke that highte Theseus; of Athens he was lord and governour', the leader of gorgeous knights and the lover of the finest ladies of the age.[17] Of these four poets, three lived while the Duchy was still in full vigour and its glories had not yet been entrusted to reminiscence alone.

Chaucer's *Knight's Tale* is a treasure-house of allusion to its fame in the mediaeval world.

During Guy's leisurely and profitable sojourn in France the victorious Prince of Achaia suffered a spectacular reverse of fortune. In the New Year of 1260 the news reached Paris that Guillaume was a prisoner in the hands of the Emperor of Nicaea. Envoys from the Morea begged Guy to hurry back to Greece and take over the government of the principality in the capacity of bailie of Achaia. Responding promptly to the invitation and without returning to Athens, the Duke landed at Glarentza and assumed his charge. He was now the effective ruler of the whole of Frankish Greece, apart from the islands, but the situation with which he was called upon to deal was extremely delicate and potentially disastrous.

The cause of the trouble was Guillaume's entanglement in the continuing rivalry between Epiros and Nicaea. In 1259, a year crowded with events, he married as his third wife Anna, daughter of Michael II of Epiros, and inevitably became the Despot's ally in the struggle between the two Greek states. This had been carried on in a desultory fashion and with varying fortunes for several years, with each side encroaching in turn on the other's territory across their common border in Macedonia. The duel began when Michael's blind but irrepressible uncle Theodore, the former Emperor of Thessalonica, encouraged his nephew to attack Nicaean territory. But the fighting did not go well for Michael and he prudently bought peace by sacrificing Theodore, who was at last put out of mischief's way in a Nicaean prison. On the death of the formidable Emperor John Vatatzes Michael again tried his luck, this time with better success. By 1258 he had made ample gains of territory, which he endeavoured to safeguard by two resounding political marriages. Besides betrothing Anna to the Prince of Achaia, he secured Manfred of Hohenstaufen, son of the Emperor Frederick II and King of Naples and Sicily, as the husband of his other daughter Helen. As the latter's dowry he was obliged to cede to Manfred Corfu and certain coastal fortresses in his native Epiros, but he now felt assured the support of two such powerful Western sons-in-law would enable him to defy the strongest pressure from Nicaea. Moreover it might help him to reconquer Thessalonica, and even give him possession of Constantinople, where Latin rule was at its last gasp. The possibility that either Manfred or Guillaume might be harbouring similar aspirations did not apparently trouble him.

Both marriages took place in 1259, but Michael was given no time to exploit his diplomatic initiatives. The Nicaean reaction was swift and effective. Since the preceding year the government of the Greek Empire had been assumed by Michael Palaeologos, a descendant on his mother's side of both the Komnenoi and the Angeloi. He was a statesman of outstanding ability and intelligence, farseeing in his plans and ruthless in action. Acting first as regent for the young John IV Vatatzes and then as co-Emperor he moved at once to counter the threat from Michael. He sent a strong army to Macedonia under the command of his brother, the Sebastocrator John, while at the same time attempting to reach a settlement by direct negotiation with the Despot and through his sons-in-law. The latters' answer, however, was to come to Michael's help with the most powerful forces they could muster. In the autumn of 1259 the two armies stood facing each other on the plain of Pelagonia (near the modern Bitola).

The battle which followed was a quite different affair from that of Karydi, which was fought out between small bodies of Western knights and men-at-arms, after the fashion of the almost contemporary English encounters between Simon de Montfort and the Plantagenets. But it would be hard to imagine a more bizarre mixture of warriors than that which was marshalled at Pelagonia. On the Despot's side the tough mountaineers of Epiros and Albania were supported by a massive concentration of Western chivalry. Manfred sent four hundred picked knights from Italy, while the army which Guillaume led personally into Macedonia included almost every feudatory of consequence in Frankish Greece. Greeks from the Peloponnese marched with their Frankish overlords, and Athens was represented by a contingent under the Duke's brother, Othon de la Roche. In order to oppose this array Michael Palaeologos went far afield in search of suitable mercenaries. For heavy cavalry he relied on three hundred German knights under the Duke of Carinthia, but the backbone of his force consisted of horse-bowmen, Hungarians, Cumans (a warlike tribe lately settled in the Hungarian Kingdom) and Turks from Anatolia. He also hired detachments of Balkan Slavs, and his own frontiersmen from Asia Minor furnished the native Greek contribution.[18]

To weld so many disparate elements into a coherent fighting force would have taxed the powers of a military genius. Before the armies collided, however, the Sebastocrator had an unexpected stroke of luck in the shape of a dispute between Guillaume de Villehardouin and one of the Despot's generals, his bastard son John. Whether the quarrel sprang, as alleged by the *Chronicle of the Morea*, from the unwelcome attentions paid by certain Franks to the bastard's wife, or from less personal dissensions between Franks and Epirotes fomented by Nicaean agents in the Epirot camp, the result was that the bastard went over to the enemy and the Despot quickly withdrew his remaining troops from the field, leaving the Franks and their Sicilian allies to fight alone. Even so the issue was not easily decided. The battle began with a tremendous melee between the western cavalry of both sides, in which the Prince had the advantage and the Duke of Carinthia was cut down by Geoffroy de Briel. While the knights were hewing and hacking at each other the Sebastocrator brought up his horse-archers, who poured volleys of arrows indiscriminately into the struggling mass.[19] As Turks and, more recently, Mongols had so often demonstrated, the Western knight, when not properly supported by infantry, was no match for the more flexible tactics of the steppe. Unable to extricate themselves, the Franks either succumbed or surrendered. Among the distinguished prisoners were the Prince himself, Geoffroy de Briel and Ancelin de Toucy, a nobleman from the almost extinct court of Constantinople. The Sebastocrator, whose triumph was complete, despatched them to the Emperor at Lampsakos, on the Asiatic shore of the Dardanelles.

The immediate military consequences of the battle were not far reaching. The imperial army duly invaded Epiros, captured its capital Arta, and penetrated as far as Thebes, where Othon de la Roche stood a siege in the Kadmeia. But at that point the Epirots pulled themselves together. As neither the Despot nor the bastard was ready to submit to Nicaea, they reconciled their differences and forced the Sebastocrator to retreat to Macedonia, thus giving the shattered Franks a breathing space. Subsequently they defeated another Nicaean general, Alexios Strategopoulos, and were themselves again beaten by the Sebastocrator, but the balance of forces, so far as the two Greek states were concerned, remained as if Pelagonia had never been fought. It did, however, profoundly and lastingly affect the relations between Michael Palaeologos and the Franks. The Emperor had now firmly trapped the most powerful of the latter, together with a substantial number of his barons, and the only question was how much, in terms of territory and other political concessions, he would be able to extract from the Prince of Achaia.

Negotiations began at once. The captives were treated with consideration and the Emperor took a liking to a man whose grasp of the Greek language and of the issues at stake were comparable to his own. Michael's objective was to restore the Byzantine realm to something like its former state by recovering Constantinople and as much of the peninsula of Hellas as he could lay hands on. Provided that he exercised patience, Constantinople was sure to fall soon. Epiros would take longer to reduce, but it now seemed that there was a chance of occupying the whole of the Peloponnese, and if that could be achieved the remaining Frankish dominions might be secured without difficulty. Michael therefore demanded the entire principality as the price of Guillaume's release. In the battle of wits that followed the Prince was at his best. He emphatically rejected the Emperor's opening bid, maintaining that according to the constitution of Achaia he was not an absolute sovereign but only the first among his peers: therefore he had no right to compromise the future of the principality without their consent. He was bound by the solemn engagements which his father had contracted with the barons. His answer gained time for the magnates of the Morea, such as were left, to consider their reaction to Michael's exigencies, but as their scope for bargaining was clearly limited, the Emperor broke off the talks and returned Guillaume and his companions to prison. They were destined to spend three years in honourable but frustrated confinement.[20]

Meanwhile Michael was strengthening his position all round. At home, with the cruel egoism which had become a convention of palace life in the Eastern Empire, he consigned his young co-Emperor to oblivion by putting out his eyes. Abroad he patched up an uneasy peace with Epiros and, by a more important stroke of policy, concluded a treaty with Venice's rival, Genoa, by which the latter received vast trading and territorial concessions throughout the Empire in return for an undertaking to aid the Emperor in his efforts to push the Venetians out of the Aegean. Lastly, in July 1261, the day came which the Nicaeans had been awaiting for many long years: Constantinople was taken without resistance by Alexios Strategopoulos. Byzantium was itself again, and the Emperor judged that the time had come to resume discussions with the prisoner Guillaume, who was brought to the capital for the purpose.

In the interval Michael's requirements had become less sweeping. Under the administration of its bailie, Guy de la Roche, the principality had partially recovered from the shock of Pelagonia and Michael realized that it would be hard to conquer by direct attack. But he could be reasonably sure of winning a foothold in the Peloponnese in exchange for his eminent hostages. He therefore restricted his demands to the cession of Monemvasia and of the castles of Mistra and le Grand Magne. He even abandoned his claim to Argos and Nauplia, because Guillaume successfully argued that since they were fiefs held by the Duke of Athens they were not his to concede. The prospective loss of

Monemvasia, which he had conquered with so much difficulty, and of the two fortresses which he had so recently built, was a severe blow to the Prince's pride, but it was plain that he could secure no better terms. He therefore agreed to them, subject to their acceptance by the barons, and Geoffroy de Briel was released with instructions to lay them before the bailie and the high court of Achaia.

He found Guy at his twin capital, Thebes. The duty which the Duke was now required to carry out in his capacity as bailie was highly embarrassing, since the critical decision before the court involved a clash between personal considerations and public policy. When the court assembled, in accordance with precedent, at Nikli it was found that of the chief officers of state and lay barons entitled to attend only two, Leonard of Veroli, Chancellor of Achaia, and Pierre de Vaux, were available, the others having been killed or captured at Pelagonia. They were therefore represented by their wives or widows, who from the Princess of Achaia downwards formed a majority in favour of accepting any concessions that might free the prisoners. Nevertheless Guy put the opposite view as strongly as possible. He insisted that once the Emperor was allowed to introduce troops into the Morea and occupy the castles he would not rest until he had recovered the whole country. The survival of the principality was in question and it was his uncle's duty to die rather than yield a yard of territory to the Greeks. In a final burst of eloquence, he offered to change places with the Prince in his Byzantine prison, or if a ransom was needed to mortgage his own duchy for the purpose.[21] But as he and his audience no doubt realized he was speaking for the record. The wives were determined to have their men back and voted accordingly, arguing that since Guillaume had taken Monemvasia and built the castle himself, he was justified in disposing of them at his own discretion. As an additional guarantee that Guillaume would fulfil his part of the bargain, two of the ladies concerned, the wives of Jean de Nully, baron of Passava, and of Jean Chauderon, Grand Constable of Achaia, volunteered to go as hostages to Constantinople.

Before the Prince was set free he and the Emperor swore to observe perpetual peace. After his release, however, both busily prepared for war. Guillaume's first move was to settle his unnecessary quarrel with Venice and the Euboean triarchs, which had been hanging fire since the battle of Karydi. With the Duke of Athens acting as mediator a conference was held at Thebes and an agreement reached restoring the status quo between the three parties, who were all awaiting a Byzantine offensive. At first the Emperor confined himself to sending his brother, the Sebastocrator Constantine, to install garrisons in the ceded fortresses. It was galling enough for the Prince to see the Byzantine eagles floating from the towers of Mistra, in full view of his palace at Lakedaimonia in the valley below, but the loss of Monemvasia was more dangerous because it gave the Byzantines a port through which its bridgeheads in the Peloponnese could easily be reinforced. It was also an excellent base for the operations of the renascent imperial navy.[22] Although the Byzantines initially controlled little territory outside the walls of the fortresses, it soon started to expand. The Tzakonians, over whom the Frankish hold had previously been shaky enough, lost no time in transferring their allegiance to the Emperor; they are almost immediately mentioned as providing sailors for his fleet. The Slavs of the Pentedaktylo (the popular name of the 'five-fingered' Taygetos massif) followed their example. These developments forced the Franks to retire altogether from the promontories of Malea and Maina, and the Nivelets and Nullys abandoned their important fiefs of Geraki and Passava.

With two jealous sovereignties jostling each other in the peninsula, an early clash was inevitable. The Franks were now on the defensive, and if the undertakings made at Constantinople were going to be broken sooner or later it was in the Emperor's interest to force the pace. He had to strike quickly before the Franks had recovered from their weakness. He was also aware that Pope Urban IV, a Frenchman from Champagne, had already assured his fellow Champenois Villehardouin that he need not consider himself bound by his sworn obligations, since they had been extracted under duress. As the immediate pretext for his attack on the principality Michael alleged that a visit by Guillaume to the latter's own town, Lakedaimonia, was evidence of his intention to recapture Mistra. Thus, in the summer of 1263, a large Byzantine army under the command of Constantine the Sebastocrator disembarked at Monemvasia from Greek and Genoese ships. Fifteen hundred of them were Turks, the first of their race to appear in the Morea. Leaving Lakedaimonia blockaded, the Byzantines struck northward and entered Arkadia unopposed. They swept across the plateau, turned westwards and made straight for Andravida, the Prince's capital.

Guillaume was in fact unprepared for the struggle. He was still engaged in filling the gaps in his baronage with knights who had escaped from Constantinople when the Greeks retook it, or who had newly arrived from France. He ordered his vassals to join him at Corinth. Meanwhile the Byzantine army was following the course of the river Alpheios, known to the Franks as the Charbon. The point at which that stream turns to the west, towards the plain of Elis, was guarded by the towering castle of Karytaina, the fief of Geoffroy de Briel, but at that crucial moment the chatelain happened to have absconded to Apulia, under the pretence of a pilgrimage to the shrine of the Archangel Michael on Monte Gargano, with the wife of one of his vassals, an elderly warrior called Jean de Catavas.[23] Consequently no resistance was offered to the passage of the Greeks, and in the absence of the lord of Skorta its highlanders joined Constantine en masse. Pressing down the valley, the Greeks soon reached the neighbourhood of Olympia, while their Turkish mercenaries burned the Latin monastery of Notre Dame d'Isova, the Gothic ruins of which still stand. There they were boldly attacked by Catavas, the injured husband, at the head of three hundred knights. The Grand Domestic Alexios Philes, commander of the Greek vanguard, counted on an easy success; he would eat up these Franks, he proclaimed, like a little snack before lunch (*proyevmatitsi mikron*). But the Frankish charge, led by Catavas himself, too gouty to wield lance or sword but with the Prince's banner (*flamouron*) tied to his arm, shattered the Greeks. Panic overtook the whole of the Sebastocrator's army, which took refuge in the hills and eventually retired to Lakonia. This action ended the campaigning season for 1263 and gave Villehardouin time to regroup his forces.[25]

In the following spring the Byzantines tried again. Once more they traversed Arkadia and marched down the Alpheios valley into Elis. Guillaume let them advance until they were within ten miles of Andravida itself. As the two armies were lined up facing each other Michael Cantacuzenos, a great Byzantine noble, member of a family which had owned large estates in the Morea before the Frankish conquest and grandfather of a future emperor, was killed in a skirmish. The death of this experienced soldier, whom the French *Chronicle* describes as 'le plus vaillant homme de Romania', caused the Greek troops to lose heart for the second time.[25] They retreated precipitately, and as they marched back into Arkadia they were deserted by the Turkish contingent, which had not received its pay. The Turkish chieftains, Melik and Salik, decided to offer their services to the Prince and an arrangement was immediately negotiated by Ancelin de Toucy, who spoke their language fluently. Thereupon the Franco-Turkish force marched rapidly southwards, parallel to the retreating Byzantines, and swinging east, caught them at the pass of Makryplagi, a few miles from Veligosti. This time a very fierce battle ensued and the Greeks were completely routed. The Sebastocrator had already returned to Constantinople but both his generals, Philes and Makrynos, were taken prisoner. Although as a result of a victory due to Byzantine ineptitude rather than to his own military skill Guillaume was able to re-enter Lakedaimonia, he made no further progress and the Greeks retained all their positions in the southern Peloponnese.[26]

For a few years after 1264, peace of a kind returned to the Morea, but the principality was no longer secure nor prosperous. Although formal campaigning temporarily ceased, the political division of the peninsula between hostile states had made guerrilla warfare endemic. Conditions in the rugged border country between Lakonia and Arkadia began to resemble those which later prevailed on the Anglo-Scottish marches. Slow but continuous pressure and harassment were maintained from the Byzantine side. In order to check raids, infiltration and the subversion of their Greek subjects the Franks were obliged to strengthen their physical defences. More castles were built, and the hills bristled with small forts and watch towers, the garrisons of which were a heavy charge on the treasury. In the threatened districts agriculture and trade were disrupted. As its wealth and strength declined Achaia lost within a very few years of the battle of Pelagonia the stability and independence which had previously established its pre-eminence among the Latin states of the Levant. Indeed, the Pope was moved to launch urgent appeals in the West to provide the Prince with subsidies and military stores. Despite his embarrassments Guillaume and his feudatories firmly rejected overtures of peace from the Byzantine Emperor, who invited him to betroth his daughter Isabelle, the heiress to the principality, to Michael's son Andronikos. This was regarded as an only too transparent attempt to bring the whole of the Morea within the Byzantines' control.

It was clear to Guillaume that the safety of Achaia would in future require a powerful protector in the West, and in 1266 he found the champion he needed in Charles of Anjou, brother of Louis IX of France and the chosen instrument of the papacy in its feud with Manfred of Hohenstaufen, King of Naples and Sicily. Early in that year Charles, having defeated and killed Manfred at the battle of Benevento, succeeded to his throne and with it to all the ambitious schemes which earlier Western sovereigns and adventurers had conceived for the domination of the Levant. As soon as he was settled in his new kingdom he began to plan a second Latin conquest of Constantinople. In addition he laid claim to Corfu and territories in Epiros which Manfred had acquired as the dowry of his wife, Helen, the Despot's daughter. Guillaume, for his part, crossed to Italy in the winter of 1266–7 and joined a conference at Viterbo between the new Pope Clement IV, Charles of Anjou and the dispossessed Latin Emperor, Baldwin II.

From that meeting two treaties emerged. The first, concluded between Charles and Guillaume, showed just how desperately the latter needed help from overseas. In effect he undertook to become the vassal of the King of Naples during his lifetime and agreed that after his death the principality should pass to the House of Anjou. It was further arranged that his daughter Isabelle should marry Philip, a younger son of Charles, who would eventually succeed Guillaume as Prince of Achaia.In the event of the latter having a son by his wife Anna of Epiros, the child would only inherit a fief corresponding to a fifth of the principality. Guillaume received nothing but promises of material support in return for signing away the rights of the Villehardouin family, but his feudatories were delighted to acquire a French King as their overlord and guardian. The second treaty obliged the Latin Emperor to renounce in favour of Charles his nominal sovereignty over the Morea and other territories in Greece. As the result of Guillaume's acceptance of Angevin supremacy, Achaia and all Hellas were overshadowed for the next fifteen years by the intense political duel which developed between Charles and Michael Palaeologos. Only the Emperor's consummate diplomatic skill in thwarting his opponent's aggressive plans, combined with fortuitous events outside the control of either protagonist, prevented the outbreak of direct hostilities between the two rulers.

Guillaume was soon summoned to aid his sovereign in the latter's struggle with the last of the Hohenstaufens, young Conradin, who in 1268 attempted to recover the Kingdom of Naples. At the head of four hundred knights from the Morea, including the Grand Constable and the barons of Karytaina, Akova and Kalavryta, he helped to overcome Conradin and his Germans at the battle of Tagliacozzo. According to the Greek Chronicle, it was Guillaume's sound military advice that decided the issue. 'May it please Your Majesty', he is quoted as saying, 'we shall not fight them as the Franks fight or we shall lose the war, for they are more numerous than we. But if we fight with craft and intelligence (*mechanian kai phrona*), as the Turks and Romans do in Romania, then with God's help and justice on our side we shall have the victory'.[27] At all events the King showed his gratitude to the Prince by paying his campaign expenses and a subsidy of two thousand ounces of gold; he also ordered the shipment of ample food supplies, barley, wheat and cattle to the Morea, which he expected to use as a base for his designs on the Greek Empire. During 1269 he pressed ahead with preparations for a grand attack on Constantinople and assembled a large fleet in Apulia. He would have liked to count on Venetian shipping for the purpose but the Republic, for which political aims always ranked second to commercial opportunities, had disappointed him by concluding a five year truce with the Emperor Michael. Even when his armada was ready he was unable to employ it immediately against Byzantium, for the King of France had at the same time inconveniently set his heart on a new Crusade and Charles, quite apart from the moral obligation to aid his brother, felt that it would be politic for him to join it. He cleverly managed to persuade Louis to divert his expedition from Palestine to Tunis, which in Western hands would greatly improve the strategic position of his own realm. Louis embarked from Aigues-Mortes on 1 July 1270, but when Charles, following somewhat tardily, appeared off Tunis on 25 August, he was told that his brother had died earlier in the day. It took Charles another two months to disengage himself from the enterprise and make peace with the Tunisian ruler: then, by a crowning stroke of bad luck, his fleet was shattered by a storm off the Sicilian coast. It was not an easy task to create a new empire in the Mediterranean.

Michael was finding it equally arduous to preserve his own state. In order to thwart his enemy he engaged in incessant diplomatic activity. His emissaries busily countered every Angevin move to enlist the kingdoms of the West, the Italian republics, Hungary and the Slav states of the Balkans in a coalition against Byzantium. With successive popes he played a more complicated game, dangling before them the prospect of a reunion of the Churches which, by ridding the Eastern Church of the taint of schism, would deprive Charles of his most plausible pretext for attacking Constantinople. The Emperor was perfectly sincere in his anxiety to heal the rift. The political advantages of achieving a formal reconciliation by which papal primacy would be recognised without prejudice to Orthodox tradition and practice were only too obvious. Despite the increased bitterness alienating the Greek clergy and laity from the Latins since the sack of Constantinople Michael judged the attempt worth making. From the time of his accession he made persistent overtures to Rome. Although he received scant encouragement from French popes who would have preferred a restoration of Latin power in the East to a negotiated settlement, he managed to maintain the dialogue until the election in 1271 of Gregory X, an Italian who had little sympathy for Charles's ambitions and wished to see Christendom united for a great Crusade in Palestine. He at once started friendly negotiations with the Emperor about reunion and invited him to send a delegation to the General Council of the Church which he had decided to convoke at Lyons in 1274. Meanwhile he insisted that Charles should hold his hand.

Michael had the greatest difficulty in persuading his prelates and advisers that the invitation must be accepted, but in the end his delegates, headed by the logothete and historian George Akropolites, appeared at Lyons. They handed to Gregory letters in which the Emperor and the Orthodox clergy acknowledged the primacy of the Roman See and promised obedience and the acceptance of its Creed. It was, however, understood that the Eastern Church would keep its rituals and that Rome would not interfere with its appointments and administration. When the Pope delightedly informed Charles that union had been restored, the King was in no position to object. Michael had won that particular contest of wits. But he was under no illusions about the attitude of his own subjects, although he tried to assure them that submission to Rome was purely a tactical measure and would not fatally prejudice the independence of Orthodoxy. Already the Patriarch himself had refused to be associated with union on the terms of Lyons. Byzantine society—the imperial family, the clergy, the magnates and the people—was radically and bitterly split between the opponents and supporters of union, and the former predominated. As time passed they became increasingly obstreperous and Michael was forced to resort to harsh repression of the dissidents. He also found to his cost that his espousal of union was condemned by other Orthodox peoples, and in particular by the Greeks of Epiros.[28]

If Byzantium could now gain a substantial grip on the Greek peninsula, as opposed to a mere foothold in the Peloponnese, Angevin aggression would clearly be made more difficult. Therefore, concurrently with his political initiatives, the Emperor deployed a considerable military effort in northern Greece as well as in the Morea. The Byzantines obtained better results in the south by infiltration than by direct assault. During this period they finally gained possession of Lakedaimonia and Jean de Nivelet, the former baron of Geraki, was stationed at Nikli with a large force to block further erosion of the Arkadian marches. But they also launched two major attacks between 1270 and 1275, which were only repelled with the aid of Angevin reinforcements from Italy. On the second occasion, when they again penetrated as far as Skorta, they were staved off by Geoffroy de Briel. It was the last act of his adventurous career, for he died of dysentery during the campaign. 'The famous lord of Karytaina', laments the Chronicle,

fell into a fearful fever, a grievous weakness. It overcame his human nature and death took him. Alas how great a loss to the Morea, how deep an affliction! The Prince was afflicted for his kinsman. All wept for him, great and small. Even the birds that have no speech wept for him. Who was there that did not groan and mourn? He was the father

101

of the orphans, the husband of the widows, the lord and champion of the poor.[29]

The conflicts which took place in Thessaly and Euboea were more spectacular, as they amounted to a serious drive by the Byzantines to reconquer those regions from both Latins and Epirote Greeks. On the death of Michael II Dukas in 1271, the Despotate had been divided into two states. The original Epiros, with its capital Arta, was held by his son Nikephoros. It stretched from the Gulf of Corinth to the borders of Albania, most of which now belonged to Charles of Anjou. Thessaly, together with the country extending southward to the Gulf between the Despotate and the Duchy of Athens, fell to the Despot Michael's bastard son, John, who had behaved so unheroically at the battle of Pelagonia. His capital was at Neopatras near Lamia. Nikephoros was colourless in character but John, despite his conduct at Pelagonia, was vigorous and efficient. As neither of the brothers wished to see his dominions incorporated into the Byzantine Empire, they were both careful to remain on good terms with the neighbouring Latin states, and Nikephoros went so far as to declare himself Charles's vassal. The Emperor tried to conciliate the Epirote pair by marrying one of his daughters to Nikephoros and his nephew to John's daughter, but they, while not refusing the alliances, remained wary. They also profoundly disliked Michael's attachment to Church union and were at pains to advertise themselves as the champions of pure Orthodoxy. Moreover, many Byzantine nobles and churchmen who had taken refuge in Thessaly, either because they found Michael's ecclesiastical policy repugnant or because they were shocked by his usurpation of the throne from the Laskaris family, enthusiastically supported John. So far as his Thessalian subjects were concerned, the bastard's position was strengthened by his marriage to the daughter of a chieftain of the Vlachs, who formed a very strong element in the local population.

In such circumstances Michael decided to resort to war against his fellow Greeks. He began by seizing, under the nose of Charles of Anjou, two of the latter's fortresses in Albania. Then, in the same year as the Council of Lyons, he sent his brother John Palaeologos, his most experienced general and the victor of Pelagonia, to invade Thessaly. At first all went well for the Byzantines. John of Thessaly was shut up in Neopatras, while his opponent's wild Cuman mercenaries devastated the country and aroused horror by desecrating Orthodox monasteries. After a while, however, the bastard escaped by sliding down a rope over the city walls and passing in disguise through the besiegers' lines. He had no difficulty in making his way to Thebes, where he appealed for help to the Duke of Athens, Jean de la Roche. The Duke's father, Guy I, had died in 1263 and his own reign had so far been equally exemplary. He had avoided becoming involved in Guillaume de Villehardouin's campaigns in the Morea. Consequently the Duchy had escaped invasion and had remained the most prosperous and the best governed state in Greece. However, alarmed by the Byzantine threat, he came to the bastard's rescue with three hundred knights. The two Johns attacked their namesake under the walls of Neopatras. John Palaeologos was decisively beaten. He retreated in disorder under the protection of the Byzantine fleet which, under its admiral Philanthropenos, was operating in the Gulf of Volo.

The Byzantine naval objective was Negroponte, strategically the key to the whole region. The Venetians and Lombards of Euboea combined to meet his dangerous challenge and attacked the Greek fleet off Demetrias. The Latin ships, commanded by a Venetian and crowded with Lombard knights and soldiers, were fitted with wooden towers and as they advanced they resembled a battlemented city. The Greeks fought better by sea than they did on land, but their admiral was badly wounded and many of their galleys were driven on shore with heavy losses. No sooner were they beached, however, than they were remanned by soldiers from the army of John Palaeologos, who fought so effectively that the Latin fleet was as good as annihilated. Many Lombards were killed and many captured and despatched to Constantinople. Negroponte was only saved for the Latins by reinforcements from Athens.[30]

There followed another two years of confused amphibious warfare around the coasts of Euboea. The Byzantines found a brilliant new admiral in Licario, a poor knight of Vicenza, who entered the imperial service as the result of a personal quarrel with the triarchs. With ships and men provided by the Emperor and a corps of adventurers collected by himself, he succeeded, in a series of whirlwind campaigns not only in seizing every town and castle of importance in Euboea with the exception of Negroponte itself, but in recovering several Aegean islands for Byzantium. The Latins were in despair, for Licario inflicted a sharp defeat on a force from the Peloponnese which tried to arrest his progress in Euboea led by Prince Guillaume himself and the Marshal Dreux de Beaumont, a high officer of Charles of Anjou, and when the Duke of Athens made a similar attempt he too was routed. Wounded and unhorsed, he was made prisoner and sent to the Emperor, along with Giberto da Verona, the triarch who had caused Licario's defection by objecting to a mesalliance between the Vicenzan and his sister. As a reward for Licario, Michael gave him a rich Byzantine bride and all his conquests in Euboea as an imperial fief.

If at this moment the Emperor's forces had also been victorious in Thessaly, he might have had a chance of realizing his ambition of overrunning all Greece. It was already a great achievement to have held in captivity, at different periods, the Prince of Achaia and the Duke of Athens. But in 1276 another Byzantine army was defeated by John of Thessaly at Pharsala and Michael abandoned his fruitless endeavours on the Greek mainland. He even released the Duke of Athens on the payment of a large ransom, without making any territorial demands. No doubt he decided that with his limited and already overstrained resources he could do no more. His military effort in Greece, never quite adequate for his purpose, had denuded his frontier garrisons in Asia Minor, where the pressure of Turkish inroads had become disquieting. Bulgaria and Serbia were openly hostile. His popularity with his own people and army was shaky. Worst of all, clouds were again gathering in the West. Pope Gregory who had held Charles in check, was dead. His successor, an Orsini, also threw his weight against an assault on the Eastern Empire, but he urged Michael to observe union more strictly, thus weakening the Emperor's authority at home. When another French Pope, Martin IV, succeeded in 1280 Charles again felt free to proceed with his plans.[31]

It looked as if the events of 1204 might be repeated. Like the earlier Frankish leaders, Charles concluded an agreement with Venice providing for a joint expedition, the object of which would be to place not himself but his son-in-law Philip of Courtenay, the titular Latin Emperor, on the throne of Constantinople. It was envisaged that in addition to hundreds of war-galleys, the parties would contribute all the shipping necessary to transport eight thousand mounted troops and their supporting infantry. Achaia too was required to send a contingent. If so enormous a force could be landed in the vicinity of the Byzantine capital the city was surely doomed. The Pope duly issued a Bull excommunicating Michael and menacing him with deposition unless he placed his empire at the disposal of the Holy See, and Michael responded by releasing his subjects from any religious obligations he had forced them to assume towards Rome.

Meanwhile fighting had already started. Before signing his pact with Venice, Charles ordered his commander in Albania, Hugues de Sully, to seize the fortress of Berat, dominating the route through Macedonia. If it could be secured as a base for the march on Constantinople, there would be no need for his expedition to take the long sea route through the Aegean. Paradoxically enough Berat was stoutly defended for Byzantium by a brother of John of Thessaly, that thorn in the Byzantine flesh. When Michael's relieving army came up, the Byzantines lured Sully's troops into an ambush and routed them. It often happened in encounters between Greeks and Franks that the latter, who carried all before them if rashly afforded the opportunity of a straightforward cavalry charge, were curiously vulnerable to tactical surprise. And once their heavily mailed leaders were unhorsed they were virtually helpless. In this case Sully, a red-haired colossus from Burgundy, was over-powered in exactly the same way as Guillaume of Achaia and Jean de la Roche, and like them he ended up in a prison by the Bosporus. The Emperor paraded him through the streets of the capital and commissioned a mural commemorating the victory for his palace of Blachernae. Unluckily that work of art has not survived.[32]

In spite of this initial success prospects still seemed black for Byzantium. Few contemporaries could foresee that the apparently overwhelming threat posed by Charles of Anjou would suddenly crumble into nothing. The story of the Sicilian Vespers is outside the scope of this book. So is the organization of the vast plot which was concerted between the exiles from Charles's own realm on the one side, and on the other the Kingdom of Aragon, the Genoese Republic and the Byzantine Empire and which, powered with Byzantine gold, paralysed Angevin aggression at the moment when the fleet intended for the assault on Constantinople was waiting to sail from Messina. The revolt of Sicily in the spring of 1282 removed all possibility of the restoration of the Latin Empire. After that date, although it could hardly have been realized at the time, the future of the Latin and Greek states of the Levant lay at the mercy of the Ottoman Turks.

The Emperor Michael did not survive his political salvation for more than a few months. Charles of Anjou lingered on, frustrated and struggling desperately against the enemies of his kingdom, until 1285. Of the minor actors on the Greek stage whose fortunes had been so closely affected by the conflict between the two sovereigns, the Prince of Achaia died in 1278 and the Duke of Athens two years later. While the Duchy simply passed to Jean's brother, the succession in the Morea, where the Villehardouins were now extinct in the male line, gave rise to a host of problems. Guillaume's latter years offered a sad contrast to the magnificence, high prestige and prosperity of the early part of his reign, when Achaia was proudly self-sufficient. All he now had to show for thirty-three years of strenuous military and political activity was a

105

principality reduced in size and to the status of a client outpost of the Angevin kingdom. Such tutelage must have been repugnant to him. Moreover his life had lately been bedevilled by family vicissitudes and feudal squabbles involving the misfortunes of certain well born ladies. These, as illustrating the changes which were about to transform the character of the principality, may be more conveniently described in the following chapter. But, notwithstanding his mistakes and failures, Guillaume's attractive personality made a very strong imprint on his century. He died in his own castle of Kalamata and was buried at Andravida, the seat of his court. 'The angels took his soul', wrote the chronicler, 'and lodged it with all the just. Remember him all of you, he was a fine ruler. His only fault, for which the great and the humble mourn, was that he left no son to inherit the realm which his father toiled to win.'[33]

CHAPTER FIVE

The Shadow of the Angevins

THE COMPLEXION OF Frankish society in the Morea began to change with the advent of the Angevins. As the sons and grandsons of the first conquerors died out they were replaced by French and Italian knights from Charles' of Anjou's dominions, ignorant of the usages of the principality and unable to speak its common language, Greek. Of the twelve chief baronies two (Geraki and Passava) had already disappeared and a third, Kalavryta, was soon to pass into Greek hands. Only four were still held by the male heirs of the families to which they had originally been granted. The wastage of war and climate had made heiresses more common than heirs, and the more eligible of them were eagerly sought in successive marriages. The most important fief-holder in the Morea happened to be the Duke of Athens, who still held Argos and Nauplia, while his cousin, Jacques de la Roche, was established at Veligosti in Arkadia and at Damala in the Troezen peninsula.[1]

Prince Guillaume himself broke up the two strategically vital fiefs of Akova and Karytaina, with the object of bringing as much of their territory as possible under his direct control. The story of Marguerite de Nully, lady of Passava and Akova and daughter of the Marshal of Achaia, provides a good illustration of the manners and procedures prevailing in the Morea, as well as of the hazards which the noble ladies of the principality were liable to encounter. Her first husband, Guibert de Cors, was killed at Karydi and the second, Guglielmo dalle Carceri, a triarch of Euboea, in the sea battle off Demetrias. It will be recalled that she herself was sent as a hostage to Constantinople when Michael VIII released Prince Guillaume from captivity. When, having spent several years in the imperial capital, she eventually returned to the Peloponnese, Passava was already part of the new Byzantine province. However, her uncle Gautier de Rosières, lord of Akova, had recently died and she, as the natural heiress of the barony, promptly claimed her inheritance. But she found to her dismay that the Prince had taken possession of the fief, declaring it forfeited on the grounds that more than the statutory interval of two years and two days had elapsed between her uncle's death and her own return. When she indignantly objected that it was solely her forced absence from the Morea on the Prince's service that had delayed the registration of her claim, he was unmoved. He replied that the usages of the principality must be strictly observed. Nevertheless, he was prepared to entertain a petition in the High Court.

Marguerite's friends thereupon advised her that her appeal would be more likely to succeed if she was supported by a new husband with powerful feudal connexions. Such a one was promptly found in Jean de St Omer, cousin of the Duke of Athens and brother of Nicholas, lord of half Thebes. By his marriage to Marguerite Jean automatically became Marshal of Achaia, thus further extending the influence of the Duchy of Athens in the Morea. It was then arranged that Nicholas, at that time the richest and most prestigious magnate in Frankish Greece, should personally represent his sister-in-law's cause when the court met in the Cathedral of Hagia Sophia at Andravida. He duly arrived with a resplendent retinue, calculated to impress the court, and demanded that the Prince should concede Marguerite's inheritance not as an act of favour but in recognition of a right. Guillaume, in accordance with the usages, relinquished the presidency of the court to the Chancellor and each contestant argued his case from the floor. After some hesitation the court decided that legality should prevail over equity, but in giving judgement for the Prince it recommended that he should behave generously to a lady who had suffered imprisonment for his sake. This gave Guillaume the opportunity to deliver a little homily to the St Omers, whose arrogance had annoyed him, to the effect that if they had been content to appeal to his liberality instead of demanding reparation, he would only have been too glad to perform an act of grace without any vexatious litigation. This done, he drew up a settlement by which Marguerite would receive eight of the twenty-four fiefs constituting the barony, while reserving the remaining eighteen for himself as an eventual dowry for his second daughter, also called Marguerite.[2]

The Prince pursued the same policy with regard to the twin barony of Karytaina. On the death of Geoffroy de Briel he appropriated one half of the domain, leaving Geoffroy's widow, Isabelle de la Roche, in possession of the other half. Before Guillaume's death she married, with his approval, one of the greatest of the Angevin vassals in South Italy, Hugues de Brienne, Count of Lecce, who thus became the absentee holder of twelve valuable fiefs in the Morea. The Prince's award, however, was twice challenged by claimants from Geoffroy's family. The first, a knight from Champagne named Jean Pestel, was easily rebuffed, but the second, a cadet of the Briels also called Geoffroy, turned out to be a more persistent and resourceful adventurer. He appeared in the Morea in about 1287, when the administration of the principality was exercised by a bailie appointed directly by the Angevin monarch. On the rejection of his claim by the high court he looked for a way of forcing the bailie's hand. According to the *Chronicle of the Morea*, which treats the episode at considerable length (348 lines of verse), it occurred to him that if he could somehow seize the almost impregnable castle of Araklovon, or Bucelet, the former stronghold of Doxapatres Voutsaras, while letting it be known that it was his intention to dispose of it to the 'captain of the Greeks', or military governor of Mistra, the mere threat of a Byzantine occupation of this key fortress in Skorta would suffice to compel the bailie to accede to his demands.[3]

Since Geoffroy's sole following consisted of eight sergeants, he had to devise some trick to gain possession of the castle. Having settled in a neighbouring village, he sent a message to the castellan of Araklovon to say that he was suffering from colic and would be grateful for permission to draw on the castle's cisterns, which contained pure water reputed to cure a complaint common to all newcomers to the Levant. In the Greek of the *Chronicle* it had 'static' qualities. The castellan, an easy-going man, readily granted the request. His name is given as Philokalos. Obviously he was a Greek, although it is surprising to find a native entrusted with so responsible a post in a district notorious for its disaffection with Frankish rule. At that moment, indeed, the castle's dungeons harboured twelve local 'Romans' suspected of disloyalty. As soon as he was on friendly terms with the castellan, Geoffroy managed to have a room (*tsampra* or *chambre*) allotted to him in the castle itself, into which his sergeants proceeded to smuggle arms, clothes and food (including—a delightfully local touch—*paximadia*, described by Patrick Leigh Fermor, that connoisseur of the Peloponnese, as 'dark-brown pumices of twice-baked bread').[4] From then on the ruse worked smoothly. The sergeants decoyed the castellan and the men-at-arms of the garrison into a taverna outside the castle walls and when they were suitably drunk, rushed the gates and shut them out. At the same time Geoffroy despatched two of the Greek prisoners to urge the Byzantine governor to seize his chance, and when they were gone informed the excluded castellan of what was in prospect.

As Geoffroy had expected, his action caused a tremendous flurry. The bailie hastily laid siege to Araklovon while the Frankish captain of Skorta, Simon de Vidoigne, effectively blocked the crossings of the river Alpheios when the Byzantine force arrived on the scene. The haggling then began. The bailie warned Geoffroy that unless he submitted, siege machines specially prepared by the Venetians at Modon would be mounted against the castle. In reply he protested that his sole wish was to join the chivalry of the Morea, which had so far treated his just claims with such lack of sympathy. The stage was thus set for a compromise. Although Geoffroy failed to obtain, as he had hoped, twelve fiefs in the barony of Karytaina, he was granted one in Skorta, while his marriage to yet another Marguerite, a cousin of Gautier de Rosieres, brought him a second in the barony of Chalandritza. The whole affair, as William Miller points out, was an interesting exercise in feudal blackmail.[5]

Under the early Angevins power tended to be concentrated in the hands of the King's bailie or of great feudatories whose main interests did not lie in the Morea itself. Significantly enough the King was unwilling that Kalamata, the ancestral barony of the Villehardouins, and the fortress of Clermont (Chloumoutzi), should remain in the possession of Guillaume's widow, Anna of Epiros, especially as she very soon became the wife of Nicholas de St Omer, the Theban magnate whom Guillaume had been so anxious to keep at arm's length, and whose brother Jean already held a third of Akova. As it did not then appear to be in the Angevin interest that the St Omers should become too powerful in the Peloponnese, it was arranged that Nicholas should receive in exchange two less important fiefs in Messenia.

Nevertheless it did not for long prove possible or politic to exclude the St Omers and their Athenian overlords and associates the de la Roches from the direction of Moreot affairs. For four years after Guillaume's death the King of Naples appointed officers from his own dominions as his bailies in Achaia. Such were Galeran d'Ivry and Philippe de Lagonesse, Marshal of Sicily. These foreigners were not popular with the Greek-born feudatories of the Morea, who complained to the King of their high-handed methods of government, and in particular of the employment of Turkish mercenaries to man the fortresses. The bailies, however, were genuinely concerned with the run-down condition of the principality, the poor showing of its defence and the decay of its finances, at a time when Charles I was preparing his grand foray against Constantinople. However, after his hopes of empire had collapsed, Charles appeased the Moreots by choosing as bailie one of their number, Guy de Dramelay, baron of Chalandritza. He also picked three leading barons from the Peloponnese, the Grand Constable Jean Chauderon, Geoffroy de Durnay and Jacques de la Roche, to accompany him to Bordeaux, where a vast tilt-yard had been prepared to enable him and a hundred of his knights to meet his rival for the crown of Sicily, King Peter of Aragon, with an equal contingent of knights, in mortal, not symbolic, combat to decide the issue between them. What would have surely ranked as the most bizarre episode in mediaeval history did not in the event take place, for even in 1283 such a procedure for settling a territorial dispute was considered embarrassingly outmoded: it was condemned by the Pope and discouraged by the King of England, in whose dominions Bordeaux lay. So the three barons returned unscathed to the Morea.

Two years later Charles I of Naples was dead and his son, Charles II, a prisoner of the Aragonese. With the Kingdom in such disarray the regency acting for Charles II sought a more prominent figure as bailie of Achaia, and it so happened that Guillaume de la Roche, who had become Duke of Athens in 1280 on the death of his brother John, was ready to assume the charge. This development made the house of de la Roche temporarily supreme in the whole of the Greek mainland ruled by Franks. Duke of Athens, bailie of Achaia, lord of Argos and Nauplia, brother of the lord of Veligosti and Damala, married to Helen Dukas of Thessaly and Neopatras, he outclassed all other Frankish nobles. Yet he was scrupulously loyal to the Angevin connexion. Any temptation that he may have felt to usurp the princely title was certainly countered by his sense of feudal propriety and by the manifest advantage of retaining the Angevin kingdom, even in its weakened state, as the protector of the principality and of his own Duchy as well. In the Morea he applied himself energetically to its defence against Greek encroachments, building a new fortress, Dimatra, on the borders of Messenia and Skorta.

Unfortunately for the Frankish cause Guillaume died in 1287. He was succeeded almost automatically as bailie of Achaia by the second greatest luminary in the Duchy of Athens and Thebes, Nicholas de St Omer. It was during his tenure of the government that the young Geoffroy de Briel played his audacious trick on the principality. It is curious that the houses of de la Roche and St Omer should have been able to maintain so amicable and lasting a co-existence within the narrow confines of Attica and Boeotia. So far as is known, no serious quarrel marred their personal concord or endangered the Duchy's stability. Both families kept brilliant courts in the Duchy and held extensive lands in the Morea. As merely co-seigneur of Thebes, Nicholas owed homage to the Duke, but his antecedents were more impressive than Guillaume's. The St Omers boasted a superior pedigree to that of the pretty lords of la Roche-sur-Ognon. While Nicholas too was a de la Roche on his mother's side, his paternal grandmother had been a Hungarian princess and he himself, before marrying the widowed Princess of Achaia, had been the husband of Mary of Antioch, descendant of the legendary Norman, Bohemond of Tarentum, who brought to Thebes not only the fading glamour of the nearly extinct Crusader states of Syria but also very substantial wealth. Thus endowed, Nicholas rebuilt the old Byzantine castle on the Kadmeia of Thebes as a superb palace with murals representing the Crusading epic in the Holy Land, while the Duke of Athens stayed content with a residence on the Acropolis which, though he may not have been aware of it, was a masterpiece of Periclean architecture.[6]

By far the most interesting of the bewilderingly frequent marriages and re-marriages of great personages with outstanding heiresses are the unions which Guillaume de Villehardouin and Guillaume of Athens entered into with Greek princesses of the Dukas family, Anna of Arta and Helen of Neopatras. Had they both produced sons, both Achaia and Athens would have acquired semi-Greek rulers in the same generation. As it was, only daughters were born to Villehardouin, but Guillaume of Athens left a young son, Guy II, to succeed him, and during his minority Helen assumed the government of the Duchy. Like her father, the bastard of Neopatras, she was distinguished by her courage and strength of character, but these personal qualities were not sufficient to sustain her in the almost exclusively Latin atmosphere of the Athenian Duchy, where Greeks counted for nothing, whereas in the principality they held many minor but useful offices and, if they were archons, fitted into the feudal hierarchy; they were in fact an essential, if not always trustworthy, element in the life of Frankish Achaia. It was therefore hardly surprising that Helen, after acting as regent for four years on her own, should seek a husband and protector in the Count of Lecce, Hugues de Brienne, whose first wife, Isabelle de la Roche, was no longer alive. The Count had vast possessions in Italy, but Greece too held a powerful attraction for him.

During Helen's regency the fortunes of Isabelle de Villehardouin, daughter of Anna Dukas of Epiros, changed abruptly for the better. She was only a child when her father signed away her rights to the principality by the Treaty of Viterbo and destined her to marry Philip of Anjou, the second son of Charles I. On his premature death she was held in seclusion in the Castel dell' Uovo at Naples, far from her native Achaia and apparently ignored by those engaged in the struggle for power. In the Morea, however, she had by no means been forgotten by either Franks or Greeks, She remained a focus for the loyalty and affection of all those who looked back with longing to the great age of the Villehardouins and deplored the decline of the principality under the Angevins. They resented the frequent changes of bailie, the mismanagement and arbitrary conduct of officials nominated from Naples and the inexperience and tactlessness of the newly arrived recipients of fiefs, Frenchmen and Italians, who did not understand the language and cared little for the customs and traditions of the country.

Depressing, too, was the intermittent but destructive warfare with the Greeks of Mistra, which consumed the resources of Achaia and impoverished its people. As is evident from the incident at Araklovon, the Byzantines were always watching for an opportunity to penetrate the Frankish defences. Any sign of disorder or faltering in the Frankish leadership encouraged them to gnaw at the boundaries of the principality and tempted its Greek feudatories to change their allegiance. Although no clear picture emerges of these sporadic hostilities, it seems that at this period the Franks finally lost control of the central basin of Arkadia and suffered some sharp setbacks in battle. Erard d'Aulnay, baron of Arkadia (Kyparissia) was made prisoner in one of such encounters. The Byzantines, gradually advancing what the Aragonese *Chronicle* calls 'la frontera de los Griegos', northward to the Gulf of Corinth, occupied Nikli, dismantled it and distributed its inhabitants among the surrounding villages. Some, if tradition is to be believed were removed as far as the Maina. Veligosti was also probably lost at about the same time.[7]

King Charles II, who was released from his Aragonese prison in 1289, was fortunately soon convinced that a change of policy in the Morea was overdue. He began by appointing a Moreot bailie, Guy de Charpigny, baron of Vostitza, in place of Nicholas de St Omer. But he was also persuaded by those paladins of the Angevin cause, Jean Chauderon and Geoffroy de Durnay, who had fought for Charles I at Tagliacozzo, as well as accompanying him on his abortive demonstration at Bordeaux, and were therefore in high favour at the court of Naples, that it was time that Isabelle de Villehardouin was allowed to return to the Peloponnese and that due reparation was made to her for years of confinement and neglect. Moreover the Moreots warned him that unless the principality was governed in future, under his sovereignty, by a descendant of the Villehardouins acceptable to all its inhabitants, he would certainly lose it. Consequently the King not only agreed to restore the honours due to his sister-in-law but also found her a second husband. This was a nobleman from Flanders called Florent d'Avesnes or de Hainault, a member of the same family as that Jacques d'Avesnes who had conquered Euboea for King Boniface and was wounded at the siege of Corinth.

Florent, an intelligent and enterprising young man, had rendered good service to the house of Anjou and Charles, with a notable display of imagination, decided to make him and Isabelle Prince and Princess of Achaia. On their wedding day he formally divested himself of the title, insisting only that they should continue to pay homage for the principality to the King of Naples and that if Isabelle's husband should predecease her, she would not remarry without the royal consent. Thus fortified, Florent and Isabelle sailed to Glarentza, accompanied by a hundred knights and three hundred archers, and were received with universal acclaim. The French *Chronicle* records that the King's message ordering the feudatories to accept them as rulers of Achaia was read out 'en vulgar' (i.e. in Greek) 'pour que cescun (chacun) l'entendit'.[8] Sustained by his wife's prestige, Florent did his best to suppress abuses and shore up the principality's defences. He carried out a thorough purge of unsatisfactory officials and castellans. But his most salutary act was to conclude a non-aggression pact, which was to last for seven years, with the Byzantine Emperor, Andronikos II. Unlike Michael VIII, Andronikos was an intellectual, not devoid of states-manlike qualities but lacking his father's determination. He had also inherited an empire exhausted militarily and financially by the effort demanded of it by the first Palaeologos. Absorbed in an unavailing struggle to stem the conquest of his Asiatic provinces by the Turks, as well as to keep up his end in northern Greece and the Balkans, the Emperor was only too glad to send a high emissary, Philanthropenos, to the Morea in order to negotiate the truce.[9]

The cessation of fighting brought immense relief to the Peloponnese as a whole. The French *Chronicle* says that it enjoyed 'ainxi bonne pais que son pays devint si cras et si plantureux de toutes choses que la gent ne savoient la moitie de ce qu'ils avoient'.[10] It also appears as if for an all too short period the artificial division of the peninsula between Franks and Greeks lost its importance. The lines of political and military demarcation became blurred and the indeterminate nature of the frontier is clear from the number of Greeks holding lands under both Byzantine and Frankish jurisdiction. Their situation did not involve a conflict of loyalties. It was simply an accommodation to circumstances, for few Greeks would have regarded their status as holders of fiefs from the Latins, or even of officials of a principality which they trusted was ephemeral, as inconsistent with their fundamental conception of themselves as 'Romans' and subjects of a theoretically supreme, if temporarily eclipsed, Emperor of the Romans.

Various striking incidents that occurred during the reign of Florent and Isabelle throw light on the complex but uneasy relationship which had developed between Latins and Greeks after nearly a century of

Latin domination, and on the extent to which the latter were regaining ground. One concerns landowners, a Frank and a Greek, living as neighbours and actually sharing a fief in the region of Corinth. We learn that the Greeks 'avoient et partoient [partageaient] avec les gentilz homes frans les fievés dou prince'; in fact the technical term applied to the frontier villages of the area was *casaux de parçon*.[11] The Frank was Gautier de Liedekerke, a Fleming who had been installed by his compatriot Prince Florent in the captaincy of Acrocorinth. The Greek, Photios, was also a man of substance and the cousin of a well-known Byzantine and Moreot soldier named Chases, the captain of the former Frankish barony of Kalavryta. Liedekerke, whose extravagance had landed him heavily in debt, had the rich Photios arrested on the pretext that the peasants of the *terres de parçon* were complaining of his exactions, and threatened to hang him failing the payment of a steep ransom of ten thousand Byzantine hyperpera. When Photios refused to pay two of his teeth were pulled out. Eventually, however, he recovered his freedom at the price of only a thousand *hyperpera* and appealed to the Prince for reparation through the good offices of the governor of Mistra. As this was not forthcoming he decided to take private revenge. Hearing that Liedekerke was sailing up the Corinthian Gulf, and guessing that he would land for a midday siesta on the beach near the modern resort of Xylocastro, he waited by the shore until, as he expected, a ship put in and a blond Frankish knight disembarked with a small escort. On the assumption that he was Liedekerke, Photios at once attacked him and cut him down. Too late he discovered that his victim was in fact his old friend Guy de Charpigny, the baron of Vostitza and former bailie. All he could do was to embrace the wounded man and beg his forgiveness, but de Charpigny died the next day and Photios fled to the Byzantine province. This tragedy caused much distress among the native Franks and Greeks, who realised that it would never have come about if Florent had not made the mistake of placing a newcomer in so delicate a post, and the claims and counter-claims from both sides were quietly dropped.

Kalamata was the scene of another curious and graver episode, which came to involve the Prince and the Emperor. One day the castle of the Villehardouins, which was poorly garrisoned, was assaulted and taken without warning by a band of Slavs from Giannitza on Mount Taygetos, led by two local archons with Greek names. They were followed by six hundred fellow tribesmen who occupied the town, proclaiming that they had acted on the Emperor's orders. Since the empire and the principality were formally at peace, Florent protested to the governor of Mistra. The latter denied that he was responsible for the attack; much as he deplored it, he confessed that he had scant authority over the Slavs, who obeyed only their own chiefs. The Prince was therefore obliged to send an embassy to Constantinople. He chose as his envoys the Constable Jean Chauderon, seigneur of Estamira in Elis and a veteran of many battles and diplomatic missions, and Geoffroy d'Aulnay, baron of Arkadia. Both were familiar with Constantinople and versed in the ways of the Byzantine court, but according to the admittedly prejudiced *Livre de la Conqueste* they found Andronikos unsympathetic and evasive. He had no wish to see Kalamata returned to the Franks, and only consented to receive the two noblemen when strongly pressed to do so by an ambassador from Charles II, who was at the time trying to negotiate a marriage between the Emperor's son and a Western princess. As the result of this intervention and that of his own brother, Theodore, Andronikos assured the envoys in public that the Kalamata would be duly given up, but he then secretly cancelled his instructions. Luckily his attempted deception was promptly revealed to Chauderon and d'Aulnay by a friend from the Peloponnese, who chanced to be the senior Byzantine officer entrusted with carrying the Emperor's real orders to Mistra. This man's name is given as Sgouromallis, 'the curly-haired', and the *Chronicle* styles him 'marshal' of Taygetos. Presumably he was one of the numerous Greek Moreots in the province of Mistra who felt sympathy for the Franks and preferred to live on good terms with them.[12]

Sgouromallis advised the envoys to seek a second audience with the Emperor and to obtain from him a written order for the surrender of Kalamata. Having given his word publicly, Andronikos was unable to avoid granting their request. He only stipulated that the castle should be delivered to d'Aulnay in person, rather than to the Prince. They then embarked for Monemvasia in the same ship as Sgouromallis, to whom they promised a reward of three thousand *hyperpera* if his assistance procured the right result. The voyage took a week. On arrival in the Morea Sgouromallis suppressed the first imperial order and in order to make quite sure of the issue, rode straight to Kalamata with three hundred cavalry. Brandishing the second order, he succeeded in overawing the Slavs and forcing them to quit the castle. He then handed it back ceremonially to d'Aulnay and Chauderon, receiving in return the promised money and the special gift of a fine charger from the Prince. Sadly enough he was disgraced for thwarting the Emperor's plan and ended his life in misery, but in the fifteenth century his family were still archons in the Peloponnese.

The peace with Byzantium was finally broken by a second incident provoked by the insolent behaviour of a Frankish knight recently settled in Achaia. Its occasion was the midsummer fair, one of the many frequented by traders from all over the Morea, which was held on the meadow at Vervena, a village on the border between Skorta and Arkadia. According to the *Livre de la Conqueste* a trivial dispute flared up between the knight, Girard de Remy, and a local silk-merchant named Korkondilos. The Frank lost his temper and felled the Greek with a blow from the butt of his lance. Deeply offended, Korkondilos considered how he might do the Franks most harm, and conceived a plan to put the Byzantines in possession of the castle of St George, one of the fortifications recently erected by Prince Florent to safeguard Skorta. His son-in-law happened to work as cellarer in the castle, while he had a friend, George Mavropapas, commanding a company of Turkish mercenaries on the Byzantine side of the frontier. With these connexions it was easy to introduce the Turks into the fortress. The Prince failed to retake it and had to content himself with building another castle, Beaufort or Oraiokastron, to block the wedge thus thrust into his territory.[13] Although the Byzantines did not immediately move to exploit this success, the truce was irreparably ruined and pressure from Mistra again posed a very real threat to the survival of the Latin principality. Florent, while working hard to build up its strength, drew little support from the Angevin connexion. Absorbed in his fruitless attempts to regain Sicily from the house of Aragon, Charles II was unable to devote much attention to the needs of Achaia, with which his feudal link had anyhow become, by his own decision, more tenuous.

Indeed the vulnerability of the Frankish state was emphasized by a rude blow from an unexpected quarter. In 1292, when Florent happened to be absent in Italy, the formidable Admiral of Aragon, Roger de Lauria, took advantage of a temporary lull in the struggle for Sicily to launch a grand piratical razzia into the Aegean, after the style of George of Antioch in the preceding century. Ominously, he made no distinction in his choice of islands to be raided between those belonging to the Emperor and those governed by local Italian dynasts such as the Sanudi and the Ghisi. Lemnos and Lesbos, Chios and Naxos were among those pillaged. On the way home Roger surprised and sacked the lower town of Monemvasia, under the eyes of the Byzantine garrison in the citadel, and then proceeded to carry off a batch of Mainotes for sale in the slave-markets. Prudently avoiding the outposts of the Venetian Republic, his galleys put in at Navarino in the principality.

Their arrival aroused the worst suspicions in George Ghisi, the captain of Kalamata, whose father's islands, Tenos and Mykonos, had not been spared by the raiders. Roger's intentions were not clear, for on his outward voyage he had called peaceably at Glarentza, but Ghisi resolved to take no chances. He assembled a small force of knights from Messenia and rashly attacked the Aragonese encampment. Although their first onset was successful and the Admiral himself was hurled from his horse by Jean de Durnay, son of the old warrior Geoffroy, they stood no chance against the Aragonese, the toughest professional fighters in Europe. The principal Franks were made prisoners and it only remained for Roger to assess their ransoms. Meanwhile he treated them all, and especially Durnay, with elaborate consideration, but his courtesy did not conceal the fact that he had Achaia at his mercy. While he protested that he had never meant to harm it, and that his men were only defending themselves against attack, he extorted 8000 *hyperpera* for Ghisi and 4000 for Durnay, both of which sums were advanced by the burgesses, Frankish and Greek, of Glarentza. He then sailed away, pausing only to plunder, for good measure, the rich port of Patras. This final act of impertinence was the more shocking as the city was a fief vested in the Latin Archbishop.[14]

It might have been wiser in the circumstances for Florent to avoid campaigning outside his own borders. But in 1291, even before the Aragonese raid, he had responded, against the advice of his senior barons, to an appeal from his wife's uncle Nikephoros, the Despot of Epiros, for help in the war which had again flared up between Epiros and Byzantium. In so doing, the Prince was in fact not breaking his truce with the Emperor, which specifically covered only hostilities in the Morea. The new conflict was typical of the complicated feuds which involved not merely the Palaeologues of Constantinople, the Dukas Despots of Epiros and their cousins in the separate state of Neopatras and Thessaly or 'Great Vlachia', but also the Angevins of Naples, who were always fishing for an opportunity of making themselves masters of northern Greece. Personal jealousies between the various dynasts were inextricably intermingled with policies of state. At the centre of the present web of intrigue was the Despot's wife, Anna Cantacuzena, niece of the Emperor Michael VIII and cousin of Andronikos II. Her purpose was to bring all the dominions of the Dukas family, in Thessaly as well as in Epiros, back into the Byzantine orbit.

As soon as Andronikos had concluded his pact with Florent, he decided that the moment had come to eliminate his father's old enemy, the bastard John of Neopatras, and sent an army to attack him in Thessaly. John's most skilled commander was his son Michael, who repulsed the Byzantines and was preparing a counter-stroke against Thessalonica when he received an invitation from Anna to visit the court of Arta. She hinted that the Epirot sovereigns might favour a marriage between him and their beautiful daughter Thamar. Michael was attracted by the idea and hastened to Arta, but when he arrived he was arrested and packed off in chains to Andronikos at Constantinople, from where he never returned. Having thus, as she thought, ingratiated herself with her cousin, Anna confidently proposed that Thamar should marry the Emperor's eldest son, shortly to be crowned co-Emperor as Michael IX. She also let it be understood that the latter could expect, on the death of Nikephoros, to succeed to the Despotate to the exclusion of her own Thomas, who was alleged to be feeble-minded.

To her amazement Andronikos would have nothing to do with this neat but unscrupulous attempt by his cousin to mend, in his favour, the old quarrel between Epiros and Byzantium. Overtly he objected on theological grounds to a marriage between second cousins, but his real reason for rebuffing Anna was that he was at the moment aiming for a Western alliance for his son with Catherine of Courtenay, granddaughter of Charles I of Anjou and claimant to the extinct Latin Empire. In the event the Emperor's project, like Anna's, came to nothing, but the immediate result of this series of treacheries and deceptions was a renewal of the Byzantine offensive in northern Greece, which this time was directed impartially against both Dukas states. Like many late Byzantine campaigns, it was well conceived, if feebly executed. A large imperial army swept through Thessaly and the passes of Pindus to Joannina, the second city of the Despotate, while a Genoese squadron in Byzantine pay penetrated into the Ambracian Gulf and threatened Arta itself.

At this juncture, however, Nikephoros was saved by his Frankish allies. Prince Florent, accompanied by the young Nicholas III de St Omer, Marshal of the Morea, came to his aid with five hundred picked men, while the Italian magnate from the Ionian islands, Count Richard Orsini of Cephalonia, brought a similar contingent. Together they advanced on Joannina, but as it turned out there was no need to fight a battle, for the Turkish and Cuman mercenaries composing the greater part of the Byzantine army refused to face the Franks and retreated in disorder. Returning to Arta, the Franks encountered a force which had disembarked from the Genoese fleet and chased it back to the ships. This episode forms the concluding passage in the Greek *Chronicle*. Florent and Nicholas are its heroes, and their triumph, with the ignominious discomfiture of the Genoese, is described in much detail and marked relish by the writer, who treats the affair as the glorious, if unbloody, climax to the splendid record of Achaian chivalry in the twilight of the Villehardouin tradition.[15]

The Despot financed the victory and, in order to hold him to his promise to pay for their aid, both Latin rulers had insisted that he should send one of his children as a hostage to each of their respective courts. Thus Thomas was taken to Andravida and another daughter, Maria, to Cephalonia. Count Richard, however, refused to return Maria to her parents, and married her to his son. Meanwhile a much more tortuous negotiation was in hand to decide the fate of the still unwedded Thamar. Using Florent as intermediary, Charles II proposed that she should marry his son Philip and that he and Thamar should inherit the Despotate instead of Thomas. Nikephoros, an unambitious prince chiefly interested in securing Epiros for himself during his lifetime, accepted this stipulation and after lengthy parleys it was also agreed that they should divide between them any territory that might in the meantime be wrested from the Byzantine Empire. Philip, for his part, promised to safeguard the practice of the Orthodox religion in his future domains. Four fortresses in Epiros, including Lepanto (Naupaktos) on the Gulf of Corinth, were handed over to him immediately and garrisoned by troops from the Morea.

While the haggling was still in progress Charles strengthened his hand by a more striking and cynical act of political chicanery. He had not forgotten that by the Treaty of Viterbo the dispossessed Latin Emperor had agreed that if his family ran out of heirs its rights and claims in Romania should pass in their entirety to the House of Anjou. In order to convert this pledge into a reality he now bullied Catherine of Courtenay, the present heiress and his own niece, into adhering personally to the Treaty and at the same time swearing not to marry without the permission of the Crown of Naples. This in effect meant that the Angevins had acquired for themselves the reversion of the Latin Empire, for what that was worth, together with suzerainty over not only Achaia, which they already exercised, but all the other mainland and island Frankish states and feudal dependencies of the former Empire, of which the most considerable was the Duchy of Athens. It pleased Charles to transfer these far-reaching rights to Philip, now created Prince of Tarentum, and the latter's wedding to Thamar was celebrated in September 1294.

While the Prince of Achaia was a willing co-operator in these Angevin designs, they were regarded more coolly at Athens. The Duchess Helen's marriage to Hugues de Brienne took place in the same year as the campaign in Epiros, from which the Duchy stood aloof. Neither objected to accepting Charles II as their feudal overlord, but they were greatly disturbed to learn that when the King had arranged for Florent to become Prince of Achaia he had also made provision, but without so informing the regent of Athens, for the ruler of the Duchy to pay homage for it to the Prince. They were vexed because a strong and wealthy Athens, which had suffered none of the Morea's recent misfortunes, was now being formally subordinated to the principality, and Hugues was personally nettled because he considered himself to be a much nobler personage than Florent, a comparative upstart and a stranger to Italy and the Levant. They therefore flatly refused to do homage to Florent, and the dispute was still unresolved when the young Guy II celebrated his coming-of-age in June 1294.

The ceremonies and festivities which graced this occasion were held at Thebes, and were lavishly planned to impress the guests with the splendour and prestige of the Duchy. As coseigneurs of Thebes and owners of the palace called Santameri, the St Omers were closely associated with the celebrations. The resplendent Nicholas II had died earlier in the year, but the family was represented by his brother Othon and his nephew Nicholas III, the Marshal of Achaia. In addition to the principal vassals from the fiefs guarding the northern borders of the Duchy, such as Thomas de Stromoncourt of Salona, the Lombard nobility of Euboea, which by this time had recovered most of its lands lost twenty years previously to Licario, attended in large numbers. Eminent Greeks from Thessaly and Epiros, and even from Byzantine territory, were also made welcome. The sensation of the day, however, according to the Catalan chronicler Ramon Muntaner, was the Duke's choice of Bonifazio da Verona to perform the service of dubbing him a knight. It was expected that this honour would have been conferred on a high dignitary, such as one of the St Omers or Guy's stepfather the Count of Lecce, but to the general surprise he called on a young nobleman who was neither well-known nor rich, but had lately attracted attention by cutting a figure at court. Nevertheless he was a member of the powerful Euboean clan of the dalle Carceri, and it was surely not a mere impulse of romantic admiration that moved Guy to attach to his person an accomplished knight of his own generation who, as well as acting as a counterweight to his existing advisers, would be useful in enchancing the influence of the Duchy in the outlying but strategically situated Euboea. That his gesture was premeditated is apparent from his simultaneous grant to Bonifazio of fiefs and castles bringing in a revenue of 50,000 *hyperpera*. The most important of those domains was Gardiki in Thessaly, guarding the northern approach to Euboea and the Euripus channel, which the Duchess had brought to Guy's father as her dowry. Another was Karystos, the port and castle at the southern end of the island, to which the Duke added the hand of its heiress Agnes de Cicon. This lady, a relative of the de la Roches, also held the island of Aegina. At that time Karystos was still in Byzantine hands, but Bonifazio soon retook it with Venetian help. It was, however, in Guy's interest that the growing power of the Venetian bailie should be balanced by the strong positions held by his own protégé.[16]

The attainment of his majority gave Guy a free hand to govern his Duchy. His mother retired to spend the rest of her life at the monastery of the Holy Luke of Stiris, while his stepfather returned to Italy and fell in battle against the Aragonese. It was only after his death that Guy at last consented, under heavy pressure from Charles II, to do homage for the Duchy to the Prince of Achaia, thus averting the very real danger of a second clash between the two chief Frankish states. But no sooner was the quarrel composed than Florent himself died, leaving the Princess Isabelle for the second time a widow and a three-year old daughter Mahaut.

As sole ruler of Achaia Isabelle wisely appointed Count Richard of Cephalonia, Florent's former comrade in arms, to act as her bailie and administer the principality. The County Palatine of Cephalonia, comprising the islands of Cephalonia, Ithaca and Zakynthos (Zante) became a fief of Achaia in the time of Geoffroy II de Villehardouin and its present lord was a perfect example of the great Latin feudatory rooted in the Greek environment. An Italian by origin, his more recent family connections were Greek and French, for his mother was a Dukas and his first wife a Stromoncourt of Salona. Three of his daughters were married to Moreot magnates, the first to Jean Chauderon and then to Nicholas III de St Omer, the second to Jean de Durnay and the third to Engilbert de Liedekerke, Florent's nephew and Constable of Achaia. No better credentials for a bailie could have been imagined. Deeply experienced in statecraft, he enjoyed the full confidence of the Princess, whose younger sister Marguerite, the lady of Akova, he subsequently married. While he directed the government from Andravida, she held her personal court in the castle of Nesi or de l'Ille at the head of the Gulf of Coron. There she was attended by her Chancellor, Benjamin of Kalamata, the Constable Liedekerke and her Chamberlain, a Greek named Vasilopoulos.

An arrangement of this kind was plainly for the best. Nevertheless

Isabelle apparently felt that more had to be done to safeguard the future of the principality. She and her advisers became convinced that the right course would be to bring about a virtual union between Achaia and Athens. The solution, as propounded by Count Richard to a parliament of peers spiritual and temporal, was that the child Mahaut should be affianced to the Duke of Athens. Sponsored by Nicholas de St Omer, who had so important a stake in both the duchy and the principality, the idea was eagerly embraced by the Duke.[17] In 1299 he came personally to Vlisiri (La Glisière) in Elis, where his betrothal to Mahaut was blessed by the local Bishop of Olena. The little girl was then removed from her mother and lodged at Thebes until the Church should decide when the marriage could decently be celebrated. From the political point of view a closer union, if not a merger, of the two Latin states was eminently sensible. Only King Charles chose to object, on the ground that his prior agreement had not been invited, but he soon gave way under pressure from the Pope, Boniface VIII, who recognized the obvious advantages of the proposal. One of these was the ending of the controversy over the homage due from the Duke to the Prince.

With her sister married to Count Richard, Isabelle's thoughts then turned towards acquiring a third husband for herself. In 1300, which happened to be Jubilee year, she undertook a pilgrimage to Rome, leaving Nicholas de St Omer as bailie in place of her ageing brother-in-law. Whether by accident or design, she was soon observed to favour the attentions of Philip of Savoy, Count of Piedmont, who, although twenty years younger than herself, was encouraged by the Pope to become her suitor. In defiance of opposition from King Charles, who regarded her choice as jeopardizing the rights accorded to his son Philip of Tarentum, she proceeded to marry the Count with the Pope's blessing and with ostentatious pomp and ceremony. Her timing of the operation was well planned, for the King was in no position to press his objections. He could not afford to alienate the Pope, especially as his war with the House of Aragon was going badly and Philip of Tarentum, like himself some years previously, was a prisoner of his adversaries. He was therefore compelled, with a bad grace, to sanction the *fait accompli*.

It soon transpired, however, that Isabelle had made a bad mistake so far as the interests of her principality were concerned. Her husband was an arrogant and insensitive young man, unversed in the customs and traditions of the Latin Levant and bent on exploiting his good fortune at the expense of the Moreot barons and his Greek subjects. He brought with him a train of greedy Piedmontese adventurers who were soon at odds with the Moreot establishment. In the knowledge that he was unfavourably regarded by the King, and that his luck might not therefore last very long, he made it his business to wring a quick personal profit out of the country. The French *Chronicle* puts his purpose quite bluntly:

> Comme cil qui avoit veu et savoit comment li thyrant de Lombardie et cil qui tenoient office ou seignorie en Lombardie ... savoient gaagnier monnoye et autres richesses, si appela Monseignor Guillerme de Monbel, son maistre chambellan, et autres qui estoient de son prive conseil et leur demanda comment et en quel maniere il porroit pourchacier et avoir monnoye.

Such an attitude towards his wife's heritage was bound to fill the four-and-a-half years which he spend in Achaia with successive quarrels and disagreeable incidents.[18]

Unfortunately for the new Prince's reputation, the archives of his own country, Piedmont, have yielded a long list of payments made to his private treasurer by Moreot individuals, Greeks and Franks, and by whole communities. They reveal a nasty record of extortion and bribery. Contributors to his coffers included Vasilopoulos, the Princess's chamberlain, and other officials, local bailies and castellans, Frankish fief-holders and the citizens of such towns as Karytaina, Glarentza and Andravida. Some of the 'gifts' amounted to thousands of *hyperpera* and as if these sums were insufficient for his needs, he raised a loan from the Peruzzi, Florentine bankers with a branch at Glarentza.[19]

It was not long before his behaviour provoked a first clash between himself and Nicholas de St Omer, the formidable ex-bailie, Marshal of Achaia, co-seigneur of Thebes and hot champion of Moreot rights. It occurred when Philip arrested his wife's own Chancellor, Benjamin of Kalamata, on a charge of peculation. Benjamin was known to be very rich and somewhat of an intriguer; consequently he was vulnerable to blackmail. But he was also a protégé of St Omer, to whom he applied for redress. The Marshal reacted furiously, accusing the Prince in public of having flouted the usages of Achaia. When Philip enquired sneeringly what those usages might be, St Omer clapped his hand to his sword. The barons, he replied, had derived their rights and customs from a compact made at the time of the conquest, and would defend them in the spirit of the conquerors against anyone who disregarded them. On the intercession of the Princess the dispute was shelved by compromise. The Chancellor was compelled to pay a fine of 20,000 *hyperpera*, but allowed to recoup it through the gift of an estate at Perachora, the peninsula facing Corinth on the mainland shore of the Gulf, which was worth an annual income of 6000 hyperpera.

The affair, however, led to a chain of unedifying transactions. The Prince suspected, perhaps wrongly, that it was Richard of Cephalonia who had prompted the charge against Benjamin. The Count was known to be on bad terms with the Chancellor, whom he in turn suspected of having advised the Princess to replace him as bailie by St Omer. Whatever truth underlay these personal enmities, Philip used the occasion to extract from Richard a loan of another 20,000 *hyperpera* against a vague promise of certain fiefs by way of compensation. Not long afterwards the Count was removed from the scene. In a fit of senile temper he struck one of his knights with a stick and was killed by the counter-blow. This gave Philip the opportunity of demanding a substantial bribe from his successor, Count John, in return for investing him with the fiefs which derived from the principality. At the same time he took John's side in a lawsuit brought in the high court by Richard's widow, Marguerite de Villehardouin, for the restitution of her late husband's movable property, valued at no less than 100,000 *hyperpera*. His partiality caused a fresh confrontation with St Omer who enthusiastically took the side of the lady of Akova. It seems that his dislike for Philip outweighed his ties with John, who was his brother-in-law. As before, a compromise was reached, but since it gave Marguerite only a fifth of the sum which she claimed, such feudatories as were still attached to the Villehardouin connection much resented Philip's mean treatment of Prince Guillaume's daughter.[20]

Besides losing credit in the eyes of the Franks, Philip's government was shaken by a dangerous uprising of the Greek archons of Skorta. One of his more disreputable advisers was Vincent de Marais, a knight from Picardy, who had already instigated his imprisonment of the Chancellor. This man now induced him to levy even heavier subventions on the Greek feudatories of the region. The archons, normally a loyal element despite the proximity of their lands to the Byzantine frontier, met at Lissistaina (not far from the ancient temple of Bassae) and decided to resort to arms under the leadership of the brothers George and John Mikronas. Joined by the 'captain of the Greeks' with troops from Mistra, they stormed and destroyed two castles, Ste Hélène and Crèvecoeur, near Karytaina. But a third, Beaufort, stood firm and gave the Franks time to muster a relieving force. As in the past the Greeks declined a pitched battle and retired into Arkadia, leaving the Prince free to confiscate the rebels' estates.[21]

The Marshal St Omer played no part in suppressing this insurrection.

Without the Prince's permission he was campaigning in the north at the side of the Duke of Athens. For several years after the intervention of Prince Florent in Epiros and his repulse of the Byzantines, the situation in the Despotate and in neighbouring Neopatras had remained quiet. When, in 1296, their respective rulers, the Despot Nikephoros and the bastard John, both died, Anna Cantacuzena, the former's widow, assumed the regency of Epiros in the name of her son Thomas, while John's son Constantine succeeded to Neopatras and Thessaly. But when Constantine too died seven years later, he left his infant son a ward of the Duke of Athens, thus turning Thessaly, with its Greek nobles and largely Vlach population, into a dependency of the duchy. Guy appointed one of his own barons, Antoine de Flamenc of Karditza in Boeotia, as his bailie and another Frank as Marshal, but confirmed the Greek archons in the possession of their castles and estates. He now controlled a territory stretching from Mount Olympus to the Gulf of Corinth.

An Athenian protectorate over Thessaly was naturally unwelcome to Anna Cantacuzena, whose dominions were now hemmed in by the Angevins to the west and the duchy, itself acknowledging Angevin sovereignty, to the east. She reacted by seizing a castle in the north-west of the country which covered the approaches to Joannina and Arta. Guy's answer was to assemble an army which was very large by the standards of Frankish Greece and more than adequate to deal with the incursion from Epiros. If we may believe the sources, it contained nine hundred Frankish heavy cavalry and six thousand Thessalian light horse. When Nicholas de St Omer joined it he was immediately given the command. It is not surprising that Anna backed down as soon as it began its advance, evacuated the fortress and agreed to pay an indemnity. Her timely retreat left Guy's vast array with nothing to do and no prospect of booty. He and St Omer therefore decided to employ it in an entirely unprovoked act of aggression against the Byzantine Empire. They marched on Thessalonica and were only deterred from an assault on the city by a personal appeal to their sense of honour from the Emperor Andronikos's wife, Irene of Montferrat, who was living apart from her husband in the Macedonian capital. Had it not been for her Latin origins the outcome of the expedition might have been very different. As it was, the army turned back and was tamely disbanded.[22]

Philip of Savoy's hold on Achaia was becoming increasingly precarious. In 1302 Philip of Tarentum emerged from captivity and it was not long before King Charles resolved to raise his son to a position of dominance in Greece. Baffled in his efforts to recover Sicily, the King turned his mind to a partial revival of his father's ambitions in the Levant. It appeared to him that a necessary step towards the realization of such projects must be the substitution for his son's formal suzerainty over Achaia by his effective rule and personal assumption of the princely title. In order to get rid of Philip of Savoy, he decided to revert to his former contention, which he had only withdrawn with great reluctance, that Isabelle had forfeited her rights to the principality by marrying without his consent. Before showing his hand, however, he invoked the Prince's help in the preliminary stage of his new forward policy in Greece, the absorption of the Despotate of Epiros. In 1303 he presented an ultimatum to the regent Anna demanding the fulfilment of the engagements contracted on her daughter's marriage to Philip of Tarentum. He insisted either that the government of Epiros should immediately be handed over to Philip or that Thomas should at least agree to exercise it strictly as an Angevin vassal and under Angevin control. Anna rejected both alternatives. She retorted that the Angevins had not carried out their part of the bargain, they had treated Thamar shamefully and forced her to renounce the Orthodox faith. In fact she had no intention of relinquishing power and was again seeking a Byzantine alliance for Thomas.

Faced with Anna's intransigence, the King ordered his generals, supported by Philip of Savoy and John of Cephalonia, to capture Arta, but they were sharply repulsed from its strong fortifications and forced to retire to their ships. He warned the Prince that he expected to renew the attack in the following year, but this time Philip made up his mind not to participate. Probably he had already got wind of the royal intentions regarding the Morea, and he also accepted a bribe from Anna, which he shared with the Marshal, to keep out of the fighting. As a pretext for eluding the King's command he summoned all the vassals of the principality to attend a grand Parliament which, he announced, would be held at Corinth in the Spring. It is conceivable that he felt that if the Angevins were determined to expel him he would at least depart with *éclat*.[23]

Indeed the last act of his reign was a model of extravagant showmanship, the most flamboyant event in the whole history of mediaeval Greece. The minor potentates of Hellas and the isles flocked eagerly to the isthmus. The Dukes of Athens and Naxos, the Count of Cephalonia, the Marquis of Boudonitza, the Euboean triarchs together with more than a thousand barons and knights, were attracted by the prospect of sumptuous entertainment and, more especially, of the tournament which the Prince had arranged to follow the proceedings of the Parliament. The highlight of the festival was a challenge issued by seven knights from the West, who seem to have been professional jousters, to the champions of Greece. Guy of Athens distinguished himself by surviving a fearful impact in the lists without being unhorsed by the leader of this troupe, Guillaume Bouchart. The French *Chronicle*, which abounds in picturesque detail of this kind, unfortunately breaks off in the midst of an account so lively as to suggest that the writer was an eye-witness of the tournament.[24]

This display of feudal exuberance undoubtedly made a great impression on contemporaries, although it did not change the disposition of Achaia's Angevin overlords in the Prince's favour. It is hard to judge to what extent it reflected the real level of prosperity in Frankish Greece at the time. There is no doubt about the flourishing state of the Duchy of Athens, and it is also tempting to infer, if only from the size of the sums said to have been exchanged in the form of bribes, ransoms and property transactions in the reign of Philip and Isabelle, that the principality had largely recovered from the effects of the recurrent hostilities with the Greeks which were terminated by the truce of 1289 and had not since been renewed on so damaging a scale. Such evidence as exists indicates that despite the division of the Morea into two semi-hostile states and the uncertainties of government under Angevin tutelage, the revenues from agriculture and trade were ample enough to make the holding of an Achaian fief a most attractive proposition. Nor was there any lack of candidates from the West to fill the gaps among the fief-holders. We have seen that the Greek archon class was drawing large profits from its lands. But it is unlikely that the Morea as a whole had regained the standard of well-being reached in the heyday of the Villehardouins.

A few months after the tournament the Prince's position was made finally untenable. Although he declared his willingness to do homage to Philip of Tarentum, the King republished his ruling that Isabelle's marriage had annulled her rights in Achaia and Philip of Savoy, considering that resistance would be futile, quitted the Morea for his possessions in the north of Italy. As might have been expected, Nicholas de St Omer resumed his office of bailie, pending the arrival of the Angevin prince, and the barons of Achaia were released from their oath to their former rulers. For Philip, his tenure of the principality had been a mere exciting interlude in the career of a young son of Savoy, but for Isabelle, who accompanied him on his departure, it was the end of an epoch. She never returned to Greece. Nor did she avail herself of the illusory compensation offered by King Charles in the form of an estate and revenues in Italy. While her husband busied himself with protecting his interests in Piedmont, she retired alone to her second husband Florent's lands in the Low Countries, which had been inherited at the age of twelve by her daughter Mahaut, Duchess of Athens in 1305. She took with her Marguerite, her little daughter by Philip, who was destined to marry a French knight and die childless. She herself survived till 1311, exiled for the second time from her homeland in Elis and Messenia. It was a sadly undeserved end for this long suffering and courageous descendant of the knights of Champagne and the high aristocracy of Byzantium.

CHAPTER SIX

The Catalans

THE REMOVAL OF Philip of Savoy left Guy II without a rival among the various rulers acknowledging Angevin suzerainty over Frankish Greece. Although such overlordship had never proved burdensome to Athens, Guy seems to have had misgivings about the prospect of Philip of Tarentum becoming an effective sovereign in Achaia. According to the Aragonese *Chronicle*[1] he put forward his own claim to the principality, based on his wife Mahaut's descent from the Villehardouins, even before the new Prince arrived in the Morea. When it was rejected by the bailie, Nicholas de St Omer, on the ground that Mahaut's rights had been extinguished along with her mother's, Guy reacted by depriving the Marshal of his hereditary half share of Thebes. Nevertheless, no breach occurred between the Prince and the Duke. The latter correctly rendered homage for Athens and his Peloponnesian fiefs, and was in turn appointed bailie of Achaia in St Omer's place. Indeed Philip showed no disposition to linger in the Morea. When he landed there in 1306 it was at the head of an imposing army of four thousand horse and six thousand foot, but after a short campaign against the Greek province in which several castles were regained he transferred his forces to Epiros. There he made no progress at all, and by the end of the year he was back in Italy without having realized any of his father's hopes.

But Guy did not survive to enjoy his favoured position. He had already contracted the fatal disease, possibly cancer, which was to carry him off prematurely in 1308. Cruelly enough, the moment when he began to fail coincided with his duchy's attainment of its highest prestige and prosperity. In the century of its existence it had never experienced a major set-back, unless the battle of Karydi can be counted as such, and had profited from long periods of peace. Outside Attica and Boeotia, it was well established in northern Morea, dominated Thessaly and spread its protective influence over Euboea. But while its successful record is hardly open to doubt, it is not easy to account for this in detail. The most exasperating feature of the Burgundian duchy in the thirteenth century is that it is so poorly documented. No Chronicle of Athens exists in any language. We are dependent on scraps of information vouchsafed by writers who were not mainly concerned with Athenian affairs. Consequently any description of life in the duchy is bound, as Sir Rennell Rodd remarked, to lack 'local charm, personal touch and a sense of realistic environment'.[2]

We are familiar with the names and personalities of a great number of Moreot Franks, but who were those Burgundians who served the de la Roche dukes? Apart from a handful of the highest feudatories, we have no idea who those vassals were; we do not know what fiefs and castles they occupied. We are not sure in what significant respects the feudal organization of the duchy differed from that of Achaia. It does seem, however, that the Duke counted for more, and the hierarchy of barons and knights for less, than in the principality, if only because his vassals were proportionately less numerous than the Prince's. He had reserved for himself a much greater share of the available lands, most of which had in Byzantine times belonged to the Emperor's private domain. In other words the constitution of the duchy was markedly more monarchic in character and the authority of its ruler less circumscribed by custom and usages. Yet, as we have seen, Guy was able to muster a powerful force of Frankish cavalry whenever he went to war.

Whereas in Achaia Greek archons and officials enjoyed a well-defined status and fulfilled important functions, there is no record of a Greek holding a comparable position in the duchy. The native Athenians certainly supplied notaries and clerks, but none of them qualified as fully free citizens except by ducal warrant. Their inferior condition is unlikely to have hampered their commercial activities, however. The French of the Levant (as distinct from the Italians) did not normally engage in trade, and it must be assumed that at Athens and Thebes this was largely in the hands of Greeks and Jews. The available evidence suggests that the economy was flourishing at the end of the century. During Guy's reign the ducal mint made three issues of silver and copper coins, and the lord of Salona worked a mint of his own. The silk industry was still busy at Thebes and Boeotia also supplied corn to Venice and its overseas possessions.

Although Guy's territory was so well furnished with harbours, he maintained no navy and left maritime trade to the Venetians. The protection of his long and indented coastline against piracy therefore depended on vigilance by coastal forts and watch-towers, which we can believe to have been well garrisoned. At no time in the Middle Ages was any part of the Greek world immune from piratical descents, but it looks as if this ineradicable plague was less rife during the last years of de la Roche rule than when the Franks were at odds with Michael VIII and the exploits of individual corsairs were eclipsed in destructiveness by the raids which Licario carried out in the Emperor's name against Frankish territories. The presence of Venetian squadrons acted as a deterrent and Turkish pirates were not yet operating from former Byzantine bases in Asia Minor. But the development of piracy as an industry or instrument of policy will be more conveniently treated in a later chapter devoted to the Aegean islands.

Guy II was attended in his last illness by Athanasius, a former Orthodox Patriarch of Alexandria, who had been expelled from Constantinople and happened to be residing at Thebes. But the prelate, although an eminent physician, failed to save him. He was buried in the monastery of Daphni. His death was much lamented, for he was esteemed for his many good qualities and his subjects were looking forward to a long and successful reign. Brave, impulsive and touchy about matters of honour, he had at the same time inherited the solid common sense of the de la Roches and a streak of the political genius of his mother's people. The Greek *Chronicle*, in a valedictory digression, praises him as an excellent knight and ruler who had won 'great glory and honour'. God, however, had not granted him an heir because 'sin had led him into wickedness', or in another manuscript, 'into whoredom'. Be that as it may, his wife was only fifteen years old when he died and can hardly have been expected to produce an heir.[3] No problem arose over the succession. The only surviving male member of the de la Roche family, Renaud, baron of Damala, was passed over for the late Duke's first cousin Gautier de Brienne, Count of Lecce, son of his stepfather Hugues de Brienne and his aunt Isabelle de la Roche. As for his girl-widow Mahaut, she was promptly betrothed to Charles, the eldest son of Philip of Tarentum by the Epirote Thamar.

Gautier was also known to be a gallant soldier. He had fought heroically for the Angevins in the Sicilian war and like so many of his peers had been captured by the Aragonese. He had presumably lived in the duchy as a boy but his subsequent training and experience had removed him altogether from the Greek atmosphere. He belonged essentially to the expatriate but fiercely French aristocracy of the Kingdom of Naples and was married to a Frenchwoman, Jeanne de Chatillon, a descendant of the Villehardouins of Champagne. In normal times all might have gone well in spite of his ignorance of local affairs and lack of political skill. Unfortunately, however, he was at once faced with a highly critical situation which had loomed up in the last two years of Guy's reign. The Catalan Grand Company was encamped on the borders of Thessaly.

By the beginning of the fourteenth century an equilibrium had more or less been reached between the Latin and Greek states of Hellas and between the Latins themselves who, with the exception of the Venetians, were at least formally united under the Angevin umbrella. Broadly speaking the mainland was divided between two Latin states, the Principality of Achaia and the Duchy of Athens, three Greek political entities, Epiros, Thessaly and Neopatras, and the Byzantine province in the Morea. The situation in the islands was a little more complicated. The Ionian group was split between the County of Cephalonia and Angevin Corfu, while the most important Aegean state was the Duchy of the Archipelago, ruled by dukes of the Sanudo family and centred on Naxos. Many Aegean islands were still, however, controlled by Byzantium. Venice, the owner of Crete, had consolidated its commercial empire and was extending its influence over Euboea. The two principal elements among the Latins, Frenchmen and Italians, co-existed with little friction, and intermarriage was common; the former, however, was encroaching on what had previously been French preserves. Finally, as has already become clear, some ruling families had acquired a strong tinge of Greek blood.

Such a division of power, together with the social, religious and cultural distinction which still sharply separated the Latin and Greek communities, had become the normal order of things for at least two generations. Now a new and disturbing national element was to be suddenly and violently injected into a Greek world which had hitherto known only French and Italian conquerors, with a small sprinkling of Flemings and Germans. These newcomers, the Spaniards, had, like the English, so far shown no interest in competing for the lands torn from Byzantium by the Fourth Crusade. The pressures which now drove a highly organized and professional army of Catalans and Aragonese to seek a career in the Byzantine Empire stemmed from two causes: the temporary cessation of the struggle for Sicily between the Houses of Anjou and Aragon, and the Emperor Andronikos's desperate need to find a new source of mercenary troops. Both of these developments require a brief explanation.

The Sicilian war began in 1282, when the islanders threw off Angevin rule and appealed to Peter III of Aragon to come to their aid. His wife, Constance, was the last legitimate representative of the imperial Hohenstaufens, whom Charles I of Anjou had ousted from Naples and Sicily and destroyed. The conflict lasted intermittently for twenty years, but all attempts by the Angevins to recover Sicily ended in failure. After Peter's death his second son James became King of Sicily. When he in turn was called to the throne of Aragon, he left his younger brother Frederick as his lieutenant in Sicily. He then proceeded, however, to negotiate a peace settlement with Charles II of Anjou and the Pope which in effect betrayed the interests of the native Sicilians. By a treaty signed in 1295 he undertook to marry Charles's daughter and to hand over Sicily to the Holy See. Predictably enough, the Sicilians refused to be sacrificed to a reconciliation between the Kings. Correctly foreseeing that the Angevins would again be imposed on them, they rejected the settlement and offered the crown to Frederick. After some hesitation he accepted and the war was prolonged for another seven years. Although he faced a coalition of Aragon, Naples and the Papacy he had on the whole the best of the fighting, and when peace was finally signed in 1302 he was confirmed as the sovereign of an independent Sicily.

No body of troops had contributed more to Frederick's triumph than the corps of Catalans and Aragonese commanded by a certain Roger de Flor, Vice-Admiral of Sicily. With the war at an end, however, their situation became precarious. Having sided with Frederick against the King of Aragon, they were understandably anxious about the welcome which they might receive if they returned to their own country. Nor could they expect to remain in Sicily, where Frederick could no longer afford to pay them and where, if they tried to live by plundering the inhabitants, they might well become the victims of a second Sicilian Vespers. They found it impossible, wrote one of their own historians, to behave '*con moderacion*'. What they needed was adventure and high pay, preferably supplemented by booty. It occurred to Roger that their best prospects of pursuing the life to which they were accustomed lay in offering their services to Andronikos, who was known to be in difficulties with the Turks. With the agreement of his captains he sent two emissaries by fast galley to convey the proposal to Constantinople.

They could not have arrived at a more opportune moment. Throughout 1302 the Byzantine armies had suffered a succession of disastrous reverses. With Osman, the ancestor of the future Ottoman Sultans, in the van, the Turks swept over the ancient Asiatic provinces of the Empire, leaving the fortified cities isolated like islands in the flood and driving hosts of refugees to the shores of the Bosporus and the sea of Marmora, hoping to be ferried to Europe and safety.[4] The Byzantine troops, even when stiffened by refugee Cretans and by a corps of ten thousand Alans (warlike tribesmen from the Caucasus whom Andronikos had confidently hired) could do nothing to hold back the invaders. He was therefore unable to resist the very stiff demands of the Catalans regarding pay and the honours to be accorded to their chiefs.

He hurriedly accepted Roger's terms, at the same time promising him the title of Megadux and the hand of one of his nieces. In his eagerness to see the last of these potential trouble-makers, Frederick gave them every help in preparing their expedition. They sailed from Messina in thirty-six ships and after putting in at Monemvasia for supplies and an advance of pay, were enthusiastically welcomed on the Bosporus.

The composition of this small but compact and extremely efficient force differed greatly from that of the Latin armies which had previously operated in the Byzantine sphere. Among the fifteen hundred mounted men-at-arms there were very few noblemen and knights and the company's prowess on the battlefield resided essentially in its well-trained infantry, the *almugavares*. Lightly accoutred but highly skilled in flexible tactics and the use of their weapons, they were especially adept at dealing with heavily armoured knights, but were to prove equally capable of putting to flight Turkish infantry and horse-bowmen. The original *almugavares*, the frontiers-men of Catalonia, Aragon and Castile, were schooled in countless campaigns against the Moslems of the Iberian Peninsula. In many respects they resembled the Byzantine borderers or *akritai*, who fulfilled the same role in Asia. They were also the precursors of the tough Spanish infantry who followed Gonzalo de Cordova in the Italian wars, of the *tercios* of the sixteenth century and of the small band which overthrew the empire of Montezuma.[5]

Their leader, Roger de Flor, was as brilliant a commander on sea as on land. His father Richard Blum, a German falconer in the service of the Hohenstaufens, was killed at the battle of Tagliacozzo. He himself ran away to sea as a boy; by the age of twenty he had become a Knight Templar and was commanding one of the Knights' galleys. When the Sultan of Egypt stormed Acre, the last stronghold of the Crusaders in Palestine, he saved the persons and property of many eminent Christians and made a fortune by his pains, but in so doing suffered expulsion from his Order and incurred the lasting displeasure of the Church. Nevertheless his Hohenstaufen connexions commended him to King Frederick of Sicily and his military abilities kept him in favour until the conclusion of peace.[6]

Far from relieving the empire of the Palaeologues from Turkish pressure the Catalan expedition shook it to its foundations, reducing it for the remainder of its existence to the status of a minor and ailing principality. Its impact on the Byzantine state was in some ways more shattering than that of the Fourth Crusade. For the next seven years the Catalans defied the Emperor's authority, smashed his armies, wasted his best provinces and dissolved his administration in chaos. They inflicted no permanent harm on the Turks and indeed facilitated their future conquests. Before finally entering Greece, they ranged destructively from the Taurus to Thessalonica. It is extraordinary that so few men managed to cause so much damage and confusion. The story of their ravages was fully recorded by several Byzantine writers[7] and in even greater detail by one of their own captains, Ramon Muntaner, a knight from Valencia. He wrote a chronicle of the Kings of Aragon into which he fitted his account of the expedition, also providing valuable information about events in Greece immediately preceding and following the Catalan irruption. His narrative, too, served as the main source of a classical work of the Spanish golden age of the seventeenth century, the *Expedición de los Catalanes y Aragoneses contra Turcos y Griegos* by the statesman and general Francisco de Moncada.

The Catalans started inauspiciously by provoking a bloody street fight with the Genoese colony at Constantinople. In the winter of 1303 they landed at Kyzikos, on the south side of the Sea of Marmora, and expelled the Turks from the district. In the spring they moved southwards, relieved Philadelphia, the most important city still in Byzantine hands, and utterly defeated its Turkish blockaders. The Emperor was delighted with their success, but from then on he lost control of the company. Instead of rescuing other towns in the rich valleys of the Hermus and Maeander rivers, in accordance with Andronikos's orders, Roger spent the whole summer and autumn in a vast plundering raid along the western and southern shores of Asia Minor. His troops marched along the coast road with the fleet keeping station and picking up the loot. Although Muntaner represents this foray as a glorious military epic, thwarted only by the ingratitude and treachery of the Greeks, the Catalans in fact encountered no serious opposition from the Turks. Their own object was pillage, not reconquest, and the chief sufferers from their brigandage were the local countryfolk, consisting mainly of Greek Christians. Roger accumulated his booty at Magnesia by the Hermus, and when the governor closed the gates of the city against him with the booty inside, he attacked it without success. Andronikos had the greatest difficulty in persuading him to lead his army back to the Marmora.

The crowded events of the next four years are not easy to disentangle. The company's relations with the Byzantine government soon deteriorated to the point of open warfare. Roger refused to undertake another Turkish campaign unless compensated for the loss of his loot. Meanwhile reinforcements for the Catalans arrived from Spain under two captains, Berenguer de Entenza and Berenguer de Rocafort. The final break occurred when the Catalan leader, having at last grudgingly consented to resume the offensive in Asia and accepted the grander title of Caesar, was incautious enough to pay a visit of courtesy to Michael IX, Andronikos's son and co-Emperor, who was commanding the Byzantine forces at Adrianople. Michael had never shared his father's confidence in the Catalans, and it was probably at his instigation that Roger was stabbed to death at a banquet by a chief of Alan mercenaries. His murder sparked off a savage series of reprisals and counter-reprisals. While the Catalans massacred or enslaved the inhabitants of Gallipoli, all members of the Company found at Constantinople, including the commander of the fleet, Fernando de Aunes, were put to death. Entenza raided the coasts of the Marmora but was captured by the Genoese with all his ships. In return the Company, now led by Rocafort, almost annihilated Michael's army in two successive battles. Finally they sought out the encampment of the Alans and wiped them out, together with their women and children.

It was now the turn of Thrace, the home province of the Empire, to suffer devastation. It was systematically ravaged, in an ever widening circle from the Aegean to the Black Sea and up to the walls of the capital. Only the fortified towns offered any resistance. Worse still, the Catalans brought over a large body of Turks to fill their ranks and share in the spoils. Even Muntaner confesses that the knights and captains could do nothing to prevent the appalling atrocities committed by the soldiery who had lost all fear of God and respect for their officers, and Moncada recalls that the expression 'Catalan revenge' (*ekdikesis ton Katalanon*) had since become proverbial in Greek lands as the most terrible fate that might befall a man.[8] The process of desolation occupied nearly three years. The Catalans affected to regard themselves as an Iberian community in arms, enjoying its own traditional institutions, freely electing its leaders and defending itself valiantly against deceitful enemies. In reality they were a huge nest of marauders, an ulcerous growth on the body of the decrepit Byzantine Empire. Many of the Catalans had their families with them and were eager to settle down and found a new Latin state. But that was impossible in a country which had been so thoroughly desolated. Dissensions arose among the leaders regarding their future plans. Entenza, who had rejoined the Company after ransom from the Genoese, challenged Rocafort's authority and was supported by a third captain, Ximenes de Arenos. At that juncture, in 1308, the Infante Ferdinand of Majorca, a cousin of Frederick of Sicily, arrived in Thrace with a commission from the King to assume the leadership of the Company in his name. If there was to be any question of carving a Catalan principality out of the wreck of Byzantium, Frederick wished to be its sovereign. But, although supported by Entenza, Ximenes and Muntaner, the Infante failed to induce Rocafort to relinquish the command. He regarded himself as the legitimate successor of Roger de Flor and as representing the interest of the common soldiers, the *almugavares*, against that of the knightly captains. Nevertheless he accepted the Infante's advice to move the Company from Thrace into the still unpillaged Macedonia. It was as its undisputed commander that he led it slowly towards Thessalonica. Before the march began the leadership broke up in confusion: Entenza was killed in a skirmish with Rocafort's partisans and Ximenes fled to Constantinople, where he took service with the Emperor. As for Muntaner, he decided to stay with the Infante, in whose company he was to undergo an unexpected turn of fortune.

The Infante was not above indulging in a little piracy, in the true Catalan manner, on the homeward voyage. The first port of call for his ship was Halmyros in Thessaly, a fief of the Duke of Athens. When four of his seamen failed to rejoin their ship he set fire to the town. Then, after plundering the Byzantine island of Skopelos, he put in to Negroponte, where he was hospitably entertained by Bonifazio da Verona and other Lombard lords. His arrival, however, was watched by a Venetian squadron escorting a certain Thibaut de Cepoy, who was on his way to make the acquaintance of the Catalans. He was acting as the emissary of Charles of Valois, a son of Philip III of France and the husband of Catherine of Courtenay, the titular Latin Empress. Nothing is more remarkable in the history of the Latins in Greece than the obstinacy with which possible aspirants pursued the unsubstantial claim of the Courtenays to the throne of Constantinople. By 1308, when the interest of the Angevins of Naples in eastwards expansion had somewhat slackened, Charles of Valois conceived the idea of asserting his wife's claim by hiring the Catalans to carry out a Latin reconquest. He thought that he might at least become King of Thessalonica. Since the Infante had been intervening on behalf of a potential rival, Frederick of Sicily, Cepoy resolved to neutralize him. By his orders the Venetians overpowered the Infante's ships and appropriated his booty. Ferdinand himself was arrested and despatched to Thebes, and Duke Guy was requested to detain him and Muntaner at the French prince's pleasure. Already in the throes of his last illness, Guy was uncomfortably aware of the disturbance created by the Catalans in the Franco-Byzantine world and its possible repercussions on the security of his duchy. He was of course irritated by the sack of Halmyros and had no hesitation in complying with Cepoy's demand, but after a while he relented and sent his prisoner home to the West.[9]

The intrigues and manoeuvres of the various parties concerned were assuming a character often described as Byzantine, but in this case equally applicable to the Franks. By that time Rocafort was encamped at Kassandreia, a deserted ancient city on one of the promontories to the south-east of Thessalonica, and dividing his time between raiding the monasteries of Mount Athos and plotting the capture of the city. He too had dreams of making himself King of Thessalonica, but thought it prudent to reinsure himself by offering his allegiance to Charles of Valois. Simultaneously he proposed himself as a vassal of the Duke, with the ultimate purpose of supplanting the latter as master of Athens and of extending his ambitions to the Morea as well. Meanwhile he spun out his negotiations with Cepoy, who had joined him at Kassandreia. As it transpired, however, he had overreached himself. His position in Macedonia was becoming insecure. A Byzantine army under a new and capable general, Chandrenos, menaced his rear and the Venetians, alarmed by the prospect of a Catalan threat to their own possessions, warned Cepoy not to continue treating with him. Finally he lost the trust of his own men and was deposed by a council of the soldiers. They handed him over to Cepoy, who seized the opportunity to smuggle him on board a Venetian ship and deport him to Naples. At the same time he abandoned his fruitless mission.

When the Catalans became aware of Rocafort's abduction, they immediately regretted him and reacted angrily against those whom they judged responsible for his deposition. They did not, however, elect a new leader. Authority was delegated to a committee of four, including a representative of the Turks. As a democratically constituted military republic, the Company styled itself 'the fortunate host of the Franks in Romania' and adopted St George as its patron. It was not a designation which commended itself to the established Frankish powers, especially as the Catalans now proceeded to move southwards. They spent the winter of 1308 between the foot of Mount Olympus and the sea, at the point where the road to Thessaly enters the defile of Tempe, clothed with hanging woods.[10]

The new Duke of Athens, Gautier de Brienne, was fully forewarned of the Catalan problem, which had preoccupied the last years of his predecessor. It was also complicated by the termination of the ducal protectorate over Thessaly. John II Dukas, the young ruler of Thessaly–Neopatras and Guy's former ward, had shaken off Frankish tutelage as soon as he came of age and made overtures to Byzantium, for which he was rewarded by a marriage with an illegitimate daughter of Andronikos. As the Emperor's ally he felt himself even more gravely threatened than Gautier by the southward progress of the Company and when the latter, in the spring of 1310, moved through Tempe into the Thessalian plain he summoned Chandrenos to his aid. The joint Byzantine and Thessalian forces succeeded in hemming the Catalans into an awkward position on the border between Thessaly and the duchy. If, at that moment, Gautier had decided to join the Greeks in making common cause against the Company, and had enlisted Venetian support, he would have stood a very fair chance of destroying it for good and all. But unfortunately for himself he tried to be too clever. Undeterred by the painful experiences of other rulers who fancied that they could use the Catalans for their own purposes, he proceeded to hire them to help restore his hegemony over Thessaly. In that enterprise they were only too successful. During 1310 the Greeks were thrust back, Thessaly was ravaged and its fortresses occupied by the Company.[11]

The Duke light-headedly imagined that at this stage he could dispense with its services. He therefore informed the Catalans that they were dismissed, with the exception of five hundred men to whom he offered permanent employment. It is hardly surprising that they declined to be disposed of so easily. They offered to do him homage for the castles and territory which they had conquered, but refused to give them up unless he made good the arrears of pay on which, they alleged, he had defaulted. Too late in the day Gautier realised that he could not afford to tolerate such dangerous neighbours on his northern borders. He broke off negotiations with the Company and summoned his vassals to join in a campaign for its extermination.

Preparations for the struggle occupied the winter of 1310. The Company mustered about five thousand Catalans and fifteen hundred Turks. Opposed to them was the whole levy of Athens, while many feudatories and sympathisers from Achaia and the islands rallied to the Duke's banner. His army is unlikely to have outnumbered the Catalans, but a large proportion of it consisted of heavy cavalry which, if properly handled, was counted as invincible. The estimate given in the Aragonese *Chronicle*—two thousand horse and four thousand foot—is very probably right.[12] Despite his experience of the Catalans in the Sicilian war, Gautier was careless and over-confident. While he was still marshalling his army at Lamia, the Company slipped past him into his own territory of Boeotia and he was compelled to follow in its tracks. But the Catalans had several days to choose the battlefield and prepare the ground before he caught up with them. The position which they selected cannot exactly be identified, but it was certainly not far from the river Kephissos and the site of the ancient Orchomenos. The surrounding country was the naturally marshy basin of Lake Copais, but (a sign of the prosperity of Frankish Boeotia) the land was well drained and traversed by dykes and canals. The Catalans took their stand among green meadows with a conveniently narrow frontage, which they flooded by damming an irrigation ditch. However, the swamp thus created was concealed by spring grass growing eight inches high and they also contrived to leave dry passages through which their own cavalry would be able, when necessary, to sally forth.[13]

The Duke does not seem to have bothered to reconnoitre these dispositions, or to have been warned by local Greeks that he was in danger of falling into a trap. As the Catalans had hoped, he ordered a frontal attack, behaving, according to Moncada, as if 'the glitter of his arms and finery would suffice to humiliate his enemies'. Chivalrous to the last, he released the five hundred Catalans still in his service when they told him that they preferred to fight on the side of their countrymen. On the other hand the Turks in the Company's army decided to withdraw from the field and await events.[14]

The massed charge of the Frankish cavalry must have been a magnificent and intimidating sight. It failed, however, to disconcert the Catalans. Before it ever reached their ranks the heavy warhorses, weighed down by riders wearing the now fashionable plate armour, sank into the artificial bog and became immobilized. Incapable of either attack or effective defence, the mailed and plated colossi were overwhelmed with missiles or stabbed at leisure by the swift-moving *almugavares* and by the Turks, who joined eagerly in the massacre. The Duke was one of the first to succumb. His barons and knights were butchered in hundreds and the rest of the army fled in confusion. 'The pursuit and the killing', wrote Moncada, 'lasted longer than the victory.'[15]

The rout of the Kephissos bore a certain, if superficial, resemblance to its near-contemporary, the battle of Bannockburn. In both cases the mounted nobility insisted in frontally attacking a strong position in defiance of sound tactical principles and were thrown into disorder by previously prepared obstacles. Both conflicts resulted in the defeat, with crippling losses, of the heavily armoured knights. But whereas the English cavalry managed to surmount the obstacles and was only routed because it was no match, when squeezed into a confined space, for a compact phalanx of spear-bearing infantry, the French and Italian knights never even came to grips with the enemy. Their defeat was more thorough and its results more fatal. According to Muntaner only two knights, Bonifazio da Verona and Roger Deslaur, escaped with their lives out of the seven hundred engaged, but he was not in Greece at the time and the Aragonese *Chronicle* simply claims that a great number were killed or taken.[16] In the circumstances the Catalans were unlikely to forego the chance of a good ransom for notables like Nicholas Sanudo, the heir to the Duchy of Naxos, who is known to have survived, though wounded. But many other important feudatories were slaughtered including Thomas de Stromoncourt, Alberto Pallavicini of Boudonitza, Renaud de la Roche and Giorgio Ghisi, lord of Tenos and Mykonos. One famous name, that of Nicholas de St Omer, is conspicuously missing from accounts of the battle. Since he lived until 1313, and it is strangely out of character for him to have stayed away when there was fighting to be done, we must assume that he was still smarting from his expulsion by Duke Guy from his Theban fief.

Apart from the fate of these grandees, the battle of Kephissos shattered and swept away the whole Burgundian upper stratum of the duchy. As the contemporary historian of Florence, Giovanni Villani, put it, 'thus was the joyful life of the Latins (le delizie de' Latini), won of old by the French, who fared there more luxuriously and prosperously than in any other country of the world, destroyed and ruined by those unruly people (dissoluta gente).'[17] Astounded by the extent of their success, the Catalans moved into a rich and peaceful land, from which its masters had disappeared, leaving intact its material structure and, what was perhaps more important, its docile working population. All fortified towns were occupied without resistance. We do not know what happened to the non-combatant French, but it would be reasonable to suppose that they made as quickly as possible for the Morea or destinations farther west. With a certain malice Muntaner and the Byzantine Nikephoros Gregoras picture the *almugavares* taking over not only the property but the widows of the fallen Burgundians, and that is indeed what may well have happened in some instances, although many Catalans had brought their wives or mistresses with them.[18]

An outstanding, if unexpected, beneficiary of the fall of the duchy was one of the Company's prisoners, Roger Deslaur. A native of Roussillon, he was doubtless regarded by his captors as one of themselves. They had hardly taken over their domain when they began to feel the need for a leader who would see them through the stage of their conversion from a rough, military republic into a stable civil community. They sought a man of sufficient local repute and prestige to convince the rulers of the other Latin powers that the Catalans genuinely intended to discard their predatory and vagabond habits and settle down on equal terms with their neighbours. With that end in view they first approached Bonifazio da Verona, but he replied that it would be dishonourable for him, as the former intimate of Duke Guy and the comrade of so many who had fallen at the Kephissos, to accept their offer. They then turned to Deslaur, who raised no such objections, and was rewarded with not only the fief but the widow of Thomas de Stromoncourt. His government, however, lasted for one year only. The Catalans wisely concluded that as a permanent arrangement they required the protection of an overseas sovereign on the model of the Angevin overlord of Achaia. They therefore placed the duchy in the hands of Frederick of Sicily, who eagerly accepted their allegiance. He designated his second son, Manfred, as the titular Duke, but until he should come of age appointed Berenguer de Estañol to act as regent, or vicar-general. It fell to Estañol, an able administrator, to lay the foundations of the new state. His death in 1316 was followed by that of Manfred, whereupon the King conferred the nominal dukedom on another younger son, William, and the regency on a bastard, Alfonso Frederick. The latter's dynamic rule was to last for another thirteen years.

The widowed Duchess, who had escaped from Athens with her son, also called Gautier, repeatedly appealed to the powers for redress. The Papacy, the Kings of France and Naples and the Republic of Venice were all outraged and alarmed by the Catalan usurpation, but when it came to expelling the usurpers they were unable or unwilling to act. The great sovereigns of Europe were otherwise occupied, and the principality of Achaia was far too weak to face a conflict with the Company. It was at least a relief that the latter did not try to annex the late Duke's Moreot fiefs of Argos and Nauplia, which were held for the young Gautier by their captain, Nicholas de Foucherolles. But many Moreot nobles had been killed at the Kephissos and the Prince, Philip of Tarentum, was clearly apprehensive lest Achaia might become the next victim of aggression from the Catalans or their overlord, the Aragonese King of Sicily. His fears prompted the King of France, Philip le Bel, to take the initiative in negotiating a new series of dynastic arrangements intended to safeguard the traditional French supremacy in the Morea. In the event, however, they very nearly miscarried by provoking what they had been expressly devised to avoid, namely an Aragonese intervention and civil war in the principality.

The plan was typical of the matrimonial chopping and changing to which the closely related royal houses of France and Naples liked to resort. It provided that Philip of Tarentum, who had never personally assumed the government of Achaia and whose first wife, the Epirote Thamar, was now dead, should relinquish his title and marry Catherine de Valois, the present heiress to the elusive Latin Empire. Since the lady had already been promised to Hugues, Duke of Burgundy, this French magnate was propitiated by the betrothal of his brother, Louis, to Mahaut of Hainault, daughter of Isabelle de Villehardouin and widow of Guy II of Athens. Her previous engagement to Charles of Tarentum, Philip's brother, was brushed aside and, in order to complete the neat diplomatic interchange, Charles was affianced to the younger sister of Catherine de Valois. Mahaut, now aged twenty, was four years older than her new husband.[19]

The object of these ingenious expedients was not only to reconcile competing interests but to restore the confidence of the Franks in Achaia. Those of French descent would naturally welcome as their Princess the grand-daughter of Guillaume de Villehardouin, and as their Prince the brother of one of the greatest feudatories of the French Crown. Unfortunately the authors of the scheme had omitted from their calculations the claims of Mahaut's aunt Marguerite, the lady of Akova and widow of Count Richard of Cephalonia. Living quietly in her own fief under the protection of Nicholas de St Omer, she regarded herself, after her sister Isabelle's death, as her father's rightful heiress. In 1313, while the marriages planned by Philip le Bel were being celebrated, she lost her protector and found herself harassed by her stepson, John of Cephalonia, with whom she had long been on bad terms. For that personal reason, but chiefly because she felt that the moment had come to assert her rights, she suddenly took a step which threatened to frustrate the French King's careful plan and make the Aragonese masters of Achaia. Entering into touch with King Frederick of Sicily, she put to him a bold and original proposal. It was that his nephew, the Infante Ferdinand of Majorca, should marry her daughter by her first marriage, Isabelle de Sabran; the pair would thus become Prince and Princess of Achaia with Frederick as the ultimate sovereign. The Infante's fortunes had taken an upward turn since his abortive attempt to gain control of the Grand Company. After fighting heroically against the Moslems in Spain, he had joined his uncle when hostilities again broke out, in the same year 1313, between Sicily and Naples. Marguerite's message was therefore received with enthusiasm, and she and her daughter were cordially invited to the King's court at Messina. To the delight of all concerned the Infante fell passionately in love with Isabelle, who, according to his faithful henchman Muntaner, was a very beautiful and intelligent girl. They were married early in the following year and Marguerite, having undertaken to transfer all her rights and properties to her son-in-law, sailed back to the Peloponnese to await events.[20]

Her idea was admittedly a gamble. It could only be realized in defiance of opposition from the partisans of Louis and Mahaut. She apparently believed that her own prestige as the daughter of the great Villehardouin would nullify their resistance. But when she landed at Navarino she was at once arrested and imprisoned in the castle of Chloumoutzi, and all her lands, including Akova, were confiscated. Shattered by this ill-treatment, she died a year later in captivity, shortly after her daughter had produced a son who was eventually to inherit the throne of Majorca. To complete the tragedy, Isabelle barely survived her mother, and her death was attributed to her grief on learning of Marguerite's fate.[21]

Nevertheless Ferdinand was still determined to enforce his newly acquired claims. While Muntaner escorted his baby son to Spain, braving the storms and the Angevin navy, he sailed straight for Glarentza in June 1315 with ships and troops provided by King Frederick. He dispersed the force which tried to obstruct his landing and easily gained possession of the town. Moreover he was welcomed by the Frankish burgesses and by the same nobles as had been guilty of incarcerating Marguerite. Convinced that he had come to stay, he even took a new wife, a cousin of the King of Cyprus. The opposition, however, was still holding out at Patras and in Messenia, where the Princess Mahaut landed towards the end of the year with reinforcements from Burgundy. These marched north into Elis and encountered Ferdinand's army near the site of the ancient city of Palaiopolis. Although the Aragonese won the battle they were unable to exploit their victory before Louis joined his wife at the head of a fresh contingent of French men-at-arms. There was a pause while both sides sought further support. Count John of Cephalonia and the Duke of Naxos ranged themselves on Louis's side, and the Greeks of Mistra, who much preferred the Moreot Franks to the Aragonese intruders, sent him two thousand men. Thus strengthened, the Prince advanced against Ferdinand. This time the Infante was at a disadvantage, for the aid which he too had summoned from Sicily and the Catalans of Athens had not yet arrived. He was forced, however, to accept a second battle in Elis. There, at Manolada, the Aragonese were crushingly defeated and Ferdinand, fighting to the last, was beheaded on the field. Even so the Spanish infantry refused to give in. They shut themselves up in Glarentza and only agreed to negotiate a capitulation when the leader of their promised reinforcements, on viewing the extent of the disaster, decided that the combat was not worth renewing. Thereupon the Catalans, who had reached Vostitza on the Corinthian Gulf, also withdrew.[22]

After the issue had been so narrowly decided, it would be pleasant to record that the triumph of Louis and Mahaut put an end to the misfortunes of the last Villehardouins; but this was not to be. Louis, who had always suffered from bad health, died immediately after the battle, and his widow found it impossible to withstand the pressures to which she was then exposed. There was no question of her being allowed to rule undisturbed as Princess in her own right. Instead she became the victim of the vacillations of King Robert of Naples. For some time this monarch had toyed with the wholly impracticable idea of negotiating with Frederick of Sicily a territorial settlement by which the latter would give up his island in exchange for Achaia, Albania and the Angevin footholds in Epiros. In 1317, however, he changed his mind and decided to re-assert the control over Achaia which he had virtually lost through the French King's sponsorship of Louis of Burgundy. On the pretext that a woman was obviously incapable of administering and defending the principality, he appointed one of his own barons captain of Achaia and sent two commissioners to induce Mahaut to marry his younger brother John, Count of Gravina.

But Mahaut was not to be persuaded or bullied. She had no intention of being used as a political pawn by the Angevins. She categorically rejected the proposition and continued to do so when taken to Naples and subjected to further threats and indignities. Although still refusing her consent, she was forced to be present at an act of betrothal and to subscribe to an elaborate convention which formally conveyed the government of Achaia into the King's hands. It also provided that as soon as the actual marriage was celebrated the Count of Gravina should be recognised as Prince. Nevertheless, Mahaut resolutely declined to commit herself to the final step. When exhorted to do so by the Pope at Avignon, she announced that she was already married secretly to a Burgundian knight. The King retorted that in that case she had forfeited her rights to the principality, since her mother Isabelle's original marriage contract with Philip of Anjou had stipulated that no daughter of hers might marry without the King's consent. This piece of shabby legalism removed the last obstacle to John's investment with the title. Mahaut had managed to hold out for five years and the King, infuriated by her obstinacy, pressed his revenge further by claiming to have uncovered a plot against his life by Mahaut's secret husband, Hugues de la Palisse. That was a sufficient excuse for him to keep her sequestered for the rest of her life in the Castello dell'Uovo at Naples, the same forbidding fortress in which her mother had spent several sad years. She died there in 1331, forlorn and forgotten. Removed from her mother at the age of four, married at twelve, widowed for the first time at fifteen and for the second time at twenty-three, perpetually enmeshed in heartless intrigues, she set an admirable example of courage and tenacity.[23]

Once the Angevins had re-established their supremacy by such brutal and devious methods, they took curiously little interest in Moreot affairs. John of Gravina was content to govern through a succession of bailies and only once visited the principality. As will be seen in the context of the spread of Byzantine power in the Morea during the fourteenth century, the bailies steadily lost ground to the Greeks. Meanwhile the decline of Achaia helped to enhance the importance of the Catalan duchy. Both Estañol and Alfonso Frederick pursued a policy of aggressive deterrence. So far as the Morea was concerned, the Catalans confined themselves to a raid on Corinth and a tardy demonstration in favour of the Infante Ferdinand, but they did not seriously attempt to seize Argos and Nauplia. In Euboea, however, they made it their business to harass Venetians and Lombards alike. They soon fitted out a corsair fleet which, besides plundering Euboea itself, interrupted Venetian commerce and terrorized the Cyclades. Bonifazio da Verona successfully reinsured himself by marrying his daughter and heiress to Alfonso Frederick, who thus acquired some valuable Euboean castles, but the Venetians lost Negroponte and suffered defeats by land and sea at Catalan hands. The despatch of a fleet under Francesco Dandolo restored the situation and King Frederick, who wished to remain on good terms with Venice and realized that the Catalans could not afford a lasting quarrel with the Republic, adjured his son to make peace. The Catalans then gave up all their conquests in Euboea, with the exception of two of the coastal fortresses. They also agreed to dismantle their naval arsenal at the Piraeus, while retaining their other base at Livadostro on the Gulf of Corinth. For the Venetians this was a major concession, because it limited Catalan piracy in the Aegean and made it easier for them to police it. They were especially worried by the Turkish sea-robbers who were operating on an increasing scale from former Byzantine harbours in Asia Minor and whom they rightly suspected of acting in collusion with the Catalans.

The second sphere in which the Catalans strengthened their grip was Neopatras and Thessaly. After the death of John II Dukas in 1318 his little state lapsed into anarchy, with the principal Greek archons carving out separate domains for themselves. While the north passed into Byzantine control, the Catalans secured the south and Alfonso Frederick assumed the title of Vicar-General of Athens and Neopatras. The duchy's defences were now so firm that the Catalans could safely discount the danger of any possible Angevin endeavour to upset them. In fact two expeditions were launched from the West in 1325 and 1333 respectively, but both left the duchy unshaken.

The first was led by John of Gravina. The inefficient rule of his bailies had caused disquiet among the Moreot barons. Alarmed by the superiority of the Catalans and the advances of the Greeks, they made overtures to Venice in the hope that the Republic might replace King Robert as their protector. When this approach became known at Naples the King and his brother were stirred into action. They decided upon a campaign in the Morea, but arranged that it should be preceded by a punitive descent upon Epiros. In the same year as the dissolution of the state of Neopatras, the Despotate had undergone a change of dynasty. Its ruler, Thomas Dukas, was murdered by his nephew Nicholas Orsini, the new Count of Cephalonia, who took over his Byzantine wife as well as his realm. Such a development was unwelcome to the Angevins, who objected strongly to their own vassals, the Orsini, setting themselves up as independent princes on the mainland of Greece. John was therefore instructed to attack them before proceeding to the Morea. This he did in his usual half-hearted fashion, expelling them from their fief of the Ionian islands but leaving their new possessions in Epiros intact. Nor was his intervention in the Morea any more successful. He failed to recover any territory from the Greeks and, since he was heavily in debt to the Florentine bankers who had financed his campaign, he was compelled to retire to Italy.[24]

The second expedition, a more formidable affair, also ended in a fiasco. It was headed by Gautier de Brienne, the titular Duke of Athens and son-in-law to Philip of Tarentum, as the titular Latin Emperor of Constantinople. These high-sounding credentials, added to papal encouragement, helped him to recruit no less than eight hundred French knights and five hundred men-at-arms from Tuscany for the invasion of Epiros, where he received the submission of the Despot (now John II Orsini, brother of the murderer Nicholas whom he had in turn assassinated). He then advanced into the Company's territory. The Catalans, who could scarcely expect him to repeat his father's errors of generalship, garrisoned the towns but prudently avoided battle. These tactics consumed the enemy's time and money and ended in baffling him so effectively that he withdrew as ingloriously as John of Gravina.[25] The only serious damage that resulted from the campaign was the destruction of the castle of the St Omers at Thebes. Some four years before Gautier's expedition Alfonso Frederick had presented it to Bartolomeo Ghisi on the occasion of the marriage of the latter's son to his daughter Simona. Ghisi, whose father had been killed at the Kephissos, was a grandee with a stake in several different regions of Romania. Lord of Tenos, a triarch of Euboea and, in virtue of his Moreot possessions, Grand Constable of Achaia, his involvement with the Catalans, like Alfonso Frederick's previous connexion with Bonifazio da Verona, was a sign that these Iberian adventurers were beginning to be regarded as respectable members of the Frankish commonwealth. But the Paris manuscript of the Greek *Chronicle* states that his castle was dismantled by the 'Catalan dogs', for fear that it might fall into Gautier's hands.[26] It will also be recalled that the French version of the *Chronicle* purports to have been derived from a book in Ghisi's possession when he was the chatelain of Thebes. Perhaps he was a man of culture as well as of substance.

The institutions which the Catalans set up for themselves differed markedly from the feudal structure of their Burgundian predecessors. When they took over the Duchy they were a compact social group numbering at the most ten thousand persons. There was little aristocratic flavour in their society, and piracy, as opposed to trade and agriculture, became the principal occupation of the men. Although a few important fiefs were allotted to prominent individuals such as the Deslaurs at Salona, the pattern was one of small and exclusively Catalan corporations or municipalities. These elected their own officers, and their own representatives, or syndics, came together from time to time in a general assembly. Such democracy at the local level reflected both the constitution of the Company at its earlier and purely military stage and the organization, on a far larger scale, of the urban communities of the Sicilian Kingdom under Aragonese rule. Ultimately however it derived from the municipal institutions of Catalonia itself. The permanence of the system in the duchy was guaranteed by the original compact negotiated between the Company and the Duke, or rather the Duke's father, King Frederick. It is curious to find the Iberian tradition of representative government, which later Kings of Spain found it so hard to eradicate, flourishing among isolated communities in alien surroundings, especially when those groups probably consisted of a few dozen citizens only in each small town or village, and when those citizens were war-hardened soldiers with a reputation for ferocity and lawlessness.

The administrative and judicial apparatus rested on the same agreed basis. The principal executive and magistrate was the Vicar-General. He was appointed at the Duke's discretion and held the widest powers, but when he took the oath to the Duke it was in the presence of the assembled syndics. Alfonso Frederick, as befitting a king's son, maintained an elaborate court and personally exercised the chief military command. Nominally, however, military affairs were the province of a Marshal, whose office became hereditary in the family of the Novelles. Lesser administrative officers, the captains, sheriffs and castellans of the towns and rural districts, were in principle appointed for three years only, and their nominations were subject to the approval of both the Vicar-General and the community concerned. In their judicial capacity they tried civil and criminal cases, while the Vicar-General presided over a higher court and appeals were referred to the King's tribunal in Sicily.

The change of masters in the duchy also led to the gradual elimination of the French clergy, although the Catalans did not violently eject bishops, canons and priests from their sees and benefices: they were already in such bad odour with the Papacy, which had more than once excommunicated their leaders, that they would have been foolish to give further offence by doing so. But as the French ecclesiastics were eased out or departed voluntarily, they were replaced by Spaniards. It is not clear to what extent this process also affected the monastic Orders, the Cistercians of Daphni, the Franciscans of Mount Pentelikon or the Knights of the Holy Sepulchre at Hosios Loukas in Stiris. The Hospitallers or Knights of St John certainly kept their castle of Oropos, facing the Euboean channel, but as they were a strong military power with a fleet based on Rhodes and other islands of the Dodecanese, in addition to holding extensive fiefs in Achaia, there was no point in antagonizing them.[27]

The Orthodox Church retained the same secondary but guaranteed status as under the de la Roches. The laity, however, suffered to some extent in the earlier years of Catalan domination from the deep-rooted aversion which the conquerors had conceived for all Greeks during their sojourn in the Byzantine Empire.[28] Their feelings were of course fully reciprocated by the Greeks, for whom the word 'Catalan' lasted for centuries as a term of obloquy in popular speech, but there is no evidence that the general condition of the *paroikoi* in Attica and Boeotia was any worse under the Catalan regime than before. It is true that the measure of democracy enjoyed by the Catalans themselves was at first strictly denied, not only to the serfs on the land, but to the majority of native townsmen engaged in trade and other civil pursuits. In theory the latter were not even permitted to deal in property among themselves, and intermarriage between Latins and Greeks was expressly forbidden. As K.M. Setton observes, 'survival was possible only by maintaining the unity and racial integrity of the Company.'[29]

The sources disclose virtually nothing about the treatment by the Catalans of the Greek landed archons of Boeotia or of the old Athenian families whom we shall find playing an active role on the eve of the Turkish conquest. We have no idea whether they were evicted from their properties or forced to seek refuge outside the Duchy. On the other hand, there are numerous references to educated Greeks of bourgeois origin who held notarial posts in the Catalan administration. Such persons soon made themselves indispensable in the office of the Company's Chancellor, who had charge of its archives and diplomatic correspondence. The best known of them are Demetrios Rendis and Nikolaos Makris, both of whom served as chief notaries at Athens.[30] They and many others were granted the Catalan franchise; in other words they received the same civil and property rights as the conquerors and, in some cases, the right of intermarriage. Indeed their status became analogous to that which Greeks had for many years enjoyed in the government of Achaia.

The final acceptance of the Catalans as reputable members of the Latin community in the Levant was delayed until some years after Gautier's futile venture. In 1334 we find the Archbishop of Patras, Frangipani, threatening them again with excommunication unless they left the duchy within six months, on orders from Pope John XXII, and the latter's successor, Benedict XII, sought to renew the sentence five years later. But on the second occasion Frangipani's colleague, Archbishop Isnard of Thebes, where a Frenchman still held the see, disregarded the order, and the Papacy's attitude was soon reversed.[31] It was obvious that no papal fulminations against the Catalans would ever restore Gautier, who was in any case losing interest in his own cause. Moreover, there was a paramount need for the Latin states to combine in checking the ominous spread of Turkish maritime power. With the Catalans neutral, or even conniving with the raiders from across the Aegean, such action would be impossible. Accordingly the next Pope, Clement VI, brought about a reconciliation with the Company and in 1344 a Latin fleet, to which the Venetians, the Genoese, the King of Cyprus and the Order of St John all contributed squadrons, destroyed the Turkish base at Smyrna and turned it into a stronghold of the West.

CHAPTER SEVEN

The Byzantine Reaction

GIBBON SAW THE later history of Byzantium as a miserable period of decline, a protracted agony which could only end in extinction. The Byzantines of the thirteenth century, however, took a more resilient view of contemporary events and of their eventual destiny. In preceding ages they had endured numerous disasters, although they had never lost Constantinople. The latest vicissitudes had been appalling but they would surely pass, and the Empire, subject to God's will, was to be regarded as eternal. They conceived it to be their duty to win back its capital and the European provinces conquered by the Latins. The rulers of Nicaea applied themselves to this task with vigour and determination. So, with varying fortunes, did the usurper Michael VIII Palaeologos. His brother's victory at Pelagonia, quickly followed by the occupation of Constantinople and by the cession of the three strongholds in the Peloponnese by Guillaume de Villehardouin, in fact marked the high tide of his success. He clearly nourished high hopes of an early reclamation of the whole Morea, and it was to that end that he fitted out the formidable expedition of 1263. Indeed it might well have fulfilled its purpose had it not been for the incapacity of the Greek generals and the perhaps unsuspected solidity of the fabric constructed by the Villehardouin princes.

Although the campaigns of 1263–4 were distinguished by signal defeats in the field, they nevertheless enabled the Byzantines to enlarge their original enclave. The latter had comprised merely one fortified harbour (Monemvasia) and two lonely castles (Mistra and le Grand Magne) in a country of recalcitrant hillmen. Communications between these three strong points were hazardous, for the Franks still occupied the greater part of Lakonia. But when the fighting was over the Greeks were left permanently in possession of Tzakonia, the Vatika (or peninsula of Cape Malea) and the Maina, together with the whole massif of Taygetos. For the time being the Franks retained a precarious hold on the Eurotas valley and Prince Guillaume's cherished abode at Lakedaimonia, but within ten years these too were lost and the Greeks were already striking deep into Frankish Arkadia.

At that period Imperial authority in the Morea was wielded by a military commander residing at Mistra and changed at frequent if not yearly intervals. The real capital of the Byzantine province, however, was Monemvasia, secure on its rocky citadel poised half-way between Tzakonia and the Vatika, both fastnesses of Greek nationalism. It was both a busy trading port and the only official and military link between the province and Constantinople. As from 1262 its Metropolitan became the senior prelate of the Greek Orthodox Church for the whole Morea. Andronikos II gave him the title of Exarch of the Peloponnese and built for him the small but lovely Cathedral of Hagia Sophia, perched on the edge of the cliff that falls eight hundred feet sheer to the sea from the upper city. Although his control over the Greek clergy in the Frankish principality was necessarily limited, his see became a vital rallying point for the political as well as the ecclesiastical allegiance of the entire Orthodox population. As for the citizens of Monemvasia, they prospered greatly under the early Palaeologue emperors, growing rich on the wine trade and benefitting from tax privileges. Its archontic families owned estates in the Vatika and were permitted, if not encouraged, to act as corsairs, harrying Latin commerce with the same freedom as Licario, also under the Byzantine flag, was operating in the northern Aegean.

The site of Mistra, a spur of Mount Taygetos looking across the Eurotas to the bare heights of Mount Parnon, was not inhabited until Guillaume de Villehardouin built the castle in 1249. Its name is said to have been derived from the shape of a local cheese called *misithra*. After 1262 the townspeople of Lakedaimonia began slowly to desert the valley floor and to settle under the walls of the castle, where the administrative business of the province was transacted. Pilgrims still frequented the celebrated shrine of St Nikon in the old town, but that too was gradually outshone by new pious foundations on the hill. The first of the surviving galaxy of Byzantine churches at Mistra, that of the Sts Theodore, was built, like the Cathedral of Monemvasia, at a time when both Byzantine province and Frankish principality were enjoying a respite from strife afforded by the truce between Prince Florent and Andronikos II.[1]

Before the truce was concluded Andronikos recognised the importance of the struggling province in the Morea by deciding that the series of ephemeral captains or 'heads' (*kephalai*) who had previously administered it should in future give way to officers of high rank with greater security of tenure. The first of these new governors was a Cantacuzenos. His first name is unknown, but he was most probably the son of the Michael Cantacuzenos who was killed fighting the Franks in Elis, and almost certainly the father of the future Emperor John VI. The latter wrote that his father was sent to govern the Peloponnese at the age of twenty one and died there after eight years of service, adding that he himself had unpleasant memories of the country which had been the cause of his being left an orphan. If the father was killed in 1264 the latest date for the son to have taken up his appointment is 1286, and the latter part of his term of office must have coincided with the truce period. When hostilities were resumed the initiative rested with the Greeks. While avoiding those frontal clashes which usually resulted in their discomfiture, they constantly probed for weaknesses in the Frankish defences. They watched for every chance of capturing or suborning a castle, for turning a Greek archon from his allegiance to the Prince to the service of the Emperor, or for advancing the boundaries of the province into the crannies of the Arkadian mountains. The revolt of Skorta, though contained by Philip of Savoy, pushed the frontier still further to the north and west. In 1306 Philip of Tarentum retook a few key points, but they were soon lost once more as the result of a defeat suffered by his bailie, Thomas of Marzano. The next governor whose name is on record is Andronikos Asen, son of the Emperor Andronikos's daughter Irene and of the dethroned Tsar of Bulgaria, John Asen III. Ever since the conquest of Bulgaria by Basil II, and even after that country had regained its independence, its court and nobility had been steeped in Byzantine culture and leading Bulgarians passed easily into the Byzantine service. Andronikos is known to have been in the Morea by 1316, but he may well have taken up the appointment at an earlier date and have inflicted the defeat on the bailie. With Asia Minor overrun by the Turks, and Thrace and Macedonia ravaged by the Catalans, the Morea was the only part of the Greek world where Byzantine fortunes were in the ascendant, while Mistra was becoming a worthy capital of the Byzantine Peloponnese. Two more remarkable churches, the Metropolis (St Demetrios) and that of the Virgin *Hodegetria* (the *Aphentiko* or 'Governor's Church') were founded about 1312 and subsequently decorated with some of the finest frescoes of the Byzantine artistic renaissance of the fourteenth century. Lakonia was no longer regarded at Constantinople as a provincial backwater.[2]

After 1316 Asen, an excellent soldier, made a damaging attack on the Frankish principality. In the absence of John of Gravina he succeeded in breaching the defensive line of the upper Alpheios, capturing or bribing into surrender the fortresses of St George, Karytaina and Akova. In the neighbourhood of the former he also routed the field army of Achaia, taking the Grand Constable prisoner and killing the Commander of the Teutonic Knights. The loss of the three almost legendary bastions of

Skorta was a tremendous blow for the Latins. Its result was that they no longer dominated the peninsula; in future the principality was to be confined to its peripheral coastlands, stretching in a semicircle from Messenia in the south-west to the Argolid in the north-east. Although these regions included the richest lands, the fact remained that the Greeks now held the greater part of the Peloponnese and that in any hostilities between Greeks and Franks the initiative had passed to the former.[3] As soon as territory passed into Greek hands, the Orthodox hierarchy was re-established under the primacy of the Metropolitan of Monemvasia. Archons were confirmed in their possessions and began to seek similar assurances in regard to lands still on the Latin side of the line. A less welcome change was the re-imposition of Byzantine taxation, which was more onerous and more efficiently collected than under the easy-going régime of the principality.

In 1321 Asen was due to be succeeded by his nephew John Cantacuzenos, the son of the earlier governor and the future Emperor, who in that year was also designated Grand Domestic, or Commander-in-Chief of the imperial armies. The stage thus seemed set for a further Byzantine advance in the Peloponnese, possibly leading to the extinction of the principality. That this did not occur was due to the exacerbation of the dynastic feuds and rivalries which afflicted the Empire even more seriously than its external enemies. Preoccupied by his ambitions at the centre of affairs, John never took up his governorship, and the history of the Byzantine province enters an obscure phase from which it only emerges on his accession as Emperor in 1347. Not even the names of its governors are recorded. We know from Frankish sources that intermittent conflicts flared up whenever the Greeks chose to press against the gradually receding Frankish boundary. Indeed the Moreot nobles and bishops, deeply alarmed by the nerveless behaviour of their Angevin overlord, were reduced to approaching the Doge of Venice with a proposal that the Republic should take over the principality. As it happened the offer was not received with enthusiasm, but it no doubt served to push John of Gravina into his fruitless attempt to restore the situation.[4]

It was not that the Byzantine government had abandoned its interest in Greece, but it seemed to Andronikos III (1328–41) and his advisers, among whom the moving spirit was John Cantacuzenos, that greater opportunities awaited them north of the Corinthian Gulf than in the Peloponnese. Their preference for the former area was shaped by internal developments in the Empire during the 1320s and by its relations with the Turkish and Slav states. By that time the old Emperor

Andronikos II was at the end of his tether. His son and co-Emperor Michael IX was dead and he had no sympathy for his grandson Andronikos. The latter was a keen soldier but was addicted to pleasure and sport. Like Manuel Komnenos in the twelfth century, he had a passion for Western-style jousting. Although he had already been crowned co-Emperor, his grandfather decided to depose and disinherit him. His attempt to do so, however, resulted in a political schism which for seven years split the Byzantines into two irreconcilable factions. The bureaucracy of the capital and the more conservative members of the aristocracy clung to Andronikos II, but the younger magnates, led by John Cantacuzenos and supported by all those who were outraged by the Empire's military decadence, the loss of its trade to the Italian republics, the incompetence of the government and the unbearable tax burden, declared for Andronikos III, who set himself up as a rival sovereign at Adrianople. Popular opinion veered in favour of the party which promised new policies and, above all, the remission of taxation. Moreover the young Emperor's cause took firm root in Thrace and Macedonia, which now that all but a very small remnant of Asia had fallen to the Turks, were the sole provinces of any extent left to Byzantium. Nevertheless it took years of civil discord, happily seldom degenerating into actual warfare, before Andronikos III finally triumphed and the old man was politely dethroned. He ended his life, as befitted his theological inclinations, in a monastery.

Spurred on by his chief adviser, Cantacuzenos, Andronikos applied himself to the task of restoring Byzantine authority and prestige. With the Empire of the Romans reduced to the dimensions of a medium sized Balkan state the problem which faced them was one of consolidating the imperial territories and of establishing a durable balance of power in the Aegean area. In framing a foreign policy they had to reckon with the Franks, the Serbs, the Bulgarians and the Turks. The former's aggressive capacity, as well as their inclination to expand eastwards, had notably diminished, and while it seemed wise not to provoke the Catalans of Athens, little danger might be expected from that quarter. Of the two Slav states concerned, the Bulgarian Kingdom was almost a spent force, but the restless Serbian monarchy posed a threat to Greek Macedonia and the north Aegean littoral which Byzantine diplomacy would find hard to contain. In the case of the Turks, one short campaign, in which Andronikos III and Cantacuzenos suffered a humiliating rebuff, was enough to convince them that there was no chance of recovering the Asiatic territories lost during the previous reign. It was equally clear, and mortifying in the extreme, that the Greek-speaking Christians of Asia

Minor had begun to prefer security and the comparatively mild rule of the Osmanli Emir, Orchan, to perpetual frontier warfare and the exactions of Byzantine tax-gatherers. Andronikos was therefore forced to seek a peaceful arrangement with Orchan, if only to postpone the day when the latter's warriors would aspire to cross into Europe. But the Osmanli or Ottoman Emirate was only one of several Turkish principalities contending for supremacy in Asia Minor, and it was a safe guess that Orchan would wish to subdue all potential rivals before invading the Balkan peninsula. Here again Byzantine diplomacy had a role to perform, and Andronikos was soon making overtures to Umur, Emir of Aydin and Smyrna and the most formidable pirate prince of the Levant. He would be a useful card to play against not only the Osmanlis but also the Slavs and the Latin maritime powers, such as the Genoese and the Knights of Rhodes, who had occupied Lesbos and other offshore islands.

A forward policy in Greece offered compensations, but it was not until 1333, two years after Gautier de Brienne's unsuccessful attack on the Catalans, that the Emperor felt it safe to intervene. Since the death of the last Greek ruler of Neopatras, northern Thessaly had been ruled by independent archons, foremost among whom was one Stephen Gabrielopoulos. When the latter died anarchy ensued and John II Orsini, the Despot of Epiros, sent troops across the Pindus to seize the provincial towns. His action, however, was swiftly countered by Andronikos. A Byzantine army expelled the Epirote garrisons and occupied the whole country as far south as the Catalan border. For the first time since 1204 Thessaly acknowledged the Imperial authority.

Two years later Andronikos was presented with the opportunity of incorporating the Despotate itself into the Empire. Since murdering his brother John, Orsini had performed a delicate balancing act between the Angevins and the Palaeologues, both of whom claimed suzerainty over Epiros. If anything he inclined towards the Byzantine connexion. He professed the Orthodox religion and his wife, Anna, was descended from the families of Palaeologos and Dukas. His Roman origins had worn rather thin. The northern part of the Despotate, with its capital Joannina, had already seceded to Byzantium. But in 1335 Anna, in true Epirote style, did away with him by poison and entered into her own negotiations with the Emperor. She offered to recognise his suzerainty for good and all, so long as her son Nikephoros was allowed to succeed to the title of Despot as a Byzantine vassal. Such an arrangement, however, was not acceptable to Andronikos. He insisted that Epiros, like Thessaly, must be totally reintegrated into the Empire. At the time he happened to be suppressing a revolt of the Albanian population in the extreme north. When he had dealt with the Albanians he marched south, accompanied by Cantacuzenos, and installed a Byzantine governor in Arta. He removed Anna to Thessalonica, while a marriage was arranged between Nikephoros and a daughter of the Grand Domestic. But in the event he nearly upset the Emperor's whole plan, as the local partisans of the Angevin connexion managed to spirit him away from Epiros to Italy.

Meanwhile Achaia had acquired a new Prince. He was Robert, son of Philip of Tarentum and of Catherine de Valois, titular Empress of Constantinople. By yet another Angevin family deal John of Gravina, disenchanted by his experience of Greece, had agreed to exchange the principality for the empty titles of Duke of Durazzo and King of Albania, together with a large sum in cash. As Robert was still a minor his mother assumed his powers and appointed bailies to govern in the Prince's name. Catherine continued to reside at Taranto; indeed it was to her court that the young Nikephoros was first taken. But in 1338 the uncertain state of the Morea demanded her presence and she established herself at Patras, bringing Nikephoros with her. Furthermore she determined to reinstate him in the Despotate under Angevin colours. She provided him with ships and troops and when he landed in Epiros his supporters rose and expelled the Byzantine viceroy. The Emperor and Cantacuzenos hurried back to quell the revolt, a task which they accomplished with little difficulty. It was the latter who persuaded the Epirotes that they would be foolish to prefer a regime which would place them at the mercy of the Latins, with all the disadvantages that such subjection would entail. Before long Nikephoros was shut up in Thomokastron, a fortress on the Adriatic coast built by the last of the Dukas Despots. But here too Cantacuzenos, by repeating his arguments and guaranteeing Nikephoros's personal safety, induced the garrison to surrender. He was in fact as good as his word, for Nikephoros was duly married to his daughter and rewarded with the title, for what it was worth, of *panhypersebastos*.[5]

The consequence of these events was that by 1340 Andronikos had become the master of the whole of northern Greece, with the exception of the Duchy of Athens, as well as of the greater portion of the Morea. No wonder that the Frankish barons were reduced to something like despair, especially when Catherine returned to Italy, leaving the administration once more in the hands of bailies. As will be recalled they had already, at the time of John Asen's campaign, offered the principality to Venice. The proposal which they now proceeded to make was more revolutionary. They sent a deputation to Cantacuzenos, headed by the Latin Bishop of Coron and a Greek or half-caste named John Sideros, inviting him to take over the government of Achaia. They announced that they were willing to accept the Emperor as their overlord, provided that they were confirmed in the possession of their fiefs and the same freedoms as they had enjoyed under their Latin princes. The offer is sufficient proof of the demoralisation then prevailing among the once proud and intransigent Frankish nobles. It also reflects the great personal prestige of Cantacuzenos, who was regarded as the true author of the imperial triumphs in the north and whose traditional connexions with the Morea were well remembered. Possibly he had never ceased to rank as governor of the Byzantine province and its actual administrators since 1321 had been his nominees. The proposal was naturally received with gratification. Cantacuzenos promised to visit the Peloponnese in the near future and sent a high officer to discuss the handover with the barons. It seemed that the grand design conceived by the Emperor and his Grand Domestic for the reunion of the Greek lands between the Albanian mountains and Cape Tainaron was on the point of becoming a reality.[6]

Yet this was not to be. When the Moreot emissaries reached Cantacuzenos at Didymoteichos in Thrace the fruitful partnership between the Emperor and himself had been dissolved by the former's unexpected death. He had already been obliged to take action to forestall attempts by Serbs, Bulgarians and Turks to take advantage of the confusion which they hoped would occur at Constantinople. Unfortunately their expectations were soon to prove correct, for in the following six years the grand design fell to pieces, while the internal unity and the economy of the Empire were shattered by a new and virulent civil war. For complex reasons outside the scope of this work Cantacuzenos missed his chance of stepping directly into Andronikos's shoes, a solution which might have spared Byzantium many years of misery.

Arrayed against him were the Dowager Empress, Anne of Savoy, the Orthodox Patriarch John Kalekas and the most powerful figure of all, his former adherent Alexios Apokaukos, Grand Admiral and head of the imperial administration. Nor was he a universally popular figure, except among the aristocracy. However, he eventually emerged the winner from a struggle in which Thrace and Macedonia were desolated by the Turkish mercenaries in his own service as well as by his opponents' Serbian auxiliaries. To these ills was added the crippling horror of the Black Death, which carried off vast numbers of the inhabitants of the capital and the provinces. It cannot be estimated how seriously the plague affected Greece, but the gaps which it left in the population were soon filled by a gradual but persistent immigration of Albanians, beginning before 1350 in Thessaly and seeping down in subsequent decades through Boeotia and Attica and into the Morea. This movement was the result of one of those mysterious demographic explosions, similar to that of the Vlachs in the eleventh and twelfth centuries, which from time to time impelled the mountaineers of the high Balkan ranges to replenish the population of the plains and valleys.[7]

On regaining possession of Constantinople John VI made a brave attempt to compose the feuds which wracked the ailing state. He amnestied his enemies and associated John Palaeologos, the son of Andronikos, with him as co-Emperor. But he was powerless to prevent the collapse of his plans for Greece. In 1348 the Serbian King, Stephen Dushan, swept into Thessaly and Epiros and succeeded in occupying, almost without opposition, all the territories which Andronikos III had so recently restored to Byzantium. Nevertheless the change made little practical difference to the condition of the Thessalians and Epirotes. Dushan, whose ambition it was to take Constantinople and to erect a great Greco-Slav realm on the ruins of Byzantium, modelled his court and administration on Byzantine lines and regarded himself as the natural heir of the emperors of the Romans.

It was only in the Morea that the Greek cause continued to prosper. In 1348 John VI took the wise step of appointing his son Manuel to the governorship and enhanced its importance by investing him with the title of Despot. The Peloponnese thus became an appanage of the imperial family and its capital, Mistra, a miniature Constantinople or Thessalonica. There Manuel ruled for the next thirty years, keeping a lively court and fostering the local flowering of the renaissance of architecture and painting which at Constantinople had illumined the darkest years of the reign of Andronikos II: 'at this time of the hopeless decay of Byzantine power, the revival of Greek supremacy in the Morea shone out like a solitary beacon'.[8] Mistra also witnessed for the first time some modest stirrings of intellectual life. Manuel himself was not a writer like his father the Emperor, who was one of the two great Byzantine historians of the period, but he was in correspondence with the other, Nikephoros Gregoras, and with various distinguished men of letters about the affairs of his Despotate.[9]

Despite their previous alarm about Greek predominance, the Franks were glad to have Manuel as a neighbour. His policy was pacific and he was not ill-disposed towards Latins in general. His wife, Isabelle de

Lusignan, was a member of the Latin royal house of Cyprus. All Christians in the Peloponnese, Greeks and Latins, including the Venetian trading communities, had a common interest in warding off the Turkish maritime raiders whose destructive incursions had only been temporarily interrupted by the Latin punitive seizure of Smyrna in 1344. The threat was still acute, and in that very year the barons of Achaia showed their lack of confidence by once more seeking a protector. Sponsored by the Archbishop of Patras, they vainly appealed to James II, King of Majorca, son of the Infante Ferdinand killed at Manolada in 1316 and great-grandson of Guillaume de Villehardouin.[10] In 1349 a fleet of eighty-five Turkish galleys swooped upon the bay of Patras and in subsequent years, when the Venetians and Genoese, the only Latin sea powers fully capable of repelling the Turks, were at each other's throats, the Greek and Frankish Moreots had difficulty in guarding their shores. Moreover the attitude of the Catalans was at the best ambiguous. Some years later their Vicar General Roger de Lluria (a descendant of the famous Aragonese admiral of the preceding century) went so far as to invoke the Turkish help in a quarrel between the duchy and the Venetians of Euboea, but the bailie of Achaia, Gautier de Lor, with the aid of Manuel's Greeks, the Venetians and the Knights of St John, caught the Turks unprepared off Megara and burned thirty-five of their ships.[11]

Another problem which required firm handling by Manuel was the unruly behaviour of the Greek archons, whose naturally anarchic tendencies had been given full reign by the lack of a strong central authority during the recent civil war. In eulogizing his son's achievements, the Despot's father drew a horrific picture of these factious local tyrants. Lawless and rapacious, feuding with each other from one generation to another, they had reduced the Morea to a condition 'worse than the proverbial Scythian desert'. Continuing the use of the stock antique allusions so dear to Byzantine littérateurs, John accused the descendants of the Spartans of 'neglecting all the laws of Lycurgus'. In all likelihood the rougher archons of the mediaeval Peloponnese had never heard of that mythical lawgiver.[12] The vision of these typical border barons of the European fringes was confined to the horizon commanded by their own peel-towers, and they had scant share in the traditional culture so tenaciously guarded by the Byzantine elite. They would have neither recognised the quotations from ancient writers so freely indulged in by its representatives, nor even grasped the meaning of the scarcely modified classical diction which they employed in their books and correspondence. Unwilling heirs of a shrinking and ossified past, most of them were less civilized than the Latin landowners living within a few miles of them, who had at least absorbed some of the light diffused in the West by the century of Dante and Petrarch. The Despot's entourage, drawn as it was from the administrative and intellectual circles of the capital and Thessalonica, could not fail to arouse suspicion and resentment among the provincials.

Consequently the early years of Manuel's reign were not free from anxieties. Local discontent came to a head when he proposed to levy a tax for the purpose of building a fleet to protect the coasts, and a rebellion broke out under the leadership of an archon named Lampoudios.[13] Although Manuel overcame it easily, he soon faced a more serious challenge to his authority posed by the situation at Constantinople, where the co-Emperors John Cantacuzenos and John Palaeologos were at loggerheads, and the Palaeologos faction was getting the better of its opponents. John Palaeologos sent two members of the Asen clan, Michael and Andrew, to the Morea with instructions to supersede Manuel, but the Despot managed to get rid of them. When in 1354 John Cantacuzenos finally gave up the struggle for power and retired into a monastery, he made his peace with John Palaeologos and was confirmed in his appanage. For the rest of his life he experienced no further trouble from the archons, and the Greek Morea enjoyed another period of quiet prosperity.

The relative concord prevailing between the Despotate and the principality was largely due to the increasing influence of Greek functionaries and landowners within the Frankish area, and to the tendency of persons of Latin and half-caste origins to adopt the Orthodox faith. The office of Chancellor (protovestiary) became virtually a Greek perquisite and the Greek Misito family, castellans of Kalamata, eventually produced a Grand Constable of Achaia.[14] A certain John Laskaris Kalopheros, who married the sister of Erard le Maure, baron of Arkadia, and named his own son Erard, was an unusually cosmopolitan figure among the Greeks of his age. By origin a Byzantine of Constantinople, he made his career in the Frankish principality, moving easily in the highest Latin society. He was employed on missions to the Pope and the King of Cyprus, and when not active in diplomacy or warfare, engaged in the silk trade. At the same time he maintained his links with Byzantium and particularly with one of its foremost intellectuals. Demetrios Kydones, theologian, philosopher, statesman and friend of successive emperors, who was deeply interested in Western thought and translated Thomas Aquinas into Greek. A life-long advocate of union between the Churches and of joint action by Greeks and Latins against the Turks, he found Kalopheros an useful intermediary in his dealings with Western leaders.[15]

Apart from such notables, who were indistinguishable from their Latin peers as regards privilege and prestige, there existed at the other end of the scale a small class of semi-independent chieftains holding their own in border areas where the authority of the Despot or the Prince counted for very little. Such a family was that of Spano or Spani, which controlled a stretch of the precipitous coast where Taygetos drops into the Gulf of Coron, and earned a bad reputation for plundering the Venetian merchants of Coron and Modon. Another prominent family in the same neighbourhood, the Zassi, was equally troublesome. Both drew their adherents from the Slav tribesmen of the region, whose separate identity and intolerance of discipline lasted at least until the Turkish conquest of the following century.

According to John Cantacuzenos, his son's energy repeopled the towns and restored the land to cultivation. There is no reason to doubt his claims, coloured as they are by family pride. While in retirement as the monk Joasaph he visited the Morea more than once, and it was there that he spent his last years; he eventually died at Mistra in 1383, aged 88. During the period the Despotate continued to flourish and expand. Its economy depended largely on the export of its agricultural products, particularly wine and silk, and consequently on the continuity and security of maritime commerce. The Greek carrying trade was almost a monopoly of the Venetians, and they maintained it in face of Turkish piracy and Genoese hostility. They used not only their own ports of Coron and Modon but also those of Achaia and the Despotate. In that respect the latter was at a disadvantage, because Monemvasia was its sole important harbour, while the principality possessed Patras, Corinth, Nauplia and Glarentza. Nevertheless, so long as peace was preserved, there is not likely to have been any obstacle to the passage of produce from the Despotate through ports controlled by the Latins.

Mistra, although it never became a great city, throve steadily on the new dispensation. It resembled to some extent a prosperous hill-town of Central Italy. With its ruler's Court and Chancery, its mercantile pursuits and its growing constellation of churches and monasteries, it was both a scene of bustling activity and as safe a refuge as any from the ultimate disaster of Turkish invasion which, as from 1355, had begun to overtake the hinterland of Constantinople. Unlike the citizens of the capital, the Greeks of the Morea did not yet feel the pressure of the barbarian flood. Art historians, it is true, have detected in the exquisite paintings of the Peribleptos church, built and decorated in the early years of Manuel's reign, a note of premonition, of a melancholy sense of the end to come. The behaviour of the men of Mistra, however, suggests not resignation but the will to survive and make a fresh start. The Despot's government was vigorous as well as benevolent and his policy adroit; neither betrayed a despairing apathy and a conviction that all was lost.[18]

On the steps of the hill crowned by Villehardouin's *château-fort* an imposing palace was built for the Despot. We can well believe that it was as luxurious as the run-down palace of Blachernae on the Golden Horn in which the Emperors struggled to uphold their dignity, and certainly more cheerful. Monastic foundations, which served not simply as pious retreats but as centres of intellectual and artistic life, housing writers, artists and copyists of manuscripts, multiplied throughout the Greek Morea. Since the time of Andronikos II it had been the custom to endow them by imperial charter and enrich them with landed property. An example is the famous monastery of Megaspelaion, nestling under its cliff in the mountains north of Kalavryta, where the Orthodox Metropolitan of Patras took up residence in 1354, waiting to displace the Latin Archbishop from his see whenever the occasion might arise.[19]

Sadly enough, these years of mutual tolerance have left no detailed record of the personal relations existing between Greek and Latin leaders in the Morea. It cannot be supposed that their contacts were anything but frequent and sometimes cordial. No doubt the appropriate visits and courtesies were exchanged. But the stability and continuity of government in the Despotate contrasted strongly with the decaying institutions of Achaia, where the fading authority of the absentee Prince yielded to that of local territorial magnates. These were almost exclusively of Italian origin and had no roots in the principality. Meanwhile, French families which had held the land for as long as a hundred and fifty years were dying out. At Patras the Italian Archbishop Frangipani ruled a little state of his own, professing allegiance to the Holy See and vitrually independent of the bailie. The important barony of Damala in the north-east of the Peloponnese had passed to the Genoese clan of Zaccaria, which had long occupied Chios but had been expelled from that island and Andronikos III. Martino, the head of the family, married Jacqueline, the last representative of the junior branch of the de la Roches, and also acquired by purchase the barony of Chalandritza. In much the same way Argos and Nauplia, the two remaining fiefs of the Burgundian duchy of Athens, had first devolved on a Frenchman, Gautier d'Enghien, married to Isabelle, last of the de Briennes, and then to a Venetian, Pietro Cornaro, married to Marie, the last of the Enghiens; and when Cornaro died she sold both these vital strongholds outright to the Republic, much to the latter's satisfaction. But the most remarkable transformation of the Latin scene in the latter half of the fourteenth century was effected by a new and supremely enterprising race of Italian adventurers, the Acciaiuoli of Florence, who, unlike the Zaccaria, had previously been strangers to the Levant. The next chapter will show how they rose to dominate the tottering principality and to oust the Catalans from their Athenian duchy.

CHAPTER EIGHT

A Florentine at Athens

THE ANCESTORS OF the Florentine Dukes of Athens were humble folk from Brescia. Their story begins with a certain Gugliarello, who migrated from northern Italy to Florence in the twelfth century and set up a factory for making steel. In the course of the next hundred years they turned from manufacturing to the more profitable business of banking. This moved them up the social scale and they were soon admitted to magistracies and offices of state, while their adherence to the cause of the Guelfs commended them to the Angevin court at Naples. In 1323 King Robert appointed a member of the family to his Council and in the following year the banking house is mentioned, along with two other Florentine concerns, the Bardi and the Peruzzi, as agreeing to finance the Greek enterprises of John of Gravina and Philip of Tarentum. From then onwards the Acciaiuoli kept a permanent agency in the Morea.

They were of course interested in the considerable trade passing through the ports of the principality and particularly through Glarentza, where the agency was situated, but more exciting prospects of profit and power were offered by the Prince's recurring need of money for campaigns, the maintenance of fortresses and state expenses of all kinds. Warfare especially had become very costly. In the great days of Achaia the Villehardouins relied on the feudal levy of their vassals and the latters' dependants, but in the fourteenth century the Latin manpower of the principality was on the wane and the only alternative was to hire professionals. Mercenaries required punctual payment and sufficient quantities of cash could only be obtained from the bankers. Even so, borrowing had its limits and that was no doubt the main reason why promising ventures like those of John of Gravina and Gautier de Brienne were prematurely abandoned. And when John bartered away his title to Achaia for that of King of Albania and a payment of five thousand ounces of gold it was the Acciaiuoli who advanced that amount. However, the bank's total investment in the Morea during the period was calculated at the immense sum of 40,000 gold ounces.[1]

That was the moment when Niccolo, the son of King Robert's councillor, came to the fore. Born in 1310, he was only twenty-one when his father entrusted him with the management of the bank's operations in the Angevin kingdom, but his brilliant abilities, combined with his handsome appearance and charm of manner, vastly impressed the monarch, who appointed him chamberlain and confidential adviser to his sister-in-law, Catherine de Valois, when she assumed power in Achaia in the name of her young son Robert. After personally negotiating the indemnity to John of Gravina, Niccolo ingratiated himself so deeply with Catherine that he was commonly regarded as her lover. In an act dated 1335 he is described as 'regius cambellanus, dilectus consiliarius et familiaris noster domesticus'. (Royal chamberlain, dear counsellor and member of our household.)[2] But he was also busily employed in turning himself into a nobleman and a landowner. King Robert made him a knight in the same year, and his position as creditor of the principality permitted him to acquire by donation or purchase a whole series of estates in Elis and Messenia as well as in the Argolid, where he secured a castle and fiefs formerly held by the Ghisi, Constables of Achaia. He was soon numbered among the chief barons and began to cut a figure in the military and diplomatic world. He built a castle near Kalamata to discourage the Greco-Slav chieftains of Taygetos, cultivated the good graces of the Venetians and contributed to the common defence against Turkish corsairs. In fact he became the most influential personage in the Frankish Morea, not excluding the bailies who came and went. When he returned to Italy in 1341 the fame of his lightning career had preceded him and he was greeted on arrival by a fulsome letter of congratulation from his countryman Boccaccio.

He went on to attain even greater heights as a statesman of the Neapolitan Kingdom. The titles which he collected, honorary or substantial, included those of hereditary Grand Seneschal of Sicily, Count of Malta and Gozo and Count of Melfi. He devoted his main energies to the service of his sovereign, Queen Joanna, who, on succeeding her grandfather King Robert in 1343, was involved in bitter dynastic warfare between the Angevins of Naples and the junior but powerful branch of the same house then occupying the throne of Hungary. Although he lived for another quarter of a century he never went back to Greece. But far from neglecting his personal stake in the Morea, he was constantly adding to it, besides providing a stream of good advice to the Prince's bailies. Indeed the latter would otherwise have been left to their own devices, for Catherine de Valois died in 1346 and Prince Robert was at the same time captured by the Hungarians. Subsequently neither he nor his wife, Marie de Bourbon, found time to visit Achaia, but in 1356 they had the sense to ask the Grand Seneschal to 'reform' the principality, with special regard to the Turkish danger. Whatever practical measures the Prince may have had in mind, Niccolo's response to his appeal was to take a great deal more power into his own hands. He came to the conclusion that the key point in the defence of the Morea against the Turks was Corinth, with its ports on both sides of the isthmus protected by the towering fortress of Acrocorinth. With Robert's approval he took over the barony and repaired the fortifications. He brought back the inhabitants of the region, who had fled inland to their homes, and remitted their arrears of taxation. For his own part he announced that, whereas he had obtained exemption from all feudal dues in respect of his fiefs in other parts of Achaia, this privilege would not apply to his Corinthian barony. The defensive works were carried out at his own expense and for the time fulfilled their purpose.

While he himself remained in Italy, a whole tribe of his Acciaiuoli relatives were waiting to undertake whatever responsibilities he might be pleased to allot to them in Greece. In the same year (1358) as he took over Corinth he drew up a will which made his intentions clear. He directed that his ample inheritance should be divided between his only surviving son Angelo and a second Angelo, the son of a cousin, whom he had adopted as his own child. The former was to have his Neapolitan dignities, Corinth and all lands in Elis and Messenia which had not been earmarked for the second Angelo. The latter was to receive the former Ghisi lands in the Argolid, but only on condition that he succeeded in marrying Fiorenza Sanudo, heiress to the Duchy of Naxos. If he did not so succeed, he would take the Messenian lands and the first Angelo would have those in the Argolid. The point of this somewhat confusing proviso was that an union between the Acciaiuoli and the Sanudi would bring a cluster of desirable Aegean islands into the former's net.[3]

As it happened, things did not work out so neatly as Niccolo, who lived until 1365, had hoped. His plans for the advancement of the second Angelo were firmly vetoed by the Venetians, who refused to tolerate so blatant an intrusion into their maritime preserves. Fiorenza was of Venetian descent, and they were determined that she should marry only a Venetian. As for the first Angelo, he showed no inclination to repeat his father's role on the Greek stage and preferred a career in Italy. Consequently the way was cleared for three more young kinsmen and brothers, Nerio (also an adopted son), Giovanni and Donato, to make their fortunes in Greece. At first it was Donato who acted as Niccolo's deputy at Corinth, but after Niccolo's death he ceded this all-important office to Nerio, the most enterprising of the second generation of the

Acciaiuoli and the author of their future aggrandisement. As soon as he was installed at Corinth, he bought from Marie de Bourbon the barony of Vostitza, one of the original Moreot fiefs, which lay between his Corinthian territory and that of the Archbishopric of Patras. With this acquisition the whole Peloponnesian coastline of the Gulf passed under the direct control of the Acciaiuoli, since in 1360 Nerio's brother, Giovanni, had been conveniently elevated to the Patras see, and when he died shortly afterwards he was at once followed by the second Angelo, who was thus consoled for his failure to secure the Naxian heiress. Thanks to the skill with which Niccolo spun the complex web of his family relationships, and of the favour which he enjoyed at the Papal court, the Florentines had already come near to founding their own state.[4]

Nerio's domain and the Greek Despotate were rocks of stability by comparison with the principality. Indeed for the next twenty years Achaia lapses into a blur of anarchy through which it is hard to distinguish the principal figures and to mark the significant events. Robert, Latin Emperor, Prince of Tarentum and Achaia, had wished all his titles to devolve on his younger brother Philip, but his widow, Marie de Bourbon, was determined to obtain the Greek principality for Hugues de Lusignan, her son by her first marriage. Hugues, titular Prince of Galilee, was the nephew of King Peter I of Cyprus, where the Lusignan sovereigns had reached the apex of their power. Founded before the Fourth Crusade, the Cypriot monarchy had turned out to be the most solid and durable of the Latin states in the eastern Mediterranean. But although its territory consisted of one of the two great Greek islands of the Levant, the Lusignan interest was for obvious reasons of geography focussed not on Greece but on the neighbouring shores of Asia, on Palestine, Syria and the regions of the Taurus, and the expulsion of the last Latins from the mainland in the late thirteenth century had not ended this preoccupation. The Kings of Cyprus had inherited the title of Kings of Jerusalem and had not given up hope of reconquering the Holy Land. Relations between the courts of Cyprus and Achaia were amicable enough. Noble persons passed freely from the service of one ruler to that of the other. Intermarriage was frequent, and a knight of Famagusta would feel equally at home in Andravida. His culture too was French and his second language the popular Greek of the Middle Ages. On the other hand the warlike and political activities of the two states seldom impinged on one another.

King Peter himself was a fervent and romantic Crusader in a hard and selfish age when such fiery enthusiasm was rarely encountered. He felt a compulsive urge to drive the infidels once more from Jerusalem. He spent the early years of his reign in raising support for his plans in Western Europe, patiently journeying from court to court. From most of his fellow sovereigns he elicited nothing but polite gestures and insincere assurances, but Venice was more forthcoming and undertook to provide the necessary ships. The Order of St John was equally co-operative and the prospect of adventure attracted individual warriors from all over Europe. In the autumn of 1365 a vast fleet and army was gathered at Rhodes, the headquarters of the Hospitallers. Peter, who was in sole command of the expedition, had prudently decided to lead it against the Sultanate of Egypt. He reckoned that if he could seize a strong base in that country he could either use it for a springboard for a later attack on Palestine, or alternatively exchange it by negotiation for his ultimate goal, Jerusalem. Consequently he sailed straight for Alexandria, the chief trading port of the Moslem world, and took it by surprise. The horrors of the inevitable sack and massacre exceeded even those perpetrated by previous Crusaders at Jerusalem and Constantinople. But as soon as the enormous plunder had been collected and shared out, the soldiers' inclination for further campaigning evaporated. The King was obliged to return in disappointment to Cyprus and to disband his armada.[5]

But although the venture had ended so tamely it temporarily enhanced the glory and military reputation of the Lusignans and aided Hugues in his bid for Achaia. Several factors favoured his candidature. His mother already possessed numerous castles and estates in the principality; he could presumably rely on the sympathy, if not the active support, of the Despot of Mistra, husband of a Lusignan kinswoman, whom King Peter himself came to visit in 1368; and he was also well supplied with funds. From the point of view of primogeniture Hugues had in fact a better right to the throne of Cyprus than his uncle, since he was the son of Peter's elder brother, but he had been content to abandon it in return for an annual indemnity of 50,000 *hyperpera*. Nevertheless the barons refused to accept him. They declared for the Angevin Philip and, headed by their bailie, Centurione Zaccaria of Damala and Chalandritza, prepared to resist his attempt to enforce his claim. The Acciaiuoli too were opposed to the Lusignan pretender. While Nerio seems to have taken no part in the struggle for the succession, Angelo vigorously defended his Archbishopric of Patras against the troops whom Hugues had brought from Cyprus and Provence, and drove them back into Messenia. Thereupon the Despot Manuel intervened on the Lusignan side and so did Guy d'Enghien, lord of Argos, who was

Marie's cousin. No major conflict, however, developed between the two evenly matched contestants. Thanks to the mediation of Count Amadeo of Savoy, who had put in at Navarino on a mission to bring aid to the Emperor John Palaeologos at Constantinople, their quarrel was patched up. Eventually, after the murder of King Peter in 1369, Hugues withdrew from the Morea on receipt of another annuity, a form of settlement which evidently appealed to him.[6] The ever recurring influence of dynastic relationships, cutting across the barriers of race and religion, on events in the area is further attested by the fact that Amadeo was first cousin to the Byzantine emperor.

Philip II of Tarentum survived only until 1373, when the title of Prince was claimed by his sister's son Jacques des Baux. The des Baux, Provençal by origin, had come to Naples with the first Angevin and belonged to the highest nobility of the Kingdom. Nevertheless Jacques proved no more acceptable to the barons of the Morea than Hugues de Lusignan and for the same reason; they had become accustomed to the loose and frequently chaotic administration of the bailies and tended to prefer an absentee Prince to one who might impose an inconvenient degree of authority on the feudatories. Despite possible risks to the security of Achaia as a whole they would rather dispense with a strong hand. Moreover the suzerain of the principality, Queen Joanna, was not only opposed on personal grounds to the des Baux, who had previously raised a rebellion against her, but also tempted to assume the title for herself, especially as James II of Majorca, her third husband, was the great-grandson of Guillaume de Villehardouin. She accordingly welcomed a delegation from the principality when it arrived at Naples to sound her out about the succession. The four nobles who composed it were an interesting racial cross-section of the baronage of Achaia in the latter half of the fourteenth century. The first, Leonardo Tocco, Count of Cephalonia, was an Italian whose father had married the sister of the last Orsini; the second, Erard, Baron of Arkadia, a Frenchman with a sister married to the Greek archon John Laskaris Kalopheros; the third, John Misito, a Greek pure and simple and the fourth, the Grand Constable Centurione Zaccaria, stemmed from a Genoese clan which had made its fortune under the early Palaeologues as lords of Chios and exploiters on the Emperors' behalf of the alum mines of Phocaea on the Asia Minor coast. They had in fact become almost more Byzantine than Italian, and the names of Centurione's son, Andronikos Asen, who acted as temporary bailie in the delegation's absence, pointedly recalled his family's imperial connexions.[7]

The barons readily agreed to recognise the Queen as their Princess, in

171

return for her promise to respect the customs of Achaia. But her new bailie, Francesco di San Severino, proved to be a trouble-maker. He began by making an unprovoked attack on Gardiki, a frontier town belonging to the Byzantine Despotate. He failed to take it but defeated a force which Manuel led to its relief.[8] Next he picked another boundary quarrel with the Venetians of Modon, which the Queen had to order him to settle. By that time she was tiring of her responsibilities in Achaia and soon hit on a way of shedding them. In 1376 she concluded a bargain by which the Knights of St John, who had held fiefs in the Morea since its conquest by the first Villehardouin, undertook to govern it for five years and pay an annual rent of four thousand ducats. Their familiarity with the Knights Hospitallers appears to have reconciled the barons to his transaction. Furthermore the Grand Master of the Order, the Spaniard Juan Fernandez de Heredia, was anxious to reassert the Frankish cause in Greece. He took as lively an interest in the principality's origins and traditions as in its survival, and one of his most notable acts was to commission the compilation of the Aragonese chronicle *Libro de los Fechos et Conquistas del Principado de la Morea.*[9]

Heredia's aim was imaginative and enterprising. He was keenly conscious of the frailty of the small Latin states of Greece in face of the all-devouring Turkish expansion and regarded it as the duty of his Order to inspire and co-ordinate a credible defence against the invaders. In northern Greece the situation was particularly alarming. The Turks were well established in the southern Balkans and under their dynamic Sultan Murad I (1326–89) were moving inexorably towards the conquest of the whole of Thrace and Macedonia. The disintegration of the Serbian Empire of Stephen Dushan after the latter's death in 1355 had fatally weakened the defence of the Slav kingdoms. Adrianople was taken from the Byzantines in 1369 and two years later the Serbian princes who had inherited Dushan's fragmented state were overwhelmed in a battle on the river Maritza. Thessalonica was attacked in 1372 and it seemed certain that Turkish spearheads would soon be penetrating into Thessaly and Epiros. After Dushan's death these regions had been unstably divided among minor dynasts of Serbian and Albanian origin. Thessaly was ruled by Serbian princes of the house of Urosh. Nikephoros II, the last of the Dukas Despots, managed to regain possession of Epiros for three years but succumbed while fighting the Albanians, who subdued the entire country down to the Gulf of Corinth.

The Grand Master was also responding to a new initiative by the Holy See. In 1373 Pope Gregory XI convened at Thebes, capital of the Catalan duchy, a meeting of all the powers, great and small, whose territories were threatened by the Turkish advance. Invitations were sent to various sovereigns, to Venice and Genoa, to the Knights Hospitallers and to local magnates such as Nerio Acciaiuoli, the Duke of Naxos in the Archipelago and the Marquis of Boudonitza. As had so often happened, the appeal was well received but ignored in practice. Only Heredia treated it in earnest and took action. As a first step in strengthening the Latin position he decided to secure the fortress-port of Lepanto (Naupaktos) on the Gulf of Corinth, which the Angevins had held for eight years but had recently fallen to the Albanian princeling John Boua Spata. The Knights duly recovered it, but their progress came to a sudden end when their Grand Master was trapped in an Albanian ambush and sold ignominiously by Boua Spata to the Turks. By the time he had been ransomed and had returned to the Peloponnese it was no longer possible for the Order to resume the offensive. Its military energies had been stultified and the allegiance of its members divided by the current schism in the papacy, some declaring for Clement VII and others for his rival Urban VI. Lepanto was lost for the second time and the Knights were forced to turn for support to Nerio and the Greeks of Mistra. When their lease of the principality expired in 1381 they were only too glad to surrender it to Queen Joanna.[10]

One of the precautions which they took during Heredia's imprisonment was to hire for a few months the services of a small body of Navarrese soldiers of fortune. These mercenaries were part of a larger company recruited from both sides of the Pyrenees, from Gascony and Roussillon, Navarre and Catalonia. The latter part of the fourteenth century, the age of the Hundred Years War, of the Black Prince, Bertrand du Guesclin and Sir John Hawkwood, was the heyday of these bands of professional warriors. This particular Company, originally raised by the King of Navarre, found after various adventures a new employer in Jacques des Baux, the enemy of the Queen of Naples, who still considered himself Prince of Achaia. He now saw new opportunities for vindicating his rights in the difficulties of the Hospitallers and in the confused situation at Naples resulting from the strife for the crown which had broken out between Joanna and a pretender, her kinsman Charles of Durazzo, and which led to her dethronement in 1381. In that struggle Jacques naturally took the pretender's side, and his Navarrese helped to expel Joanna's adherents from Corfu.

Their subsequent movements are not easy to trace, but they are next reported as launching a surprise and apparently uncalled for attack on the Duchy of Athens. It is possible that this was undertaken on the orders of Jacques des Baux, who, although he was primarily interested in

Achaia, could well have aspired to revive the claim of suzerainty over the Duchy which the Princes of Achaia had frequently asserted in pre-Catalan times. More probably, however, the leaders of the Company, Mahiot de Coquerel and Pierre de St Superan, were tempted to intervene in favour of a faction among the Catalans opposed to the rule of the reigning Duke, King Peter IV of Aragon, and the Vicar-General, Luis Fadrique, Count of Salona. Without exploring for the moment the causes of this rift, which dangerously undermined the solidity of the Catalan state, we may suspect that the Navarrese captains scented advantage for themselves in putting an end to the existing government at Thebes and Athens. It is doubly ironical that the blow which struck the descendants of the Catalan invaders of 1311 should have been inflicted by a very similar company of mercenaries originating from much the same corner of Europe as their predecessors.

The date of the Navarrese aggression is uncertain but it cannot have been later than 1380. The Company entered the duchy from the north and at first made good progress. The Marquis of Boudonitza, who controlled the pass of Thermopylae, let them through unopposed. The castles of Lamia and Salona withstood their assaults, but they took by storm the two strongest fortresses of Boeotia, Livadia and Thebes. They then pressed on into Attica and laid siege to the Acropolis. However, its castellan, Romeo de Bellarbe, assisted by Demetrios Rendis, the Greek notary who had achieved Catalan citizenship and high office in the duchy, beat them off and gained time for reinforcements from Aragon, under the King's new Vicar-General, Felipe Dalmau, Viscount of Rocaberti, to come to the rescue. When they sailed into the Piraeus the Navarrese found themselves in an awkward position, squeezed between the relieving forces and those of the Count of Salona advancing on Thebes from the north. Diplomatically, too, they were isolated, as Peter of Aragon was busy pressing the Latin powers with interests in the Levant, as well as the Duchy's immediate neighbours, to combine against the new intruders. They therefore proceeded to seek an accommodation with the Vicar-General, who himself thankfully grasped the opportunity to get rid of them on easy terms. It was arranged that they should retire to the Morea, where they still had to perform the task intended for them by Jacques des Baux.[11]

Having thus disengaged themselves, they crossed into the Peloponnese and marched along the coast to Glarentza without encountering any opposition. Indeed the barons had already tried to make the best of an uncertain future by recognising des Baux, the Company's employer, as their Prince. But Jacques still showed no inclination to come to the Morea. In appointing Mahiot de Coquerel as bailie, he was either accepting the inevitable or indicating his preference for the Navarrese over the Moreot barons as the guardians of his personal authority. Thenceforth the real power was shared between the Company and a group of established feudatories, among whom the Zaccaria were the leading figures, with the former, the *Societas Sistens in principatu Achaiae*, as the dominant partner. The installation of the Navarrese involved nothing like the disruption of the existing order which the Catalan Company had brought about at Athens. At the same time the change can hardly have occurred without friction and the ejection of some of the existing land-owners to make room for the newcomers. It is certain that the Acciaiuoli lost the numerous properties, the heritage of Niccolo, which they possessed outside their Corinthian domain.

Jacques des Baux, the shadowy Prince who never showed his face in Greece but took so much trouble to vindicate his title, died in 1383. For the next twenty years the Navarrese leaders, first de Coquerel and then St Superan, administered Achaia, or what was left of it, without paying overmuch attention to the intrigues of different princely claimants, French and Italian, who bickered in the background about their presumed rights to the title, while the ultimate sovereignty was also disputed between rival contenders for the Neapolitan throne. Louis d'Anjou of France, Louis de Clermont, Duc de Bourbon, and Amadeo of Piedmont were all involved in complicated diplomatic manoeuvres and military plans concerning the Morea, and even the Grand Master of the Hospital was tempted to join the competitors, but all their schemes and combinations tended to cancel each other out. Whenever the dust raised by the activities of the various pretenders clears sufficiently for us to discern what is actually happening, it is always the same scene that is revealed—the Navarrese firmly established in the seat of power and playing off one eager potentate against the other. The air of total unreality investing the projects of the Western princes contrasts pointedly with the starkness of the supreme danger facing the Christian states of Greece, the imminent prospect of a Turkish invasion in overwhelming force. Apart from the offshore duchies (Cephalonia and the Archipelago) those communities had in effect been narrowed down to a truncated Achaia, an expanding Despotate, a still intact but exhausted Duchy of Athens and the dispersed but formidable bulwarks of Venetian sea power. And at the centre of events Nerio Acciaiuoli, anything but a spent force, was watching his opportunities from the vantage point of Corinth.[12]

In the same year as the Navarrese settled in the Morea a new Despot, Theodore Palaeologos, began to rule at Mistra. He was the fourth and youngest son of John V and Helen Cantacuzena, daughter of John VI. His appointment was part of a political rearrangement by which his harassed father hoped to prolong, so long as Sultan Murad might permit, the survival of the remaining fragments of the Byzantine realm. The whole course of John's long reign had been marked by disastrous decline. While the difficulties of the age might have daunted a sovereign of much higher talents than he himself possessed, he was not only unfortunate but incapable. His earlier years had been bedevilled by the civil conflict with his father-in-law and the later period by similar strife with his son and co-Emperor Andronikos IV. The interval had been filled with his well-intentioned but futile efforts to enlist military assistance from the West against the Turks. In vain he visited Hungary, Naples, Rome and Venice: in vain he prostrated himself before the Pope, to the scandal of the enormous majority of his own subjects, and announced his adherence to the Roman Catholic faith. His activities evoked only indifference abroad and disloyalty at home. So he took the only alternative available to him, which was to purchase comparative safety and tranquillity by a humiliating transaction with Murad. By the later seventies the Byzantine Empire had become a tribute-paying ally, if not a plain vassal of the Sultan, and was even compelled to render him military service when called upon to do so.

So high a degree of subservience to the Turks may not have been initially demanded from John's sons Manuel, who deputized for his father at Thessalonica, and Theodore who commanded in the Morea. Nevertheless the latter made a shaky start. His predecessor's long and successful viceroyalty had endeared him to the Moreots, who would have probably preferred another Cantacuzene to a Palaeologue. An obvious candidate from the former family was indeed at hand in Manuel's elder brother Matthew, a tried soldier and administrator who had shared the throne with his father shortly before the latter's fall. He had also been residing quietly in the Peloponnese at his brother's side for about ten years. On Manuel's death he appears to have taken temporary charge of the government but to have relinquished it when, in 1381, the old ex-Emperor, the monk Joasaph, arrived for the last time at Mistra from Constantinople bearing the news that he had personally agreed with his former rival, John V, that Theodore was the right choice for the succession. Even so the Emperor's wishes were challenged by Matthew's son Demetrios. Furious at being passed over, he headed a revolt of his own partisans, and called in Latin—presumably Navarrese—and

Turkish troops to his aid. It was two years before Theodore managed to pacify the country. He and Nerio had learned to distrust the Navarrese, and began to develop a community of interest.[13]

Nerio had long detected signs of weakness in the Catalan state. Outwardly little had changed in the duchy since the days when its masters had been treated by Popes and Princes as the outcasts of mediaeval society. When this hostility faded, as it was bound to do, the Catalans came to be regarded as respectable vassals of the Sicilian Crown. Moreover it was recognised that their compact and easily defensible territory, protected by natural barriers and by fortresses in depth, constituted an almost impenetrable obstacle for invaders from the north. So long as the Catalans maintained their guard, the approaches to the isthmus of Corinth were safe from Byzantines, Serbs or even Turks. But, as Miller justly observes, 'soon after they became respectable they ceased to be formidable'.[14] The Company lost its sting when it ceased to be a people in arms and settled down as a community of land-holders and burgesses. Nor was the system of sovereignty by which the absent Duke, the King of Sicily, entrusted the government to a Vicar-General who was often also an absentee and represented by a deputy, conducive to efficiency or harmony. Much the same system indeed prevailed in the principality, with its rapid changes of bailie, but whereas the barons of Achaia could usually be trusted to act in concert, the quarrels of the higher feudatories of the duchy were harder to compose. Only a very strong Vicar-General was capable of imposing his authority. If he was not at loggerheads with the hereditary Marshal, he was more often than not guilty himself of irresponsible behaviour, as happened when Roger de Lluria took a body of Turks into his service and allowed them to garrison Thebes.[15]

This incident seems to have thoroughly shocked the other states of Greece. Even Frederick III of Sicily, the sovereign Duke, who was not given to forceful intervention in the affairs of Athens, ordered the replacement of Lluria by Matteo de Moncada, a leading Sicilian nobleman of Aragonese descent who had once already filled the office. But Moncada's previous experience had made him reluctant to resume it. While not refusing the charge outright, he resorted the to time-honoured Spanish expedient of *obedezco pero no cumplo* (I obey but do not comply) and avoided setting off a second time for Greece. His attempt to administer the duchy through deputies proved a failure; it only sharpened existing dissensions, and the King was eventually forced to restore Lluria for want of a better man. By now, however, the neighbours of Athens were in no doubt that its stability had been seriously impaired and suspected that it was ready to succumb to a sudden *coup de main*. Such an attempt was in fact mounted in about 1370, after Lluria's death and his succession by Matteo de Peralta, by the two Enghien brothers, the heirs of the de Brienne dukes. The elder, Louis Count of Conversano and titular Duke of Athens, happened at that time to be bailie of Achaia, while his brother Guy held the family fief of Argos which had come down to them from the de la Roches. The pair applied to Venice for leave to use Negroponte as a base for their expedition but the Republic, seeing that it stood to gain nothing for itself from an old-fashioned enterprise of this kind, would have nothing to do with the proposal. Consequently the Enghiens got no further than the walls of Athens, from which they were easily repulsed. But in their advance and subsequent retreat they passed in full view of Nerio's Corinth.[16]

In 1374 Nerio felt that it was his own turn to strike. He had spent nearly ten years building up his resources and had plenty of money to hire ships and troops. His target, modest enough for the first stage of his plan, was the little city of Megara, one of those tenaciously long-lived communities, very typical of Greece, which has preserved its name and essential character unchanged since pre-Classical times. In the Middle Ages, as at other epochs, it was a point of strategic value, covering the northern approach to the precipitous cliff road (the Kaki Skala) which led to Corinth, and in the other direction guarding the two roads which forked left and right to Thebes and Athens, as well as an useful anchorage just outside the bay of Salamis. For the time being Nerio was content with this successful probe and attempted no further advance.[17] Fresh disturbances broke out in the duchy after 1377 when the Duke, Frederick III of Sicily, died leaving no male heir. This event divided the Catalans into two factions, those who were content to accept his daughter Maria as sovereign and a more influential party which preferred his brother-in-law Peter of Aragon, and it was their quarrel that enabled the Navarrese to break into the duchy and bring it close to collapse. Nevertheless Nerio was no longer in a position to apply the decisive blow. He had suffered equally rough treatment from the Navarrese when they reached Achaia and was looking round for an ally. He soon found a suitable one in Theodore Palaeologos, who was beset by internal difficulties and equally nervous of Navarrese aggression. The Despot hurried to reach an understanding with Nerio and was glad to take his beautiful daughter Bartolommea as his wife. Thus a Florentine girl from Corinth succeeded a French princess from Cyprus as chatelaine of Greek Mistra.[18]

As soon as the Navarrese had gone Peter and his vassals seem to have discounted danger to Athens from any other quarter. A man of some culture, the King was delighted with his dukedom and with the Acropolis, which he described as 'the most precious jewel that exists in the world and such that all the Kings of Christendom together could in vain imitate'.[19] The Catalan notables for their part, meeting at Athens and Salona, proceeded to address detailed petitions to their sovereign, under the name of capitulations, specifying the status, privileges and immunities which their communities expected to enjoy in future in return for the formal renewal of their homage. These documents suggest that the democratic principles on which the original constitution of the Company had rested had largely fallen into abeyance and that the real power had passed to a few large feudatories and castellans of fortified towns. The former political organization of a citizenry in arms is no longer in evidence. On the other hand we find the representatives of Athens asking the Duke to grant them autonomy from Thebes and the remainder of the duchy, on their own merits and as the reward of their successful defiance of the Navarrese. This was not, however, a concession which Peter was willing to grant, although he was otherwise most liberal in his response to his subjects' requests. Among the individuals favoured was Demetrios Rendis, the Athenian notary who acted as a kind of State Secretary to successive Latin governments in his homeland throughout the second half of the fourteenth century. As early as 1366 he had won the right to Catalan franchise which was awarded to very few Greeks, and later he had taken part in the defence of Megara against Nerio and that of Athens against the Navarrese. In recognition of his loyalty he was now appointed hereditary Chancellor of the city of Athens with a substantial salary payable from the customs receipts, and confirmed in all his former properties and perquisites. Another recipient of Catalan rights was a Megarian woman, the mistress of Romeo de Bellarbe, the warden of the Acropolis.

Despite the general euphoria the duchy still lacked a firm and lasting central authority. At first it looked as if this might be provided by the Vicar-General Rocaberti and strengthened by the projected marriage between his son and the heiress to the County of Salona, the most important of the Catalan fiefs. The last holder of the title, Luis Fadrique, died in 1362. He was a former Vicar-General and a kinsman of the Duke, and his domain comprised the whole region between the Gulf of Corinth and the Spercheios valley, studded with fortresses and little towns, ethnically and in sentiment very Greek. He was also the husband of a Greek lady of extremely high rank, Helen Cantacuzena, daughter of the co-Emperor Matthew and first cousin of the Despot Theodore. But Rocaberti, in the manner of Catalan Vicars-General, became so deeply involved in Spanish affairs that he left his office to a deputy, Ramon de Vilanova; and when the latter, too, abandoned his charge for similar reasons authority, so far as it was at all effective, was divided between the Countess Helen of Salona, the two sons of Roger de Lluria in Boeotia and the new military commander at Athens, Pedro de Pau.

Nerio waited until the disunity among the duchy's defenders was at its height. When in 1385 he at last sent his troops forward from Megara he encountered little resistance. His Albanian and Turkish cavalry easily brushed aside the Llurias and Pedro de Pau was shut up in the Acropolis.[20] Obviously Nerio had very carefully prepared the ground. His venture would have stood no chance of success unless it had enjoyed at least the tacit support of the Venetians of Negroponte, and unless they had been satisfied that their own interests would be better served by the presence of a vigorous Italian ruler at Athens than by the continuance of an increasingly feckless and unsteady Catalan regime. Fortunately Nerio's wife was a Saraceno from Euboea, and the Saraceni were citizens of Venice. Even so we are told that Venetian policy would not permit him to maintain a fleet of his own either at Corinth or at Athens, and that he captured the Piraeus with a single hired galley. Yet, although the Acropolis held out for three whole years, Nerio's mercenaries overran the rest of Attica and Boeotia without any trouble; perhaps the surrender of so many strong castles was prearranged. The only serious failure which he sustained was at Salona. When he suggested that his brother-in-law, Pietro Saraceno, might be a suitable match for the Countess Helen's daughter, he was contemptuously rebuffed. After her disagreeable experience with Rocaberti, the grand-daughter of John VI Cantacuzenos was taking no chances with a similar proposition from a Florentine money-broker, even if he had disposed of his own daughter on her Palaeologos cousin. She betrothed hers to a petty Serbian prince, who at least had the advantage of being Orthodox, and preserved the independence of her domain for a few more years.[21]

Whatever inducements or threats Nerio may have employed to discourage opposition, it is hard to account for the smoothness with which he took possession of the duchy. Apart from the one small engagement with the Llurias and a bloodless blockade of the Athenian citadel, we hear of no battles or sieges. Even more puzzling is the speed with which all trace of the Catalan occupation vanished from the scene. The big feudatories, a mere handful, no doubt made their bargain with

Nerio and found a comfortable refuge in Spain or Aragonese Sicily, but it is curious that the whole Iberian element in the population of the duchy should so suddenly have been dissolved after seventy years of apparently solid settlement, leaving the word 'Catalan' to linger in Greek folklore solely as a bogy to scare children, or as a term of intemperate abuse. What can have happened to the main body of Catalan citizens?[22] A few, we may suppose, took ship to Spain; others may have stayed behind to be absorbed by their Greek neighbours; others perhaps took service with the Navarrese in the Morea, just as the followers of the French knights who fell at the Kephissos were surely made welcome in Angevin Achaia. As for the Catalan state, capitulations and all, it was transformed, as it were overnight, into the private property of a house of Florentine traders. Its feudal structure was promptly dismantled and the administration, directed by salaried agents of the Acciaiuoli, Florentines and other Italians, was thenceforth run on strictly commercial lines.

The new dispensation favoured a revival of the Greek national element which had been so long damped down under the Burgundians and the Catalans. The proportion of Latins to Greeks in the population was further reduced after Nerio's coup and he was forced to rely to a much greater extent on the support, or at least the consent, of his Greek subjects. He began his rule with a number of overtures calculated to win their sympathy. They were increasingly encouraged, under Florentine supervision, to conduct their own municipal affairs, while the indispensable Demetrios Rendi and other members of the notarial class multiplied their functions. Greek became the official language of Nerio's secretariat. A more popular and indeed almost revolutionary step was the reinstallation, after the lapse of 180 years, of a Greek Orthodox Archbishop in the metropolitan see of Athens. At Nerio's invitation, the Byzantine Holy Synod appointed a certain Dorotheos from Thessalonica (then temporarily under Turkish occupation) to the place once filled by Michael of Chonae. His title of 'Exarch of All Hellas' emphasized the political nature of his mission, as viewed from the Byzantine angle, and it was not long before he came under suspicion for working against the Latin interest and even for devious intrigues with the Turks. Nevertheless, once the concession was made it could not be reversed, and the Acciaiuoli could only hope that the advantages of the philhellenic policy to which they were now committed would continue to outweigh its drawbacks. Nerio only insisted that the Exarch should reside and have his church in the lower town, on the edge of the ancient

Agora, while a Catholic Archbishop, now reduced to the status of the ruler's private chaplain, continued to officiate in the resplendent Parthenon.[23]

Whereas Nerio sought tranquillity within his boundaries by offering toleration to the Greeks, his external security depended heavily on the maintenance of good relations with Venice, the sole Levantine power capable of blocking the progress of the Turkish Sultans. Though weakened by the long and inconclusive struggle with its rival, Genoa, the Republic was still enormously strong and was steadily strengthening and extending its network of bases in the eastern Mediterranean. Crete, Kythera, Euboea, Modon and Coron it already held; in 1386 it seized Corfu from the Angevins of Naples and two years later it moved to take possession of Nauplia and Argos. The ensuing developments revealed the fragility of Nerio's alliances and demonstrated all too clearly that he could not afford to offend Venice.

When Marie d'Enghien, the last holder of the two former Peloponnesian fiefs of the Duchy of Athens, lost her Venetian husband, Pietro Cornaro, she sold the Argolid, complete with its castles and vital strategic and trading harbour, outright to the Republic. This turn of affairs was equally distasteful to Nerio and to his son-in-law, the Despot Theodore, whose respective domains were separated from one another by the thin strip of the Argolid. Each of them would have been glad to grab it, or at least to partition it with his ally. Moreover, the Despot was anxious to forestall any Venetian encroachments on what he regarded as a Greek preserve. In the event the Venetians were able to take over Nauplia unchallenged, but before they could occupy Argos Theodore snatched it for himself. Rightly suspecting Nerio of collusion, they retaliated by breaking off commercial dealings with Athens and stopping its essential imports and exports. Further, they called on the Navarrese, no friends of Nerio or of the Greeks, to intervene on their behalf.[24]

As neither Venice nor Mistra was willing to yield, the weakness of Nerio's position was suddenly exposed. In an attempt to find a way out of his embarrassment he hastily arranged a meeting with St Superan, the Navarrese leader, but incautiously agreed on the strength of a safe-conduct that it should be held in Achaian territory. As soon as he crossed the border from Corinth he was arrested by the Grand Constable, Asen Zaccaria, and locked up in a castle near Patras. So blatant a breach of mediaeval propriety produced a furious outburst of international activity from the more influential of Nerio's kinsmen. His brothers Angelo, Cardinal-Archbishop of Florence, and Donato, a

Gonfaloniere of the city, prevailed on the Signoria to press his cause at Venice and with the Holy See. Meanwhile his wife Agnes Saraceno, whom he had left at Corinth, offered Theodore a heavy bribe to evacuate Argos and appealed to her other son-in-law Carlo Tocco, Count of Cephalonia and a feudatory of Achaia, to put pressure on the Navarrese. When these urgings had no effect Donato undertook to place the cities of Athens, Thebes and Megara in Venetian hands as guarantees for the eventual cession of Argos, and added to the pledge fifteen thousand ducats' worth of merchandise lying in Nerio's Corinthian warehouses. Yet the Venetians remained obdurate. They had little confidence in Nerio's ability to shift the Greeks from Argos and only came to terms when threatened with Genoese intervention in his favour. At length a compromise was reached whereby they accepted Megara and the available merchandise as guarantees, but with the additional requirement that Nerio's daughter Francesca, Countess of Cephalonia, should be detained as a hostage at Negroponte. Finally, before he could obtain his release, Nerio was obliged to pay a separate ransom to the Navarrese. By that time his formerly ample resources had become so depleted that he could only raise the necessary cash by denuding the Parthenon of its treasures, and particularly of the silver panels which had adorned its doors since the days of Basil II.[25]

Very probably it was the sharpening of the Turkish menace, and the Venetian Republic's anxiety to end the chaotic squabbles between the Christian states of Greece, that prompted its government to settle with Nerio before gaining possession of Argos, which the Despot gave up only in 1394. While the dispute between Venice and the Acciaiuoli was at its height, the completion of the Turkish conquest of the northern Balkans seemed to portend the early fall of the encircled city of Constantinople and the overrunning of Athens, the Morea and all the mainland of Hellas still in Greek or Latin hands. The crushing defeat of the Serbian Tsar Lazar on the Kossovo Polje, the 'Field of Blackbirds', firmly assured Turkish hegemony up to the Save and the Danube. Though Murad himself fell in the battle, his son Bayezit, known as Yilderim (the Thunderbolt) proved an even more merciless and dangerous enemy, disinclined to tolerate the surviving Christian excrescences on the fringe of his empire. For a century and a half Greece had known the Turks as mercenaries and freebooters; it now faced organized attacks by Ottoman forces led by Evrenos Beg, the Sultan's most formidable and fanatical lieutenant. The first of his intrusions is hard to date, but it seems to have occurred even before Murad's death when the Despot Theodore, intent upon seizing Argos, acknowledged

Turkish suzerainty and invoked the aid of Evrenos, who responded by raiding Navarrese territory.

By all logic Nerio would have been wise to pack up and retire to Florence. Yet he refused to behave as if he were ruined and discredited, and still less as if he expected his hard-won domain to be engulfed at any moment by the Turkish flood. Indeed he returned to Athens bent on saving as much as possible from the wreck. Throughout 1391, the year following his release, he plunged into a tortuous negotiation with Amadeo of Piedmont, the most persistent of the pretenders to the principality of Achaia, with the object of helping the latter to expel the Navarrese from the Morea and of thus recovering his lost estates. At the same time St Superan was assuring Amadeo, who was preparing to bring an army to Greece, of the Company's willingness to accept him as their Prince, on condition that they retained their fiefs. However this diplomatic duel was cut short when Amadeo suddenly abandoned his Greek projects. Again seeking support in the West, Nerio then turned to Ladislas of Anjou, King of Naples and theoretical sovereign of both Achaia and Athens, from whom he extracted the title of bailie of Achaia.[26] Since the Navarrese were still in control of the principality, the appointment was a pure formality and brought its holder no profit, but his next step was to induce the King, who was mindful of the former services of the Acciaiuoli to the house of Anjou, to recognise him as the legitimate Duke of Athens, thus confirming the duchy's direct feudal link with Naples and excluding any intermediate vassalage to Achaia. Nerio was inordinately proud of his success in obtaining the ducal title. In his eyes it raised him to a more glorious pinnacle than any hitherto attained by the Acciaiuoli, offspring of bankers and traders. It also consoled him for his grievous material losses and, in some measure, for the terrifying insecurity which overhung the duchy's northern approaches. As the new Duke had no legitimate son, the King designated his brother Donato as his successor and, much to Nerio's gratification, entrusted his other brother, the Cardinal-Archbishop Angelo, with his investiture. Angelo also succeeded to the honorary bailieship of Achaia and as a further rebuff to the Navarrese, the Pope conferred upon him the Archbishopric of Patras.

This shower of honours descended on Nerio and his kinsmen in January 1394, just nine months before his death and while the Turks were already encroaching on his border. With Bayezit busy in Asia, and incidentally heaping humiliations on the two helpless Emperors of Byzantium, John VII and Manuel II, his general Evrenos finally extinguished the Serbian principality in Thessaly and in a further advance occupied the region of Neopatras and Lamia, together with the County of Salona. The Byzantine historian Laonikos Chalkokondylas, the son of an Athenian subject of the Acciaiuoli, later recorded a lurid version of the events which ended in the disappearance of the County and the relegation of Helen Cantacuzena and her daughter to the Sultan's harem. Popular legend made her the mistress of an unscrupulous Greek priest who usurped her authority and treated her people so brutally that his Archbishop appealed to the Turks to intervene, adding as an inducement to the Sultan that the glens of Parnassos would make a fine hunting estate.[27] No doubt the underlying truth is that the higher Orthodox clerics had made up their minds that once Turkish domination was inevitable the national and religious survival of the Greek community could be best preserved by a timely and voluntary submission. A quick accommodation with the Moslem conquerors was surely preferable to a precarious existence under Latin rule on a battleground exposed to periodic devastation. When the Turks started to raid the duchy itself, Nerio suspected, probably with good reason, that his own Greek Metropolitan was in clandestine touch with their leader. Dorotheos confirmed his fears by quitting Athens in a hurry, while Nerio protested vainly against his treachery to the Patriarch at Constantinople.[28]

1394 was a year of crisis. Shortly after becoming Duke, Nerio recovered Megara as part of a three-cornered deal by which Theodore surrendered Argos to Venice and the latter reluctantly refused an offer from Paul Mamonas, the leading archon of Monemvasia, to hand over the city. In the knowledge that the Turks could only be held back by a Christian alliance based on their own fleets and fortresses, the Venetians worked hard to reconcile St Superan with Nerio and the Despot and to persuade all three to concert a common plan for defence. One of the measures mooted was the building of a protective wall across the narrowest part of the isthmus of Corinth, where Justinian had once erected a rampart against the Slavs. The Navarrese leader, however, preferred to seek support from the Sultan. Mamonas too made overtures to the Turks and the prospects of saving Greece looked even bleaker when Bayezit peremptorily summoned Manuel II, his brother the Despot and various Slav client princes to meet him in Macedonia. Uncertain whether they were to be strangled on the spot or merely terrorized, Manuel and Theodore did not dare to disobey. According to Manuel's own account, the Sultan actually gave the order for their execution but was pleased when he learned that for some reason or other it had not been promptly carried out. While the Emperor was allowed to return to the confines of Constantinople, Theodore was told to be ready to accompany Bayezit in a triumphal progress through Thessaly leading, for all he knew, to a campaign for the final subjugation of all Greece. It says much for the Despot's resourcefulness and firmness of nerve that he soon managed to escape and to annul instructions which he had been compelled to issue to his officers in the Morea to surrender its strong-points to the Turks.[29]

As it happened the Turkish invasion was delayed until the next winter, by which time the death of Nerio, which occurred in September 1394, had plunged Greek affairs into even worse confusion. Like his predecessor Niccolo, the Duke left a complicated and controversial will. Instead of simply bequeathing the duchy and his other possessions to his brother Donato, as envisaged by his sovereign the King of Naples, he disposed of his inheritance in such a way as to provoke the highest degree of dissension. It was an act curiously uncharacteristic of so practical a politician and man of business. By way of reparation for his dispersal of the Parthenon's treasures in payment of his ransom, he gave the city of Athens, with all its dependencies and revenues, to the Cathedral of the Virgin. He gave detailed instructions for the conservation of the building, for the replating of its doors and for the future maintenance of an appropriate number of Catholic clergy, while any deficiency in the endowment was to be made good by the income from Nerio's stud farm. On the other hand the whole of Boeotia was left to his bastard Antonio. This young man, the son of his mistress Maria Rendis (the daughter of the notary) thus inherited the richest but most insecure portion of the duchy.

Nerio's principal heiress, however, was Francesca, Countess of Cephalonia and Duchess of Leucadia; she was to take Megara, Corinth and all the surrounding country. As for Bartolommea, the Despot's wife, who had fully expected to have Corinth, she was to receive only the sum of 9700 ducats which her husband already owed Nerio. This slap in the face was certainly meant as a penalty for Theodore's obstinacy in hanging on to Argos, but just as had happened over Argos six years earlier, the Despot intervened before Francesca's husband, Carlo Tocco, was ready, seized all the lands around Corinth and laid siege to the fortress itself. His action sparked off an unedifying struggle between the two brothers-in-law, in the course of which Tocco did not scruple to enlist Turkish aid. Nevertheless, on realising that he was in no position to enforce his claims, he soon withdrew and relinquished Corinth to the Greeks. Theodore, after spiting his father-in-law and narrowly saving his skin from the Sultan, had won a signal triumph for his nation and further constricted the area of the Peloponnese still controlled by the Latins.[30]

At Athens too Greek national sentiment asserted itself after the Duke's death. The provision of his will which reduced the city to a mere annex of the Catholic cathedral was bound to turn the loyalty of its inhabitants into disaffection, and the new Metropolitan, Makarios, immediately appealed to the Turks to put an end to Latin rule. A Turkish force duly invested the Acropolis, which was defended by its castellan, Matteo de Montona, one of Nerio's executors. This officer decided in his predicament to invoke a vague clause in the will requesting Venetian help in fulfilling its dispositions and generally committing his former territories to Venetian care. Nerio had correctly estimated that in the last resort Venice would not allow the Turks to occupy so vital a stronghold as the citadel of Athens. When Montona's messengers arrived at Negroponte its bailie, Andrea Bembo, responded with alacrity and sent a sufficient force to drive the Turks away. With the banner of St Mark already hoisted over the Acropolis, the Venetian Senate resolved, after long deliberation, to approve his action. Directing him to assure the Athenians that Venice would respect their former rights, they set up in the course of 1395 a regular colonial administration under a Podesta, Albano Contarini. The Acropolis received a Venetian garrison with twenty *ballistarii* (artillerymen), and certain Athenians who had made themselves useful over the transfer of power were rewarded with sums of money. In order to conciliate the Greeks the obnoxious injunctions of the Duke's will were dropped. On the pretext that many of Nerio's valuable mares had been stolen from his stud farm during the recent troubles and that little income from that source was consequently available, the Parthenon establishment was reduced to eight priests only and entrusted to the management of two 'procurators'. Together with Negroponte, Argos and Nauplia, Athens was ranged in the line of Venetian fortresses guarding the eastern coasts of Greece and once it had taken its place in the system no question seemed to arise of another Acciaiuoli emerging as the ruler of a resurrected and united duchy. The Republic could have nothing to fear from the young Antonio at Thebes.[31]

When the Turkish blow eventually fell it was less heavy than might have been feared. It soon transpired that Evrenos Beg, who again led the Ottoman army, was bent not on total conquest but simply on the chastisement of the Despot, whose conduct had particularly irritated the Sultan. The campaign also seems to have been undertaken partly at the request of the Navarrese, for instead of making for Mistra the Turks joined them in storming the old Frankish castle of Akova and sacking the town of Leontari, both Byzantine possessions on the fringe of the dwindling principality. But as soon as this limited result had been achieved Evrenos withdrew swiftly to Thessaly, leaving Theodore free to rally his forces and inflict a severe reverse on the Navarrese. Both St Superan and the Grand Constable Zaccaria were taken prisoner by the Greeks and only Venetian insistence procured their release.[32]

It can be no fantasy to assume that the retirement of Evrenos from the Morea was hastened by the impending challenge to Ottoman power which had begun to take shape north of the Danube. Bayezit could not fail to be already aware that Sigismund, King of Hungary and brother of the Holy Roman Emperor, was profoundly alarmed by the presence of the Turks on his southern frontier and was trying to form a coalition of Western sovereigns with the avowed purpose of driving the infidels from Europe. After two hundred years of vain efforts by Popes and princes, it suddenly seemed that a new Crusade on a vast scale was about to become a reality. During 1395 Sigismund's envoys travelled to Germany, France and Italy in search of contingents to serve under the Hungarian banner. They received firm and enthusiastic promises of men and money from the Emperor, the Kings of France and England and the Duke of Burgundy, while both the Pope of Rome and the rival pontiff at Avignon gave their blessing to the enterprise. Warships were to be provided by Venice, Genoa and the Hospitallers. But while diplomatic exchanges and preparations for the muster of an enormous Christian host went slowly ahead Bayezit too took his precautions. He attacked the Romanian Prince of Wallachia and after a bitter struggle, wrested from him the control of the lower Danube crossings. The Turkish field army, swollen by levies from the Slav vassal states, reached a strength of a hundred thousand men. We can only guess with what anxious excitement the small communities of Greece looked forward to the prospect of a colossal clash, on the issue of which their destiny inevitably hung.

CHAPTER NINE

The Defence of Hellas

COLUMNS OF CRUSADERS from the West reached Buda in the summer of 1396. King Sigismund's own army, drawn from all quarters of the huge Hungarian realm, was said to total sixty thousand men, and the whole joint host which moved south-eastwards along the Danube was equal in numbers to the opposing Ottoman array. Unfortunately it proved no match for the Turks in cohesion and discipline. At first all went well. Eight days were needed to ferry the troops across the river at Orsova, below the Iron Gates, but they passed over unchallenged. They then pursued their march to the east along the right bank of the Danube until they were checked at Nikopolis, an old fortress guarding the centre of the river line half way to the Black Sea and performing the same function for the Ottomans as it had in former days for the Byzantines. Its walls were strong and it was still untaken when Bayezit came up to confront the besiegers. The battle which followed showed that the Western Christians had forgotten the tactical lessons learned by hard experience in former Crusades; nor was there any real confidence or co-ordination between the impetuous French knights and the more cautious warriors of King Sigismund. The outcome was a complete triumph for the Sultan. The toll of slain and captured French nobles recalled the calamities of Crecy and Agincourt, while the Hungarians were hurled back in confusion over the Danube. The King escaped by boarding a Venetian vessel which carried him to the Black Sea, and thence through the Bosporus to the safety of the Mediterranean.

For the Emperor Manuel at Constantinople and his brother Theodore in the Morea this dismal collapse of their allies could only portend, short of divine intervention, their own very speedy eclipse. It also tended to confirm their innate cynicism about either the will or the ability of the two greatest kingdoms of Catholic Europe, France and Hungary, to rescue Orthodox Christendom from the Turks. They were not surprised when after his victory at Nikopolis Bayezit returned to supervise the investment of Constantinople, which had already lasted for two years and was to be prolonged for another six. The blockade by land, tightened or relaxed at the Sultan's pleasure, brought great suffering to the population, but in the absence of an effective Ottoman

189

navy communications between the city and the outside world, and the passage of essential supplies, were never completely interrupted. Meanwhile the Despotate had to provide for its own safety; it could expect no support from the beleaguered capital of a vanished empire.

Theodore's first reaction to the shattering news of Nikopolis was to offer his latest acquisition, Corinth, to the Venetians. Presumably he thought that this gateway to the Morea would be safer in their hands. The Republic, however, declined the responsibility, either from traditional reluctance to assume a new commitment or because it did not possess sufficient resources at the moment to defend the isthmus. The Despot's worst fears seemed to have been fulfilled when, in the summer of 1397 sixty thousand Turks under Evrenos Beg and Yakub Pasha descended upon Greece. As before they did not linger in Boeotia or Attica; Antonio Acciaiuoli at Thebes and the Venetian Podesta in the Athenian Acropolis simply closed their gates and hoped to survive. Sweeping over the isthmus and leaving Corinth undisturbed as they entered the Peloponnese, the invaders divided their forces into two columns. While Evrenos made for Leontari, as he had done two years previously, Yakub flung himself upon Venetian Argos, which was in no condition to resist his assault. The castle was destroyed, the town sacked and its people netted for slavery, but no attempt was made to storm the much stronger fortifications of Nauplia. Meanwhile Evrenos, after an indecisive engagement with the Despot's forces and a demonstration before Venetian Modon, marched back to the isthmus and the united Turkish army retired as swiftly as it had advanced. We may wonder why Bayezit was content with yet another punitive expedition and did not decide to conquer Greece for good and all. The answer is surely that he was not yet ready for a long and costly struggle with Venice. The sea coasts of Greece were studded with fortresses which he would not be able to reduce unless they were blockaded from the sea as well as from the land, and he still lacked the necessary ships and artillery. Moreover, if the remaining Greek and Latin rulers could be terrorized into compliance with his wishes, he was prepared, at least for the present, to accept them as obedient vassals on the same level as the satellite princes of Serbia or Bosnia. Greece could await its final subjection until he had achieved his major aim, the capture of Constantinople.[1]

Unlike the Navarrese and Antonio Acciaiuoli, Theodore was unwilling to hold his territory on the Sultan's terms. On the other hand he did not see how he would be able to prolong his resistance without substantial backing from the Latin powers. Venice had already declined the role of protectress of the Despotate. In a mood of pessimism, if not of despair, Theodore resolved to approach the Order of St John. When Heredia had been its Grand Master, shortly before Theodore became Despot, the Hospitallers had taken charge of Frankish Morea for five years, and now they were playing a vigorous and determined anti-Turkish role in the eastern Aegean from their strongholds of Rhodes and Smyrna. If the Venetians would not buy Corinth, the Knights might be glad to have it.

Theodore's decision was not taken without the blessing of his brother Manuel. Much to his credit, the Emperor had not lost his nerve after Nikopolis. While resolutely defending Constantinople he continued, despite his own deep-seated scepticism, to address appeals for aid of any kind to the sovereigns of Europe. By 1399 the King of France, Charles VI, agreed to send a small force of royal troops under Marshal Boucicaut, a stout soldier who had survived the Nikopolis campaign, to assist in the defence of the city. Their arrival so heightened Byzantine morale that Manuel judged it safe for him to reinforce his pleas by personal visits to Western courts. Accordingly he set off at the end of the year, accompanied by Boucicaut, on a tour which was to take him to Venice, Milan, Paris and London. Constantinople was left in charge of his nephew, the co-Emperor John VII, and of Boucicaut's deputy, the Sieur de Châteaumorand. On the way he touched at Modon, where he deposited his wife and children and approved his brother's proposal to dispose of Corinth to the Knights. But when Theodore sailed to Rhodes in order to conclude the deal, he found the Hospitallers intent on acquiring Kalavryta as well and even on establishing themselves at his own capital, Mistra. Perhaps in a moment of weakness, he accepted all their demands and agreed himself to retire to Monemvasia. His own Moreots, however, indignantly repudiated concessions which would have subjected them once more to Latin control. While the Knights took over Kalavryta and Corinth and began to fortify the isthmus, the Bishop, with the full support of the people, denied them access to Mistra.[2]

The Turks, too, protested to Theodore and offered to leave him undisturbed if he went back on his commitments to the Order. But strange as it might seem Turkish exigencies were no longer the all-important factor in the politics of the Peloponnese. In 1401 reports were reaching Greece and Western Europe that the Ottoman Empire was in serious trouble on its eastern limits. The first stories of disaster were exaggerated, but it was true that the Sultan had fallen out with the great Turco-Mongol conqueror Timur, then at the height of his power and the lord of an immense empire in Central Asia and Iran. After 1390 the two potentates faced each other across a common frontier in the Caucasus and friction inevitably developed into armed clashes. A Mongol army invaded Anatolia in 1400 and destroyed the town of Sivas with peculiar barbarity. During the next year, while Timur was devastating Mesopotamia and Syria, insults and provocations flew to and fro. Bayezit was determined on revenge and assembled a vast army in Asia Minor. It included a large corps of Christian Serbs and another of Janissaries, picked troops composed of young Christians removed from their homes and brought up as fanatical Moslems. But Timur moved more quickly and in the summer of 1402 came up with Bayezit near Ankara. Though the Turks and Christians fought with obstinate bravery, they were routed and the Sultan fell into Mongol hands. His life was spared but in a few months he died in captivity, some said of sheer mortification.

Asia Minor was ravaged far and wide after the battle. When Timur eventually returned to his capital, Samarkand, the Ottoman domain dissolved temporarily into a number of independent Turkish emirates. In Europe, Bayezit's eldest son Suleiman established himself at Adrianople. Ottoman prestige was, however, in ruins, and an immense surge of relief swept over the Christian Levant. Further west, the news was received with delighted surprise, more especially by Manuel whose protracted negotiations with England and France had reached a dead end. On his return journey from Paris to Constantinople, now released from its blockade, he again stopped in the Morea and discussed with Theodore what should be done about the Hospitallers. Now that the Turkish tide had ebbed, the problem was what to offer to the Knights as sufficient inducement to abandon Kalavryta and Corinth. This task the Despot accomplished with his usual dexterity. It so happened that the Mongols, in the course of their terrifying razzia through Asia Minor, had stormed and sacked Smyrna, from which the Grand Master of the Hospital had been fortunate enough to escape with his life. Consequently the Order was in a chastened mood and not disposed to drive a difficult bargain. It was glad to give up the territory in the Peloponnese in return for a cash payment and the County of Salona, which Theodore, cousin of the former Countess, had been quick to grab after the Turkish débâcle. But here again the Greek inhabitants refused to accept a renewal of Latin rule, and again the Knights did not persevere when faced with popular resistance. Salona, Lamia and Southern Thessaly shook off Turkish domination and enjoyed a brief period of freedom under local leaders.[3]

Thus by good luck, skilful diplomacy and a measure of cool fortitude

Theodore had managed to hold on to his Despotate and to extend the boundaries of Byzantium when they were contracting everywhere else. Furthermore his reoccupation of Corinth coincided with a modest Byzantine revival at the centre. When Manuel reached Constantinople he found that John VII had already concluded a pact with Suleiman whereby the latter ceded to the Greeks Thessalonica, much of the Thracian hinterland of the capital and several Aegean islands. Constantinople now had a little room to breathe and the Palaeologues could make provision for the immediate future without the Turks gripping their throats. They were not of course so naive as to suppose that the recent change in their fortunes would last. Though Suleiman had proclaimed himself an ally and even the vassal of the Emperor, such a gesture was likely to lose its value once the Ottomans began to recover from the Mongol shock. The solution adopted was that while Theodore continued to govern the Morea, John was entrusted with Thessalonica and any other lands that the Byzantines might regain in the north.

The Turkish setbacks also procured a respite for the two precarious footholds still maintained by the Latins in continental Greece. In the principality of Achaia, now confined to a narrow strip of territory in the Western Peloponnese, Navarrese rule came to an end in 1402 with the death of St Superan. As soon as he was out of the way Centurione Zaccaria, the most prominent of the remaining barons and son of the former Grand Constable, usurped the power which should have passed to St Superan's children, his own cousins. He also prevailed on the King of Naples to recognise him as Prince of Achaia, the last, as it turned out, of the line which had begun with Guillaume de Champlitte. But his prospects were hardly promising. The Greeks were encroaching on his uncomfortably restricted domain, he was at loggerheads with his neighbours, the Venetians of Modon, and Carlo Tocco of Cephalonia, nominally a vassal of the principality, not only refused to acknowledge his title but seized his chief port, Glarentza, and most of Elis. But though the territory under his control was at times no more extensive than his own barony of Arkadia, he was not finally dislodged for another quarter of a century.[4]

North of the isthmus Antonio Acciaiuoli had only survived at Thebes by lying low as Ottoman armies crossed and recrossed Boeotia. Like the Navarrese, he had cynically courted the Sultan's favour while it was politic to do so, and even joined the Turks in raiding Attica. Nor had he ever given up hope of reuniting both halves of his father's duchy under his own rule. He was not even to be deterred by the fact that Athens now belonged to Venice. The risks which a political adventurer like himself would run in openly challenging the power of the Republic were all too obvious. Yet, as an Athenian and half Greek by birth, he had many sympathizers in the city, and he reckoned that if he were initially successful his father's influential kinsmen in Italy could be relied on to intercede on his behalf. He had also noticed that Athens was feebly held. Therefore, in the summer of 1402, he decided on a bold stroke. Before the Podesta knew what was happening Antonio had taken possession of the whole of Attica and of the lower city, and the garrison was isolated on the Acropolis. When the news reached Venice, the Senate's reaction was one of outraged fury. Antonio was denounced as an 'enemy of the Christian faith'. The bailie of Negroponte was instructed to place the sum of 8000 *hyperpera* on his head and to proceed against him with the utmost rigour. If necessary, Thebes was to be burned to the ground. Spurred on by these orders, the bailie raised an army of six thousand men, a very considerable land force by Venetian standards, and marched on Athens. But Antonio, who was waiting for him in an unnamed mountain defile, put his troops to flight and returned to the siege of the Acropolis. Its defenders resisted manfully for seventeen months and only surrendered when there was nothing left to eat on the rock.

After Antonio's victory the Venetians, for whom practical considerations were apt to rank higher than prestige, changed their tune and consented to negotiate. They were genuinely scared lest Antonio might go on to take Negroponte itself. His ambitions, however, were confined to Nerio's duchy, and he was quite content to spin out the talks over the next three years. The eventual result of these exchanges, in which Sultan Suleiman as well as all the interested Christian parties were concerned, was that the Venetians agreed to cut their losses on condition that Antonio paid suitable compensation and declared himself the Republic's vassal. As a yearly token of his dependence he was to contribute a valuable silken cloak to the treasury of St Mark. But in return he kept all his gains and was acknowledged in 1405 as legitimate Duke. He had fully succeeded in his shrewd gamble and ruled at Athens for the next three decades.[5]

The despot Theodore died at Mistra in 1407, after a troubled reign of twenty-six years. The need to forestall anarchy, as well as to settle the succession, soon prompted the Emperor to pay a third visit to the Morea. Whereas Theodore was childless, Manuel had six sons and had already decided that the second of these, also named Theodore, should be the next Despot. However, since he was still an infant, provisional arrangements had to be made for the administration. The Emperor also took the opportunity to publish, if not to deliver, an elaborate funeral panegyric of his brother, praising the political skill which he had displayed during his long stewardship and insisting in particular that his offer of Moreot territory to the Knights was to be considered not as a betrayal of the Hellenic cause but, in the circumstances, as an act of higher statesmanship. The Emperor was presumably anxious to counter the unpopularity which Theodore had incurred on that issue and to scotch any lingering feelings of discontent with Palaeologue rule. But he was certainly right in his assessment of Theodore's record, if that is considered as a whole. Although the Despot notably misjudged, or chose to ignore, Greek national sentiment when he approached the Hospitallers, it was not right to reproach him for cowardice or lack of resolution for having sought to draw them into the defence of the Morea at a time when Venice was refusing further commitments and nobody could possibly foresee that Ottoman pressure would suddenly be relaxed.

In fact Theodore had performed wonders in fending off the Turks while steadily strengthening the Despotate at the expense of the Latins. His worst enemies had been his own archons, many of whom had resented his original appointment and had always been inclined to deny him their co-operation when times were difficult. Some, like Mamonas of Monemvasia, had not hesitated to intrigue against him with the Turks or the Venetians. All were quarrelsome and, as the Cantacuzenes too had discovered, prone to fighting among themselves. It was their bad habits, as much as the intermittent Turkish incursions and hostilities with the Latins, that created the sense of insecurity which prevailed in the Morea just at the time when the Greek element had at last achieved a clear paramountcy over the Latin. The Peloponnese was still regarded as a desirable country, abounding in metals, in silk, cotton, wine, wheat, wax and honey, but in many districts the population had declined since the high Frankish period of the thirteenth century. The Moreots were tending to quit the open towns of the plains and to regroup in the less accessible mountain villages. Nevertheless, the tally of inhabitants removed by the Turks from a small part of the Argolid—thirty thousand according to one account—suggests that the more favoured regions were still thickly populated.[6] Moreover Theodore had encouraged large numbers of Albanians to cross the Gulf of Corinth and settle permanently in the Peloponnese. Besides filling the agricultural gaps, these mountaineers provided him with excellent soldiers, the hardy infantrymen and nimble light horsemen needed to harass and disconcert the ponderous Latin men-at-arms.[7] From the Turks however there was ultimately no military salvation. Not only were their forces always superior in numbers to any which the Greeks or Latins, or a combination of both, could put into the field, but they also presented a superbly balanced and disciplined concert of all arms, to which a formidable artillery was soon to be added.

We do not know who governed the Despotate during the young Theodore's minority. The period was not rich in events. Venetian diplomacy, however, was busily employed in improving the Republic's own defences and in composing Centurione's squabbles with the Greeks and Carlo Tocco which threatened the existence of the principality. The once powerful Achaian State, now whittled down to a handful of baronies held by the few remaining French, Italian and Navarrese families, had become the weak point of the Morea. In their anxiety to restore peace and order before the next Ottoman attack, the Venetian Senate were prepared to depart from their usual cautious policy and take the principality under their protection. In 1407 they had made the Gulf of Corinth secure by acquiring Naupaktos (Lepanto) from the local Albanian chieftain. The possession of this immensely strong fortress and harbour, with its triple *enceinte* of walls, completed the triangle of maritime bases—Negroponte, Naupaktos, Nauplia—covering the northern approaches to the peninsula, and amply compensated for the loss of direct control over Athens. It was supplemented by the lease of Patras for five years from its Archbishop, Stephen Zaccaria, Centurione's brother. At the same time the Senate offered to make Centurione a citizen of the Republic and to guarantee the integrity of Achaia, demanding in return the cession of sufficient territory in Messenia to include the port of Navarino (known to the Franks as 'Port de Jonc') in the existing Venetian colony of Modon. The Prince, however, demurred and, with singular lack of prudence, made approaches to Genoa, Venice's inveterate rival. No settlement had been reached when in 1415 the Emperor Manuel took over the initiative and paid his third and best advertised visit to the Peloponnese.[8]

This time he came to Mistra in some state, not as a harried vassal of the Sultan nor as a disappointed suppliant of the Western monarchies, but as a sovereign who had held his own against the Ottomans and abated none of his claims to an Empire far surpassing the limit of his present authority. To the Orthodox people of Europe and Asia he was still, by favour of Christ, the Emperor of the Romans. Even the new Ottoman Sultan, Mehmet I, formally acknowledged him as overlord and 'father'. Although there was no doubt where the preponderance of power resided, Manuel had been outstandingly adroit in the hair-raising task of handling Byzantine relations with the sons of Bayezit. Ever since their father's death three princes had contended for the succession and struggled to reunite the Ottoman realm. Manuel helped Suleiman until he was killed by his brother Musa, and when Musa displayed anti-Byzantine tendencies he aided Mehmet to do away with him in his turn. For the moment there was no outward enmity between the two sovereigns, and Mehmet had also assured the other independent rulers of Greece that he desired to remain at peace with them. It therefore seemed an opportune moment for an imperial progress through the Morea.

Manuel had spent the preceding winter at Thessalonica. In the spring he sailed to Negroponte, where the bailie received him with due pomp. Relations between Venetians and Turks in that area were less than cordial, since Mehmet's newly built fleet had lately ravaged Euboea while on the mainland opposite his troops had extinguished the old marquisate of Boudonitza, whose lord was a Venetian dependent and citizen. In April the Emperor moved on to Corinth and immediately caused work to be resumed on his brother's project for a wall across the isthmus, which had been interrupted by the previous Turkish invasions. This rampart, known as the Hexamilion, was completed, according to contemporary accounts, in twenty-five days and garnished with castles at each end and 153 interlying towers. If that is true, its construction is unlikely to have been very solid, but the achievement was nevertheless impressive and carried the imperial touch. Even the Venetians were stirred to admiration, although they characteristically declined to share in the expense. From Corinth Manuel proceeded to Mistra, where he formally invested his son, now of age, with authority to govern the Despotate. He dealt personally, however, and very firmly with a revolt of archons professing to be outraged by the imposition of a special tax to pay for the wall.[9]

Manuel remained at Mistra for about six months. The little city under Taygetos became briefly the centre of the Byzantine world, the hub of an incessant diplomatic activity ranging from Trebizond to the Thames. It was full of aristocrats, courtiers, officials and literati from Constantinople, curious to see how their compatriots lived in the unfamiliar surroundings of old Greece. Most of them had been accustomed to regard the Morea as a semi-barbarous country. Nevertheless it was the cradle of that Hellenism which they themselves were proud of having preserved and of which they considered themselves to be the heirs and living representatives. They were conscious, too, of their sovereign's deep interest in the safety and welfare of the province. If his concern and presence were not exactly welcome to the local archons, they were a sign that Byzantium had not lost its vitality and faith in its recuperative power.

They also manifested themselves in two of the most interesting products of Late Byzantine literature. The authors of these works, the satirist Mazaris and the philosopher George Gemistos, both took a close look at the Peloponnese in the context of the imperial visit. Each, however, surveyed the scene from a very different angle. Mazaris composed what is essentially a bitter and disillusioned political pamphlet attacking the evils and abuses which he found rampant in the Despotate. At the other end of the spectrum Gemistos Plethon, a scholar of dazzling erudition and an international figure who was to emerge as one of the most original of Renaissance humanists, drew up for the benefit of the Moreots an elaborate plan for the reform of the system of government and for radical changes in the economic and social order.

The satire of Mazaris is a curiously disjointed work. It starts as a 'Dialogue of the Dead' in the same genre as that employed by the author of *Timarion* in the reign of Manuel I Komnenos. Mazaris describes how he fell ill of the plague at Constantinople and found himself, like Timarion, in Hades. There he falls in with a certain Holobolos, formerly a close friend and an imperial secretary who had accompanied Manuel on his journey to France and England: had it not been for his premature death, he would certainly have attained the highest office. This personage suspects that Mazaris (again like Timarion) has descended into Hades before his appointed time, and urges him to return to the upper world as swiftly as possible. Why does he not settle with all his household in the Morea, where he can fill his stomach with good food and drink, win the respect of the inhabitants and earn good money into the bargain? Furthermore he might do well to seek the patronage of a certain Eudaimon, who occupies a high place at the Despot's court. Mazaris is grateful for this advice, but before he returns to the world above he has to reply to many eager questions from Holobolos about the state of affairs in Constantinople, and to converse with a variety of the Byzantine dead. These encounters provide the writer, who had a lively talent for vituperation, with an excellent opportunity to abuse his contemporaries, denounce their intrigues and indulge in every kind of malicious gossip.[10]

The dialogue breaks off with a remark by Mazaris that he has written it to instruct rather than to amuse. We then find him talking to Holobolos once again, but apparently in a dream. It seems that he had emerged from Hades and taken his friend's advice to set up house in the Morea, but that the experiment has not been a success. None of his hopes has been realized; he has been ill-treated by the provincials; he has been living in penury and neglect for fourteen months and worse still, surrounded as he is by the barbarized Tzakonians, he has almost forgotten how to speak correct Greek. He berates Holobolos for his bad counsel and appeals to him for help in his predicament. Holobolos is suitably horrified; he cannot imagine how things could have changed so greatly since he himself was in the Morea with the Emperor and has been treated so kindly and generously. He begs Mazaris to tell him exactly what has gone wrong. When Mazaris objects that his life will be in danger if the violent Moreots ever find out that he has been denouncing them, he tells him to write him a letter and confide it to an individual on the point of death to carry it to him in the underworld. In any case Tainaron, the entrance to Hades, is quite near Sparta (Mistra), and there are always boats running thence to the infernal regions. He promises, as soon as he has the leisure, to study Mazaris's memorandum with due care. Meanwhile his friend had better stay in the Peloponnese, much as he may dislike it, in the hope that he may secure better treatment and a prosperous future by favour of the young Despot Theodore II. If all else fails he had better settle in Crete (a Venetian possession) or apply to the Count of Cephalonia (Carlo Tocco, husband of the philhellene Countess Francesca Acciaiuoli).

The letter itself follows, meticulously dated 21 September (old style) 1416. It is a furious philippic pronounced by an 'Anatolian', or eastern Greek from Constantinople, or from a province of Byzantine Asia already conquered by the Turk, against the Greeks of the Morea. It looks as if Mazaris[11] (or the real man lurking under a pseudonym) had been induced to leave the capital and try his luck in the Despotate in the wake of the Emperor's visit, and had found himself out of his depth and out of sympathy with the raw and uncongenial society of his new home. He has conceived a profound antipathy for the Moreot archons and his scathing castigation of their behaviour, though exaggerated by every rhetorical trick, is consistent with the frequent condemnation of their irresponsibility and unruliness by earlier Byzantine writers. These men were the thorns in the flesh of every authority, Frankish or Greek, unless kept severely in order as they had been under the Villehardouins or the Cantacuzenes.

Mazaris does not bother to examine the condition of the Despotate in detail, as Holobolos had requested, but concentrates his venom on the archons, or as he calls them the 'toparchs'. He describes the population in general with some contempt as a mixture in which seven races are severally represented, not to speak of plenty of half-castes. He lists them as 'Lacedaemonians, Italians, Peloponnesians, Sclavinians, Illyrians, Egyptians and Jews'. The first are of course the Tzakonians, and the Peloponnesians are all the other native Greeks; the 'Italians' are the various kinds of Franks, the 'Sclavinians' the Slavs of the southern Morea and the 'Illyrians' the recent immigrants from Albania, while it is not strange to find Gypsies and Jews also included.[12] Each of these, says Mazaris, has infected the others with its own special vices and defects, but they are all treacherous, violent, greedy, corrupt and uncivilized, to mention only a few of the epithets applied to them. But what draws his strongest invective is the disloyalty of the toparchs, for they have attempted to frustrate at every turn the efforts of the 'most sacred and unconquered Emperor' to regenerate and defend their country. In enthusiastically commending Manuel for having built the Hexamilion, he again denounces the archons, whose reaction to this wise measure has been to rebel, thus forcing the sovereign to suspend his constructive labours and waste his time and resources in bringing them to heel. Manuel's own comment on the situation is contained in a contemporary letter to a friend: the trouble with the Moreots, he complains, is that 'they are all in love with weapons'. If only they would use them in the right cause, instead of in civil war![13]

Mazaris warmly supported the Emperor's aims, but the whole tone of his satire implies that he doubted whether they would be realized. Apart from his solitary satirical piece he is an insubstantial figure; equally shadowy are the numerous friends and enemies whom he introduces into it under pseudonyms and punning nicknames. With George Gemistos Plethon we are on firm ground.[14] So far at least as his writings are concerned, he is a well known and documented personality. 'Gemistos' and 'Plethon' are synonyms meaning 'full' or 'brimming', but the philosopher preferred to use the latter and more classical term as his surname. It matched both his longevity (he almost reached the age of a hundred) and his vast literary output. Until he was over fifty he seems to have lived mainly at Adrianople, already the capital of the European part of the Ottoman Empire. One would not imagine it to have been the ideal residence for a Platonist polymath in the age of Murad and Bayezit, but when he finally moved he went not to Constantinople but to Mistra. We do not know exactly when he reached the Morea, but he was certainly there shortly after the death of the Despot Theodore I. His intellectual talents made him *persona grata* in the imperial circle and he was appointed mentor of the young Theodore II. Other learned persons, both lay and clerical, soon assembled around him.

Plethon wrote voluminously on a great number of subjects including philosophy, history, rhetoric and music. As a thinker he was an idealist and an eccentric to the point of rashness. His preoccupation with the Hellenic past and in particular his addiction to Plato and the Neoplatonists, turned him gradually away from the Orthodox Christianity to which the great majority of cultivated Byzantines, steeped as they were in the classics, remained scrupulously faithful. Eventually he rejected Christianity altogether and composed hymns to the ancient gods in excruciatingly incorrect hexameters. Towards the end of his life he embodied his beliefs and views in a book which, in imitation of Plato, he entitled *The Laws,* and in which he preached a revival of the ancient Hellenic religion, slightly tinged with Zoroastrianism. It is hardly surprising that this work was at once denounced as heresy and burned by order of his old friend and intellectual opponent Gennadios, the first Patriarch of Constantinople after the Turkish conquest, and survives only in fragments. In 1415, however, he had either not yet developed heretical tendencies or was keeping them discreetly to himself.

It was his feeling for the Hellenic past, as much as his Byzantine patriotism and admiration for the Emperor, that moved Plethon to present to Manuel and Theodore respectively two addresses containing his proposals for the future government of the Peloponnese.[15] In the first of these he begins by stressing the need to consolidate and exploit the advantage recently won by the Greeks over the Latins. For that purpose it is imperative to revive and foster the national spirit. Ignoring the racial distinctions drawn by Mazaris, he boldly claims,

> We, whom you lead and rule, are Greeks by race, as witnessed by our language and our traditional culture. There is no country more intimately and fittingly associated with the Greeks than the Peloponnese, adjacent as it is to both Europe and the neighbouring islands. Greeks seem always to have lived in it since time immemorial.

Also it can be considered as the mother country of Byzantium itself. It has an excellent climate and a fertile soil. Moreover it is eminently defensible. Each mountain fastness is like an acropolis which can hold out even when an enemy has occupied the plains. The Palaeologues have reconquered this land by their own exertions, and it is in their power to confer even more lasting benefits upon it.

After this introduction Plethon unfolds his scheme for a new Greek commonwealth, the prescriptions for which are divided between the two addresses. At its head stands the monarch, for in such troubled times no form of government but monarchy is conceivable, provided that it is upheld by proper institutions, by good, durable laws and by suitable advisers. The Council of State should not be too large nor too small, and its members should be well-educated and not too rich. In a just social order each class of the population should be required, in Plethon's view, to stick to its own job, and he divides his Moreots into three classes, the peasants or primary producers, the merchants and craftsmen and the ruling element, that is to say the Despot's councillors, officials, judges and all soldiers. The whole of the third category would be exempt from taxation but forbidden to engage in trade. The soldiers, a full-time professional army composed of natives, not mercenaries, would neither own nor work the land, which would be nationalized and held in common by peasants cultivating their individual plots and owning their own cattle and implements. Plethon calculates that the product of one peasant (or 'Helot' as he cannot resist calling him, although his Moreot peasant is destined for a much more tolerable lot than the Helot of ancient Sparta) would support one infantryman and that of two would suffice for a cavalryman. Officers, functionaries and bishops would be entitled to the product of three. He is, however, strongly opposed to giving the monks any benefit from the public treasury. Let this 'swarm of drones', he says, who contribute nothing to the good of the state, be satisfied with exemption from taxes, and it would indeed be more appropriate if they gave unpaid service in return for holding untaxed property. But the long and strongly worded passage attacking monasticism was hardly likely to commend itself to a society in which it was held in deep respect, and at a time when emperors chose to end their days in the cloister.[16]

The philosopher was much concerned with problems of taxation and of the equitable distribution of the country's products. In principle the landworkers, the sole tax-paying class, would keep one-third of their produce for themselves, pay one-third (in kind) to those who provided them with their capital (seed, tools and animals) and one-third in tax (also in kind) for the support of the rulers and soldiers. He is sure that the system will bring prosperity to all and prevent the exploitation of the peasants by the landowners whom, like Mazaris, he roundly condemns for their greed, love of luxury and lack of public spirit. The bellicose instinct of the archons would be diverted into the safe channel of regular military service, and he estimates that a standing force of six thousand men could be maintained without overburdening the producers. As regards the economy in general he is a convinced protectionist. Indeed, in his view, the less international trade the better. Since the Morea is self-sufficient in agricultural output, including textiles, there is no need for that kind of import. What is the point of bringing in wool 'from the Atlantic Ocean', or clothes made up abroad? Only iron and arms have to be purchased overseas, and they can be paid for by the export of Peloponnesian cotton. Other exports should be subject to a fifty per cent export duty. He argues that a system of self-sufficiency would lead to a salutary diminution in the supply of currency, especially of the debased coinage circulating in the Morea—a hit at the product of the Latin mint at Glarentza.

Plethon's proposals are pervaded by a sense of extreme urgency. He looks upon the Peloponnese, and not Constantinople, as the last refuge of Hellenism and the Roman idea. In his summing up he admits that what is at stake is survival. 'We can see to what a state the mighty empire of the Romans has been reduced. We have lost everything except two cities in Thrace and the Peloponnese (and not all of that is ours) and a little island or two.'[17] Nevertheless the Greeks need not despair provided that they choose the right institutions and rulers. With those they can balance the military might of their enemies. The task should not be too difficult and their chances of survival are not yet hopeless. Although he does not say so in as many words, he was probably thinking of the Ottoman Sultan in terms of Darius and Xerxes.

In this somewhat pathetic passage Plethon achieves a real eloquence. His pure and supple style is no disgrace to his classical models. It has been suggested that he saw himself as a new Plato advising a new Dionysios of Syracuse, with the Turkish danger substituted for the Carthaginian. Although Manuel II was a far finer character than the unscrupulous Sicilian dynast of the fourth century B.C., the parallel is an attractive one. Indeed there is something anachronistic about Plethon's ideas for a tightly regulated State socialism. They would have been comprehensible in Plato's time and they strike a not unfamiliar note in our own. But they do seem alien to the atmosphere of the late Middle Ages in the Morea, from which the culture that had inspired them had so long disappeared. Much as they were doubtless appreciated by the Emperor and the educated Constantinopolitans who surrounded him, they meant nothing to the feudally minded archons sheltering in their fortified manor houses, the neighbours of hostile Franks and unamenable Albanian colonists.

The programme was of course inapplicable. However it was not just an intellectual exercise devoid of practical significance. Plethon was not entirely a visionary and no crackpot. He saw clearly, as did the Emperor, that what the Despotate required was a strong central authority, stable and civilized institutions, a prosperous peasantry and a professional army. These had once been the essential props of Byzantine supremacy. But even if the recalcitrance of the fifteenth-century Moreots could have been overcome and their character transformed, the Morea would still have remained only a microcosm of the old Byzantium, perilously poised between Byzantium's Ottoman successor and the Latin West. Under the best conditions its survival was problematical indeed.

Just how precarious its situation continued to be was demonstrated by another Turkish invasion. Manuel had been careful to tend his good relations with Mehmet, and the latter's power was diminished by the destruction of his fleet by the Venetians in 1416. But when the Sultan died five years later, the ageing Emperor, under the influence of his eldest son John, unwisely promoted the claims of a pretender, Mustafa, in opposition to Mehmet's son Murad II. Murad, an Ottoman of the old conquering and fanatic breed, was justifiably incensed and retaliated by attacking Constantinople. This time it was no mere blockade but a full scale assault which, however, was sharply repulsed. The Sultan withdrew his troops, but in 1423 he sent Turakhan, the Pasha of Thessaly, to raid the Morea. Once again the Turks easily broached the defences of the isthmus. The truth was that the hastily built Hexamilion, unless strongly and permanently manned by professional soldiers, was no obstacle to a resolute mass attack. Turakhan's blow fell equally on the Greeks and on the Venetian settlements in Messenia, but achieved no lasting result. His purpose, as that of Evrenos in 1397, was to punish and not to annex. As it was the Despot's troops put up a fierce resistance and defeated the Turks in at least one encounter. The main sufferers were the Albanian colonists, who stood up on their own to the invaders in a pitched battle near Tripolis in Arkadia. They were utterly routed and the conquerors raised a grisly pyramid of eight hundred of their heads.[18]

It might have seemed to the Moreots that such Turkish visitations were destructive but merely transitory phenomena which, though destined to occur every twenty or thirty years, would make no permanent difference to their lives. With Turakhan out of the way, the only question was who would absorb the remaining fragments of the Frankish principality. Centurione Zaccaria held his barony of Arkadia and little else, while Glarentza had first been seized by an Italian adventurer named Oliverio Franco and then sold by him to Carlo Tocco of Cephalonia. A third Latin enclave, Patras, retained its independence under its Archbishop. In 1422 Venice was considering whether the best course might not be to take over the whole Western coast of the Peloponnese. Such a policy would have involved a partition of the peninsula between Venice and the Despotate and the reduction of

Centurione to the status of a minor Venetian vassal. A special envoy, Dolfin Venier, was despatched to the scene with instructions to report on the prospects. The account which he rendered was uniformly favourable. The Morea, he declared, was infinitely to be preferred to Crete; it was more fertile and productive; it had a livelier trade and it was full of wealthy towns and strong castles. On receiving his recommendations, the Senate authorized him to pursue the necessary negotiations with the Despot, Centurione and Carlo Tocco. Little, however, emerged from these exchanges. Understandably the Greeks dragged their feet and Tocco proved equally evasive. All that was achieved was a truce between the various Christian states and an undertaking to form a common front against the Turks, and even that arrangement was stultified when Tocco made common cause with Turakhan. The only advantages, though not to be despised, gained by Venice were the acquisition of Navarino and a protectorate over Patras.[19]

The way was thus open for the Palaeologues to put an end to Frankish Achaia. After 1425, when John VIII succeeded Manuel on the Byzantine throne, three of his brothers, the Despot Theodore II, Constantine and Thomas, were working together in the Morea. The Emperor himself joined them in 1427 and led the attack against the Tocchi. Glarentza soon surrendered to George Phrantzes, the historian of the late Palaeologues and a native of Monemvasia, and Carlo's fleet was dispersed by a Greek squadron. When peace was restored in the following year Carlo's niece, Maddalena, was married to Constantine, who received Elis as his apanage. Two hundred and twenty-three years had passed since Champlitte and his knights had swept across it in their triumphal progress from Corinth.[20]

The brothers' next objective was Patras, where Pandolfo Malatesta, a kinsman of the lords of Rimini, had succeeded Stephen Zaccaria as Archbishop. Although his sister, Cleopa, was the wife of Theodore of Mistra, he held the city obstinately against the Greeks, expecting aid from Venice which never came, and it was only taken at the second attempt. Phrantzes, to whom we are indebted for a detailed account of the event, was wounded and captured during the siege. The recovery of the historic city, and the restoration of the Orthodox Archbishop to his see, were treated as a great triumph. On the other hand Constantine had little regard for Glarentza, the creation of the Villehardouins, which he dismantled and left deserted. Meanwhile Thomas had been assigned the task of dealing with Centurione. Encircled in his last stronghold of Chalandritza, the Prince made the best terms he could for himself and his family; he gave his daughter, Caterina, to Thomas and was allowed to keep his barony of Arkadia. Thus, in 1430, the whole of the Peloponnese, with the exception of the Venetian possessions (Modon, Coron, Navarino, Argos and Nauplia) acknowledged the sovereignty of Byzantium.[21]

Under the perpetual Ottoman menace Mistra enjoyed no golden age. Yet the first half of the fifteenth century was a kind of Indian summer and its fourth decade in particular a time of peace and recuperation. Plethon was writing his *Laws* and the painters were completing their last masterpiece, the frescoes of the chruch of the *Pantanassa*, the Queen of Heaven. Quite naturally the Emperor's brothers preferred the free and adventurous life of the Peloponnese to the stifling atmosphere of Constantinople, where John wrestled with the eternal problems of Western aid and the reunion of the Churches. Theodore bestowed very extensive domains on both Constantine and Thomas. Those of the former stretched from Vostitza on the Gulf of Corinth to the tip of Maina, but after the early death of his wife, Maddalena Tocco, he made his home at Kalavryta, while Thomas took Glarentza in exchange and revived it. Yet another brother, Andronikos, came to the Morea after Thessalonica, which he had governed for Manuel II, was traded to the Venetians in 1423, in the expectation, soon to be deceived, that they would make it impregnable.

The Greek triumph ended the endemic struggle between the two communities but left social conditions largely unchanged. Most of the landowners, even on the Latin side of what had always been a very flexible frontier, were already Greek by race or in some degree hellenized by the use of the Greek language, by contact with the population and by intermarriage. The Palaeologues, from the emperors downwards, regularly married Latin women, while Antonio Acciaiuoli of Athens, himself half a Greek, was wedded to Maria Melissene, a member of a Byzantine family which had never ceased to hold lands in various parts of Greece throughout the Latin occupation. In the fifteenth century they held vast properties in Messenia and the country of the Tzakones. Byzantine feudalism, which differed very little from the Latin system and had borrowed many of its features, flourished exceedingly in the period immediately preceding the Turkish conquest and its anarchic tendencies were more effectively held in check than in previous times by the Despot and his brothers. Even Plethon, who loathed it in principle, was glad to accept Theodore's gift of two small fiefs, Phanari in Argolid and Brysis in Lakonia.[22]

Plethon was no solitary phenomenon, but the most eminent

representative of a large group of Byzantine intellectuals living and working at Mistra during the first half of the fifteenth century. Most were churchmen and included two future Greek champions of the union of the Churches and Roman Cardinals: Isidore, Abbot of the monastery of St Demetrios at Constantinople and Metropolitan of Monemvasia and Kiev, and Bessarion, Metropolitan of Nicaea. These great scholars and theologians were balanced by the equally learned and strenuous opponents of unionism, George Scholarios and John Eugenikos. The former was chosen by Mehmet the Conqueror to be the first Orthodox Patriarch of Constantinople under Turkish rule, while the latter ended his career in the Morea as Bishop of Lakedaimonia. All four, however, belonged to the same milieu before they were divided by the controversy concerning union. We know little of the cultured members of the laity, landowners and officials of the Despotate, beyond the names mentioned in the correspondence of the intellectuals. One of them was the John Frangopoulos who restored, in 1428, the monastery church of the *Pantanassa* and commissioned the frescoes described by Robert Byron as 'the very flower of later Byzantine art', outstanding in their colouring and composition. 'Only El Greco in the west, and later Gauguin', adds David Talbot Rice, 'would have used their colours in just this way.'[23] Another, John Dokeianos, is recorded as possessing an ample library of the classics (including Homer, Hesiod, Xenophon and Aristotle), the Church Fathers and Byzantine writers. Many such collections no doubt existed, and the copying of manuscripts was very diligently pursued at Mistra until the last days of the Despotate.[24]

CHAPTER TEN

The Last Years of Athens and Mistra

ANTONIO ACCIAIUOLI, an agile politician, clung to his Duchy on sufferance from the Turks and under the somewhat grudging protection of Venice. He was especially adept at placating Turkish rulers and quickly aligned himself with Turakhan when the latter invaded the Peloponnese. On the other hand his close ties with the first Theodore, and with the Greek world in general, saved him from quarrelling seriously with the Despotate. His elder half-sister, Bartolommea, died at Mistra in 1407. The younger, Francesca, the flamboyant wife of Carlo Tocco, was the moving spirit behind her husband's political ambitions. Besides the southern Ionian islands (Cephalonia, Levkas, Ithaca and Zante) and his foothold in the Morea, Carlo held most of Epiros. By 1418 he had gained possession of both Joannina and Arta, its northern and southern capitals, and even assumed the title of 'Despot of the Romans'. His consort, who had been brought up by her father Nerio at Athens and Corinth, affected a thoroughly Greek style at her court, identified herself with the interests of her Greek-speaking subjects and signed official documents in the imperial purple ink of Byzantium. It was clearly in Antonio's interest to cultivate the friendship of this impressive, if ephemeral, Latin state with its Florentine connexions. But after the death of Carlo in 1429 the mainland empire of the Tocchi crumbled away. The Turks occupied Joannina in the following year and established their authority throughout Epiros, but Carlo's nephew, Carlo II, was allowed to retain Arta as the Sultan's tributary.

In 1430, too, Thessalonica fell to the Turks for the second time. Its capture, which was personally directed by Murad II, and accompanied by spectacular excesses of massacre and pillage, was intended as a rehearsal of an eventual assault on Constantinople and as a ghastly warning to John VIII of the inevitable extinction of his Empire. It also served as a salutary demonstration of the military impotence of Venice, whose garrison had put up a very poor fight.[1] For the time being, however, the Sultan forebore to attack Venetian Euboea, the conquest of which would have almost certainly entailed the disappearance of the Duchy of Athens. Antonio was thus enabled to prolong his balancing act for the last five years of his life. His personal generosity and the easy-going nature of his rule had endeared him to his Greek subjects and also induced a considerable number of Florentines to settle in the Duchy. A Medici had already arrived at Athens in Nerio's time and in the course of years the family hellenized its name as Iatros. William Miller has also traced the presence of other renowned Florentine names, including the Pitti and a Niccolo Machiavelli who was a grandson of Antonio's uncle Donato. There must have been something peculiarly alluring in the Athenian ambience to attract these young Italians to Greece at a moment when Florentine life was at its most stimulating. Perhaps the rural pleasures of the Duchy, so hauntingly evoked by Shakespeare, had a quality which not even Tuscany could rival. Despite occasional Turkish depredations, during which Antonio prudently removed the famous Acciaiuoli stud to the shelter of Euboea, the agriculture of Attica and Boeotia blossomed under the care of assiduous Albanian peasants and the wooded mountains invited Antonio's guests to hunting and hawking. Foremost among the Florentine immigrants were Antonio's own kinsmen, especially the five sons and three daughters of his father's brother Donato. One of these, Franco, was rewarded with the lordship of Sykaminon, the former fief of the Hospitallers near Oropos. A second, Giovanni, became Archbishop of Thebes and a third, Nerio, obtained the bishopric of Cephalonia, thanks to the family link with the Ionian islands. But the ties between Athens and Florence were also strongly commercial, and we find the Prince and the Signoria concluding in 1422 an agreement granting freedom of trade to Florentine merchants in all ports of the Duchy.

On the Greek side the principal citizen, a confidant of the Duchess Maria Melissene, was the archon Chalkokondylas, whose son Laonikos, the historian, was the Athenian counterpart of the Lakonian Phrantzes. Duke Antonio himself was as Greek as he was Italian, and so long as he lived there was no antagonism between the Greek and the much smaller Latin communities, for Florentine rule was infinitely preferable to Burgundian or Catalan. Moreover the city of Athens, which had dwindled under previous regimes to the dimensions of a large village crouching under the fortress rock, was enjoying a brief revival. Athens, not Thebes, became the normal residence of the Duke. According to the younger Chalkokondylas, Antonio, who had inherited great wealth from his father, used it to adorn his capital with new buildings. No sure trace of such has remained, but a Greek document of the fifteenth century establishes that he remodelled the Propylaea to serve as his palace. It would be interesting to know how a Florentine architect of the age of Brunelleschi accomplished this task. That he did so successfully is evident from a letter from Niccolo Machiavelli to Nerio, Bishop of Cephalonia, urging him to visit Athens, where 'you have never seen so beautiful a country nor so fine a castle'. Antonio is also thought to have built the so-called 'Frankish tower' which stood by the southern wing of the Propylaea, opposite the little temple of the Wingless Victory, until 1874 when, in the words of Gregorovius, the German historian of mediaeval Athens, 'it fell a victim to modern Athenian purism'.[2]

Unfortunately Antonio's heir Nerio II, the son of Franco of Sykaminon, possessed neither the ability nor the panache of the Acciaiuoli, and the succession was immediately contested by the Greek party. The Dowager Duchess Maria and Chalkokondylas occupied the Acropolis. Armed with a large bribe, the latter then rushed to the Sultan's court in the hope of enlisting Turkish support for ousting the Florentine. Murad's reaction, however, was to throw the Athenian into prison, and when he succeeded in escaping to Constantinople, the ship in which he embarked for Greece was intercepted by a corsair who sent him back to the Sultan, but by another erratic turn of fortune he was pardoned and set free. Meanwhile the Duchess had sought to reinsure herself in another quarter. For some time she had been negotiating with Constantine Palaeologos, through his confidential emissary Phrantzes, an arrangement whereby the Duchy would be annexed to the Despotate and she herself compensated out of the lands already owned by the Melissenoi in the Morea. Thus, when Chalkokondylas failed to achieve her object Maria summoned Constantine to the rescue. Phrantzes was duly sent back to Athens with an armed force, but on arrival he found not only that Turakhan's Turks had anticipated him by seizing Thebes, but that the adherents of the Acciaiuoli had obtained possession of the Acropolis. The solution of this slightly comic imbroglio, an Athenian *journée des dupes*, was reached by compromise. Nerio II married the widowed Duchess and kept his dukedom as the Sultan's vassal, while Turakhan abandoned Thebes and the Venetians, for their part, undertook not to intervene provided that something like the status quo was maintained. The only losers were the Palaeologues, whose vision of the union of Athens with the Peloponnese was frustrated.[3]

A major disappointment for the student of the Greek Middle Ages is the lack of personal accounts of the Greek scene by any of the numerous visitors to Hellas from the Latin West, while the picture drawn by Byzantine writers is usually obscured by rhetoric or prejudice. Suddenly, at the very end of the era, there appears a traveller of the most articulate kind. Cyriacus of Ancona, or Ciriaco dei Pizzicolli, had nothing mediaeval about him. His approach to Greece was one of a fully fledged product of the Renaissance and of an impassioned student of Classical antiquity. His purpose was to observe and classify the monuments of the past, and in particular to copy and record inscriptions. In that respect he was in advance of his own age and notably of his Byzantine contemporaries, those literati who for all their pride in the purity of their Greek style were apparently indifferent to the relics of old Greece which surrounded them in such abundance. Cyriacus, on the other hand, inherits after eleven centuries the tradition of Pausanias. He is also the ancestor of 'Athenian' Stuart, of Byron and Colonel Leake, and of Chateaubriand musing among the oleanders of the Eurotas. And when he could spare time from antiquities he had a keen eye for the realities of his own age.[4]

The antiquary, a merchant by profession, was born about 1391. His travels in the Levant, of which he kept a fascinating if not always very accurate record in Latin, seem to have begun in 1422 and to have continued for over a quarter of a century. His earlier journeys included Asia Minor and Egypt. His first visit to Greece lasted from Christmas 1436 until the late spring of the following year. After crossing from Corfu to Epiros he was warmly welcomed by Carlo II Tocco at Arta. On the Gulf of Corinth he saw Greek Patras and Venetian Lepanto, and having inspected the remains of Delphi passed through Boeotia to Negroponte and thence to Athens, which he reached in early April. For the next fifteen days he stayed there with a friend, Antonio Balduino. On that occasion he appears not to have paid his respects to the Prince (Nerio II), but to have been totally absorbed by ruins and inscriptions. He then rode southwards over the isthmus of Corinth, noting the shattered state of the Hexamilion, and was entertained at Kalavryta by George Cantacuzenos, grandnephew of the Despot Manuel and an adherent of Constantine Palaeologos. This noble Byzantine was also a scholar and lent Cyriacus books from his fine library. The traveller described his host as 'virum hac aetate graecis litteris eruditum, ac librorum graecorum omnigenum copiosissimum, qui mihi Herodotum historicum ac alios plerosque suos optimos et antiquos libros accommodavit'. (A man of that age learned in Greek letters and possessed of a vast library of all kinds of Greek books, who lent me a History of Herodotus and many other of his old and best books.) It is intriguing to discover this islet of Classical culture in the highlands of the Morea, on the spot where the Greek War of Independence was to break out in 1821. On his way back to Italy Cyriacus again visited Patras, where his host was another Cantacuzene, John, at that time governor of the city. During Cyriacus's third tour in Greece some years later the same man was administering Corinth and the Anconitan referred to him as 'pacis bellique artibus praestantem . . . qui cum me ex Patra veterem novisset amicum perquam benigne suscepit et munifice ex venatu rediens magna cervi parte aliisque haud indignis muneribus donaverat'.[5] (Outstanding in the arts of peace and war—who, when he had recognized me as an old friend from Patras, received me extremely kindly and, on returning from the hunt, presented me generously with a large portion of the stag and other not unworthy gifts.)

Such glimpses of the contemporary Peloponnese are rare and instructive. Perhaps it may be hard to reconcile the supposedly doom-laden milieu on the eve of the Turkish conquest with the spectacle of a cultivated Italian antiquary being entertained by Byzantine magnates in the well stocked libraries of their houses and plied with game from the estate. Perhaps the magnates, being without benefit of hindsight, felt no such sense of doom. At all events Cyriacus was always to be found in the best of company and was no doubt passed on with solicitude from one distinguished host to another. A further friend in the Morea was Memnon, one of the numerous Italo-Greek bastards of Carlo I Tocco, whom he found occupying, on behalf of Constantine Palaeologos, an old Frankish fief by the 'springs of the Alpheios'. There he attended a hunting-party and was presented with the skin of a bear. Evidently, Cyriacus was pleased by the sporting proclivities of Moreot landowners. It was Memnon who accompanied him subsequently to Mistra, where he was introduced to the Despot Theodore II and clambered happily over the debris of ancient Sparta. During the same journey he was at Mycenae and Monemvasia, in the Maina and on the island of Kythera. As we shall see he revisited Mistra in later years and was made much of by the Palaeologues. Athens, too, he saw again, probably in 1444, completed his archaeological studies and was greeted by Duke Nerio 'on the Acropolis, the high castle of the city'. Nerio's tenure of the Dukedom was to last until 1451. It was, however, interrupted for two years from 1439, when he was temporarily supplanted by his brother Antonio II. Until the latter's death permitted his restoration he lived quietly at Florence, where he owned substantial property. The situation in the Morea was more complex, because the Palaeologue brothers were treading on each other's toes. In order to prevent them from lapsing into civil war John VIII sent for Constantine, the most enterprising and pugnacious, and appointed him to act as his agent at Constantinople while he personally headed the imposing Byzantine delegation to the Councils of Ferrara and Florence at which a final effort was to be made to achieve the union of the Eastern and Western Churches. The Emperor took with him his remaining brother, Demetrios, and among the galaxy of clerics and scholars in his suite was Plethon, who had been included not for his soundness as a theologian, which was more than questionable, but for his reputation as the doyen of Byzantine intellectuals.

Rightly or wrongly, John was convinced that only aid from the Catholic West could save Constantinople and that the only hope of obtaining such aid lay in the acceptance by the Orthodox of union and papal supremacy. Among the minority of his subjects who agreed with him were some of the most intelligent, but the majority were as little disposed as in the past to yield over essential points of doctrine and the supremacy of the Holy See. His father Manuel had always maintained that neither force nor persuasion would prevail against the implacable obstinacy of the anti-unionists. It would therefore, he thought, be more politic not to try to bring the issue to a head, but to leave the Turks guessing. The Greeks of the Morea, who had recently expelled the Latins and their clergy after two centuries of struggle, were in no mood to readmit them in any guise. They were horrified to hear that their Emperor, after more than a year of discussion in Italy, had given in and actually signed the fatal Act of Union. When, at the beginning of 1439, he put in at a Peloponnesian port on his return voyage to Constantinople, they bitterly reproached him for deserting the Orthodox cause. And on reaching the capital he found the people divided into two camps, the larger of which remained irreconcilably hostile to union.

Nevertheless the Pope, Eugenius IV, did his best to honour his undertaking to organize a fresh Crusade as soon as union was concluded. As he well knew, the times were not conducive to Crusading. Fervour was conspicuously lacking in the West. France and England were locked in the final stage of the Hundred Years War and no substantial aid could be expected from Germany. Venetian policy was directed by strict considerations of expediency and by the need not to offer unnecessary provocation to the Sultan. Only the Hungarian Kingdom had the interest and the will to fight. The young sovereign, Vladislas of Poland, responded eagerly to the Pope's call, if only for the reason that his frontiers were already under Ottoman attack. In 1439 the Turks overran what was left of Serbia and proceeded to besiege Belgrade. But this fortress was defended for Hungary by the greatest Christian captain of the day, the Transylvanian John Hunyadi, and the assault was beaten off. Subsequently, in 1443, another Ottoman army which had invaded Transylvania was crushed in two successive battles, and the way seemed open for a successful counter-offensive in the Balkans. Indeed the so-called 'long campaign' of 1443 brought victory after victory to the Christian army, which consisted of Hungarians and Serbs reinforced by a small contingent from Western Europe under the Papal Legate, Cardinal Cesarini. Much of Serbia was liberated and Hunyadi pressed forward into Bulgaria.

For the moment it looked as if the Ottoman grip on the former European provinces of Byzantium had been nearly broken. The Sultan, detained in Asia Minor by a revolt of non-Ottoman Turkish emirs, could do little to stop the Hungarian progress. In Albania George Kastriotes, the famous 'Skanderbeg', rose at the head of his countrymen and, in evident co-ordination with the Hungarian advance, a similar drive was launched from the Peloponnese by Constantine Palaeologos.[6] This prince had returned to Greece in the same year, after exchanging places with his brother Theodore, and was now titular Despot of the Morea. As soon as he perceived that the Turks were on the defensive, he acted with speed and decision. While the isthmus was refortified, he marched into northern Greece and was soon in control of the entire country south of Mount Olympus. Nerio was permitted to keep the Duchy on condition that the tribute previously paid to the Sultan would in future accrue to the Despot.[7] Murad had lost so much territory and so many soldiers in Europe that he was glad to agree to a settlement with the King of Hungary and his allies by which the Turks evacuated Serbia and both sides undertook to respect the Danube frontier. In Buda a procession escorting thirteen captive pashas and nine Turkish standards attested the Magyar triumph.

The victory atoned for the disaster of Nikopolis. It also afforded relief, and a prospect of survival, for Constantinople and an opportunity for the Despot Constantine to found an enduring Greek state within the limits of the classical Hellas. On the other hand the balance in the Balkans still swung uncertainly and it was hardly to be expected that the ten year term of the pact concluded in the summer of 1444 between the two chief adversaries would last its course. A further confrontation was inevitable and it came very soon. The Cardinal Legate, Cesarini, had been flatly opposed to the pact. Convinced that a renewal of the campaign would drive the Turks permanently from Europe, he managed to persuade the King of Hungary that an engagement signed with the infidel was not binding on a Christian and could be violated at will. Hunyadi, who would greatly have preferred to rest his forces, reluctantly yielded to his sovereign's insistence, but the Serbian leader, George

Brankovich, and the Albanian Skanderbeg, who had gained all they wanted in the previous fighting, refused to be further involved. It was thus with a much reduced army that the Christians moved through Bulgaria towards the Black Sea. Murad met them at Varna and after a fearful contest practically wiped them out. The King and the Cardinal both lost their lives, but Hunyadi escaped to prolong for another twelve years his unending struggle to stem the Ottoman advance.

The battle of Varna was the decisive calamity for the Greek cause, and the fall of Constantinople only the unescapable aftermath. It is interesting, though unfruitful, to speculate on the course of events had the issue gone the other way. Would, for instance, a Christian victory have reasserted the freedom of the Balkan Slavs, or rescued Constantinople from its isolation in the midst of Ottoman held territory? Would it have saved old Greece, or would its effects have proved merely temporary? In 1444 it was unhappily clear that the West had struck its last blow on behalf of Byzantium. Even so two years passed before Murad, who had been much weakened by the Hungarian war, was ready for a riposte against the Greeks. On this occasion he led his army in person, as if to underline the enormity of Constantine having dared to intrude upon Ottoman territory. The veteran Turakhan accompanied him as subordinate commander. Before this display of power Constantine and Thomas evacuated northern Greece and prepared to stand on the isthmus. But Murad was taking no chance of a repulse. The cannon with which seven years later his son was to breach the walls of Constantinople were deployed against the Hexamilion, and when they had done their work, the onslaught of the Janissaries was as usual irresistible. The Greeks fought bravely enough but were dispersed with severe losses, and separate bodies of men who surrendered were slaughtered on the spot. Events then took much the same course as they did when Turakhan, and before him Evrenos and Yakub, had invaded the Peloponnese. The Turkish army split into two columns, and while Turakhan pursued the Palaeologue brothers in the direction of Mistra, Murad himself marched along the north coast, ravaging it systematically as far as Glarentza. Vostitza was burnt, and the lower city of Patras, but the Turks failed to storm its citadel. Constantine and Thomas evaded capture in the fastnesses of the south. Above all, Mistra defied the invader and the united Ottoman host withdrew from the Morea carrying with it, according to contemporary estimates, sixty thousand prisoners. Although the damage suffered by the Despotate was more grievous than in previous irruptions, it was not yet reduced to the status of a Turkish province. The brothers retained the government, subject to the payment of a heavy tribute and to an undertaking not to oppose the Sultan.[8]

The reluctance of the Turks to take over the Morea outright can only be explained by their well-founded assessment that it was a tough nut to crack, and by the reasonable expectation that it was bound to be theirs anyway before very long. Experience had shown them that a razzia would always succeed in terms of booty and political deterrence. Conquest, however, threatened to be a long-drawn out affair of sieges and ambuscades, the cost of which many Ottoman armies were to feel in succeeding centuries. As Plethon had rightly pointed out, every peak in the Morea was a potential Acropolis.[9] Nor was it in the Turkish interest to waste and destroy beyond a certain point a province which was about to become a prized possession of the Ottoman monarch. Furthermore Murad was wise, in 1446, not to fritter away his military resources in the gorges of Arkadia. His priorities were to strike another blow at the Hungarians, and if necessary at the Albanian Skanderbeg, and then to concentrate his effort on the reduction of Constantinople. In 1448 Hunyadi forced the issue by advancing as far as Kossovo, the field where Bayezit had crushed Lazar of Serbia nearly sixty years earlier. But this time Hunyadi had no allies; Skanderbeg failed to march to his assistance and the Serbian George Brankovich had decided that his advantage lay in placating the Turks. So Hunyadi lost another closely contested battle, and the Greeks of Constantinople and the Morea were left on their own.

Yet, in 1448, the fatal point did not necessarily seem to have been reached. Constantine and Thomas were still in power. For three generations the Moreots had endured Turkish onsets like successive acts of God. Each time, however, the tide had receded and the country had again flourished under its native Orthodox rulers. There seemed no reason why the cycle should not continue to revolve as previously. The untiring traveller Cyriacus returned to Mistra in the year following the Sultan's invasion and found life there proceeding exactly as before. Plethon was still alive and active and he also met the younger Athenian Chalkokondylas, whom Constantine had unsuccessfully tried to use as an intermediary with the Sultan and who now obligingly translated a sonnet by Cyriacus into Greek.[10] The Anconitan observed that the Morea still appeared flourishing and well cultivated. He presumably missed, however, the most splendid and poignant occasion which Byzantine Mistra had ever witnessed, the coronation of the last Emperor of the Romans.

The childless John VIII died at the end of October 1448, nominating

Constantine as his successor. Of all his brothers, the sons of Manuel II and of his Serbian basilissa Helen Dragas, Constantine was undoubtedly the most able and courageous and the least oppressed by the grim inheritance of the Palaeologues. All his life he had fought with varying fortunes to sustain the imperial dignity and to widen the limits of Greek rule. The only other possible candidate, the former Moreot Despot Theodore II, had predeceased John. Despite the latter's express wishes both Thomas and Demetrios made bids for the throne, but the intervention of their mother in Constantine's favour was decisive. When it came to the point, it was found preferable that he should be crowned at Mistra by a bishop professing the pure Orthodox faith than by the Patriarch of Constantinople, Gregory, who represented the dominant but unpopular unionist faction in the Church. The insignia of empire were sent to the Morea and Constantine was solemnly invested with them on 6 January 1449.

Two months later he was in Constantinople, where he held a conference with his two brothers. It was agreed that the latter should divide the Morea between them, each taking the title of Despot. Demetrios was to have the central, eastern and southern parts of the peninsula, with Mistra as his capital, while Thomas, from his seat at Patras, governed the western rump of the former principality of Achaia and the littoral of the Corinthian Gulf. They swore faithfully to respect each other's rights. Given the need to satisfy the claims of both, the Emperor's dispositions were sensible enough, but they had no sooner returned to the Morea, out of range of Constantine's restraining influence, than they were revealed as a pair of selfish and short-sighted intriguers. Not only did they covet each other's portions, but they also nourished all too apparent designs against the Venetian outposts in the Peloponnese, especially Argos and Nauplia, at a moment when it was clearly vital for them to cultivate the favour of the Republic. Both invoked Turkish help in their mutual quarrels and the new Sultan, Mehmet II, who had succeeded his father Murad in 1451, ordered Turakhan to take the side of Demetrios. After a reconciliation of a sort had been effected by Constantine's good offices, it was the last act of Plethon's life to congratulate Demetrios on what was to be only an uneasy truce.

Late in 1452, as Mehmet drew the net tighter around the doomed city of Constantinople, he called on Turakhan to create a diversion by again invading the Morea. Supported by his sons Achmet and Umur, the old pasha initiated the campaign by the now classic attack on the defences of the isthmus, which the Despots had once more repaired. Here again the Greeks put up a strong fight and when the Turks again burst through, Matthew Asen, a brother-in-law of Demetrios, caught Achmet in the same narrow pass between Corinth and Mycenae where an Ottoman army was wiped out during the Greek War of Independence, destroyed his force and took him prisoner.[11] Meanwhile, the old feudal castles of the Arkadian marches stubbornly resisted Turakhan. Military honours were perhaps even, but the purpose of the operation had been achieved, for no soldiers nor supplies from the Peloponnese reached Constantinople in its final agony. When the Despots received the appalling news of the fall of the city on 29 May 1453, and of the Emperor's heroic death in the mêlée below the walls, they had no choice but to beg the Sultan to confirm their state of vassalage on the existing terms and subject to the payment of the same tribute.

They were now, however, threatened by an uprising of their own subjects, exasperated by years of insecurity and tribulation. It was inspired by the Albanian element, under a chief named Peter Boua, but the movement was immediately joined by the Greek archons. Greeks and Albanians found a common leader in Manuel Cantacuzenos, apparently a member of the former imperial family who had been governing the Maina. Acclaiming him as counter-Despot, the insurgents appealed for support to Venice, but while the Senate was still hesitating Demetrios and Thomas called in the Turks to quell their own people. As Umur duly engaged the rebels, the situation was confused by the appearance of a second popular aspirant to power. This was Giovanni Asan Zaccaria, the son of Centurione, who had been incarcerated by Thomas for some years in the castle of Chloumoutzi, and who now took the field as the champion of the still active Latin element in the Western Morea, proclaiming himself Prince of Achaia. In order to clear up the resulting anarchy, and to restore the authority of the two thoroughly humiliated Despots, Turakhan was forced to mount another full-scale campaign. Of the chief rebels, Cantacuzenos managed to escape, Boua was pardoned by the Turks and reinstated as the spokesman of his people, and Zaccaria ended his days as a pensioner of Venice and, subsequently, of the papal court.[12]

No further event of importance occurred during the next four years. The Despots still hoped for support from the West, and each on his own sounded out at various moments the Holy See, Venice, the King of France and, more insistently, King Alfonso of Aragon and Naples, who let it be known that he had not forgotten his family's ancient claim to the principality of Achaia. Nothing, however, came of these approaches. Meanwhile the Sultan regarded with increasing irritation the failure of the Despots to remit to him their annual tribute. When payments were three years behindhand and all his warnings had been disregarded, Mehmet at last lost patience and sent them an ultimatum. With incredible folly, this too was rejected. The Sultan decided to enforce his will with the full strength of his army of Europe and in May 1458 he crossed the isthmus. The campaign which followed was largely an affair of small but hard fought sieges. Dozens of small castles, the relics of the Frankish overlords, and of hilltops fortified by Greek and Albanian villagers, needed to be stormed one by one. The Sultan found it costly, for the Moreot countrymen resisted desperately, refusing to be overawed by Mehmet's professional warriors, the terror of all Europe. The most formidable task of all, the reduction of Corinth, was entrusted to Mahmoud Pasha, a renegade of Greek race. Its defenders, under Matthew Asen, held out against three months of continuous artillery bombardment and when he eventually surrendered he was sent to carry the Sultan's terms to the Despots, who were skulking in the recesses of Mount Taygetos. For all his military exertions half the Morea was still unsubdued with the campaigning season already over. Mehmet was anxious to break off the fighting and therefore offered to allow Thomas and Demetrios to retain two-thirds of the peninsula. He removed from them, however, the whole of the north from Patras to Corinth and made it into a Turkish province. Having placed it under the administration of Umur Pasha, he retired for a few days to Athens, a city for which he had developed a strong personal interest.

It had already been his for two years, the Duchy was extinct and the Acciaiuoli were dispersed. Their last years were not without incident. Nerio II, Murad's obedient vassal, had died in 1451, the same year as the Sultan, leaving his second wife, Chiara Zorzi, a Venetian from Karystos in Euboea, in charge of their young son Francesco. At the Turkish court there resided, in the capacity of favourite or hostage, or possibly both, a cousin of Francesco named Franco, the son of the Duke Antonio II who had for a short time displaced Nerio. These personages became the chief actors in a lurid drama of the Italian Renaissance played out on an Athenian stage. It began when the Duchess fell in love with a young Venetian, Bartolommeo Contarini, the son of the castellan of Nauplia, who had come to Athens for reasons of trade. As the lady insisted on marriage, and Bartolommeo already had a wife in Venice, it was perhaps inevitable that he should remove the latter by poison in the course of a sojourn at home. On his return to Athens the pair were married by the apparently unsuspecting Archbishop and Bartolommeo became guardian of the boy Francesco and *de facto* Duke of Athens.

Before long complaints from the citizens about his arbitrary behaviour were reaching the Sultan, who on straightforward political grounds was displeased at the prospect of the Duchy coming again under Venetian influence. He accordingly summoned Contarini and his stepson to his court and held them there while he despatched Franco, the cousin, to take over the Dukedom. At first the latter's government seemed acceptable to the Athenians, but he soon shocked them by imprisoning the deposed Duchess in the castle of Megara and secondly by putting her to death, some said with his own hands. When the news reached Contarini he confessed the whole truth to the Sultan, whose reaction was to order Umur to seize Athens, expel Franco and put an end to Florentine rule. It is not known what happened to Francesco, but presumably, like many other personable youths, he was reserved for the seraglio. The pasha occupied the city in June 1456 but as had so frequently occurred before, the Acropolis held out. The Turks had to besiege it for two years until Franco was convinced that neither the Venetians nor any other Latins would take the fortress off his hands. Finally, while the Sultan was still engaged in the Morea, he accepted the offer of Thebes, with the whole of Boeotia, to be held as an Ottoman fief. Two years later, when serving his masters in a campaign against the Tocchi, he was quietly strangled and Boeotia went the way of the rest of Greece. His three sons became Moslems and Janissaries.[13]

Following in the rare footsteps of two Byzantine sovereigns (Constans and Basil II) and of one Latin (Henry of Flanders) Mehmet was the first and only Ottoman Sultan to visit Athens. According to the Byzantine historians of the conquest he was delighted with it. This strange young man, only twenty-one at his accession, could be a monster of inhumanity when reasons of state or personal inclinations were concerned. His other face was of a civilized man. He was a polished linguist, full of intellectual curiosity and an avid student of the past. He loved to hear about vanished civilizations and the exploits of former conquerors. One of the Westerners whose acquaintance he had made at about the time of the fall of Constantinople was Cyriacus of Ancona, who was still travelling in the Aegean area and whom he employed to read history to him. In all probability Cyriacus had told him about classical Athens and perhaps had shown him his own drawings of the Parthenon and other buildings, a few of which have survived. He is likely to have given him the usual inaccurate information which prevailed until the nineteenth century about the identity of the ruined monuments which existed in greater profusion at the time of the Acciaiuoli than after the liberation of Greece. At all events Mehmet seems to have derived much pleasure from his visit. He treated the Athenians kindly and granted them a number of unspecified civic and ecclesiastical privileges. The Latin Archbishop, Protimo of Euboea, was at once expelled while the Greek clergy were confirmed in the possession of most of their churches and monasteries and in their liberty of worship. The Parthenon, however, was soon converted into a mosque, and a minaret rose from the midst of its roof.

The Palaeologues did not long outlast the Acciaiuoli. If Demetrios had been left as sole Despot he would in all likelihood have acquiesced quietly in his role of vassal prince. He was unambitious and like many Byzantines, had come to prefer Turkish to Latin ways. Thomas, however, was an inveterate and adventurous intriguer who never learned his lesson. He listened far too readily to irresponsible native advisers and to unreliable voices of encouragement from the West. He soon became embroiled with his brother over boundary questions and at the same time began to harass the Turkish garrisons on the northern Morea. He even attempted to suborn Umur Pasha, but the Sultan got wind of the affair and replaced the latter with an Albanian, Hamsa. Nevertheless, with the aid of Italian mercenaries Thomas managed to hold off the Turks while enlarging his territory at his brother's expense. In the spring of 1460 another Turkish commander, Zagan Pasha, drove him back into the southern part of the Peloponnese and compelled him to beg for peace. Since, however, he was unable to raise the tribute demanded, the Sultan at last decided to get rid of him, and for good measure to remove Demetrios as well. The latter object was achieved by negotiation. Demetrios surrendered Mistra and placed himself under the Sultan's protection, while his wife, Theodora Asen, and their daughter Helen, who had taken refuge at Monemvasia, were induced to leave its shelter for that of Mehmet's harem. As for the ex-Despot, he was consoled with the lordship of the little islands of Lemnos and Imbros, facing the entrance to the Dardanelles.

Mehmet's full fury was then turned on Thomas and such of his archons as continued to offer a brave but futile resistance to Ottoman arms. Every cruelty was employed, under his personal direction, to terrify the recalcitrant Moreots into submission. At Kastritza the local landowner, Proinokokkas, was flayed alive and his followers beheaded or impaled; at Gardiki six thousand persons were indiscriminately slaughtered after the surrender of the castle. Many more thousands were rounded up and shipped to Constantinople, which the Sultan, like certain of his Byzantine predecessors after past wars and plagues, was endeavouring to repopulate. In some places frightfulness merely stimulated defiance, as in the case of the fortress of Salmenikon in the mountains behind Patras. There Constantine Graitzas Palaeologos, perhaps a kinsman of the imperial family, held out for a whole year, and was chivalrously allowed by the Grand Vizier to go free. Kritoboulos of Imbros, the Sultan's Greek panegyrist, claimed that Mehmet had captured two hundred and fifty castles in the course of his final campaign in the Morea. The figure may be exaggerated, but it illustrates the nature of the difficulties faced by one Turkish host after another, and especially between 1446 and 1460, in grinding down the embittered resistance of the last independent corners of Hellas. The fight put up by the obscure heroes on those Peloponnesian hilltops was worthy in each case of the last stand by Constantine Palaeologos in his capital. Thomas's behaviour, on the other hand, was ignominious in the extreme. He took no part in the fighting of the summer of 1460, but lay low on the Messenian coast and on the approach of the Turks slipped away to Corfu from the Venetian harbour of Navarino. A few months later he crossed the Adriatic to Ancona, bringing with him the head of St Andrew, which had been preserved for many centuries at Patras. His possession of one of the most notable relics of the Greek Church, and his willingness to present it to Pope Pius II, ensured him a cordial reception in Rome, as well as pensions from the Holy See and the Venetian Senate. He died there in 1465. His brother Demetrios later lost the Sultan's favour and had difficulty in maintaining a livelihood. In 1470 he ended his days as a monk at Adrianople.[14]

A sole Greek city, Monemvasia, was left in Greek hands. Its governor, a Palaeologos, refused to surrender it to the Turkish envoys who came to fetch the wife and daughter of Demetrios, and the Turks rightly judged it too strong to be worth attacking. The city thus reverted to Thomas, who placed it under the protection of his new patron, the Pope. This arrangement, however, did not last long. It was not practicable to maintain a papal administration on the coast of the Morea and after three years Palaeologos, with the agreement of the citizens, transferred the government to a Venetian podesta. In its long deferred but imminent confrontation with the Ottoman power, the maritime empire of St Mark needed all the bastions on which it could lay its hands.

CHAPTER ELEVEN

Duchies of the Islands

THE GREEK ISLANDS are a world in themselves. Greece would be unimaginable without them; yet each group, each unit has its separate identity and character, very real but subtle and hard to define, distinguishing it from its sea-girt neighbours, from the maritime communities of the mainland coasts and from the secluded environment of the mainland mountains. In the Middle Ages, as at other times, the sea endowed the islanders with its traditional advantages and drawbacks. While preserving them from mass invasion and providing them with ever available channels of communication with the rest of the Mediterranean, it left them peculiarly vulnerable to the raider and the pirate. Once the Latin Conquest had deprived them even of the limited degree of protection against these plagues afforded by the Byzantine navy, their only hope of security lay in subjection to a feudal lord who was an effective guardian of his territory against corsairs as well as a successful corsair himself. Unfortunately for the subjects, the Catalans of Athens became the most proficient sea-robbers of the period and the Turks, as soon as they had accustomed themselves to seafaring, were not far behind them.

The history of the Aegean and Ionian islands in the Frankish age of Greece is of course intertwined at many points with that of the mainland, but not so inextricably that the threads of insular events cannot easily be traced. The partition agreement concluded between the conquerors of Constantinople in 1204 assigned to Venice both the Ionian islands and the principal groups in the Aegean (Cyclades, Sporades, Dodecanese). The Republic, however, had too much on its hands to assimilate anything like all the new possessions to which it had assumed so dubious a title. To acquire trading privileges was a comparatively simple affair; to conquer and hold a territorial empire was infinitely more laborious and costly. Since Venice lacked the necessary resources to enforce the totality of its claims staked out in the partition treaty, these had to be realized with strict regard to economy and priorities.

Therefore, when it came to occupying the islands of the Aegean archipelago (the term is an Italian corruption of the two Greek words

223

aigaion pelagos), the Republic was glad to delegate, as it were, its rights to private individuals, provided that they had the right qualifications. Preferably they should be Venetians of good family, imbued with a basic loyalty towards their mother city and with willingness to further its commercial interests. At the same time they must be prepared to risk their lives and fortunes in the Levant without being able to count on official Venetian support for their enterprises. In return, however, they were not necessarily expected formally to acknowledge Venetian sovereignty. Such a loose arrangement proved ideally favourable to Marco Sanudo, a nephew of Doge Dandolo who had given useful service to his aged uncle in the political and military fields during the expedition against Constantinople. As soon as he could release himself from those responsibilities he recruited a company of like-minded adventurers, and, with a small fleet fitted out at his and their expense, succeeded in taking possession of seventeen islands. Most of them were undefended; no opposition was encountered from the Greek side and the only fighting of the cruise took place at Naxos, which had to be captured from a band of Genoese freebooters.

It is curious to observe these Venetian aristocrats and their retainers playing the part of Vikings in the Greek archipelago. Sanudo lost no time in proclaiming himself Duke and establishing his capital in Naxos, a fertile and populous island which in classical times had been capable of putting eight thousand heavy armed infantry into the field. For himself he also appropriated Paros, Melos, Syra and Kythnos, Siphnos and Sikinos, Ios and Amorgos. Other islands were reserved as fiefs for his principal followers, whose names sound like a roll call of the patrician families of Venice. A Dandolo had Andros, a Barozzi Thera (Santorin), a Quirini Astypalaia. Anaphe fell to a Foscolo, Kythera to a Venier. More acquisitive were the Ghisi, who obtained not only Tenos and Mykonos but also Skyros, Skiathos and Skopelos, while the Giustiniani occupied Keos and Seriphos.[1]

The insular domain which each of these petty tyrants found waiting for him was admirably self-contained and suited to men whose lives were normally spent in adventurous seafaring and trade. It would already have its own port, its castle, an island village or two, a clever and hard-working population of sailors, merchants and tillers of soil which was not always ungrateful. The larger Cyclades, such as Naxos and Andros, were well worth cultivating, but there is no evidence that the Italians at first made much effort to exploit their mineral resources, such as the gold and emery of Naxos and the marble of Paros. What the islanders thought of their rulers can only be conjectured, but it is certain that the vigorous Italian lords offered their Greek subjects a far greater measure of security then they had enjoyed under the decaying regime of the Byzantine Angeloi, when the archipelago had been at the mercy of every stray pirate, not to mention the massively organized operations of the Normans of Sicily.

Having won his duchy with so little trouble Marco turned for a short while to higher politics. He saw himself as a feudal ruler of the same stature as the Prince of Achaia and the Seigneur of Athens, and his prestige was notably advanced when the Latin Emperor Henry accepted his homage and, as his immediate sovereign, confirmed his title of Duke, thus relieving him of any shadow of formal obligation towards Venice. His ambitions for the future were directed towards Crete, the purchase of which he had formerly helped to negotiate for Doge Dandolo. In 1212 the Venetian governor of that great island, a Tiepolo, was in difficulties with a native rebellion and Marco, now acting as a good Venetian, went to his aid. But when the uprising was duly quelled he decided, with some local connivance, to try to seize Crete for himself. He calculated that if he could rely on the support of native Greeks and his gamble was initially successful, Venice might conclude that the price of reconquest would be too high. Moreover it was probable that the Latin Emperor, his sovereign, would back him up. The reward of his audacity would be a realm comparable in size and importance to the Lusignan kingdom of Cyprus and, in addition, he would continue to hold the galaxy of islands which he had previously conquered. The Aegean would henceforth be his lake; he would emerge as a sort of mediaeval Minos, the new sea-king of Crete.

The conception was grand enough and the risk worth taking, but in the event the venture misfired. Tiepolo proved as bold and resourceful in defence as Sanudo in attack. When Marco, after overrunning most of the island with the aid of the Cretans, took its capital, Candia, Tiepolo slipped out disguised as a woman and directed the Venetian resistance from another and stronger castle. His rival set to work to eliminate the remaining Venetian garrisons, but this slow process was interrupted by the arrival of powerful reinforcements from the Adriatic. Sanudo soon realized that without the element of surprise, he was no longer likely to succeed; Crete stood at the head of the Venetian priorities and neither side was anxious to prolong what was mainly a civil conflict between Venetians and did not help the Latin cause in general. So a truce was arranged, amicably enough, between the two commanders by which Sanudo gave up the towns under his control but was permitted to retire to the archipelago, taking with him the principal Cretans who had adhered to him. Oddly enough, the Republic does not seem to have harboured much resentment against him for his disloyalty. It was no doubt satisfied that his failure would serve as a deterrent to any other private adventurer with an urge to challenge Venetian sea-power. It certainly showed no inclination to punish him for his presumption by expelling him from his duchy. There was no advantage to Venice in administering a host of small islands. Their capture would be arduous and unprofitable, and so long as they remained in the hands of Italians (provided that the latter were not Genoese) little harm was likely to spring from them.[2]

In the next year the Duke of Naxos tried another bold but futile *coup de main*, this time against the Emperor of Nicaea, Theodore Laskaris. Launching his small fleet across the Aegean, he seized the port of Smyrna. The aggression was as unexpected as it was unprovoked, but in attacking the Latin Emperor's most dangerous opponent, Marco may well have counted on acquiring merit with his sovereign as well as on effacing the bad impression caused by the Cretan fiasco. However, his second attempt to assert himself was as injudicious as the first. The Nicaean forces were much stronger than his own and when they counter-attacked he lost Smyrna and was taken prisoner. From his predicament he was saved by his luck and charm, for Theodore found his personal qualities so attractive that he set him free and gave him his sister in marriage, an outcome which enhanced his prestige with his Greek islanders and even, perhaps, with his Latin overlord. Since the twelfth century there had been frequent intermarriage between the sovereign houses of Europe and the imperial family of Byzantium, but Marco was the first of the great Latin magnates of Greece to take a Greek bride.[3]

The Venetian lords of the archipelago adapted themselves more easily to local conditions than the Burgundians and Champenois who settled at the same time in continental Greece. They had fought and traded for many generations in the Christian Levant, while the only experience which the French conquerors had to guide them was that of the mainly Moslem Outremer. Throughout the early thirteenth century a thin but steady stream of enterprising young Italians flowed towards the Aegean, where they found the service of the Duke and his lords preferable to the restraints and disciplines of their native cities. Few possessed knightly status or were so closely enmeshed in feudal custom and prejudice as the French of Achaia. Few, too, brought wives with them. In their social relations with the Greeks they were from the first easy-going and tolerant. There was a notable absence of religious bigotry in the islands and the Orthodox Church was neither displaced nor harried. The Greek

Metropolitan was confirmed in his office. Nevertheless a parallel Roman hierarchy, too elaborate for the immediate needs of the immigrant Italians, was established throughout the archipelago and as time passed it struck much deeper roots than the similar system set up by the Franks in northern Greece and the Morea. Whereas the *gasmouloi* or half-breeds of the mainland tended to cling to their mother's faith, the islanders of mixed blood were just as likely to gravitate to Rome. Hence the flourishing Roman Catholic community which is still to be found in the Cyclades.

These Venetian expatriates and their bilingual Levant-born children derived their livelihood from the sea, from commerce or from preying on the commerce of others. From their capital in Naxos the Sanudi were well situated for controlling the shipping lanes, and these were very busy in the first decades of Frankish hegemony. Traffic from Egypt and Outremer, Cyprus and Crete. Smyrna, Constantinople and Thessalonica, grain and cotton ships from Thessaly, cargoes of wine and silk from the Morea, long-distance freight from the Black Sea, from Provence, Italy and Sicily, all passed through the Aegean. It was easy enough for the swift galleys belonging to the Duke and his vassals to slip out of their island harbours and intercept merchant vessels. Moreover no stigma was attached to the levying of charges, or to the confiscation of ship and burden if flight or resistance were attempted. Such activity was not regarded as illegal piracy unless pushed to extremes and calculated to ruin profitable trade; it would have been foolish for the Duke to cause needless offence by excessive exactions to the Republics of Venice and Genoa, to the Hohenstaufens of Sicily and to local Latin rulers. So long as the island lords confined themselves to what were considered as normal perquisites by the standards of the day, they were free to enrich themselves by those means, as well as by straightforward trading in the products of the archipelago.

In 1227 Marco was succeeded by his half-Greek son Angelo, whose prosperity enabled him to cut an even greater dash among his fellow princes. His fleet was much in demand to uphold Latin interests. Like a good vassal he responded readily to calls from his sovereigns, the Latin emperors, for aid against his kinsmen, the emperors of Nicaea. He gave particularly sterling service in 1236 when, along with Geoffroy II de Villehardouin, he helped to frustrate a dangerous move by John III Vatatzes to regain Constantinople. The Emperor Baldwin's slightly wayward reaction to this feat of arms was to make him a vassal of the Prince of Achaia and a peer of the principality, but Angelo does not seem to have taken amiss his subordination to the Frenchman. He

loyally supported the next Prince, Guillaume II, in his attack on
Monemvasia and the Tzakonians and joined him eleven years later, in
1259, for the disastrous campaign of Pelagonia. With his feudal superior
he was taken prisoner, but it appears that Michael VIII soon allowed
him to return to Naxos. He died there in 1263, profoundly regretted, we
are assured, by his subjects. Like the principality of Achaia, the duchy of
the archipelago never flourished so vigorously as in the first half-century
of its existence.[4]

Writing of the sixteenth century, the French historian Fernand
Braudel describes the Adriatic and Ionian islands linking Venice with its
Aegean possessions and 'running along the axis' of Venetian power as
the Republic's stationary fleet'.[5] In the thirteenth century, however, the
chain was far from complete. Although the Ionian, like the Aegean,
islands had been allotted to Venice by the partition treaty, there were
practical difficulties in enforcing its provisions. In the general
dissolution of Byzantine authority under the Angeloi, Corfu had been
seized by a Genoese corsair, Leone Vetrano, while Cephalonia, Zante
and Ithaca had fallen to an adventurer of allegedly Roman origin,
Matteo Orsini, at the time of the last Norman attack on the Empire. It
took the Venetians two amphibious expeditions and much fighting to
get rid of Vetrano. After he was caught and executed the Republic
entrusted the government of the island to ten Venetian nobles, provided
that they made themselves responsible for its defence and paid a
substantial sum for the privilege. At the same time it gladly confirmed
Orsini in his possession of the other three islands on condition that he
acknowledged Venetian overlordship. Hardly, however, had these
economical arrangements been concluded than Corfu was again lost,
this time to the Despot Michael Dukas of Epiros. Under the pretence of
recognising Venetian suzerainty over his dominions Michael, as well as
challenging the Frankish occupation of northern Greece and the Morea,
succeeded in evicting the Republic's lessees from Corfu and, further
south, in annexing Leukas. So Corfu remained under Greek rule until
1259, when the Despot Michael II gave it to King Manfred of Naples
and Sicily as the dowry of his daughter Helen. And when the
Hohenstaufens were supplanted by Charles of Anjou, it duly passed to
the Angevin crown. Modon and Coron were the only Greek staging
points left to the Venetians on the sea-route to Crete.

The Treaty of Viterbo, which in 1267 conferred on Charles of Anjou
suzerainty over Achaia, automatically brought the archipelago as well
under the Angevin umbrella. In practice, however, this reshaping of the
feudal structure made little difference to the fortunes of the new Duke,

Marco Sanudo II. It failed to protect him when Michael VIII Palaeologos deployed his counter-offensive against the Latins which in turn stimulated Charles's own plans for a second Latin conquest of Constantinople. For some years he was hard put to it to defend his islands against the Byzantine admirals Philanthropenos and Licario. The latter, himself a hired Italian freelance, was the more dangerous and effective of the two. In a series of bitter maritime encounters Marco and his vassals lost all the Sporades and, of the Cyclades, Keos, Siphnos and Seriphos, Sikinos, Polykandros, Ios and Amorgos, Astypalaia, Santorin, Anaphe and Kythera. His sister, the widow of Paolo Navigajoso, Grand Admiral of the defunct Latin Empire, was expelled from Lemnos. But most of these Byzantine successes proved only transitory, and the Latin lords gradually filtered back. The Duke himself clung resolutely to the main islands: at Melos, for example, he drove out the Greek rebels who had captured the castle and ordered their leader, a monk, to be fettered and flung into the sea.[6]

Hostilities with Byzantium ceased with the death of Michael Palaeologos in 1282 and three years later his son Andronikos II signed a pact with Venice by which the Empire and the Republic undertook to respect the integrity of each other's territories. Unconstitutionally, because Naples and not Venice was Marco's suzerain, the duchy was included in this arrangement which, though it brought relief to the islands, gave Venice an excuse to re-open the issue of overlordship. It would of course have been neater and more logical for all the islands occupied by Latins to have counted as Venetian dependencies. Most of their lords were Venetians by origin; some, like the Quirini of Astypalaia (Stampalia), maintained palaces in Venice; others possessed and frequently resided on estates in Venetian Crete. Nevertheless it suited Duke Marco to remain a vassal of Charles of Anjou, to whom he carefully renewed his oath of allegiance. He reckoned that by admitting the Venetian claim he would surely be forfeiting all hopes of real independence. The dispute came to a head in respect of Andros, the affairs of which afford a good illustration of the continuing involvement of Venice in the archipelago. When Marino Dandolo, the lord of Andros, died childless, Duke Angelo, acting correctly according to feudal custom, divided the island between his widow and Geremia Ghisi. The latter, however, a forceful character, proceeded to appropriate the whole fief and it was to Venice that the widow, who quickly married a Quirini as her second husband, appealed for redress. The Republic saw its chance and instructed Ghisi to hand over the island, pending a permanent decision, to its own representatives, but as the usurper happened to have married his daughter to a son of the reigning Doge, the instruction was never carried out. The suit was still pending long after both Ghisi and Dandolo's former wife were dead. Marco, its overlord, eventually moved to assume direct authority over Andros, but his action was challenged, within the period allowed by Frankish custom, by the lady's son by her second marriage Niccolo Quirini. While the latter renewed his mother's appeal to Venice the Duke took care to lodge his case with the court of Achaia at Andravida, from which he was sure of obtaining a favourable decision. At the same time he gave the Republic to understand that if it persisted in supporting Quirini, it would be risking an unnecessary and impolitic quarrel with the Angevin kingdom. This was the signal for the Venetian government, always realistic in such matters, to back down. The Sanudi were confirmed in their hold on Andros, and Quirini was mollified by an indemnity.[7]

Despite this diplomatic victory over so formidable an opponent, and the gradual resumption of Marco's authority over islands lost to the Greeks, the prosperity of the archipelago declined sharply throughout his long reign, which lasted until 1303. Licario's operations fatally impaired the order which the galleys of the first two Sanudi had imposed on the maritime scene and after the death of Michael VIII the Byzantines made no effort to police the Aegean. Finding it too expensive to maintain a fleet of his own, and relying for the defence of his coasts on his alliance with Genoa, Andronikos II dismissed his sailors, who turned all to readily to piracy. Venice and Genoa, when not fighting one another, were strong enough at sea to guarantee a measure of protection to their commerce, but Marco could not save his scattered domains from the continual depredations of the corsairs. The smaller islands suffered more severely; some of them were deserted by their own inhabitants and became, like those of the Caribbean in a later age, the regular retreats of buccaneers. From those bases they haunted the channels most frequently used by shipping and plotted their raids on the still flourishing larger islands in which the population now tended to concentrate.

The general disorder was accentuated by local warfare between Latin magnates and by occasional destructive irruptions from outside the area. A typical incident, ridiculous in itself but originating in the traditional feud between Sanudi and Ghisi and involving the intervention of two of the greater Western powers, is described by one of the few contemporary Latin writers who took an intense personal interest in Romania. This was Marino Sanudo, called Torsello or the Elder to distinguish him from a later historian of the same name, who began to record his experiences of Frankish Greece some years before the compilation of the *Chronicle of the Morea*. Born at Venice about 1270, he was a cousin of Duke Marco, who welcomed him at Naxos as a young man, while his subsequent visits to the court of Achaia gave him an intimate knowledge of Peloponnesian affairs. It was at Glarentza that he composed the most historically significant of his books, the *Secreta Fidelium Crucis*, the purpose of which was to awaken the Latin world to the very real danger threatening it from the nascent expansion of the Ottoman Turks. Although his foresight was to be fully justified by events, few listened to his warnings at the time. A later work, the *History of the Kingdom of Romania*, is less rich in detail, but more accurate in its presentation of the facts, than the *Chronicle of the Morea*, as also are his surviving letters and memoirs. Hence the value of his glimpse of the turbulent life of the archipelago.[8]

Marino was at Naxos in 1293 and the squabble in question broke out seven years earlier. It concerned, of all things, the theft of a prize donkey, surely an animal bred for carrying distinguished personages over the rough island tracks. Corsairs carried it off from Ghisi territory and sold it to Guglielmo Sanudo, son of the Duke, who refused to give it up although it bore the Ghisi brandmark. Thereupon war between the two families ravaged the Cyclades, centering round the key harbour of Syra, which Guglielmo held against the Ghisi besiegers. At the critical moment the attackers were foiled by the unexpected arrival of a squadron of ships flying the flag of Charles II of Naples, the Duke's Angevin overlord, which duly came to the rescue of the King's vassal, but the quarrel was only settled, after both sides were exhausted, by the arbitration of the Venetian bailie of Negroponte, and the eventual fate of the donkey is not recorded.[9]

Even fresher in the minds of the Naxians was a ruinous raid by the Aragonese admiral Roger de Lluria, that inveterate enemy of the Angevins, which the Cyclades endured in the year before Marino's visit. Apart from the endemic piracy, the prevailing insecurity was prolonged by a seven-year war between Venice and Genoa, which began in 1296 and absorbed the energies of both Republics in Levantine waters. For the duchy of Naxos, however, it demonstrated the advantages of the Venetian connexion, or rather of the adroitness which the Duke displayed in leaning for support now on Venice, now on the King of Naples, as occasion demanded. Since the Byzantines were allied with Genoa and Venetian strength was based on the central and southern Aegean, the war enabled the Duke and various independent adventurers siding with Venice to complete the eradication of Greek power from the archipelago just at the time when Byzantium was recovering ground in the Morea at Latin expense. Among the last of the islands to be wrested from the Greeks was Kythera, an important stopping-place on the route to Crete, which from being a dependency of Greek Monemvasia reverted to the Venetian Venieri. Simultaneously Latin rule was greatly reinforced by the installation of the Knights of St John at Rhodes. Duke Guglielmo, quick to enlist them as allies, sent a squadron to assist them in taking the island from the Turks and invited them to establish a second maritime base in his own Delos, where their castle dominated the wide field of Hellenistic ruins.[10]

These developments resulted in a temporary improvement in the affairs of the duchy and encouraged Guglielmo and his eldest son, Niccolo, in their penchant for chivalrous gestures, in which they resembled conventional Frankish nobles rather than canny overseas Venetians. They were very meticulous in the performance of their feudal obligations, especially in respect of the Princes of Achaia. Guglielmo was present at Philip of Savoy's grandiose tournament on the isthmus of Corinth and Niccolo led the knights of the Cyclades to join Gautier de Brienne, Duke of Athens, at the fatal battle of the Kephissos. He was lucky to survive that ordeal at the price of wounds and a ransom, whereas his rival, Giorgio Ghisi of Tenos, lost his life. Later, in 1316, he fought for Princess Mahaut of Achaia against Ferdinand of Majorca at the battle of Manolada. After his father's death in 1323 he sought, as Duke of Naxos, every possible opportunity to indulge his taste for military glory, without much concern for or against whom he fought. In the eighteen years of his reign we glimpse him battling with the Byzantines of Mistra in the Alpheios valley and the plains of Elis, helping the Byzantine Emperor Andronikos III to recover Chios from the Zaccaria, allying himself with the Knights of Rhodes on different occasions against both Greeks and Turks and implacably prosecuting the family feud with the Ghisi.

Such feverish bellicosity, and the chronic reluctance of the Latin powers of the Aegean to combine with the Greek Emperor in resisting the Turks, appalled Marino Sanudo, who in old age was still bravely preaching unity and vainly exhorting his own kinsmen to more rational behaviour. The duchy, though presenting a bold front to the world, was being drained dry by war and piracy. Squeezed between Catalans and Turks, the Cyclades were plundered and devastated year after year. If the Catalan raids could be dismissed as a mere harmful nuisance, the Turkish inroads, as predicted by Marino, promised to denude the islands of their resources and population. Nothing is more remarkable in the early history of the Ottomans than the speed with which, following in the steps of earlier Turkish emirs, they took to the sea, at the same time as they were overrunning by land the last Byzantine provinces in Asia Minor. The sad truth is that their fleets were largely manned by Christian sailors, or by recent converts to Islam, from the same coastal districts as had immemorially provided crews for the Byzantine navy. Operating on each raid with hundreds of small vessels and tens of thousands of men, the Turkish commanders systematically stripped the Aegean islands of their inhabitants, carrying them off to the slave markets, or, with a greater sense of statesmanship, to restock with industrious folk the lands which the Ottomans had recently conquered. Two centuries later Venice and the Spanish Hapsburgs were to discover that their most terrible enemies in the maritime wars which they waged with the Ottomans were the renegade Aegean Greek admirals, Dragut and the brothers from Lesbos, Khaireddin and Amrudj Barbarossa.

The next Duke of Naxos, Niccolo's brother Giovanni, was also the last of the direct line of the Sanudi. The best that can be said of him is that in the course of his twenty years reign he did not lose his duchy altogether. He shared his brother's addiction to warfare, and when another major conflict broke out in mid-century between Venice and Genoa he ranged himself unreservedly on the former's side. The consequence of this zeal, however, was that while his galleys were elsewhere a Genoese force attacked Naxos, stormed the city and carried him prisoner to Genoa. It was fortunate for him that the peace concluded between the rival republics in 1355 allowed him to return to his impoverished and desolated domain. Nevertheless the Sanudi could justly congratulate themselves on having emerged as the longest lived dynasty in Frankish Greece. They had outlasted the Villehardouins, the de la Roches and all other princely and ducal houses.

The only record which could compare with theirs was that of their counterparts in the Ionian Sea, the Palatine Counts of Cephalonia. Whether or not the Orsini of Cephalonia were a branch of the ancient Roman family of that name, it is certain that in the twelfth century they were settled in Apulia and that Count Matteo, or Maio, had already held Cephalonia, Zante and Ithaca for some years before the Fourth Crusade broke up the empire of the Angeloi. Matteo was an extremely shrewd politician. As we have seen, he dodged any threat to his position which might have arisen from the allocation of the Ionian islands to Venice under the partition treaty by promptly recognizing the Republic's sovereignty over his territories. He was also so successful in avoiding friction with his neighbours that he enjoyed peaceful and undisturbed possession of his rich and beautiful islands for well over half a century. The powers which he was chiefly at pains to conciliate were Greek Epiros and Frankish Achaia. It was clearly necessary for him to cultivate the friendship of the Dukas dynasty, masters of Epiros, Corfu and Leukas, and Matteo did so by marrying an Epirote princess. At about the same time he found it politic to switch his feudal allegiance from Venice, which, having lost Corfu, wielded little influence in the Ionian Sea, to the principality of Achaia, which under Geoffroy de Villehardouin was rising to the zenith of its power. Having thus reinsured himself, the Count was able to offer his subjects, both Greeks and Italian immigrants from Apulia, a high degree of security and well-being. He himself filled the role of elder statesman to whom the Villehardouins could always turn for advice and military support. As late at 1248 we see him assisting Prince Guillaume in his capture of Monemvasia.

His son, Richard, was almost as long-lived; the two of them spanning the whole of the thirteenth century. He was also a striking personality, although he lacked the more subtle traits of Matteo's character. His own restless and impulsive temperament drove him to play a much more active part in the internal affairs of Achaia and to figure, as was indeed his right, as one of its wealthiest and most powerful feudatories. He was conspicuously proud of his title of 'Most high and mighty Count Palatine' and his arrogance and tactlessness tended to irritate his fellow peers and cause them to resent him as an interfering outsider. Like Angelo Sanudo, he followed Prince Guillaume to the battlefield of Pelagonia. By his first wife, a Stromoncourt of Salona, he had a son, John, and three daughters whom he succeeded in marrying to Moreot nobles, Jean Chauderon, Jean de Durnay and Engilbert de Liedekerke.[11] But it was not until the last seven years of his life that he attained the highest position in the principality by his marriage to Marguerite de Villehardouin, the lady of Akova, and his appointment as bailie for his sister-in-law, the Princess Isabelle. However, as we have already learned in a previous chapter, his administration was not a success. Whether he was considered too old or unpopular for the task, or had made too many influential enemies like the Chancellor, Benjamin of Kalamata, he was forced to make way for his only real rival in power and prestige, Nicholas de St Omer, and was murdered in 1304 at Glarentza by one of his own knights, whom he had offended in a fit of irascibility.

It might perhaps have been better policy for him to have spent his old age in his island possessions. Nevertheless before becoming so heavily absorbed in the Morea, he had rounded off the County Palatine by the acquisition of Leukas, which the Despot Nikephoros Dukas of Epiros presented to the young John Orsini, the husband of his daughter Maria. The fact that both girl and island had been obtained by unscrupulous pressure by Richard on Nikephoros as the price of his military aid in the Despot's squabble with the Byzantine Emperor, did not affect the value of this addition to the County's territory. It now comprised the whole line of islands stretching from the Ambracian Gulf to the Peloponnesian coast and covering the approach to the Gulf of Corinth.

John's reign, which lasted until 1317, was undistinguished but brought no changes to the islands. He inherited two awkward feuds from his father's involvement in the Peloponnese. The first, with Richard's old enemy Benjamin the Chancellor, cost him for a while the favour of the new Prince, Philip of Savoy, which he was only able to regain by lavishly subsidizing his feudal superior. The second was a lengthy and bitter dispute with his stepmother, Marguerite de Villehardouin, about money and property which she accused the Orsini of having filched from her. Despite the enthusiastic support of Nicolas de St Omer, Marguerite was only able to recover, by decision of the Prince, a fifth of what she demanded, and the enmity which she felt towards her stepson lasted until her death. It was fully reciprocated by John, who subsequently was one of the strongest opponents of the claim to the principality advanced by Marguerite's son-in-law, Ferdinand of Majorca. Together with Louis of Burgundy, the Count commanded the Frankish army which crushed Ferdinand at Manolada. There was no doubt about his bravery, but his arbitrary and quarrelsome disposition alienated the Moreots, with whom he was even less popular than his father. Indeed, when Louis of Burgundy died suddenly after the battle, local rumour proclaimed that John had poisoned him, but as the Count made no attempt to turn the situation to his personal advantage, there were probably no grounds for the charge. He too died of natural causes in the following year.

In his two sons, Nicolas and John II, the violent streak which had first appeared in their grandfather Richard displayed itself in an exaggerated form. Whether this can be attributed to their Dukas blood is a matter of conjecture, but in most respects the inclinations and interest of both these princes were less Frankish than Greek. They had plenty of ambition and imagination but no scruples. Whereas their father and grandfather had been content to outshine their French peers in Achaia, Nicolas and John reckoned that their future lay in Epiros. In the circumstances of the day the Orsini could no longer aspire to dominate the principality. Moreover even their formerly secure base in the islands was now threatened by the more lively concern which the Angevins of Naples, to whom the rulers of Achaia and Cephalonia owed allegiance, were showing for the whole area. The sovereign rights of the King of Naples were at the time exercised by his brother of Taranto, who had long cherished plans for conquests in northern Greece, while the second brother, John of Gravina, had become Prince of Achaia in 1318. Nicolas saw no reason why his islands should merely serve as stepping-stones for an Angevin expansion in which he was reduced to playing a secondary role. If anyone seized Epiros it must be himself. He therefore decided to ignore the Angevins and to strike first. As the grandson of Nikephoros Dukas he saw himself, with some justification, as a more capable ruler of the Despotate than the latter's inept son Thomas. So, in the year after his father's death, he carried out a swift and devastating *coup d'etat*. His uncle the Despot was surprised and assassinated and his territory of southern Epiros taken over without a fight, and, to complete the usurpation, he appropriated Thomas's wife Anna Palaeologina, granddaughter of the Emperor Andronikos II. The stroke must have been very well planned, and was of course a slap in the face for the Angevins, but for the moment John of Gravina, who was the murdered Despot's cousin, confined himself to ordering Nicolas to do homage for his new dominions to the bailie of the principality.

Once established at Arta, Nicolas was necessarily caught up in the politics of the Byzantine sphere. As a mark of his decision to turn his back on the West, and of his transformation from a Latin feudatory into a Greek princeling, he publicly adopted the Orthodox faith, and the Greek hierarchy seems to have raised no serious objection to his conduct on moral grounds. The only flaw in his scheme was the refusal of northern Epiros and its capital Joannina, an important centre of trade, to accept his authority. It preferred that of the Byzantine Emperor, and Nicolas was unable to persuade its inhabitants to change their minds in his favour. So long as his wife was alive he abstained from trying to annex northern Epiros by force, but on her death in 1321 and the outbreak of civil war in the Empire he decided to make the attempt. Before doing so he sought to enlist the help of Venice by offering to acknowledge its suzerainty and to grant commercial privileges. The Venetians, however, saw no attractions in his proposal. They politely declined it, pointing out that the suzerainty was already theirs by virtue of the original partition treaty. His subsequent attack on Joannina was repulsed, and in 1323 John Orsini, from motives of personal ambition, or more probably because he was alarmed by the rashness of his brother's policy, murdered him and stepped into his place. He no doubt realized that the Orsini could not afford to be at loggerheads with both Angevins and Palaeologues. So far as the Ionian islands were concerned, his fears were justified. In 1324 John of Gravina, leading an expedition for the purpose of combating the Greeks in the Morea, stopped at Cephalonia and deposed the Orsini from their tenure of the County Palatine. For the next thirty years the islands were to be administered directly by the Angevins. Only Marguerite, the sister of Nicolas and John, was allowed to retain a fief consisting of half of Zante.

Cut off from his base, John II inevitably made his peace with Byzantium. The settlement which he obtained was eminently favourable, for he gained thereby the whole of Epiros at the price of accepting imperial sovereignty. At the same time he married another Anna Palaeologina, daughter of a Byzantine general. He ruled the united Despotate for the next ten years. However the invasion of Walter de Brienne, on his way to challenge the Catalans of Athens, cost him some anxious moments and he was again obliged to recognize Angevin instead of Byzantine overlordship. Unfortunately for him, the Despotate now contained two irreconcilable factions, one favouring the Western and the other the Eastern connexion. His wife, Anna, was so fanatically inclined to the latter that she eventually poisoned her husband, and on behalf of their son Nikephoros once more placed Epiros under Byzantine protection. But, as explained in a former chapter, the Emperor Andronikos III resolved to do away with the Despotate altogether and to substitute for it direct rule from Constantinople. We have also seen how the Angevin party in Epiros, by contriving the escape of Nikephoros from Byzantine custody, made a final but unsuccessful bid for supremacy. Its failure, and the surrender of Nikephoros to the Emperor, ended the bizarre history of the Orsini. The last scion of the dynasty, a Greek in everything but his paternal ancestry, became a Byzantine governor in Thrace, while Epiros was destined to become part of the Serbian Empire of Stephen Dushan.[12]

The melodramatic events which accompanied the downfall of the Orsini may well obscure the very real interest of the attempt by these semi-hellenized Italians to perpetuate the existence of an autonomous Greek state balanced between the Angevin and Byzantine monarchies. With the possible exception of John I and Nikephoros, all these Counts and Despots were original and energetic personalities, ranging from the canny Apulian Matteo to the vigorous but unprincipled half-breeds Nicolas and John II. Their hundred year cultural evolution which converted them from Franks into Greeks was unique in the history of

Romania. At the end of it the sons of the Latin-orientated John I were easily absorbed into the thoroughly Byzantine atmosphere of Arta, where their entourage, the magnates, the clerics and the people were exclusively Greeks or Albanians. They zealously identified themselves with the traditions and beliefs of their subjects. As William Miller recalls, John I added the names of Angelos, Komnenos and Dukas to his own, and as a pious Orthodox Christian repaired the Cathedral of Arta, the Panagia Paregoritissa which his Dukas ancestors had built. He even commissioned one Constantine Hermoniakos to 'compose a paraphrase of Homer in octosyllabic verse'. The existence of a strong pro-Orsini and anti-imperial party suggests that these efforts to win the sympathy of the Epirotes were by no means fruitless.[13]

The Angevins were now supreme in the whole Ionian region, while in Corfu their rule had already lasted since 1267. The reputation for harshness which they rightly earned in their own Kingdom of Naples was not borne out by their treatment of the Corfiotes. It is true that the Orthodox Church, which had been especially favoured by the Dukas Despots, was reduced, as might have been expected, to a secondary status and the Greek Metropolitan ousted by a Catholic Archbishop, but the native clergy was nevertheless permitted to retain many of the privileges and immunities granted to it by the previous regime. Its head, styled the *megas protopapas*, was still a very considerable personage and the recognised leader of his community.[14] He was elected by an assembly of thirty-two town and eight country priests and by a corresponding number of Greek landowners. With so wide a degree of autonomy the national element was far from being downtrodden. Although a considerable number of nobles from the Angevin dominions in Italy and Provence obtained fiefs in the island, local Greeks were similarly rewarded for their services to the Crown and there seems to have been very little friction between them and the newcomers. Among such fiefs, whose productivity compensated for their small size, various estates were reserved for the royal domain.

The higher administration was staffed exclusively by Latins. It was a mixture of the feudalism prevailing elsewhere in Romania with a more bureaucratic system imported from Naples and inherited from the Hohenstaufen and Norman eras. For so small a territory it was remarkably elaborate. The royal governor, entitled the Captain or Vicar-General, was assisted by a Council or Curia and a galaxy of officials and judges. When, as often happened, the Captaincy was conferred upon a great vassal of the kingdom, such as the Prince of Achaia, the office became purely honorary and the administration ran itself. In 1294, however, King Charles II, appointed one of his sons, Philip of Taranto, who, whether resident or not, took a keen view of his personal responsibilities and conferred very real benefits on the islanders. Corfu was carefully cherished by the sovereigns of Naples for a variety of reasons. Strategically it was the key to the Adriatic and a possible springboard for ventures in northern Greece. It was also a convenient base for the control of the few but vulnerable outposts held by the Angevins on the Epirote mainland. Its commercial importance stemmed equally from its geographical position and from the exuberant fertility of its soil, from the abundance of oil, wine and fruits and the profitable exploitation of salt-pans and fisheries. Jewish and Venetian traders were encouraged to settle in the town. Had it not been for the ravages of the Aragonese sailors who several times attacked it during the long drawn out wars between Aragon and Naples, Corfu would have enjoyed an uninterrupted boom; indeed the government of Philip of Taranto was perhaps the longest period of unbroken prosperity in any part of Greece ruled by Latins.[15]

The County of Cephalonia was revived in 1357, after thirty years of direct and uneventful Angevin rule. One of the high officials who administered Corfu for Philip and his son Robert was a certain Guglielmo Tocco. This Neapolitan married Margherita Orsini, sister of the Despots Nicolas and John II, and their son Leonardo both retained the confidence of the Angevins and strengthened his own prestige in Romania by marrying a niece of Niccolo Acciaiuoli. As a reward for his loyalty Robert created him Duke of Leucadia and Count of Cephalonia and Zante. We have observed how three generations of his family played a leading part on the Greek mainland, together with other Italo-Greek dynasties such as the Zaccaria and the Acciaiuoli, and how a Maddalena Tocco became the wife of Constantine Palaeologos, the future Emperor. The Tocchi survived without difficulty the sudden decline of Angevin power in the Ionian Sea which occurred after 1380 and resulted in Venice again becoming mistress of Corfu. Ever since the Republic had been dislodged from this vital point by the first Dukas Despot of Epiros it had been patiently awaiting an opportunity to regain it. This at last came when the Angevin hold was fatally enfeebled by the dynastic struggles between the various contenders for the throne of Naples, Queen Joanna, Jacques des Baux and Charles of Durazzo (Charles III of Naples). Their strife unsettled the previously contented Corfiotes, who were particularly incensed when des Baux seized their island with the help of the Navarrese Company. Although these mercenaries were soon expelled by the adherents of Charles, the leading men of Corfu, Italians, Greeks and

Jews, had become disillusioned with the Angevins and attracted by the idea of substituting for their increasingly erratic rule the stable and efficient administration of Venice. They therefore listened eagerly to Venetian blandishments, supported by well placed bribes, and when Charles III died in 1386 the change of sovereignty was smoothly effected. In order to discourage possible competitors, a Venetian garrison was promptly landed, while delegates from the Corfiote community sailed to Venice and procured from the Doge ample guarantees of its traditional customs and privileges. The arrival of a bailie to assume the government inaugurated a four hundred year period of Venetian domination. After surviving two grand Turkish assaults, it ended only with the extinction of the Republic itself at the hands of the republican French.

Venice left the Tocchi undisturbed. Once Corfu had been recovered, it re-established good relations with the Kingdom of Naples and the latter's influential vassals. It went so far as to pay the new King, Ladislaus, a very substantial sum for the formal surrender of his rights to Corfu. In the south Ionian sphere the first Tocco Duke and Count, Leonardo, had recently died and his widow, the Duchess Maddalena, was exercising the regency for her young son Carlo. A Buondelmonti from Florence, and an Acciaiuoli on her mother's side, she held her own for twenty years until in 1401 Carlo attained his majority. She must have been a woman of remarkable ability and resource. She also had a brother called Esau, whose career was even more unusual than that of most contemporary Italian fishers for power in the Levant. After the collapse of Stephen Dushan's Balkan empire, the former Despotate of Epiros was split between a bevy of Albanian chieftains in the south and the Serbian prince Thomas Preliubovitch, who ruled the north from Joannina. Thomas, an efficient but arbitrary tyrant, alienated both his Greek and his Albanian subjects and was eventually assassinated by his own guards. At that moment, for reasons that are not entirely clear, Esau happened to be on the spot and the tyrant's widow, with the ready approval of the Epirotes, chose him as her new husband. Inevitably enough, he was suspected of having already been her lover, but his availability at Joannina may equally have been a mere coincidence. At all events his family connexion with Cephalonia, as well as with Nerio Acciaiuoli who was on the point of becoming lord of Athens, marked him as a suitable candidate for the not wholly enviable task of governing Epiros.[16]

It is intriguing to find this Florentine of the age of Boccaccio ruling over a turbulent mixture of Greeks, Albanians, Serbs and Vlachs, but in his day the society of Joannina was relatively sophisticated, independent in its outlook and commercially inclined. The abject era of Ali Pasha, so minutely described by British travellers, lay centuries ahead. With the Ottoman Turks as his uncomfortable neighbours in Thessaly and Macedonia, and jealously watched by the Albanians in the south, Esau manoeuvred with skill and vigour, leaning whenever it suited him now on the Byzantines, now on the Turks. After the death of his Serbian wife he married the daughter of his principal Albanian rival, John Boua Spata. His political virtuosity maintained him in power until his death in 1408 and prepared the way for return to the mainland of the Counts of Cephalonia. Against all probabilities, the Tocchi in fact succeeded to the Epirote inheritance of their predecessors, the Orsini. For ten years, from 1408 to 1418, the whole of the former Despotate was in Albanian hands, but the confusion which reigned during this interval enabled Esau's nephew, Carlo Tocco, to assert his claim. The Epirotes, northern and southern, rallied to him gladly and in the latter year he emerged as Duke, Count and Despot, master of the islands, Joannina and Arta, peer of Achaia and kinsman of the Duke of Athens.

In the twilight of Latin ascendancy in Greece, Carlo was its most active and vigorous champion. He dissipated his energies, however, in strenuous and rather selfish endeavours to add to his dominions by seizing territory in the Morea, and these ventures achieved only temporary success. Although he had few scruples about invoking Turkish aid against his Christian opponents when it suited his immediate aims, he was finally squeezed out of the Peloponnese altogether by the Palaeologues. However his reign brought peace and well being to the islands and particularly to Cephalonia, where the Duchess Francesca kept her splendid court. In a rare contemporary glimpse of life in Romania, the chronicler Froissart portrays her entertaining there the French knights captured at Nikopolis on their return after release by the Sultan. But she also presided over the government, shrewdly favouring, like her father, Nerio, the interests of the Greek population. Epiros too prospered under Carlo and it was at Joannina that he died in 1429. He left no legitimate children but adopted the son and two daughters of his younger brother Leonardo.

His nephew Carlo II (1429–48) had a rougher passage. At the beginning he nearly lost Epiros altogether. His hold on the southern half of the country was disputed by his uncle's five bastards, who sported names like Memnon and Hercules. They claimed that the land had been divided among them under their father's will and sought the Sultan's intervention on their behalf. Murad, however, was more anxious to gain possession of Joannina and sent against it his commander in Europe,

Sinan Pasha. He faced its inhabitants with the choice of resistance, in which case he threatened that the city, when eventually taken, would suffer the same ordeal of plunder and massacre as had been inflicted six months previously on Thessalonica, or of immediate surrender, in return for which he promised the most liberal treatment. When they not unnaturally chose the second alternative the pasha scrupulously abode by his undertaking. All classes of Epirotes were allowed to retain their religion, lands and personal property; no houses or churches were destroyed; no captives were dragged away. The publicity value of this gesture was potentially immense, but although it was clearly designed to soften the determination of Constantinople and the Morea to withstand the Turks, it was hardly effective. As for Carlo, he was allowed to keep Arta and the south as the Sultan's tributary; in that capacity he welcomed Cyriacus of Ancona and provided him with a guide to the country's classical antiquities. Meanwhile, in order to strengthen his position in the islands, he turned for support to Venice. He duly obtained satisfactory guarantees, together with honorary membership of the Republic's Grand Council.[17]

In the latter part of his reign, and in the general reaction against Turkish domination which followed the earlier successes of John Hunyadi's Balkan campaign, Carlo repudiated his vassalage and was fortunate, when captured by the Turks, to be permitted to revert to his former status without further punishment. But a worse crisis arose on his premature death. This time the Ottomans resolved to terminate for good the rule of the Tocchi on the mainland. His son Leonardo, who was still a minor, could do nothing to stop them from occupying the whole of southern Epiros, with the exception of three isolated fortresses. Alarmed by the Turkish advance to the Ionian seaboard, the Venetians made a rapid counter-move; they took over Zante and prepared to annex all the islands. On reflection, however, they preferred, while establishing a firm protectorate over the whole group, to retain Leonardo as Duke and Count, and so things stood when Mehmet II carried out his conquest of the Morea.

The Duchy of the Archipelago also survived the Turkish conquest of mainland Greece. Indeed it struggled on well into the sixteenth century, but its new dynasty, the Crispi, never wielded the same influence as their predecessors, the Sanudi, or their counterparts in the Ionian Sea, the Tocchi. The Crispi came into power in the wake of an interregnum and as the result of particularly lurid political crime. Giovanni Sanudo, when he died in 1361, left only a daughter, Fiorenza. Her husband, a dalle Carceri from Euboea, had also died, leaving her with a small son, the heir to the duchy. The prospect of this lady's remarriage immediately became a source of friction. Venice, then at the height of its enmity with Genoa, was especially worried lest, by choosing the wrong husband, she might take the archipelago out of its own sphere of influence into that of the rival republic. It was equally perturbed because the young Nerio Acciaiuoli, backed by his powerful adoptive father Niccolo, was regarded as a likely suitor for Fiorenza. For the Venetian government, a Florentine protectorate over the islands was almost as unacceptable as a Genoese. Nerio, too, could count upon the support of the Angevin Robert of Taranto, titular sovereign of the archipelago.

In such a situation Venice could not afford to take risks. Before Nerio could press his suit any further a Venetian warship hovering off Naxos abducted the Duchess and carried her off to Crete. There she was warned that she would not be permitted to return home unless she consented to marry her cousin, another Niccolo Sanudo, whom the Republic considered to possess all the appropriate qualities, both personal and political, for the role of Duke–Consort. A Venetian by descent, a landowner in Venetian Euboea, lacking independent ambitions, he could be relied upon to further the aims of Venetian policy. But he was also famous as a soldier and somewhat of a swashbuckler, his bravery and panache having earned him the nickname *Spezzabanda*, the man who routs armies. In fact this paladin made an admirable Duke, and all went well in the islands until his stepson came of age and began to rule on his own. His misgovernment and general irresponsibility soon alarmed his Venetian sponsors. He neglected his islands and spent most of his time in Euboea, where he was finally involved in an obscure conspiracy aiming at seizure of Negroponte with the help of the Navarrese Company, which was at that time active on the mainland. When the Venetians ascertained that their protége was actually plotting to deprive them of one of their most valuable strongholds in the Levant, they were naturally infuriated by his disloyalty. Characteristically, however, they did not move directly against him but left the initiative to a private individual, Francesco Crispo. Like the dalle Carceri, the Crispi were a Veronese family long settled in Euboea, and Francesco's wife was a niece of Duke Giovanni Sanudo; in her name he held the barony of Melos in the Cyclades. It is therefore unlikely that he would have acted without Venetian encouragement or at least connivance. At all events the operation seems to have been carefully prepared. In 1383, some three years after the discovery of the plot against Negroponte, he landed in Naxos with a band of accomplices and laid a trap for Niccolo. According to one picturesque but not implausible account, he joined the ducal party for a day's hunting and having contrived to separate the Duke from his entourage, he had him brutally stabbed to death.[18]

Presumably the Naxiots had become seriously disillusioned with their ruler, for they readily accepted Crispo in his place. Venetian diplomacy was at pains to damp down the scandal which the murder caused throughout the archipelago. The chief objectors were eventually appeased by the offer of attractive fiefs, and the end of the crisis found the Cyclades firmly held by faithful adherents of the Republic. It was important enough for Venice that they should not be controlled by any of her commercial competitors, but quite vital that they should remain intact as the outer screen of its defensive line Negroponte—Nauplia—Crete. The Republic could not afford to garrison them all, but their harbours and anchorages were now in safe hands and could at all times be used by its fleets, to which the galleys of the Aegean barons made a welcome addition. Although the islands could not altogether shield the Greek mainland from Turkish maritime thrusts, they at least afforded a useful measure of forward protection for the Venetian mainland bases. In fact the Peloponnese was less harried from the sea at the end of the fourteenth century than in the days of the later Sanudi, while the whole region also benefitted by their elimination of Catalan piracy.

One result of Venetian hegemony was a loosening of the Duke's authority over his vassals, some of whom were newcomers to the Levant but who all found it more convenient to treat on their own with the representatives of the Republic. Such were the Zeni of Andros, the first of whom was the son of the bailie of Negroponte, the Sommaripa of Paros, the Gozzadini of Anaphe and Thermia and the da Corogna of Siphnos. As for Tenos and Mykonos, they were administered directly by Venetian officials when the Ghisi clan died out. Other island fiefs were bequeathed by Duke Francesco to his numerous sons on his death in 1397. The new system was to some extent effective in holding off the Turks, especially during the short period of Ottoman weakness which followed the battle of Ankara and more or less coincided with the reign of Giacomo I (1397–1418). The respite, however, ended in 1416, when a strong Turkish expedition ravaged the whole archipelago. It created such havoc that Venice was provoked into instant retaliation and, in one of the few great sea-battles of the age, thoroughly trounced the Sultan's fleet off Gallipoli. Nevertheless, just as the Christian states of continental Greece were incapable of withstanding incursions by land, the scattered Aegean baronies were fatally vulnerable to raids from the sea. The ensuing decades brought to the Greek islanders nothing but insecurity and misery, caught as they were between the cruel but never decisive pressure from the East and the evident determination of their Italian masters, under the aegis of Venice, to persevere in their tough but, in the final issue, hopeless resistance.

The process of depopulation, which had begun with the Turkish slave-raids of the preceding century, had accelerated alarmingly. Many of the smaller islands were deserted except by fishermen and goatherds, while on the larger the inhabitants abandoned their farms and huddled behind the walls of the little towns. Even so the barons recolonized energetically by transfers of population between the islands and by bringing in new settlers from the mainland. Thus Astypalaia was restocked from Tenos and Mykonos, and quantities of Albanians, of whom there seems to have been an inexhaustible supply at this period, were shipped over to Andros and Ios. Such measures barely sufficed to maintain a necessary balance. At no time, however, did these overseas Venetians despair of their situation and decide to quit the archipelago. Their castles, estates and ships still endowed them with an adequate livelihood and, what was perhaps more important, a degree of freedom only to be sampled in the outposts of the Venetian Empire. Despite a precarious present and an uncertain future they had not lost the zest for their peculiar existence on the fringe of Christian Europe. Many of them would have been unhappy anywhere but in the Levant. Their upper crust must habitually have spoken Italian among themselves and could probably have been reassimilated without much difficulty into the ways of the Italian cities, had it been necessary for them to return there, but that was certainly not the case with their very numerous dependants and retainers. The latter were a mixed race, Catholic by religion but speaking Greek by preference and utterly committed to a mode of life that had already endured for two centuries and still exercised a powerful attraction over those who followed it.

Nevertheless, during the reign of Duke Giovanni I (1418–33), it looked as if the duchy was about to founder. The Venetian government were finding it more and more difficult to protect its outlying dependency. It was not that they lacked the will to do so, but their resources were not adequate to maintain constantly in those waters a naval force of sufficient strength to ward off the Turks. While conscientiously including the duchy in any truce which they might from time to time conclude with the Sultan, they privately advised its ruler to negotiate his own terms, provided that they did not prejudice the Republic's interests. Thus the archipelago became both a Venetian protectorate and an Ottoman tributary. And when the Duke made a similar arrangement to buy off that other inveterate enemy of Venice,

Genoa, the Republic protested in vain, but his prudence, however undignified, brought some relief. The reign of his successor Giacomo II (1433–47) was relatively tranquil, especially as the Ottomans were heavily engaged on the Danube.

It was then that Cyriacus of Ancona visited the islands. Later he recorded a leisurely conversation about local antiquities with his host Crusino Sommaripa, lord of Paros and Andros.[19] Like Cyriacus, Crusino was a cultivated gentleman of Renaissance tastes who liked to excavate Classical statues and send them to his friends in other corners of the Aegean. There can be no greater contrast between this vignette of civilized life and the scenes of dereliction painted by an earlier Italian traveller, the Florentine cleric Buondelmonti (doubtless a relative of his namesake the ruler of Joannina), to whom we are largely indebted for our knowledge of the sad state of the archipelago when Turkish depredations were at their worst. Conditions had certainly improved in the twenty years or so that separate the two accounts, both of which are based on first-hand acquaintance with the Cyclades, but not to such an extent that they had in interval become quiet havens of culture. Raiders always lurked below the horizon and made occasional descents.

The Duke had a posthumous son, Gian Giacomo, who did not long survive him. He was followed, in the year that Constantinople fell to the Turks, by his elderly great-uncle Guglielmo Crispo, baron of Anaphe, who had been acting as one of the regents for the boy. The Crispi were a highly prolific and competitive family, so the last two successions did not take place smoothly, but after the quarrels between the various claimants had been composed, Guglielmo was left in firm possession of the Duchy. No ruler understood better than this veteran the difficult technique of balancing between Venice and the Turk. While always counting as a Venetian and enjoying the Republic's confidence, he paid his tribute regularly to Sultan Mehmet II and for the ten years of his reign the Conqueror let him be. Thus, in 1460, he and Leonardo Tocco, Dukes of the two seas enclosing Hellas, were the only Latin princes left. The subsequent fate of the Islands belongs to the history of Venice and can only be touched on in the brief epilogue which follows.

CHAPTER TWELVE

Venetian Epilogue

1460 IS THE OBVIOUS DATE on which to bring the history of feudal Greece to an end. It marks the beginning of the Turkokratia, the subjection that lasted until the War of Independence. But it would be confusing as well as untidy to check the narrative abruptly in mid-fifteenth century and not to round it off with a brief account of the period during which the Venetians were still obstinately disputing the Turkish hegemony.[1] The Ottoman conquest of the Morea left them entrenched in Crete and Negroponte, overlords of numerous Aegean and Ionian islands, supreme at sea and clinging doggedly to their positions on the Greek mainland. They held all Euboea, Pteleon at the entrance of the Gulf of Volo, Naupaktos (Lepanto), the island of Aegina facing the Piraeus, Argos and Nauplia, Modon, Coron and Navarino. Within a year or two Monemvasia was added to this already impressive list. As a defensive posture it could hardly have been bettered.

Yet it was not to be expected that Sultan Mehmet would wait long before trying to remove these awkward excrescences on the fringe of his empire. His forces immediately started to probe possible weak spots in the defences; they took Argos by surprise and threatened Modon. This move led to a sternly contested war which lasted for sixteen years and produced no decisive result, although it caused infinite distress to the Greeks living in the battle area. At first the Venetians acted with energy and their general, Bertoldo d'Este, appealed to the Moreots to shake off Turkish rule. Elated by the prospect of strong leadership in place of the disastrous vacillations of their last Despots, they sprang to arms and soon expelled most of the Turkish garrisons from the fortresses of the peninsula. D'Este himself, supported by a fleet under Loredano, laid siege to Acrocorinth and rebuilt the isthmus wall which had already been so many times raised and demolished. Unfortunately he was soon killed in action, while the Grand Vizier, Mahmoud Pasha, swept down from the north with the Turkish relieving army, broke through the Hexamilion and undid most of the successes previously gained by the Christians.

Both sides then settled down to a war of attrition. The Greeks resorted to guerrilla warfare and the new Venetian commander, Sigismondo

Malatesta, directed an attack on Mistra, now the capital of the Ottoman administration. He failed to take it, but before giving up the attempt he disinterred the remains of Gemistos Plethon and later had them solemnly reburied in the Cathedral of his native city, Rimini. Further north the Republic's admiral, Vettore Cappello, raided Athens, burned the Turkish ships in the harbour of Piraeus and went on to blockade Patras, while his colleague, Barbarigo, and the Moreot magnate Michael Rallis led the assault from the land side. But the venture failed lamentably; both leaders were captured and impaled, and the Greco-Venetians suffered a further defeat under the walls of Kalamata.

After a few more years of desultory fighting the Sultan assumed personal control of the war. His objective was Euboea, except for Crete the most valuable but at the same time most vulnerable of the Venetian possessions in the Levant. But in order to make sure of success he had gathered just as massive resources and had prepared the operation just as carefully as for his siege of Constantinople seventeen years earlier. He by no means underestimated the defensive capacity of Negroponte. The fortress lay in the strait itself. A bridge, easily broken, connected it with the Boeotian mainland, and strong walls and a moat protected it on the Euboean side. An army of a hundred thousand men, with its full complement of artillery, assembled in Boeotia and marched to the Euripos channel. Three hundred ships, carrying many more thousands of combatants, blocked the channel on both sides, landed troops in Euboea and invested the town from the east. Meanwhile the powerful Venetian fleet based on Crete, which had previously never failed to overcome the Turks in a straightforward sea-battle, unaccountably omitted to intercept the Ottoman armada on its way from the Bosporus, and its subsequent efforts to break the ring were half-hearted and unavailing.

Unlike Constantinople, Negroponte might have been rescued if the Venetian admiral, Canale, had shown more spirit. As it was the fortress and its tiny but valiant garrison were doomed. Nevertheless it took Mehmet almost as much time (about five weeks) to overwhelm Negroponte as it did to reduce the Byzantine capital. A heavy bombardment by the same batteries as had breached the Roman walls of Constantinople failed to break the defenders' resolution and two assaults were repelled with huge losses. But the third attempt succeeded. The attackers forced their way into the town and fought their way from street to street, slaughtering the inhabitants, Italians and Greeks, as they advanced. The bailie, Erizzo, withdrew into the castle and parleyed with the Grand Vizier for its surrender. Mahmoud indeed undertook to spare the lives of all those who had taken refuge within its walls, but was disavowed by his master. When the gates were opened the bailie was seized and sawn in half and all the surviving male inhabitants were butchered with atrocious refinements. The women and children were shipped to Constantinople for slavery or eventual ransom.

The fall of Negroponte involved the loss of the whole of Euboea and the flight of its Latin population. It also dealt a grievous blow to Venice's political and military prestige. Having forfeited the initiative in its struggle with the Turks, the Republic was unable to regain it. The incompetent Canale was disgraced and his successor, Mocenigo, raided Smyrna and recovered many captives, while Loredano and Zorzi foiled a dangerous Turkish threat to Lepanto. But in the Peloponnese the Venetians again lost Argos and were driven back on their virtually inexpugnable strongholds of Modon, Coron, Nauplia, Monemvasia and Navarino. These they retained when a formal treaty was concluded in 1479 between the Republic and the Ottoman Empire. Venice had taken some hard knocks, but the balance was redressed by their acquisition of Cyprus when, through its last Queen, Caterina Cornaro, they succeeded to the heritage of the Lusignan dynasty. With Crete, Cyprus and Rhodes still in their hands the Christian powers were well placed to block further Ottoman expansion by sea.

For the next twenty years there were no hostilities between the Republic and the Sultans. However, the Moreot Greeks, whose hopes had been so cruelly frustrated, did not tamely submit to the Turkish reconquest. Among the Greek captains serving under Venetian command was a certain Korkodeilos Kladas, a landowner of sufficient status to have been granted estates in Lakonia when Sultan Mehmet first overran the Peloponnese, as a reward for submitting to the Turks. Now, in the style of a Klephtic leader in the future War of Independence, he pursued the fight for freedom and routed one Turkish army. When an overmastering force was sent against him he first retreated into the Maina and was finally taken off by a Neapolitan galley. Later he is heard of fighting the Ottomans in Epiros. But this was the last upsurge of the national spirit. Judging that no reasonable hope subsisted either of independence or of Latin protection against the infidels, the Moreots fled the country in their tens of thousands.[2]

While the young and adventurous took service with Venice and the King of Naples as light-armed horsemen (*stradioti*), large numbers of ordinary peasants and townsmen settled in the southern Ionian islands, where they were enthusiastically welcomed by the Count–Duke. Leonardo II Tocco, married to a grand-daughter of Thomas

Palaeologos, was the only Latin prince on the western side of Hellas who still preserved the feudal traditions of Romania, ruling over a mixed population with a strong majority of Greeks. Cephalonia and Zante were thriving and peaceful. But Leonardo was not strong or clever enough to cope with the competing ambitions of the greater powers. After the death of his first wife he tried to fortify his position by marrying a niece of King Ferdinand of Naples, but by doing so he lost the protection of Venice, which resented any revival of Neapolitan interest in the Ionian. By pointedly excluding the Tocchi from the treaty of 1479, it exposed them to Turkish aggression. Convinced that resistance would be useless, Leonardo and his family fled to Naples, while the Turks wasted and occupied his islands. Two years later, however, he set out to recover his domain with Neapolitan help. His brother Antonio drove the Turks from Zante and Cephalonia, but he had hardly done so when the Venetians intervened to snatch them in their turn. This cynical piece of statecraft yielded them permanent possession of Zante, but the Turks, who already held Leukas, insisted on the retrocession of Cephalonia. In any event the old order in the islands was destroyed.

The conflict between Venice and the Ottoman Empire was resumed in 1499, with even more damaging consequences for the former. This time Bayezit II, the new Sultan, launched a carefully planned campaign against the Republic's remaining bastions. His first goal was Lepanto. Here the Venetian naval commander, Grimani, was guilty of the same inertia as had lost Negroponte, failing either to ward off the Turkish fleet before it reached the Gulf of Corinth or to relieve the fortress when already beleaguered. The garrison and citizens thereupon surrendered at discretion and were treated with scrupulous humanity. But a year later, when Bayezit in person conducted the siege of Modon, the defenders refused to give in and suffered the familiar ordeal of massacre and enslavement. This blow entailed the immediate fall of Coron and Navarino, but not of Nauplia and Monemvasia, whose elaborate fortifications defied any attempt at attack. Although fighting dragged on for another two years the Turks scored no further successes. The Venetians, for their part, contented themselves with the recovery of Cephalonia, their solitary victory in what was otherwise a calamitous war. Both sides were glad to sign a second treaty, which kept the status quo for another thirty years.

Greece, however, remained a theatre for the rivalries of the chief Mediterranean powers, France, Spain, Venice and Turkey. In 1494 Charles VIII of France burst upon the scene and, before undertaking the conquest of Naples, made an offer to Andrew Palaeologos, the exiled son of the Despot Thomas and the nephew of the Emperor Constantine. In return for the surrender of his rights to the Empire the King promised him a subsidy and his restoration to the Despotate of the Morea as soon as it had been wrested from the Turks. Charles's well advertised intentions aroused much excitement in Greece and apprehension at Constantinople, but it may be doubted whether he entertained any serious hope of crossing the Adriatic and reviving the grand design of the Angevins. At all events his own retreat from Naples and return to France soon dispelled such illusions, and after his death in 1498 the efforts of his successor, Louis XII, to re-establish French rule in Naples were shattered by the victories of Gonzalo de Cordova, the Great Captain, whom Ferdinand and Isabella, the Catholic King and Queen of Aragon and Castile, appointed to lead their army in Italy. The consequent conversion of Naples into a Spanish viceroyalty resulted in the increasing involvement of Spain—and as from 1516 of the whole vast Hapsburg monarchy of Charles V—in the waging of amphibious warfare against the Turks in Greek waters. The struggle was to assume the character of a duel between Charles and the most formidable of all Ottoman Sultans, Suleiman the Magnificent, and to extend over the whole Mediterranean, while the role of Venice, though still crucial in the Levant, became for a time subsidiary to that of imperial Spain. This was the era when the Ottomans emerged as a maritime power of the first order, when their fleets were commanded by renegade Greeks, the two Barbarossas and Dragut, and largely manned by Greek sailors from the Aegean.

Suleiman's first feat of arms was the expulsion of the Knights of St John from Rhodes in 1523. Eight years later, after Charles had resettled them in Malta, they unsuccessfully attacked Modon and in the following year the Emperor's admiral Andrea Doria, made a more serious descent on the Morea. He took Coron and Patras and provoked a considerable Greek revolt. The effort, however, was not sustained. Venice, when invited to resume possession of its colony in Messenia, declined the responsibility and Charles, judging the outpost to be untenable ordered its evacuation. Its inhabitants, terrified by the impending reprisals, were shipped to Italy and Sicily.

The Venetians were frankly worried by the massive Hapsburg intervention in the affairs of the Levant. For the purpose of containing the Ottoman menace they were inclined to put more faith in their own diplomatic ability and military resources than in any untried ally, however outwardly powerful, and they took an instinctive dislike to the imperial command being entrusted to a Genoese. Nevertheless, they had no choice but to accept an alliance with Charles V, especially as the Turks reopened their attacks on the whole chain of Venetian strongholds from Corfu to Monemvasia. Corfu underwent a particularly savage siege and all the Ionian islands were fearfully ravaged; the colony of Aegina was wiped out and even Nauplia barely held out. In 1538 the combined squadrons of the Empire and the Republic met the Turkish fleet off Preveza on the Epirote coast and were ignominiously dispersed by Khaireddin Barbarossa, the Greek from Lesbos. Placed in a desperate predicament, Venice was obliged to negotiate its own terms with the Sultan, the price of peace being the abandonment of the two positions on the Greek mainland which had hitherto defied all Turkish assaults, Nauplia and Monemvasia. To the credit of the negotiators, they at least secured that all the loyal Greeks who had assisted in the defence of the fortresses should be allowed to migrate to Venice, Crete or the Ionian islands. But no vestige was left of the Latin presence in the Morea.

It may seem anomalous that amidst these tumults, and the collapse of one Western bulwark after another, the minor Latin baronies of the Aegean should have been permitted to prolong their precarious semi-independent existence well into the sixteenth century. Successive Sultans treated them with contemptuous tolerance. Thus the Duchy of the Archipelago survived the fall of Negroponte, the war of 1499–1503 and that of 1537–40, and was not finally snuffed out until 1566. The latter year also witnessed the disappearance of the rich Genoese colony in Chios, which the Turks had hitherto left undisturbed for commercial reasons. Five Crispo dukes spanned the century that followed the death of Guglielmo II, and the penultimate member of the dynasty, Giovanni IV, reigned from 1517 until 1564.[3]

There were, however, two short periods during which Venice intervened to set aside the Crispi and administer the islands directly. On both these occasions (1494–1500 and 1511–17) the Republic acted to safeguard its own interest and those of junior members of the ducal family, to whom it duly handed over the government as soon as they came of age. Giovanni III, who died in 1494, had irritated the protecting power by his scanty regard for its dignity and by his arbitrary treatment of his own subjects, but in his illegitimate son Francesco eccentricity degenerated into madness. In 1510 he murdered his wife, a Loredano, by stabbing her in the stomach, and when the Naxians came to arrest and depose him he tried to kill his son too. Fortunately the youth escaped by jumping out of a window and the crazy Duke was locked up in Crete until his death. After attaining his majority Giovanni IV was faced with the perennial problem of preserving the right political equilibrium between his Venetian protectors and his immensely powerful Ottoman neighbour. This was not an easy task. Whenever Venice and the Turk were at war the Cyclades were laid waste and their Western lords shut themselves up in their castles. But when peace prevailed—and there were long periods of peace—the islands achieved a modest prosperity, impaired only by the attentions of freelance corsairs from east and west, such as Black Hassan and the Sicilian Paolo de Campo. The Duke himself was once made prisoner by a Turkish pirate, but his release was promptly procured through diplomatic channels.

On the whole he steered his way skilfully through the reefs. Highly honoured at Venice, he only fell foul of its government when he from time to time sought to extend his personal domain at the expense of other fief-holders such as the Sommaripa of Paros and Andros or the Gozzadini of Siphnos and Keos. But such domestic squabbles between baronial families were of minor importance. Between the wars the islands drew profit from the products of their quarries and agriculture, and even greater returns from their share in the carrying trade of the whole Aegean area. Above all, they were concerned in the business of supplying the needs of Constantinople, for the essential economy of the region had not been altered by the transition from Byzantine to Turkish rule.

The respite was too good to last, for the war of 1537 unleashed Khaireddin Barbarossa on his hapless fellow-islanders. In the course of his first cruise he expelled the barons of Amorgos and Astypalaia, Ios and Anaphe, Seriphos and Antiparos. Having sacked and depopulated Paros, he besieged the Duke in his Naxian capital, while his men plundered the island. In order to avoid a worse fate Giovanni surrendered and was allowed to retain his diminished duchy for an annual tribute of 5000 ducats. The Sultan even presented him, as a sop to his docility, with Paros and Keos. The Sommaripa of Andros also escaped at the cost of tributary status. Subsequently Khaireddin mopped up the northern Sporades (Skyros, Skiathos and Skopelos). Tenos alone bravely repulsed the Ottoman fleet, kept the Venetian flag flying and avoided any form of subjugation.

Venice recovered nothing by the treaty of 1540 and the wretched Duke, crippled by his tributary obligation and stripped of wealth and territory, appealed in vain to the Christian powers for rescue. Moreover his Greek subjects, from whom the money was necessarily exacted, began at last to discard their attachment to their Latin lord. When great careers were the reward of apostasy, and security and profit were to be obtained from collaboration, there was clearly no point in staying loyal. Nor, if the lords themselves acknowledged Turkish mastery, did there remain any significant gap between Latins and Greeks. Nevertheless the habit of centuries, and the fact that many of the islanders were Catholics, precluded any change during the old Duke's lifetime. It was only when his son, Giacomo V, succeeded him in 1564 that the Naxians petitioned the Sultan to replace their Latin ruler by a nominee of his own. Armed with a huge bribe, Giacomo hurried to Constantinople in the hope of averting his deposition, but the Sultan ignored and imprisoned him. After 359 years the Latin state of the archipelago was painlessly dissolved, leaving no trace but the persistence of the Roman Catholic faith, a crop of Latin surnames and a few decaying escutcheons on the walls of churches and castles.

At this point events took an unexpected turn. A whim of the Sultan, Selim II, conferred the government of Naxos, Andros and other islands on one of his cronies, a Portuguese crypto-Jew named Joseph Nasi, or sometimes Joao Miguez or Micas. This strange and picaresque figure had roamed for many years through Western Europe, exchanging one lucrative business for another, until in about 1550 he turned up in Constantinople and became factotum to Selim 'the Sot', heir to Suleiman the Magnificent. Once established in favour he reverted to open Judaism. He also proceeded to amass a huge fortune, and among his more profitable activities was farming the customs duties on wines from the Aegean islands. He was even allowed to assume the ducal titles. But as political adviser to the Sultan, and the channel by which secret links were maintained between the Ottoman government and the courts of France and Spain, the Jewish adventurer remained at Constantinople, delegating the administration of the islands to another Iberian Jew, a Dr. Francisco Coronello. The latter's principal function was to wring from their inhabitants as much money as possible, for, apart from the need to make a profit from the duchy, its annual rent had now grown to 14,000 ducats. While acting as Nasi's deputy Coronello led an abortive expedition to conquer Tenos, after which he was himself grabbed by irate islanders and delivered to the Venetians for incarceration in Crete.[4]

At that time the eastern Mediterranean was convulsed by the new war (1570–3) which once more opposed the Ottomans to the combined forces of Venice and the Spanish monarchy, and in which the most striking events were the Turkish conquest of Cyprus (an enterprise promoted by Nasi) and the crushing defeat of the Turkish fleet off

Lepanto by Don John of Austria. For a brief moment the Venetians regained the upper hand in the archipelago and Giovanni Crispo, who after his release from Turkish captivity had ceaselessly solicited Venetian and papal aid, was restored to his duchy, only to lose it permanently by the peace of 1573. Naxos again became the preserve of Nasi and Coronello, until the former somewhat surprisingly died in his bed, still full of riches and honour. As for Giovanni, he ended his days at Constantinople, a pathetic petitioner at the Sultan's court. Turkish governors were then appointed for all the Cyclades with the curious exception of a group of seven minor islands centring on Siphnos. There the Gozzadini were allowed to rule as Turkish tributaries until as late as 1617.

Lepanto reduced, if it did not remove, the latent Turkish threat to the Ionian islands and the Adriatic coasts. So in 1572, the year after the battles, the Hispano-Venetian fleet hovered uncertainly off the Morea, while Don John hoped for a Greek insurrection that never occurred. Nor did he succeed in bringing the Turkish navy, reconstituted by a tremendous effort since the disaster of 1571, to a decisive encounter. The Ottoman commander, Euldj Ali, held off the Christian armada by skilful tactics and an intelligent use of the former Venetian bases, and was soon able to counter-attack. Before long Ottoman resilience again caused Venice to seek, to the fury of its ally, a separate peace. Thereafter Crete, the Great Greek Island, stood alone, the Republic's last and most impressive dominion in the Levant, linked with its Ionian dependencies and the mother city by only one intermediate station, the island of Kythera. This valuable outpost and observation point guarded its integrity until 1797, together with a peculiar form of land ownership which was shared in more or less equal proportions between the Republic itself and the Venieri, the original barons to whom it was allotted in 1207.

CHAPTER THIRTEEN

East and West

ONE CANNOT PRETEND that the period of Frankish domination in Greece was rich in cultural achievement. No great works of art or literature were engendered by the encounter and lengthy symbiosis on Greek soil of two types of mediaeval civilization, one indigenous and the other imported, derived from divergent traditions and from different interpretations of the truths of the same religion. The rival cultures resembled two streams like the Rhone and the Saone at Lyons, flowing parallel to one another but reluctant to fuse. The simile must not be overdone, for the two rivers do eventually mingle their waters. But the Greek and Latin currents in mediaeval Hellas obstinately refused to blend. Relations between Franks and Greeks were characterized by many compromises and concessions, but by scant understanding or real accord.

The antipathy which had long divided the two halves of Christendom reached its highest point in 1204. The ever widening rift between the Churches, the bitter recriminations of the earlier Crusades and a whole century of Norman aggression against the Empire preceded the sack of the two greatest Greek cities in Europe, Constantinople and Thessalonica. On the Byzantine side these events left a legacy of shame and exasperation, feelings which were shared equally by the aristocracy, the clergy and the populace. For a short time, during the reign of Manuel I Komnenos, the court and nobility had flirted with Latin ways, but the rape of the capital had united all classes in a common detestation of their conquerors. The attitude of the Western invaders towards the Greeks was less straightforward, but its two main elements were contempt and irritation. They despised, or affected to despise, the Greeks for their presumed lack of martial virtues, a habit of mind which had grown up and become fixed during the long decline of Byzantine military power from the late eleventh century onwards. It therefore riled them exceedingly that the 'grifons' obviously despised them in return for their lack of culture and good manners. They felt it as an affront to their pride that the Byzantine upper class and all educated Greeks should so openly regard them as barbarians and, what was worse, that the whole subject population should obstinately reject the blessings of submission to Rome. On the other hand the invaders grasped that their future

256

existence as lords of the land would largely depend on the services, and to some extent, the good will, of Greek peasant serfs, domestics, craftsmen, tradesmen, stewards and clerks.[1]

At the same time the sentiments of outraged distaste for the Latins which prevailed in Constantinople, Thessalonica, Thrace and Asia Minor were hardly so pronounced among the simple inhabitants of the Greek peninsula between Mount Olympus and Cape Matapan. The Greeks of Hellas proper were humble folk. Wherever sophisticated persons were to be found, they were likely to be landowners, clerics and imperial officials hailing from somewhere east of Hellas, or from Thessalonica which had always been a source of intellectuals. The local archons too, as distinguished from absentee landlords living in the capital or elsewhere, were a rough and unruly lot whose feudal ways and cultural standards differed little from those of Western knights. It was clearly in their interest, if they wished to keep all or some of their lands, to come to a speedy arrangement with the Franks. For one Sgouros or Voutsaras, there were a dozen who compounded with the invaders. As for the peasants, it mattered little to them if they worked for a Greek or a Frankish lord, so long as they were free to practise their religion and to keep their own lower clergy. They soon realized that the Greece of the Villehardouins and the de la Roches was going to be a more secure and prosperous country than that of the Angeloi.

The same considerations applied to all those engaged in that essentially Greek occupation, trade. One may safely conclude that the population as a whole was ready to put up with Frankish rule, subject to the religious reservation and on the understanding that it did not forfeit the limited rights and freedoms which it had enjoyed under the Empire. Apart from the serfs, who had no say in the matter, society in Frankish Greece was two-tiered. The thin superimposed Frankish layer was 'a part of France transplanted to Greek soil',[2] while the Greeks continued to be governed in accordance with their own customs and institutions. Inevitably, of course, they had to endure social and juridical inferiority, but such secondary status became less marked with the passage of time, and was less irksome for the archontic class. The national sentiment outlasted all vicissitudes, and 'foreign dominion only served to emphasize Byzantine awareness of their own cultural and religious way of life'.[3] It only needed the appearance of an aggressive native leader on the scene, such as a Dukas in Epiros or Thessaly and a Cantacuzene in the Peloponnese, for this feeling to assert itself and for his compatriots to rally to him. The Frankish rulers knew that however submissive the Greeks might seem at any moment, they looked on their subjection to a small Latin minority as a temporary evil which was bound to be corrected in God's good time. And when Byzantium regained a foothold in the Morea it must have seemed that the time had arrived.

The dominant minority brought with it its own languages, French and Italian, and continued to employ them within its own restricted circle. But for the purpose of communicating with the mass of the population it was obliged to learn Greek. The linguistic situation invites comparison with that which arose in England after the Norman Conquest, when French was similarly superimposed upon the native speech, but in Greece it evolved differently. The French (or Italian) speaking minority was smaller in relation to the native majority than was the case in Norman and Plantagenet England, where a sizeable proportion of the French-speakers did not necessarily have to resort to Anglo-Saxon for their daily requirements. So far as language was concerned, they were to a large degree self-sufficient, and the business of the kingdom was anyway conducted in French and Latin. Consequently the native tongue wilted, was profoundly simplified and ultimately merged with that of the conquerors in a new and composite language. In Romania, on the contrary, there was never any question of the disappearance or radical transformation of Greek, or of the emergence of a compound. The Greek language remained essentially the same throughout the *Frankokratia*, while temporarily absorbing into its everyday vocabulary a substantial number of words of romance origin, relating chiefly to feudal organization, war and navigation. The only wonder is that the Franks, in communicating with each other and their cousins overseas, managed to keep their speech, even after many generations of bilingualism, so pure and free from Hellenisms.

The Greek which the Frankish settlers learned to speak with fluency was the popular or demotic language which, as the American editor of the Greek *Chronicle of the Morea* observes, 'is closely connected with that of the present day, much closer than the language of Chaucer with modern English'.[4] It is true that the educated Byzantines used among themselves a somewhat more refined and, by classical standards, correct version of that idiom, and we may surmise that Guillaume de Villehardouin conversed in it with Michael Palaeologos when he was the latter's prisoner. It is highly improbable that any Frank succeeded in expressing himself, or even tried to do so, in the literary language modelled on Thucydides, Plato and Plutarch, which was normally employed by Byzantine historians, philosophers, theologians and letter-writers. There is no doubt, however, that bilingualism in the demotic tongue had become the rule among the Franks by the second generation after the Conquest at the latest. In a revealing passage of the Greek *Chronicle* the old knight Geoffroy de Briel remarks, before the battle in which the allied Franks and Greek Epirotes are about to confront the Byzantine army, that 'we [Franks and Epirotes] speak one language', whereas 'they' (the Byzantine forces mostly composed of non-Greek mercenaries) speak 'various tongues'.[5]

There was apparently no enthusiasm among the Greeks to acquire more than a smattering of the Frankish languages, although knowledge of Italian in the islands was no doubt more common than that of French on the mainland. However the numerous Greek clerks in the princely and ducal chanceries were certainly capable of correctly translating Latin, French and Italian documents and of conducting their masters' diplomatic correspondence with Greek rulers in the correct literary form. When in the fourteenth century the Byzantine theologian, Gregory Palams, was censured by the historian Nikephoros Gregoras for maintaining an amicable correspondence with the Grand Master of the Knights of Rhodes, we can hardly doubt that this was framed from the latter's side in an idiom as impeccably Classical as Gregory's.

It is true that certain works written in Greek supply evidence of a kind of cultural rapprochement. The Greek *Chronicle of the Morea* is at once a product of Greek literature and a panagyric celebrating the deeds of Frankish heroes. As we have already learned it was composed in Greek, either by a Frank or a *gasmoulos*, because Greek was the medium in which it would reach the widest public. Five manuscripts of the *Chronicle* have come to light in that language against one text each in French, Italian and Aragonese. The *Chronicle* is not of course a literary masterpiece. The author, whoever he was, was no Homer of the Middle Ages. His style is pedestrian and flat and his narrative is seldom enlivened by flashes of imagination. Linguistically he 'wavers between forms transmitted by literary tradition and those used in the common language', and he sprinkles his text with words of Latin origin.[6] Although the content of his work possessed vast historical interest he fails almost invariably to rise to the occasion. He yields no impression that he realized the potential grandeur of his theme. He was a plodding chronicler and propagandist but no poet. When the scene was so thickly peopled with paladins of both races, what a picture he might have painted of the lives of the Villehardouins and their Frankish and Greek peers. What an opportunity he missed of rivalling the epic of Digenis Akritas, the cycle of poems which celebrates the struggles between Byzantine and Saracen border barons.

The Franks had their own romances in plenty. Their settlement in

Greece coincided with the flowering of the chivalrous and courtly literature of the Western Middle Ages, of the *Chansons de Geste*, the Arthurian cycle and the prose *romans d'aventure*. These works either slightly predated the Fourth Crusade or were being written at the exact moment when the Franks were setting up their feudal states in Hellas. The songs of trouveres, and recitations from this enormous output of writings were the favourite entertainment at the courts of Andravida and Thebes and in countless castles scattered over the length and breadth of Romania. Soon the Greeks began to feel the attraction of Western romantic literature, especially as they too had inherited a long tradition derived from the novels of late Antiquity and revived in twelfth century Constantinople, where various authors produced popular romances in both prose and verse. Their content, however, was unoriginal and it was only when the Byzantine would became familiar with Western love-stories that writers began to produce fresh and lively tales more likely to find favour in the minor courts of the Latin-ruled Levant than in the back streets of Constantinople. At all events Latin influence resulted in a crop of Greek poems inspired by, though not directly imitated from, Western models. Interest in this genre was admittedly confined to the lighter and more exciting type of fantasy, for the full range of the emotions experienced by a Tristan or a Lancelot was perhaps too intense to appeal to the taste of the Levant. Nor, conversely, would it have occured to the overseas Latins, even when they had been domiciled in Greece for two centuries, to demand a translation into their own tongue of the Iliad and Odyssey, the staple literary diet of every Byzantine gentleman. Such a requirement was first voiced by the Italian humanists of the fourteenth century.

The best known of the Greek romances tinged by Western influence are the *Belthandros and Chrysantza* and the *Lybistros and Rhodamne*. The first dates from the thirteenth century and the second probably from the fourteenth. Both, like the *Chronicle of the Morea*, are composed in fifteen-syllable verse and both recount the trials, astounding adventures and eventual reunion of a pair of suitably high born lovers.[7]

In the first poem Belthandros, whose name recalls the Frankish Bertrand, is one of the two sons of Rodophilos, an imaginary Emperor of the Romans. He falls out with his father, who prefers his brother to himself, and runs away to seek his fortune in the service of an infidel prince, accompanied only by three squires (*paidopoula*). He rejects his father's entreaties to return and kills the emissaries despatched to arrest him. Making for Antioch, he traverses Anatolia and the 'mountains of the Turks', where he slaughters a whole band of brigands which

attempts to waylay him. He then descends into the plain of Tarsus which
the poet, with historical correctness, places in the mediaeval kingdom of
Lesser Armenia. Here he leaves the real world for a while and passes into
a realm of marvels. Following a fiery star which he perceives glowing
through the current of a stream and beckoning him onwards, he arrives
after ten days' march at a magic castle of supreme magnificence, built
entirely of sardonyx and packed full of the wonders of art and
mechanical invention. It is, he discovers, the Castle of Love.

On its gate of adamant, Belthandros reads an inscription declaring
that the man who has never felt the pangs of love will immediately suffer
them a hundred thousand fold if he succeeds in entering. Naturally he
does enter and finds the castle apparently uninhabited except for a
sculptured gryphon guarding the fountain of love, which comes to life at
his approach and flies away. He then comes upon two statues, both of a
young man, one in an attitude of despair and the other with his heart
pierced by an arrow. He realizes that it is himself who is so depicted, and
inscriptions explain that he is destined to be stricken with love for
Chrysantza, daughter of the King of Antioch, but that the God Eros has
separated them one from the other.

The bizarre adventure continues with the appearance of the God
himself, who announces that he has charged Belthandros with the task
of conducting a large scale judgement of Paris. He had to select the most
beautiful from among forty lovely girls, all daughters of Kings. They
come before him one by one and the choice narrows to three; one is
rejected because of the down on her arms, a second for a defect in her
eyes. But the survivor is perfect, and he presents her with the God's
golden staff, whereupon Eros and all the girls suddenly vanish.

Belthandros is obliged to leave the splendours of the empty palace and
proceed on his way to Antioch. Before he reaches the city he encounters
its Moslem ruler hunting with his nobles and is taken into his service. He
gains much favour by shooting an eagle which has attacked the King's
favourite falcon. One day, when in the King's presence, he catches a
glimpse of his daughter and duly recognises the winner of the
competition in the Castle of Love. To his delight recognition is mutual,
but as Chrysantza is secluded in the harem, he has to wait many months
before he can contrive to win access to her. However he is discovered
lurking in the royal garden and arrested. He is only saved from death by
a ruse invented by the princess, who complains to her father that
Belthandros has climbed into the garden for a rendezvous with her maid
Phaidrokatza. The stratagem succeeds, but the trusting monarch
promptly gives orders for a marriage between Belthandros and the maid.

Although this decision momentarily disconcerts the lovers, it works out in their favour, for the marriage, though celebrated, is not consummated and enables the liaison between Belthandros and the princess to proceed happily under the nose of the King and Queen.

But this state of affairs cannot last for ever. The couple abscond, taking with them the faithful Phaidrokatza and the three squires. They are pursued, and squires and maid are drowned while crossing a river. Only the prince and princess escape. Eventually they reach the sea and find a ship which takes them to Byzantium. The Emperor, who in the meantime has lost his other son, receives them with joy and they are wedded with full ceremony of church and state.

Lybistros, the hero of the second and later romance, is a Frank, not a Roman. The atmosphere of the poem, too, suggests the Latin Orient rather than Byzantium. It opens with a meeting between two knights errant, Lybistros and Klitobos. They swear friendship with one another and the former recounts the troubled history of his love for Rhodamne. His trials begin, according to his account, when he shoots a dove one day and is astonished to see the bird's mate fall dead of grief at its side. His old counsellor instructs him in the laws and mysteries of love, and in a series of dreams he is conducted to Erotokratia, the palace of Eros, and into the God's presence. Eros explains that he is fated to love Rhodamne, daughter of King Chrysos, who rules over the city of Argyrokastron, the 'castle of silver'. So he sets out with an escort of a hundred knights to claim his princess.

Like the magic castle in *Belthandros*, the King's palace is full of marvels, including a host of allegorical statues in marble and bronze. Lybistros does not find it easy to approach the princess because she is already affianced to Frederick, King of Egypt. But he manages to correspond with her through one of her eunuchs (a Byzantine touch but a somewhat out-of-date one) and one day meets her as she rides out hunting. He then reveals his intentions to the King, who decrees that the two claimants to his daughter's hand should fight it out in a tourney. Not unnaturally Lybistros wins the contest; he is immediately married to Rhodamne and associated with the rulership of Argyrokastron. All would be perfect but for one ominous inscription on a statue in the princess's garden which foretells that before settling down with his bride he will have to endure two years of suffering and separation.

It turns out that the vanquished Frederick is no mean magician and has sent his sorcerers to punish Lybistros. During a hunt (this Frankish pastime recurs time and again) Lybistros and Rhodamne come across a 'merchant of Babylon' (Cairo), accompanied by an old hag riding a camel, and inspect what he has to offer for sale. The prince selects a ring and his wife is interested in a splendid horse. But as he slips the ring on his finger he faints away, and when he comes to both horse and princess have disappeared. It is during his apparently fruitless search for Rhodamne that Lybistros encounters Klitobos, and they ride on together. At last, guided by another opportune dream, they again meet the old witch, who is fortunately disenchanted with Frederick for not having properly rewarded her services. After a long and blood-curdling digression on the power of magic she discloses that Rhodamne is alive and, moreover, has virtuously resisted Frederick's advances. She is in fact keeping an inn on the shores of the 'Egyptian sea'. Mounted on the witch's magical horses the knights hurry there and remove her in triumph to Argyrokastron, where Klitobos is wedded to Rhodamne's sister.

Who wrote these poems and others like them? For whom were they written and before what audiences were they intended to be recited? No very clear answer is provided by the internal evidence. The romances are written in good popular Greek of the period and contain much fewer verbal Latinisms than the *Chronicle of the Morea*. So far as the content is concerned, Latin and Byzantine elements are combined in both poems, but the flavour of the *Belthandros*, despite its hero's Latin-sounding name, is more markedly Byzantine. The action takes place in Asia and begins and ends at the imperial court. The characters are for the most part recognisably Byzantine types and behave in a Byzantine way. The specifically Latin touches are few, but the conception of the Castle of Love seems to have been inspired by a Provençal original. We may conjecture that the author was a Greek who was familiar with both the Greek and Western romances of the period. We may also surmise that he was writing for a mainly Greek public (outside as well as within the frontiers of the Empire), though not for the classically educated élite. His work may well have appealed to the archons of the Morea and of the Despotate of Epiros.

The *Lybistros*, on the other hand, has a definitely Latin slant. The hero is portrayed as a blond Frank, shaven, clothed and armed and mounted like a Westerner. He is the perfect knight errant of chivalry. Frederick of Egypt, despite his inappropriate name, and the witch of Babylon are stock Oriental villains as conjured up by the Crusading imagination. Chrysos of Argyrokastron exhibits more Byzantine traits, but his daughter is described as wearing Latin dress and confesses to her father that she loves the Latins. 'They are a brave race', she says, 'and among them I especially like those who fight for love and glory'. Thus the writer, like the author of the Greek *Chronicle*, takes pains to stress his Latin sympathies. His preoccupation with dreams, allegory and magic also suggest Western rather than Byzantine leanings. At the same time the court of Chrysos displays all the familiar Byzantine features and the poet's ennumeration of the statues adorning his palace is derived from Byzantine models. Perhaps he was a Greek or *gasmoulos* living under Latin rule and catering for mainly Latin audiences. Those Latins who read his poem, or more probably listened to its recitation, were bilingual and had no difficulty in following the popular Greek in which it was composed. This type of literature emphasizes the modest character of the cultural fusion achieved within a narrow field. It does however, seem to establish that there were in Byzantium or outside Greeks capable of understanding the French and Provencal romances which influenced their work.

Greece is so thickly strewn with relics of mediaeval architecture that it may seem paradoxical to lament that they are on the whole a disappointment.[8] The sites are uniformly magnificent, but the ruined monuments themselves are more remarkable for their quantity than for their quality. The Latins built nothing in Greece to compare with what they left behind them in Syria and Cyprus. They evolved no new regional style of their own, and the surviving buildings in which Western and Byzantine features are combined are no more than curious. It is sad that such second-rate work was produced in that grandest age of Gothic architecture, the thirteenth century. But in the circumstances the Franks of Romania could hardly have been expected to achieve their best. Time and history have treated with unusual harshness castles and churches raised hurriedly under hostile pressure and in the almost total absence of the skilled Western workmen who would have been available in their countries of origin. Materials and methods of construction were alike inferior.

What reminders, for instance, of the long Frankish presence are left in the heart of the principality of Achaia, the triangle Andravida–Glarentza–Chloumoutzi? Only the bulky ruins of the castle of Clermont, which are reasonably well preserved and have been carefully restored in recent years, attest the power and dignity of the Villehardouins and their successors. They are a solid but provincial version of the superb military architecture of Le Crac des Chevaliers and Aigues-Mortes. Of the town of Glarentza, dismantled by the Palaeologues in 1429, nothing is left. Even the meagre remains of its plain but imposing church were demolished by the German occupants in the last War. Further away, little can be traced of the capital, Andravida, which is known to have contained several monuments of the Latins, St Sophia, St Stephen, St Nicolas of Carmel, the Hospital of St James, the palace of the princes. The eastern extremity of St Sophia alone survives to show that this was an entirely Gothic church. According to Sir Osbert Lancaster, it was 'northern rather than Italianate in feeling, and indeed the exceptional width of the central aisle may well have given it an almost English look'. Essentially it was a simple French church of the late thirteenth century, although blocks of antique cut stone were used in its construction. On the two sides of a capital are engraved the coats of arms of the Villehardouins and of Florent of Hainault, and a funerary stone, decorated with Byzantine carvings in relief, marks the tomb of Prince Guillaume's third wife Anna (Agnes) of Epiros. Its inscription reads 'Ici gist Madame Agnes jadis fille du Despot Kier Mikaille.' Here lies Madame Agnes, once daughter of the Despot Lord Michael.[9]

Not far from Glarentza is the convent of Blachernai, a Byzantine foundation of the late twelfth century which appears to have been taken over for the Latin rite. It is described by A. Bon as 'un exemple curieux d'architecture mi-grecque mi-occidentale', (a curious example of half Greek, half Western architecture). He points out that its church exhibits pointed arches and other Western features and goes on to deduce that it was still unfinished at the time of the Frankish invasion and completed later under Frankish direction.[10] Western forms and motifs are to be found in many other Greek mediaeval churches, but it is not easy to discern whether they have been added after 1204 to a church built before the Conquest or have been incorporated in the design of one constructed at a later date. Ogival arches are to be seen in buildings of Byzantine style all the way from Epiros to the Maina, even at Geraki and Geroumana in that part of Lakonia which the Villehardouins only held for a short while in the mid-thirteenth century. Another novelty introduced from the West was the bell-tower or bell-cote. Good early examples exist at Merbaka in the Argolid and Samari in Messenia, and there is a particularly fine free-standing specimen at Karytaina. From the fourteenth century, however, the belfry became a normal feature of Orthodox churches.

One single Gothic church among all those built by the Franks, Hagia Paraskeve at Chalkis (Negroponte), has endured almost intact. It was originally a Franciscan foundation. Although the sum of their surviving work is pitifully small, the religious orders were all active builders. St Sophia at Andravida was a Dominican house; Notre Dame d'Isova in the Alpheios valley, which was ruined in 1263 by the Turkish auxiliaries in the service of Michael Palaeologos, probably belonged to the

Benedictines. The Cistercians are represented by the remains of the cloister which they added to the Byzantine monastery of Daphni in Attica and by their own new foundation of Zaraka in the remote region of Lake Stymphalos in north-eastern Arkadia. The churches at all these places were Gothic edifices of the first half of the thirteenth century, simple and austere, with the dimensions of a large parish church. In none of them does the nave exceed fifty metres in length. If the Franks ever planned a cathedral in the Morea or elsewhere on the scale which they realized in Cyprus, they never built it. Their early churches were the work of pioneers in a strange land and from the moment when the Greeks began the counter-offensive which in the end expelled the Franks altogether the latter lost the will to attempt anything grander. They lacked the leisure, the wealth and the security to reproduce a vestige of what was being achieved in their homelands. Nor did circumstances favour the emergence and development of a hybrid architectural style. Whatever resources they could find for building had to be devoted to the imperious requirements of defence.[11]

In a country which bristles with fortifications of all epochs from the pre-hellenic to the Venetian, and in which the principal sites of military vantage have been continuously utilized, it is not always possible to distinguish which are of purely or even mainly Frankish construction. There are no more fascinating fortresses anywhere than Acrocorinth and Acronauplia, the Larissa of Argos and Patras, but in all these cases the Franks adapted for their own use strongholds which had existed in Hellenic and Byzantine times, and their thirteenth and fourteenth century work has been overlaid and obscured by later accretions, notably from the period of the Turco-Venetian wars. Both Argos and Patras were Byzantine castles; the latter had repelled attacks from the invading Slavs and the former, when defended by Leon Sgouros and Theodore Dukas, defied the Latins for seven years. Both were strengthened by the Franks and refashioned by Venice. Kalamata and Arkadia (Kyparissia) were also occupied from antiquity until the Turkish era. Byzantium had always been renowned for its military architecture; so were France and all Western Europe in the high Middle Ages, and the Crusaders developed it splendidly in Outremer. But in Greece the Franks fell short of these high standards; only Clermont (Chloumoutzi), a vast and carefully designed polygonal structure dating from 1220, has an air of massive permanence.[12]

Yet the mountain castles, large and small, which seem to crown every other hill, compulsively attract the traveller. The grander examples, Salona towering above the surrounding olive-groves, and Karytaina perched on its cliff over the deep gorge of the Alpheios, are quite irresistible. But the simplicity of their design, the roughness of their construction, the absence of all decoration and provision for comfort, soon tell a sad tale. They were clearly built to satisfy the pressing military needs of the moment. No master-masons from the West accompanied the invaders. They were forced to rely on their own improvisation, a reluctant and unskilled Greek labour force and whatever materials were available on the spot. Wherever there were antique ruins to be used as a quarry they took all the cut stone they could find, but usually they resorted to the local limestone and Byzantine brick, and to grosser material for filling. It is a wonder that so many walls and towers have nevertheless withstood warfare and weather.

Of course the Franks did not spend all their time crouched behind fortifications. The Dukes of Athens, Princes of Achaia and Counts of Cephalonia, with their principal lieges and clerics, lived in great style. Unfortunately we can form little idea of what their palaces were like. We know that the Kadmeia of Thebes was luxuriously appointed and, like similar residences, adorned with frescoes, but the only trace of Frankish wallpainting which still exists (or did exist until lately) is to be found in a tiny chapel at Geraki. There Joshua was depicted leading a charge of mail-clad horsemen against the Amorites, dressed in white and carrying a shield decorated with a coat of arms, possibly that of the Nivelets who were the local barons. They chase the enemy towards a city gate, and the defenders shower them with missiles. Above this scene stands a row of personages also clad in white, but one wears high boots and a hauberk. It is suggested by A. Bon, from whose book these details are extracted, that 'Amorites' is a pun and the fresco commemorates the conquest of the Morea.[13]

Neither in literature nor in the visual arts was any real cultural accord reached between Franks and Greeks. Nevertheless over a region much wider than the Greek peninsula, a very significant change of mental climate had slowly been taking place in the relations between East and West. After 1204 the schism, not only in the religious but also in the political and cultural spheres, was virtually complete, but by 1400 Western hostility and incomprehension were rapidly giving way to a genuine understanding of what Byzantium had to offer to the humanists of the early Renaissance who were groping their way towards the rediscovery of Classical culture. Petrarch, Boccaccio and their followers had come to realize that only the Greeks could help them in their search for enlightenment. On the political plane it had also become obvious to the Western monarchies that Turkish encroachments in Europe posed a real threat to their own security. This, however, might yet be kept at bay by a tardy support for the moribund but still desperately struggling Eastern Empire. Hence there was no longer any political obstacle to a reconciliation between East and West.

True, the sectarian barrier loomed as impassable as ever. Those emperors, from Michael VIII onwards, who acknowledged with or without reluctance that the salvation of the Empire depended on a transaction with Rome were obliged to admit that a solution of this kind could not be enforced against the obstinate resistance of their own subjects. Such measure of *rapprochement* as came about was achieved in the teeth of the stiff intransigence of the papacy and of the stubborn antagonism of the Byzantine people, including the majority of Byzantine intellectuals. The popular attitude stemmed from a mixture of temperament and bitter experience; that of the élite from profound differences of ideology and tradition.

Gradually, however, independent spirits in Byzantium began to show interest in the secular as well as the religious aspects of Latin culture. At the time when Michael VIII was pursuing his policy of uniting the Churches the monk Maximos Planudes, an all-round scholar and editor of the Anthology of Greek epigrams, was engaged in a thorough study of the Latin language. He translated Ovid, Cicero, Boethius and St Augustine into Greek and served as Ambassador to Venice. A grasp of Latin was of course essential for a proper understanding of the Western mind and of the vast corpus of Western scholastic thought, of which the erudite Byzantines, basking in the assumption of their intellectual superiority, had long remained supremely ignorant. Platonists to a man, they had failed to realize how deeply the scholastics had become versed in Aristotle and how they were using him as a pillar of Christian theology. It was not until about 1340 that Demetrios Kydones, the polymath and intimate friend of the Emperors John Cantacuzenos and Manuel Palaeologos, published a Greek translation of the *Summa Theologiae* of St Thomas Aquinas.[14]

Kydones, whose life spanned the whole of the fourteenth century, was an enthusiastic partisan of Church union and alliance with the Latins, but ended his days, in characteristic Byzantine fashion, as a monk in Crete, his country of origin. A frequent visitor to Italy, he was the precursor of all the brilliant scholars who later fled from the collapse of Byzantium and found a haven in the West, which received them with open arms. The sympathy which they encountered was paralleled in the political field by the final Western Crusades which came to grief at Nikopolis and Varna. But all these moves towards reconciliation and union came too late to save Constantinople and Greece from the Ottomans. It was a tragedy that in the mid-fourteenth century, when the energies of the failing Empire should have been concentrated on combating the Turks and on establishing a basis for concord with the Latins, they were consumed in civil war and, on the religious and intellectual plane, in the exhausting quarrel which opposed the Hesychasts, champions of a mystical movement that came to be regarded as the core of national Orthodoxy, to the less numerous supporters of union with Rome, or of a less intransigent point of view.

It must be confessed that these controversies and ferments created less stir in the Greek peninsula itself, where Latins and Greeks maintained an uneasy co-existence. The former, whether of French or Italian stock, still took a minimal interest in Greek culture, Greek theology and the intellectual movements of the fourteenth century and onwards. The fact that their bilingualism was limited to popular Greek would have prevented them from exploring those fields, even if they had felt any inclination to do so. But the majority of their Greek neighbours were equally untouched by such influences, and the only cultural trait which distinguished them from the Latins was their firm attachment to Orthodoxy. After the expulsion of Michael of Chonae and other clerical literati at the conquest there was practically no cultivated Greek society left in Hellas. The indigenous archons were just as unpolished as their Frankish counterparts. However, as the fourteenth century wore on and Mistra became the capital of an expanding Greek principality, the Morea began to reflect the culture of Constantinople and Thessalonica. The re-establishment of Byzantine rule brought scholars and artists in the wake of the soldiers. In the course of time and under the patronage of successive Despots, they created a new, if short-lived, focus of Hellenic culture. The result was the remarkable outburst of intellectual and artistic activity which illumined Mistra in the decades preceding the extinction of the Despotate.

The churches of Mistra displayed the flower of Palaeologan painting; libraries were founded and manuscripts copied. While Plethon and his circle were at work the little city became an obligatory port of call for all leaders of Byzantine intellectual life and the bridge over which the Greek humanists passed on their way to Italy. Meanwhile Moreots formed in the schools of Mistra filled high posts at Constantinople. Such was Joseph Bryennios, head of the Patriarchal Academy (or Institute of Higher Theology) under Manuel II. He too knew Latin well and had studied the scholastics, but differed from Plethon in that he was a Hesychast and strictly Orthodox. The Greek intelligentsia no longer ignored nor affected to ignore Western thought. Flattered by the difference paid to them, they were happy to speed the progress of the Italian Renaissance with the resources of their own learning. Personal relations between like-minded men in both worlds multiplied, and even in the highlands of the Peloponnese George Cantacuzenos placed his classical library at the disposition of Cyriacus of Ancona. But whereas this intellectual revival was certainly stimulated by contacts with the West it was not inspired by them; it was a purely Greek phenomenon. Experts have detected a faint Italian tinge in the culture of Mistra, perhaps deriving from the Despots' Italian marriages. 'The arcades of the Church of the Pantanassa', wrote David Talbot Rice, 'are thus rather Florentine in style',[15] and Runciman draws attention to an interesting manuscript in the Bibliothèque Nationale of Paris of Oppian's *Cynegetica*, a classical Greek treatise probably copied at Mistra and containing delightful and realistically drawn scenes of hunters in obviously Western dress and attitudes. 'Lay life in the Peloponnese', he comments, 'had been too deeply affected by Frankish rule not to show its reflection.'[16] Such examples, however, are evidence of little more than a natural improvement in the association between Greeks and Latins just at the point when the latter, with the exception of the Venetians, were losing their last footholds in Hellas. Any prospect of a more fruitful development of that relationship was due to be blighted by the Turkish conquest.

While Mistra played its crucial part in implanting true Greek culture in the Italian Renaissance, the Frankish interlude in Hellas struck other chords in the minds of the masters of European literature. It was Gibbon who first remarked that three great poets, Dante, Boccaccio and Shakespeare, conferred upon Theseus, the national hero of ancient Athens, the mediaeval title of Duke. Dante, the contemporary of the de la Roches, leads off by making Vergil say to the Minotaur, in the twelfth canto of the *Inferno*,

> . . . Forse
> Tu credi, che qui sia il duca d'Atene,
> Che su nel mondo la morte ti porse?

(May be you think that the Duke of Athens is here, who in the world above did you to death.) Boccaccio, the friend of the Acciaiuoli, goes further in vivifying classical legend drawn from Plutarch's *Life of Theseus* with the lustre of the ducal court. To quote John Addington Symonds, the Florentine writer's *Teseide* 'is a narrative poem in which the Greek hero plays a prominent part, while all the chiefs of Theban and Athenian legend are brought upon the scene' in a grand effusion of mythological learning. In this romantic epic appears for the first time the story of Palamon and Arcite and their rivalry for the love of Emilia, which it is possible that Boccaccio derived from a Greek popular tale. He also brings the Duke of Athens into one of his stories in the *Decameron*, where the Princess of Babylon is introduced at the Athenian court.[17]

Chaucer, with singular skill and felicity, very soon adapted the theme and content of the *Teseide* for his *Knight's Tale* and in doing so he unconsciously captured better than any of his fellow poets the flavour of feudal Athens. The poem, the action of which oscillates between the twin ducal capitals of Athens and Thebes, is packed with lines recalling the pomp of the de la Roches and St Omers:-

> There was a duk that highte Theseus;
> Of Athens he was lord and governour.

> His banner he desplayeth, and forth rood
> To Thebes-ward, and al his oost bysyde.

> The reede statue of Mars with spere and targe
> So schyneth in his white baner large,
> That alle the feeldes gliteren up and down;
> And by his baner was born his pynoun
> Of gold ful riche, in which ther was i-bete
> The Minatour which that he slough in Crete.
> Thus ryt this duk, thus ryt this conqueror,
> And in his oost of chevalrie the flour
> Till that he came to Thebes, and alighte
> Fayre in a feelt when as he thoughte to fighte.

No more apt a description could be imagined of Gautier de Brienne riding to his destruction at the Kephissos, among

> The scheldes bright, testers and trappures
> Gold-beten helmes, hauberks and cote armures.[18]

We are more familiar, perhaps, with the Theseus of *A Midsummer Night's Dream*, but in Shakespeare's Athens the mediaeval echoes have grown more faint. He enrols himself, however, on the side of those who have felt the fascination of Burgundian horns and hounds in the classical landscape. 'My hounds', exclaims the Duke,

> are bred out of the Spartan kind . . .
> A cry more tuneable

Was never holla'd to, nor cheered with horn,
In Crete, in Sparta, nor in Thessaly.[19]

Lastly, it is Goethe who pays an enigmatic though unmistakable tribute to feudal Mistra, where he unites Faust, the personification of the young, invigorating north, with Helen, the spirit of the ancient Ewig-Weibliche.

'So viele Jahre', says Phorkyas to Helen in the third act of Part II of Faust,

> stand verlassen das Talgebirg,
> Das hinter Sparta nordwärts in die Höhe steigt,
> Taygetos im Rücken, wo als muntrer Bach
> Herab Eurotas rollt und dann, durch unser Tal
> An Rohren breit hinfliessend, eure Schwäne nährt.
> Dort hinten still im Gebirgthal hat ein kühn Geschlecht
> Sich angesiedelt, dringend aus cimmerischer Nacht
> Und unersteiglich-feste Burg sich aufgeturmt,
> Von da sie Land und Leute placken, wie's behagt.

> [So many years the hill-girt vale neglected stands,
> Which behind Sparta ever to the North ascends,
> Taygetos to rearwards, whence, a brawling stream,
> Eurotas falls, and broadening twixt its reed-crowned banks
> Flows down the valley where it nourishes your swans.
> There in the mountain-gorges has a daring tribe
> Esconced itself, emerging from Cimmerian night,
> And reared a lofty citadel, unscaleable;
> From whence at will they sally, harrying men and crops.]

This is an astonishingly accurate evocation of Villehardouin's 'Burg', whose courtyard, in Goethe's stage directions, is 'umgeben von reichen, phantastischen Gebärden des Mittelalters' (Surrounded by rich, fantastic figures from the Middle Ages), and in which Faust appears 'in ritterlicher Hofkleidung des Mittelalters' (in knightly mediaeval court apparel) and sings

> Germane du, Korinthus Buchten
> Verteidige mit Wall und Schutz!
> Achaja dann mit hundert Schluchten
> Empfehle ich, Gote, deinem Trutz.

> Nach Elis ziehn der Franken Heere,
> Messene sei der Sachsen Los!

Normanne reinige die Meere
Und Argolis erschaff er gross!

Dann wird er jeder haüslich wohnen,
Nach aussen richten Kraft und Blitz;
Doch Sparta soll euch überthronen,
Der Königin verjährter Sitz.

[Thou, German, must with men and walls
O'er Corinth's bay keep watch and ward;
And, Goth, on thee the duty falls
Achaia's hundred vales to guard.

The Frankish host to Elis goes;
Messene is the Saxon's prize;
Thou, Norman, clear the sea of foes,
Till Argolis to greatness rise.

Then each shall dwell in house and hall,
And flash his lightning strokes around;
But Sparta shall be lord of all,
The Queen's domain, for aye renowned.][20]

The whole passage repays quoting at length. Goethe, of course, never visited Greece, and it is unlikely that he could ever have read the *Chronicle of the Morea*. No matter that he heavily overstates the Germanic character of the Franks; no matter, either, what source inspired the unerring stroke of imagination that placed the fabulous fabric of the Faustburg on the towered outcrop of Taygetos.[21]

CHAPTER FOURTEEN

Crete (from 1204 to 1669)

HOMER'S 'BROAD' CRETE, the Great Greek island, was first lost to Byzantium in or about 825, when it was seized and held by a body of daring freebooters from Moslem Spain.[1] Until the reconquest of the island in 961 by the future Emperor Nikephoros Phokas, these corsairs disrupted Aegean trade and spread terror throughout the Archipelago. It was they who, under the leadership of Leo of Tripoli, sacked Thessalonica in 904. Seven years later, in a sea-fight off Samos, they destroyed the armada which the Emperor Leo VI had despatched against them. In 949 a second Byzantine attempt to dislodge them from Crete also failed. But subsequently the island remained in Byzantine possession for nearly two and a half centuries, undisturbed by enemies from East or West.

According to the original arrangements concerted between the Latin conquerors of Constantinople for the partition of Byzantine territories, Crete was first allotted to Boniface of Montferrat, but as we have already seen Venetian pressure compelled the future King of Thessalonica to sign a *Refutatio*, dated 12 August 1204, by which he renounced his claim in favour of the Republic for a cash payment of 1000 marks of silver. It only remained for Pietro Ziani, the new Doge who succeeded Enrico Dandolo, to assert his authority in the dominion which he had so cheaply acquired.

He did not find it an easy task. In the first place the Venetians had to overcome competition from their inveterate rivals the Genoese. Before they had time to establish their own garrisons they were forestalled by Genoese corsairs led by Enrico Pescatore, an adventurer who called himself Count of Malta. Apparently unopposed and perhaps assisted by the Cretans, Pescatore quickly fortified a number of strong points and prepared to resist a Venetian attack. That was not long delayed. A powerful squadron commanded by Renier Dandolo, son of the former Doge, appeared in Cretan waters after driving out the equally dangerous Genoese freelance, Leone Vetrano, who had momentarily seized Corfu. At first Dandolo was repulsed, but in the following year (1207) he returned with a larger force and succeeded in capturing some of Pescatore's castles. He also made himself master of Chandax, the former Saracen slave-market, the future Candia and modern Heraklion.

An obstinate struggle was waged for the next three years, as Pescatore, after receiving reinforcements, managed to take Dandolo prisoner, and the captive starved himself to death. Finally the Genoese, finding that in the long run he could not expect to outfight Venice, negotiated a truce, accepted compensation in cash and retired from the island. When he was gone Giacomo Tiepolo, a future Doge of Venice, was appointed governor of Crete with the title of Doge or Duke, and took up residence at Candia. His office soon assumed a viceregal character, for the Venetians were proud to style their new dominion *Regno di Candia,* or *Regnum Cretae.*[2]

We have no firm information about the role played by native Cretans during these conflicts. It can only be supposed that they were disinclined to support either of the alien combatants and had not yet sufficiently recovered from the shock of the fall of Constantinople to produce a positive national reaction. The structure of Cretan society at the time did not appreciably differ from that of other Greek lands in the thirteenth century. By then memories of the earlier occupation of Crete by Andalusians and other Saracens had become dimmed. We may perhaps assume, in the absence of firm evidence, that the Arab presence, concentrated as it was around a naval base and slave-market, had not involved an overwhelming Moslem immigration nor a mass conversion of the Cretans to Islam. Most probably the majority of the islanders remained Hellenes and Orthodox Christians during the years of Arab rule and their ethnic and cultural character was not profoundly modified.[3] That is not to say that numerous apostasies did not occur, and we know that the task of reconverting those who had fallen away from Christianity was entrusted to St Nikon, also the evangelist of the Peloponnesian Slavs, after the reconquest in 961.[4] In 1204 the descendants of Saracens and apostatized Cretans were known as *douloparoikoi* and regarded as the most humble class of labourers bound to the soil. Thus such traces of Moslem influence as lingered on had been virtually effaced before the advent of the Venetians and the Arab racial element had been absorbed. It did not constitute a separate and viable community like the Arabs in Sicily.

Just as in mainland Greece, the Cretan archons were headed by representatives of the great families of Byzantium. Among the latter we find, for instance, the Phokades, the Argyropouloi, the Melissenoi, the Mousouroi and the Gabalades. Known as the *archontopouloi* or *archontoromaioi,* they themselves maintained that they were descended from twelve noble Byzantines despatched to Crete from Constantinople by the Emperor Alexios Komnenos (1081–1118).[5] These rich and powerful magnates were supplemented by a more modest class of landowners of native Cretan origin. Below them came a broad category of freemen whom the Venetians called *franchi*. The Orthodox clergy was as numerous and influential as in any part of the Byzantine world, and the monasteries owned extensive estates. The *paroikoi* who tilled the land did so in the same conditions as the peasantry of Attica and the Peloponnese.

As soon as opposition from outside Crete had been disposed of, Venice proceeded to impose its own pattern of administration. At its head was the Duke, a nobleman appointed by the Venetian Senate for a two-year but renewable term of office and assisted by two counsellors (*consiliarii*). Together they formed the *Signoria* or government of the island and exercised supreme authority in both civil and military affairs. Immediately subordinate to them, and also appointed directly from Venice, were the rectors or governors of the two smaller cities, Canea and Rethimnon, and the six captains commanding the military forces in the six districts into which Crete, as we shall see, was divided. At a later date these officers were placed under the overall authority of a captain–general. In addition upwards of twenty fortresses with their surrounding territory were independently administered by their own *castellani*. Economic affairs were directed by two, and later four, *camerlenghi* (Chamberlains), also appointed from the metropolis.

Judges, two for Venetians and one for Greeks and Jews, were nominated by the local *Signoria*. So were the many minor officials of the administration, who might be either resident Venetians or, in some instances, native Cretans. All members of the bureaucracy, high and low, were subjected to strict discipline meticulously regulated in writing by so-called capitularies and enforced by fierce penalties. Senior officials from home were forbidden to bring their wives, children and other relations to Crete during their period of service; they were not allowed to accept presents or even invitations to meals from the natives. Moreover they were periodically checked and supervised by *provveditori*, commissioners despatched from the metropolis with full powers of inspection and control, as well as for the occasional exercise of various kinds of special function, such as the building and maintenance of ports, docks and arsenals.[6]

This edifice of government was founded on the introduction of military colonists. The first batch of these landed in Crete as early as 1211; others followed in 1222, 1233 and 1252. The party which arrived in 1211 was composed of 132 *milites* or *cavalieri* and 48 *pedites* or sergeants. Each colonist was presented with a contract defining his rights and duties. For the purpose of Venetian settlement the island was divided into six districts or hexarchies, corresponding to the *sestieri* of the city of Venice, and the captains of the districts were initially entrusted with the task of allotting fiefs to the settlers. These were carved partly out of existing public lands, but chiefly out of estates expropriated from Cretan owners. A sergeant obtained only one-sixth of the land reserved to a *cavaliero*, or noble knight.

Each feudatory was allotted one or more villages or farms for his upkeep, together with a minimum of twenty-five *paroikoi*. He was also granted a house in Candia and a share in common grazing rights. A fief was the full property of the colonist; he could sell or mortgage it to another, but not to a Greek. For the first four years he was not required to pay taxes, but was liable at any moment for military service. All noble colonists formed a Great Council, which in turn appointed a committee to work with the *Signoria*, as well as any other boards or committee that might be found necessary. In fact the whole administration was a microcosm, suitably simplified, of that which existed at home.[7]

The arrival of the colonists, followed by the confiscation of Cretan lands in order to provide them with fiefs, sparked off the first of a long series of revolts against Venetian rule. It is hardly surprising that the native landowners should have been outraged by these intrusions, especially as they contrasted so unfavourably with the generally tactful treatment of Greek archontic interests by the easy-going Frankish princes of mainland Greece. The Moreots, according to the French version of the *Chronicle of the Morea*, 'se acorderent avec le Champenois en tel maniere que li gentil homme grec qui tenaient fiez et terres et les casaux dou pays eust cescun et tenist selonc sa qualité, et le surplus fust departi a nostre gent'. (Agreed with the man of Champagne that the Greek gentlemen who held fiefs and lands and villages in the country should each have and hold them according to his quality, and that the surplus should be distributed to our people.)[8] But in Crete the Venetians were not satisfied with the surplus. Instead of being confirmed in their possessions, the Cretans often found themselves ousted. The spirit of cold self-interest in which the Venetians grabbed the property of their subjects caused lasting disaffection and frequent uprisings over a period of 150 years.

A further cause of Greek resentment was the expulsion of the higher Orthodox clergy, the Metropolitan of Crete and his ten Bishops, from their sees and their replacement by a Latin episcopate. That process, similar to what occurred in other parts of the Byzantine realm occupied by Latin invaders, involved the confiscation of church buildings and properties. In addition to the new hierarchy, a full complement of Latin priests and members of religious orders was installed in the towns and wherever a sizeable number of Venetians had taken root. Only the lower Orthodox clergy remained to serve the Cretan population, and all recruits to the priesthood were obliged to incur inconvenience and expense in travelling overseas in order to be ordained. The numerous existing Orthodox monasteries were also left undisturbed, with the result that they inevitably came to serve, as in subsequent periods of Cretan history, as centres of passive or active resistance to alien rule. Needless to say, the Cretans totally rejected papal supremacy as well as Catholic doctrines and rites.[9]

The first Cretan rebellion broke out in 1212. It was not a mass uprising of the native population, for a partial change of masters is unlikely to have worsened the lot of the *paroikoi* to any appreciable extent, but a sudden coup mounted by one of the leading archontic clans, the Argyropouloi or, as they were usually known in Crete, the Hagiostephanitai. No doubt it was their reaction to the seizure of some of their properties, which seem to have been located around or to the east of Candia. The Duke Tiepolo was taken by surprise and his strongholds in the eastern part of the island were quickly taken. But, as mentioned in the previous chapter, he promptly called the Duke of Naxos, Marco Sanudo, to his aid, and their joint forces very soon mastered the rebellion. The Hagiostephanitai seem to have avoided capture and to have removed themselves for a time from Crete.

We have already observed how Sanudo, whether from motives of personal ambition to found an Aegean realm of his own, or from sheer annoyance that Tiepolo had been unwilling or had not received permission to implement his promise of thirty knights' fees in Crete, changed sides and joined the Cretan rebels in a renewed attempt to overthrow Venetian authority. This time the Cretan leader was another prominent *archontoromaios*, Constantine Sebastos Skordilis, but it is unclear how important a part Cretan forces played in the ensuing duel between Sanudo and Tiepolo. The two sides were well matched and each possessed fortresses that were virtually impregnable. It was only when the Duke was reinforced from Venice and succeeded in retaking Candia that Sanudo decided to seek a compromise. In return for surrendering his remaining castles, he was compensated in cash and kind and retired from Crete with his prestige unimpaired. The most interesting clause in the agreement which ended the war was that which permitted twenty Cretan allies of Sanudo to leave the island unharmed and to dispose of their property as they wished. We do not know whether or when they were allowed to return, but both Skordilis and the Hagiostephanitai figure in the records of the succeeding years.[10]

The chronology of the period is somewhat confused and it is uncertain how long the struggle lasted. It was over by 1217, when Paolo Quirini succeeded Tiepolo as Duke of Candia. Not much later certain Cretan notables, ecclesiastics, citizens of Candia and individuals styling themselves the 'loyal' Hagiostephanitai, addressed a bitter remonstrance to the Doge of Venice complaining of the oppressive character of Quirini's rule, of expulsions, confiscations and other arbitrary acts. It looked forward to the appointment of a new Duke of Candia and expressed the hope that neither Quirini nor any member of his family would be given a new appointment in Crete. The document, drafted in poor Latin, was probably conveyed to Venice behind Quirini's back. He was in fact reappointed Duke in 1223. As for the 'loyal' Hagiostephanitai, it can only be assumed that their former dissidence had been forgiven to the extent that some of them were still living in Crete.[11]

In any case, it was Quirini who had to face the second Cretan insurrection, which can be dated within his first term of office. As before, its leaders were archons, Skordilis and his brother John Skordilis Skantzeas, with Theodore and Michael Melissenos. This time the insurgent area was the west of the island. The trouble arose from a trivial incident involving the theft of animals belonging to John Skordilis by the Venetian castellan of a fortress near Rethimnon. When hostilities began the Duke's forces suffered a sharp reverse and the death of one of his commanders, Giovanni Gritti. Peace was however restored in 1219 when a new Duke, Domenico Delfin, replaced Quirini and concluded a pact with the rebels. This settlement was markedly favourable to the archons, to whom the Venetian government surrendered thirty four and a half knights' fees in exchange for a moderate yearly rent and guarantees of loyalty to the Republic. It also contained provisions for protecting the interests of the *paroikoi*. Seventy of the latter were to be set free altogether. For the rest, it was agreed that a villein might be allowed to become a priest or monk, while his obligations in kind towards the fief-holder were exactly specified.

Such concessions to the Greeks suggest that the Venetian grip on the island was not very strong. Indeed we see the Venetian authorities and the Cretan magnates treating with each other on almost equal terms. That is presumably why the Republic decided to strengthen its occupation by sending out, three years later, a fresh body of colonists, numbering sixty knights and a corresponding complement of sergeants. Their advent immediately provoked a second rebellion by the

Melissenoi. Although a relatively minor affair, it again emphasized the precarious nature of the Venetian hold on Crete. It ended in an agreement negotiated with the unpopular Quirini, now entering on his second term as Duke. The Melissenoi thereby recovered two knights' fees in return for renewed promises of loyalty and the restoration of property and *paroikoi* appropriated from the settlers.[12]

For the next seven years a frail balance was maintained between the sovereign interests of the Republic and those of the stubborn Cretan magnates. By contrast the years 1230–36 were ones of continuous dissidence. In addition to the Skordilai and the Melissenoi, other leading families, such as the Arkoleoi and the Drakontopouloi, emerged as champions of the national cause. Also a new and important factor in the confrontation was the assistance afforded to the Cretans by the renascent Empire of Nicaea under John Vatatzes. While the Duke of Naxos, Angelo Sanudo, provided help for the Venetian Duke, Giovanni Storlado, and fortified a secure base in Suda Bay, the Emperor fitted out a squadron of thirty-three warships for the support of the insurgents. They landed a small but efficient body of troops from Asia Minor (Anatolikoi).

This revolt of the 'two Syvritoi' took its name from two small districts (Ano and Kato Syvritos) lying to the south of Rethimnon and between the two massifs of the White Mountains and Mount Ida. At first it made some progress. Rethimnon and several fortresses were captured, but the Venetians managed on the whole to maintain their ground. The Duke of Naxos, probably not wishing to be embroiled with the Nicaean Emperor, soon withdrew his contingent. On the other hand the Greek fleet was shattered by a storm off Kythera, and two Venetian envoys whom it was carrying to Nicaea for the purpose of negotiations with the Emperor lost their lives. The Greek troops, however, remained in the island until the end of the insurrection. Sieges and skirmishes dragged on inconclusively until 1234, when the Duke, Bartolommeo Gradenigo, tried to arrange a truce with two of the principal Cretan leaders, Markos Melissenos and Nikolaos Sebastos Daimonoyannis. But the latter were disavowed by other Cretan archons and by the Nicaean commanders. At that stage Gradenigo died and the government devolved on his two Counsellors. While one of them was besieging Seteia in eastern Crete, a new Nicaean squadron appeared in Suda Bay and engaged the Venetian fleet in an indecisive battle. The Venetian commander was seriously wounded and forced to break off the contest, but the Nicaeans too had had enough and sailed away. Thus, when a new Duke was appointed in the person of Gradenigo's son Angelo, the way became clear for further negotiations with the Cretan leaders.

As in the case of former rebellions, the resulting agreement was based on the restoration of the *status quo*. All free Cretans, nobles and *franchi*, were amnestied and confirmed in their former properties, rights and privileges, on condition that they swore loyalty to the Republic and undertook to help the Duke to deal with the Nicaeans and the Drakontopouloi brothers, the only Cretans who still refused to submit. All runaway *paroikoi* were to be returned to their former masters. It only remained to draw up a separate agreement with the Nicaean generals, Gregorios Loupardas and the Primikerios Mavrangoulos, who were still occupying the fortress of Hagios Nikolaos and other strongpoints. This was concluded without delay and the Anatolikoi returned safely home. We do not know what eventually happened to the recalcitrant archons.[13]

None of the clashes between the Cretans and the invaders during the years 1212–36 was fought out to the bitter end. Indeed each rebellion ended in compromise and mutual concessions. Hostilities were expensive and damaging for both sides and only worth sustaining so long as either felt that its vital interest was affected. Although both defended themselves stubbornly, they were not engaged in an irreconcilable conflict. Given their new and vast commitments in the Levant, the Venetians were obliged to build up their position with care and if possible with tact. They were in Crete for the purpose of commercial profit and the very nature of their long-term interest required a gradual approach. In any case there could be no question of a large and rapid influx of colonists at a time when so many demands were being made on the Republic's manpower. It has been estimated that the total Venetian population of Crete in the thirteenth century did not eventually exceed 3500.[14] The survival and expansion of the Venetian element depended on its ability to keep possession of secure ports and fortresses in the island while at the same time patiently proceeding to exploit its economic advantages.

In the end nearly a century passed before a real *modus vivendi* could be attained between Venetian and indigenous interests. Nevertheless the Cretan notables, for their part, were no doubt shrewdly aware that, provided that they were able to maintain their privileges and possessions, they might reasonably expect to receive a fair share in the prosperity that seemed likely to accrue to Crete as a Venetian dominion. They knew that they had no practical prospect of subsisting as a state on their own, and that they might well be better off as Venetian subjects than as those of a Byzantine state robbed of its capital and European provinces and surrounded by dangerous potential enemies. Clearly they had nothing to lose from the development of local trade and agriculture by the Venetians, and they might equally have all to lose from too fanatical and obstinate an opposition to Venice. On the other hand, they were bitterly and understandably resentful of encroachments on their domains and on the privileges which they had enjoyed under Byzantine rule.

Our sources for the period are almost exclusively Venetian and therefore not likely to be well disposed towards the Greeks of Crete. Moreover, so far as the thirteenth century is concerned, no contemporary writer devoted his attention exclusively to Cretan affairs. Crete has nothing to correspond with the *Chronicle of the Morea*. The earliest Venetian source for the thirteenth century and after is the *Chronicon de rebus Venetis* of Laurentius de Monacis (Lorenzo de'Monaci), written about 1404 and not published till 1758. The author was appointed Chief Secretary or *cancellarius* in the administration of Crete in 1388 and died there in 1429. He wrote in Latin and his description of events, while heavily weighted from the Venetian point of view, is concise and accurate, although he admitted to a learned correspondent that in spite of having lived for many years in the island he had thought it a waste of time to learn Greek. In 1755 Flaminio Cornelio published at Venice two volumes entitled *Creta Sacra*, in which he drew on various Venetian annalists and on the copious official records of the Republic. It is to the latter work, and especially to the reports of Venetian *provveditori* which it embodies, that we are chiefly indebted for exact information about developments in Crete.[15]

The natural tendency of Venetian chroniclers was to fasten on the native dissidents the full responsibility for revolts and disturbances. It was, in their view, entirely the fault of the insurgents that Crete failed to settle down. They blamed the Cretans for their intransigence, their unruliness and their alleged propensity for violence and rapine. But very similar complaints were levelled at the Venetian authorities and colonists by the Cretans themselves in their remonstrance of 1212, the only document of native origin that has happened to survive from that period. The truth was that each side was purposely exaggerating the misdeeds of the other, and many decades had to pass before the inevitable tensions were even partially resolved. Venice's urge to exploit a colonial situation with its strategic and commercial advantages was countered with some success by the tenacity of the Cretans in clinging to their own. During the thirteenth century Cretan society and culture were still essentially Greek outside certain towns and fortresses and the richer agricultural areas where, to the detriment of the archons, the colonists were apt to hold the best lands. Signs of a society in any sense integrated were as yet hardly apparent.

Despite latent discords, the island was quiet for twenty-five years after the revolt of the two Syvritoi. No outbreak followed a fresh colonizing enterprise in 1252, when the town of Canea was founded by Venetian settlers and ninety new knights' and sergeants' fiefs were distributed. But from 1261 international events threatened to upset Venetian rule. After his recovery of Constantinople from the Latins (25 July 1261) the Emperor Michael Palaeologos despatched to Crete a small expedition under an officer whose name figures in the *Chronicle of Laurentius* as Stengos,[16] with orders to provoke an uprising. Such action was designed to embarrass Venice and was no doubt connected with Michael's newly concluded treaty of Nymphaeum (13 March 1261), by which the Genoese, Venice's enemies, were accorded far reaching commercial and financial privileges in Byzantine territory. But Stengos made little progress. The Cretans were not inclined to support him to the full unless he himself was supported by a much larger force than that which the Emperor, concerned as he was with the reconquest of other provinces from the Latins, could afford to spare. Moreover in 1263, when a Genoese fleet was decisively defeated by the Venetians in the Gulf of Nauplia, Michael felt obliged to mend his relations with the Republic. He offered the Venetians a treaty granting them privileges as ample as those conceded to the Genoese four years earlier. It is therefore not surprising that his commander in Crete received no reinforcements and that the revolt petered out in 1265, the year in which the Emperor's treaty with Venice was signed. Until the end of his reign he adroitly played off one Italian republic against the other. When Venice was slow to ratify the pact of 1265, he negotiated a new agreement with Genoa, but as soon as ratification had been secured the Venetian treaty was twice renewed, in 1275 and 1277. By those instruments he explicitly recognised Venetian sovereignty over Crete.

The archons who had taken part, with varying degrees of enthusiasm, in the revolt once more made their peace with the Venetian government, and made it on favourable terms. As usual a general amnesty was announced, and the relevant agreement contained a long list of Greek nobles who received concessions in land and guarantees of privilege. They included the leaders of the revolt, George Chortatzes and Michael Skordilis. Again according to precedent, Stengos and his imperial contingent were permitted to depart from Crete unharmed.[17]

Such a display of Venetian tolerance was doubtless prompted by a desire to reward loyalty as well as to appease the disaffected. However that may be, it signally failed to ensure lasting quiet. In the succeeding years we find George Chortatzes and his brother Theodore again taking up arms whenever the Venetians showed any sign of weakness. Descended from an archontic family settled in Crete in the reign of Alexios Komnenos (1081–1118), they were great landowners in the region of Rethimnon.[18] They also gave proof of outstanding military talent. In 1271 they took advantage of a withdrawal of Venetian troops to start an extremely dangerous insurrection. They lost the first battle but won the second, and it began to look as if the Venetians were losing control of the situation. Then, two years later, the Duke Marino Zeno allowed himself to be trapped in an ambush at a place called Xylodema. His army was cut to pieces and he himself lost his life. Many other noble Venetians also fell, including, as Laurentius tells us, two Cornari, three Avrami, four Gradenighi and two Foscoli. For the first time the Cretans showed an ability to defeat knights and professional soldiers in the field. Nor was Zeno's successor, Marino Morosini, able to make headway against the rebels. They had virtually overrun the island by 1276 and shut up the Duke in Candia. Only in 1278, when Marino Gradenigo arrived with strong reinforcements, did the Venetians succeed in breaking the siege. The Cretans were at last crushed in the ensuing battle, but the Chortatzes brothers made their escape to Constantinople.[19]

This time there was no question of an amnesty or of an amicably negotiated compromise between the authorities and the rebels. Faced with so nearly successful a challenge, the Venetians outlawed the leaders of the rebellion and took firm measures of repression. The critical nature of the struggle suggests that the uprising enjoyed wide popular support and was not merely the work of a few disgruntled magnates. Indeed a number of influential archons, such as the Skordilai and the Hagiostephanitai, had carefully disavowed it. Consequently no steps were taken against them and they were able to contribute to the pacification of the island.

More important, but also enigmatic, was the part played by Alexios Kallergis,[20] the man who was shortly to emerge as the acknowledged leader of his people. His imposing personality dominates the Cretan scene for some fifty years. We first catch sight of him during the abortive Byzantine intervention. At that time he had a foot in both camps, first warning the Venetian Duke about the designs of Stengos and then assuring the latter that he was ready to join him if only the Emperor would increase his aid. In 1266 he was protesting his loyalty to the Duke Andrea Zeno and offering to intervene on his side in a clash between rival Venetian factions at Candia. During the revolt of the two Chortatzai, of whom he was said to be jealous for personal reasons, he frankly supported the Venetians and fought with them against the insurgents in more than one battle. There is no mention of him as having been present either at the rout of Xylodema or at the final defeat of the Chortatzai, but he is reported to have been received with honour at Venice as soon as the revolt had been quelled.

His equivocal attitude does not seem to have damaged his reputation in the eyes of his countrymen. He helped to mitigate the effects of repression that followed the revolt, and soon figured as the Great Archon, the wealthiest and strongest of all the Cretan magnates. He owned vast estates near Mylopotamos and property in Candia. On the former he lived in feudal grandeur, breeding war horses (a very profitable occupation) and supporting a host of armed retainers, while in the town he was a welcome and familiar guest at the ducal palace. He had great personal qualities, courage, eloquence and a quick mind, together with the defects of an ambitious egoist. The Venetians, although they flattered and courted him for obvious reasons, distrusted him as a crafty opportunist, a potentially dangerous soldier and an expert double-dealer in politics. As a matter of fact his general attitude was perfectly consistent. He liked to be on the winning side, but in his view there was no chance of Crete surviving on its own, nor was there any foreseeable and acceptable alternative to Venetian rule. Thus he saw every advantage in upholding it, provided of course that it continued to recognise his preeminence among the Cretans and to safeguard his privileges, immunities and riches.

Yet he soon became disenchanted, either because he was a patriot at heart or because he saw a new threat to his personal position. All was well until 1282 when Andrea Gabriel, known as the 'good' Duke by contrast with his harsh predecessor Gradenigo, was recalled and Gradenigo was given a second term of office. He may have thought that Kallergis had lately grown too powerful and needed to be cut down to size. He also suspected, rightly or wrongly, that Kallergis was plotting against him and warned the Venetian government accordingly. He himself died in the following year, but his successor, Giacomo Dandolo, was ordered to arrest Kallergis and deport him to Venice. But before he could be seized the Cretan leader got wind of the danger and slipped out of Candia by night. Having reached a place of safety he gave the signal for a rebellion which was to last for sixteen years.[21]

His call was answered by his fellow archons and by the whole Cretan people. In the long drawn out struggle that followed he displayed consummate tactical skill, avoiding pitched battles and direct assaults on major Venetian strongholds and exploiting the genius for guerrilla warfare for which the Cretans have become famous in later times. His men drove the Venetians from their prosperous fiefs in the plains, destroyed isolated garrisons and ambushed the expeditions sent to relieve them. They soon became masters not only of the mountainous and less accessible regions but of the greater part of the island, the Venetians being confined to Candia and other inexpugnable fortresses on the coast. Successive dukes, employing professional mercenary forces, failed for ten years to make any sensible progress against them.

The deadlock was loosened by a sudden change in the balance of sea power. In 1293 the Venetians, after two devastating defeats at the hands of the Genoese admiral Doria, one off the Dalmatian coast and the other at the Dardanelles, temporarily lost control in the eastern Mediterranean. Doria lost no time in attacking Crete, their key dominion in the area. He took Canea and invited Kallergis to join him in expelling the Venetians from the island altogether. To the disappointment of many if not most of his supporters, Kallergis flatly rejected the admiral's proposals, thereby indicating that the aim of his insurrection was not to put an end to the Venetian presence, and still less to replace it by subordination to Genoa, but to establish once and for all that Venetian rule could never prosper unless it properly respected the rights and traditions of the native Cretans, whom the Republic would be wise to treat as partners rather than subjects.

As a result of this incident the Cretans' loyalty to Kallergis waned and so did their enthusiasm for the fight. When Doria had sailed away the Duke Andrea Dandolo retook Canea and made some progress against the rebels. Nevertheless guerrilla warfare on a smaller scale persisted for another four years until Giacomo Tiepolo won a notable victory in Sphakia. His successor, Michael Vitali, arrived in 1299 with a mandate to arrange a truce, that task he managed to fulfil, but not without some difficulty in finding a formula that did not imply that the Republic was treating with Kallergis on the basis of equality. Nevertheless that was just what it was doing. The outcome of the Duke's parleys with Kallergis was a generally and freely negotiated settlement, the provisions of which were embodied in a long document signed by the Duke and one of his counsellors and by two notaries, one Latin and one Greek. It made sweeping concessions to all classes of Cretans. In the first place Kallergis and his heirs were not only confirmed in all the possessions which they had held before the rebellion but were granted a batch of new fiefs with the right to dispose of them at will. It was specified that when summoned by the government Kallergis and his dependents were not obliged to attend in person, but were entitled to send representatives. No penalties were exacted from the other Cretan feudatories, and they were granted for the first time the right of intermarriage with Latins of the same class. The social categories to which all Cretans belonged were exactly defined and persons who could prove that they had become freemen at any time between 1265 and the beginning of the rebellion were confirmed in that status. Kallergis was authorized to grant freedom to one hundred *paroikoi* of his choice and all free Cretans, as well as Jews and gipsies, were permitted to reside wherever they pleased on the island. Nor might they be compelled to serve the Republic in any capacity outside Crete. A special clause permitted the Monemvasiotes who had come to fight on the Cretan side to return freely to the Morea.[22] Generous provision was made for the remission of debts and tax obligations which had accumulated during the rebellion, and judgments rendered by Kallergis and his subordinates were declared valid.

The Cretans could hardly fail to be satisfied with the terms obtained by their leader. In return he gave away nothing beyond a formal oath of loyalty to the Doge of Venice, his successors, and his representatives in Crete, and the delivery of twenty hostages, including one of his sons, for a period of two years. It is remarkable that no other Cretan, with the exception of Michael Chortatzes, was named in the act of settlement. Kallergis was implicitly recognized as the sole authentic spokesman and champion of the Cretan people and treated almost as if he had been an independent sovereign. In the longer term, the concession which he exacted as regards intermarriage paved the way for the partial hellenization of the Venetian feudatories and the consequent development of a mixed culture among the whole ruling caste.[23]

Two matters only, one of trifling and the other of crucial importance, were remitted for decision in Venice itself. The first concerned the Cretan magnate's passion for horses. The settlement authorized him to buy fifteen war horses a year and if he could not find them in the market, to acquire them from the government, but a disagreement seems to have arisen over the ownership of ten mares to which he laid claim, and the Signoria was asked to decide what should be done with them. Of a quite different order was the controversy which resulted from the insistence by

Kallergis that the vacant bishopric of Agrion or Arion, held before the rebellion by a Catholic prelate, should be conferred on an Orthodox ecclesiastic.

It was not to be expected that he might succeed in abolishing altogether the existing discrimination against the Orthodox hierarchy. Nevertheless he made a well timed attempt to re-introduce Greek bishops in certain sees which their Latin occupants had left vacant during the rebellion. These were Agrion, Mylopotamos and Kalamon (Rethimnon), all three situated in Western Crete where Kallergis was especially strong. What he demanded was that Agrion should be handed over unconditionally to a Greek and that the two other adjoining sees should be leased from their absentee Latin bishops and conferred on Greeks for a yearly rent of 350 *hyperpera*, this arrangement to be renewable for the next fifty-eight years at five-year intervals. Despite the Signoria's traditional tendency to flout papal authority when politically convenient, the Venetians at first objected strongly to Kallergis's proposals. They finally agreed, however, to try to persuade the Latin Archbishop to accept them, and although it is not clear what arrangements eventually prevailed in all three sees, it seems that so far as Agrion was concerned Kallergis achieved his object for a time at least. At the end of the first five-year period the other two Latin absentees complained of their exclusion to Pope Clement V, who in turn protested to the Republic over the latter's 'nefarious pact with that Greek'. He summoned the Venetian government to reinstate and compensate the bishops, only to be assured, with a touch of malice, that they themselves had abandoned their sees and could now return to them if they so desired. We do not know if they made the attempt, or how the matter was in the end resolved.[24]

Alexios Kallergis lived until about 1319. When the walls of Candia were shattered by an earthquake in 1304 and some of his compatriots urged him to start a new rebellion, he firmly refused, telling them that the Cretans would never gain freedom by such action, the only result of which might well be to subject them to the far less tolerable yoke of the Genoese or Catalans. On his death bed he sent for his four sons and made them swear loyalty to Venice. After a hero's funeral attended by the Duke, Venetian and Cretan notables and the Greek and Latin clergy, his remains were buried in the monastery of St Catherine of Sinai at Candia. His descendants were later inscribed in the Golden Book of the Venetian nobility and became members of the Great Council of the Republic.

The settlement so cleverly negotiated by Kallergis lasted for over sixty years. It restored peace and quiet, in so far as such a state of affairs has ever existed in Crete, and gave its internal economy time to recover from a century of almost continuous disturbance. Even so the Signoria had to face two revolts originating in the west of the island, where the craggy recesses of Sphakia offered the insurgents a convenient base for their raids and fairly sure refuge from reprisals. Dissident members of the Kallergis clan were prominent in both these movements, while kinsmen who had remained loyal to the Republic participated in their repression. Indeed, it was the policy of the Duke Andrea Cornaro to set one Cretan to catch another. One of his victims, Leon Kallergis, was denounced, seized, tied up in a sack and hurled into the sea. The first outbreak, in 1333, was an insignificant affair but the second, which started in 1341, was still smouldering six years later and caused the government some anxiety when it spread to the central region of the Mesarea and as far as Lasithi in the far east. It was finally extinguished and all its leaders were executed.

When not distracted by such troubles, Crete prospered. Its more fertile regions produced in plenty the corn, wine and oil common to all Greek lands. Although it was not for their sake that the Republic went to the labour of occupying and partially colonizing that unruly island, they fully sufficed to support the Venetian fief-holders and to feed the garrisons and ships' crews. It was from corn that all Cretan landowners, Venetian and Greek, as well as the free smallholders, derived the bulk of their income, and corn of course provided the main sustenance of the *paroikoi* who tilled the soil. It also yielded, in the early years of the fourteenth century, a substantial surplus for export, subject to very strict controls by the government.[25] Wine, too, was a profitable article of export. The heavy, dark wines of Crete, so popular in the Middle Ages, were shipped in quantity to Western Europe, together with those of Monemvasia with which they shared the name of Malvasia (Malmsey). Oil production, though of minor importance, was carefully fostered, and Cretan forests furnished timber for shipbuilders and coopers.

Venetian occupation of Crete greatly helped the Republic's merchants to secure their very substantial share of sea-borne trade throughout the Mediterranean and beyond. Their sturdy cargo ships of new design (cogs) carried to and fro such basic commodities as grain, wine, timber and salt (much of it from the government's salt-pans in Crete). This commerce slowly gathered momentum during the thirteenth century and was in full swing by the fourteenth. Much more lucrative, however, was the specialized traffic in the spices which Western Europe so insatiably demanded. Venetian ships picked them up in Cypriot, Syrian, Palestinian and Egyptian ports and, as the textile trade developed through Italian intermediaries, exchanged them for the products of Western European looms, together with luxury goods from Venice itself. Other Eastern exports for which a keen demand developed in the West were sugar and cotton, while the Orientals, for their part, welcomed the slaves and furs which Venetian traders brought from the Black Sea. As the fourteenth century progressed and the Eastern traffic became more highly organized, the importance of Candia and Canea, both strategic and commercial, was immensely enhanced. Their arsenals, docks and warehouses were indispensable for the preparation and protection of the convoys, or *mudas*, which formed up in Cretan waters at regular intervals for the outward and inward voyages. These installations were designed to equip both the war galleys of the Venetian state and the new merchant galleys which were granted a strict monopoly of the spice trade. Publicly owned though privately operated, they were manned by large and well-armed crews, maintained and supplied from Cretan resources.[26]

The voyages were hugely profitable until about 1350, when Venice began to go through a lean period. While suffering acutely from the consequences of the Black Death, the Republic was involved in exhausting and unsuccessful struggles with Hungary and Genoa. These were hardly concluded when a great and wholly unexpected revolt in Crete (1363–7) threatened to destroy the main overseas prop of the whole Venetian commercial empire.

The causes and course of the insurrection are minutely described by the chronicler Laurentius de Monacis, who took up his official appointment in Crete twenty-five years later. On this occasion it was not the native Cretans but the Venetian colonists, some of them the descendants of settlers who had arrived a hundred and fifty years earlier, who rose against the government. They had indeed for some time been voicing complaints about the heavy and increasing financial burdens which they were obliged to bear on behalf of the State. For defence purposes they were required to pay a yearly contribution in cash as well as to give personal service. They were forced to sell their corn at an artificially low price either for the upkeep of the garrison and the fleet or for export by the government; at the same time they were forbidden to make their fiefs more economic by mergers with their neighbours. Their losses in previous revolts had never been compensated, and they had been driven to borrow at exorbitant rates from the Jews of Candia. Their pride as overseas Venetians had been offended by the arbitrary behaviour of Castellans fresh from the homeland and by blatant discrimination in favour of metropolitan Venetians in official posts. Their request for permission to send a delegation of twenty to Venice in order to present a petition for the redress of these and many other similar grievances was summarily rejected by the Duke of Candia.[27]

The last straw was a fresh tax levied for the repair of Candia harbour, half of which was to be paid by fief-holders and half by the free citizens, merchants and Jews of the capital. The former denounced this requirement as unconstitutional and contrary to their charter. On 8 August 1363, after a mass meeting at the church of St Titus in Candia, they told the Duke, Leonardo Dandolo, that unless they were allowed to send a deputation to Venice they would refuse to pay the levy and would defy the Signoria. Finding the Duke still adamant, they arrested him and his Counsellors, proclaiming that the rule of Venice was at an end and would be replaced by that of an independent republic under the protection of St Titus, as opposed to St Mark. The head of the new government (governor and rector) was Marco Gradenigo; he was to be assisted by four counsellors and a great council which Greek magnates were invited to join. Meanwhile all Venetian authorities were held to be deposed and replaced by Creto-Venetians, equality of cults was proclaimed and some Venetians in their enthusiasm even embraced the Orthodox faith. Freedom of import and export was conceded, and preparations set in hand for the defence of the island.

As soon as the news of the secession of Crete was relayed to Venice by the governor of Modon and Coron and the baile of Euboea, deep consternation prevailed. Conscious that they had completely misjudged the mood of their overseas citizens, the government hastily despatched a mission of five *provveditori* to Candia with orders to negotiate, if possible, a peaceful settlement. At the same time, in case they should have to resort to military measures, they enlisted the moral support of the Pope and of the sovereigns of Europe in their condemnation of the rebels' disloyalty to Christendom and the Republic. But in Crete, although the mission was accorded a hearing, the talks broke down through intransigence on both sides. The insurgents were deaf to appeals and threats, while the envoys insisted on absolute submission. Nor was the atmosphere improved by an incident at Seteia in eastern Crete when a Venetian convoy on the way to Cyprus and Alexandria was attacked by the local population and many seamen were killed.

Throughout the winter an elaborate expedition was fitted out at Venice for the reconquest of the dominion. Mercenaries (a thousand cavalry and two thousand infantry) were hired from Italy and Germany and placed under the command of Luchino Dal Verme, a Veronese *condottiere.*[28] A fleet of thirty three galleys and twelve transports was entrusted to the admiral Domenico Michieli. Supplies and horses were purchased from the Turks. On May 6, 1364, the armada put in at an anchorage seven miles west of Candia, and the soldiers disembarked. One hundred of them who set out in search of plunder were promptly cut off and killed.

The insurgents, however, were ill prepared to put up an effective resistance. The Latins were united in their determination to fight but the Greeks, while glad to join them if there was a serious chance of shaking off the Republic's yoke, were more hesitant. They distrusted the Latins' newly found enthusiasm for reconciliation or identification with their Orthodox brethren and they were frightened by the prospect of Venetian retaliation. And even if the rebels won the initial conflict, how could an independent Crete survive the ever-growing power of the Turks, especially as the Byzantine Empire was in a state of dissolution? Therefore their response to the overtures made to them was friendly but cautious, and in the event they did not commit themselves until it was too late. In the confusion of the moment strife broke out between the two communities and was with difficulty quelled. Nevertheless the Greeks, led by the brothers John, George and Alexios Kallergis, professed themselves ready to co-operate.

The invaders moved too quickly for them, and it was the Creto-Venetians who bore the brunt of the decisive battle against the expeditionary force, which took place on 9 May. The former fought bravely but were no match for Dal Verme's professionals. They were instantly crushed and Candia surrendered at once. Marco Gradenigo and his Counsellors were beheaded on the spot and the new Venetian authorities launched a thorough-going programme of repression against the islanders: executions, torture, banishments, imprisonments and confiscations of property. Their forces met with no resistance in occupying the other towns in the island, Canea, Rethimnon and Seteia. Indeed their task seemed so facile that the bulk of the expensive mercenary troops were withdrawn within a few months. The Republic had had a bad fright but had reasserted its authority with apparently triumphant ease.

But while the reconquest was celebrated by solemn rejoicings at Venice, the Cretan Greeks tardily took up the struggle. They were joined by such Latin leaders as had survived, notably Francesco and Antonio Gradenigo and Tito and Theodorello Venier, all with heavy prices on their heads.[29] No sooner had the mercenaries departed than the Kallergis brothers—perhaps but not certainly sons of Leon

Kallergis—called for a national insurrection and began to attack Venetian garrisons. As on previous occasions, their family strength lay in the western region and was anchored in the almost impenetrable redoubt of Sphakia. Again as in former revolts, their campaign took the form of a guerrilla movement on the widest scale which soon affected the whole island. The fighting seems to have been particularly bitter and destructive; the rebels ravaged the rich plains and the government's men burned the mountain villages. Before long the devastation caused widespread famine and misery. Venice once more poured in reinforcements, including Turkish mercenaries, and by 1366 they were closing in on the rebels' mountain bases. Even Pope Urban V was moved, in December of that year, to deplore their savagery. In the spring of 1367 four hundred horse and five thousand foot were grouped for the last operation, in which the remaining centres of resistance in Sphakia were systematically reduced. Of the rebel chiefs, the three Kallergis brothers were all executed; the brothers Gradenigo and Venier were also beheaded and only a third Gradenigo, Tito, managed to escape. All Cretan members of the latter families were removed to Venice for life and their descendants were not amnestied until 1391.

Such a pitiless lesson ensured that this was to be virtually the last uprising in the history of Venetian Crete. The *provveditore* Giustiniani reported to the Senate in that sense and his prediction proved to be correct. For greater emphasis some mountain districts were stripped of their inhabitants and left desolate and uncultivated for many years. The worst example was Lasithi in the east, which was condemned to lie fallow for a century. Lands confiscated from Latin and Greek rebels were sold by public auction and their purchasers became fief-holders. For the future, however, all fief-holders were released from the obligations imposed on them by charter; they were solely bound to swear fealty to Venice and its local representative. Real security was firmly entrusted to the Republic's paid professional troops.

The great revolt may be considered as the watershed between the feudalized Crete of the first hundred and fifty years of Venetian rule and the formation of the mixed society which emerged there as the Middle Ages gave way to the Renaissance. The damage which it inflicted was serious but not irreparable, and a new period of growth followed. In the early fifteenth century the island's economy revived briskly when Venice, having at last got the better of Genoa in the war of Chioggia (1378–81), embarked on a determined policy of consolidation in the Levant. In an endeavour to counter the advance of the Ottoman Turks, the Republic added a chain of new bases (Nauplia, Corfu, Corinth,

Thessalonica) to its existing possessions around the coasts of Greece. Underpinning this whole defensive structure was Crete, with its vital military installations at least temporarily proof against Turkish conquest, and the Venetians did not hesitate to put more capital and effort into strengthening their hold on it. Candia was refortified on a massive scale and many new coastal castles were built in order to deter Turkish pirates.

Apart from military expenditure, agriculture was diversified by the development of sugar plantations[30] and fostered by an increase in the class of free cultivators. Economic change and social mobility slowly gathered momentum but were favoured by a number of factors. One was a rise in the population. Figures are sadly lacking, but it is safe to assume that the losses caused by internal strife were swiftly made up. Secondly, divisions between the social classes were becoming less rigid and clear cut. In particular, the decline of feudalism was leading to the gradual emancipation of the peasant serfs. We hear, for instance, that in 1432 *paroikoi* in state service enjoyed the right to purchase their freedom at a price. Such persons would probably be reclassed as citizens of the towns (*cittadini* or *politai*), but the majority of the *paroikoi* released from feudal subjection became peasant cultivators (*contadini, agrotai* or *chorikoi*) extracting a living from their own rural plots. Their liberty and productivity were, however, circumscribed by their liabilities towards the state. Compulsory service in the galleys, the fortifications and the coastguard was much resented and occasionally caused disturbances among the peasantry.[31]

Although less and less effective as a defence force, the fief-holders were at least in theory liable to military service and, like all other free persons, to the onerous demands of the Venetian treasury. But parallel to the strictly administered fiscal system there grew up in Crete an equally elaborate and anomalous network of privileges and exemptions (*pronomiai*) covering members of all classes and even extending to some categories of *paroikoi*. Whole areas were eventually recognized as being protected by *pronomiai* and people of course tended to flee to them. In the more inaccessible parts of the island, however, it may well have been less trouble for the government to allow exemption than to try to enforce the fiscal regulations.[32]

The Orthodox clergy too enjoyed immunities and for that reason alone priests and monks multiplied. A spirit of toleration increasingly prevailed throughout the fifteenth century. The Orthodox Church was permitted to grow and prosper so long as it had no bishops of its own. On the other hand Catholic nominees were frequently absent from their sees, if only because of shrinking congregations, and the chief Orthodox priest (*protopapas*) in each community was treated by the authorities as a person of consequence and prestige. In places where there were no Catholic clergy the descendants of Venetian settlers, many of them half Greek by blood and culture, depended on the ever available Orthodox priests for the normal spiritual offices. If an Orthodox hierarch from outside were to slip into Crete from time to time in order to ordain and exhort, the authorities would be ready to turn a blind eye. But any hopes which they may have entertained of an effective union of the Churches springing from the Council of Florence in 1439 were not fulfilled. On the contrary the fall of Constantinople in 1453, followed by the Turkish conquest of the Morea, resulted in a considerable migration of refugee Greeks to Crete, and the majority of these were strongly nationalist and Orthodox in their sympathies. Indeed their influence gave rise to an anti-Venetian conspiracy which took its name from one Siphis Vlastos, a magnate from Rethimnon. It was discovered in time and easily stifled, but the Duke was thereafter authorized to dispose of any suspect Cretan secretly and without trial.[33]

The acquisition of Cyprus in 1489 more than compensated the Republic for the loss of Negroponte in 1479 and of its outposts on the Greek mainland, all of which had been yielded to the Turks by 1540. It thus retained two great island dominions, both Greek-speaking, as its bastions of power and sources of wealth in the Levant. Although its empire was in slow decline and commercial prospects were gradually becoming less attractive, the islands still amply repaid the expense and attention lavished on them. Their sugar plantations continued to be profitable, while trade between Western Europe and the Turkish realm, now about to embrace the whole eastern and southern coasts of the Mediterranean, persisted and prospered amid intermittent wars and incessant piracy. Neither the Christian nor the Moslem world could do without the commodities exchanged and the Venetians, though less and less able to dictate the terms of trade, were still conveniently poised between the two.

So far as Crete was concerned, conditions were at last stable enough to permit the flowering of a real Veneto-Cretan culture. Whereas Cretan literacy had been at its lowest ebb during the first two hundred years of Venetian rule, Candia developed 'into a significant centre of Greek learning and piety' as from the mid-fifteenth century.[34] Under the stimulus of migrants from Constantinople and Mistra, Crete became the last refuge in former Byzantine lands where scholars could be trained in the traditions of the Palaeologan renaissance before passing on to the wider fields of opportunity in humanist Italy and beyond. Once they had departed they seldom returned. Nevertheless Crete produced an ever increasing flow of scholars, writers and artists until the Turkish conquest. Among the earlier intellectuals the most prominent were the Aristotelian philosopher George of Trebizond (born in Crete) and the brilliant scholar and critic Markos Mousouros of Rethimnon, editor of Plato and Aristophanes. Before printing became general, classical manuscripts in quantity were being copied in Crete for export to Italy, and Cretan residents in Venice subsequently helped the Aldine press to bring out its famous series of ancient Greek writers. Greek presses too were set up at Venice by Cretan printers. One of them, Zacharias Kalliergis, also a native of Rethimnon, was financed by a rich fellow citizen, Nikolaos Vlastos. It published, in 1499, a great lexicon known as the *Etymologicum Magnum*, to which Mousouros contributed a proud preface in impeccable elegiacs.

During the sixteenth and early seventeenth centuries the school domiciled in the monastery of St Catherine at Candia offered courses in theology, the Greek classics and the elements of philosophy and rhetoric. Many scholars and clerics who later won fame on a wider stage studied and taught there. When their preparatory training was over they usually completed their education at the University of Padua, where a chair of Greek had been set up as early as 1463. Thus equipped, they not only sustained the standards of Greek learning but also infused a new vigour into the spiritual and intellectual life of the Orthodox Church in the lands subject to Ottoman rule. Meletios Pigas, for example, after returning from Padua to the school of St Catherine, became Patriarch of Alexandria and took charge of the patriarchate of Constantinople while the oecumenical see was temporarily vacant. Another Cretan, Maximos Margounios, presided over the patriarchal academy in the Ottoman capital. A third, Nektarios, became Patriarch of Jerusalem. Lastly Cyril Lukaris, a cousin of Pigas, the most distinguished pupil of St Catherine and of Padua and a determined foe of Roman Catholic expansion at the expense of Orthodoxy, occupied the patriarchal throne at Constantinople at intervals for seventeen years (1621–38), and died a martyr at the hands of the Turks.[35]

These men were prodigies of talent and learning, but they formed an intellectual élite mainly active outside Crete. Many more of their compatriots contributed to the remarkable explosion of popular literature which occurred at the same period. Peculiarly Cretan in character, these writings drew their inspiration from Italian sources but were expressed in vigorous demotic Greek. The language 'strikes one by its unity and the absence of obsolete forms; the goal toward which the Greeks had strained in vain for centuries seems almost to have been reached.'[36] This happy synthesis of Italian styles with the Greek of everyday life was fostered by the foundation of a local society known as the Accademia dei Extravaganti, itself a significant example of cultural fusion between two communities so long divided by enmity.

The writers were certainly prolific. They continued to pour out thousands of lines of verse, their favourite medium, until the fall of Candia, after twenty-five years of struggle against the Ottomans, put an end to all literary activities. Some of their themes hark back to Byzantium; for instance the old device of a satire based on a dream-journey to Hades crops up more than once. Others are concerned with contemporary events, such as the earthquake of 1508, the siege of Malta in 1565 and the final war of Candia itself, while one contains a lively description of low life in Candia among gamblers and whores. Closely reflecting an Italian original is a pastoral poem in rhyming eleven-syllable verse by one Nikolaos Drymitinos entitled *Omorphi Boskopoulla* (The Fair Shepherdess). The finest work in a varied collection is the *Erotokritos* of Vitzentios Cornaros, a romantic story of love and war in 10,052 fifteen-syllable lines, also rhyming. It reflects the chivalrous epics of the Byzantine and Frankish eras, as well as later Italian works, and is above all distinguished by its striking language and stout national spirit. Cornaros, a native of Seteia, wrote it when the Turks were already at the gates, and it soon caught the imagination of the whole Greek world.

Cretan authors were also much attracted by the theatre. Most of their plays were closely modelled on Italian prototypes, ranging from blood-stained tragedy (the *Erophile* of George Chortatzes) to biblical subjects (*The Sacrifice of Abraham*), pastoral love stories (the *Gyparis*, in which the action takes place on Mount Ida) and broad comedies which feature the stock characters of antiquity and its Italian imitators. The dramatists experimented successfully with rhyme and metre and often wrote with real poetic feeling.

Many of these writers had obviously Greek names. Others, like Cornaro, Foscolo and Caliero, sound purely Venetian, but they all wrote in Greek and no significance need be attached to their presumed origins. By the seventeenth century persons of inextricably mixed descent must have predominated in the literate and semi-literate class of town-dwellers which produced them. It is curious how many of them came from the little town of Rethimnon.[37]

The activity of Cretan artists in the sixteenth century rivalled that of the men of letters. Varying opinions have been advanced by art historians regarding the origins and development of the contemporary Cretan school of painting, but there is no doubt that an easily identifiable style evolved in the island and quickly spread throughout the eastern Mediterranean. No doubt it grew out of the general revival of Byzantine art under the Palaeologues which was so suddenly extinguished in its main centres by the Ottoman conquest. Icons painted in Crete were especially esteemed and commanded good prices. The artists signed their panels, usually adding the word *Kres* (Cretan) as a guarantee of their proficiency. The best known of them is Michael Damaskinos, who worked at Candia before migrating to Venice in 1574 in order to decorate the new church of San Giorgio dei Greci. From the purely aesthetic point of view the frescos with which Theophanes and other Cretan painters adorned monastery churches on Mount Athos possess greater significance, but as Robert Byron, the most percipient analyst of their works, has pointed out, few have escaped the attention of clumsy restorers.

Damaskinos is also important as an innovator, for he was the first prominent icon painter who sought to apply Venetian technique to the uncompromisingly stark requirements of Byzantine tradition. He was succeeded by a host of imitators working in a hybrid idiom which satisfied the popular taste until quite modern times, but of all the Cretan artists who absorbed Venetian influence the only one who achieved a perfect combination of Greek tradition, Venetian dynamism and individual genius was Domenikos Theotokopoulos of Candia (El Greco), a slightly younger contemporary of Damaskinos. He may be claimed as the greatest Cretan of all times since, if the truth be admitted, the island has produced few outstanding personalities since the legendary King Minos.[38]

Despite the flourishing state of culture in sixteenth century Crete and the relative lack of strife between two communities which had attained a high degree of fusion, the external threat was increasing and social conditions were causing anxiety. Sporadic raids by Turkish pirates gave way to organized expeditions commanded by the principal Ottoman admirals which wrought havoc in the dominion. In 1538 Khaireddin Barbarossa, fresh from a devastating cruise through the archipelago, swept down on Crete, destroyed Rethimnon and narrowly failed to take Canea. A razzia by Dragut in 1562 was almost equally destructive and in 1567 the Algerian Euldj Ali sacked Rethimnon for the second time. Many thousands of Cretans were slaughtered or enslaved in these attacks. Six years later the Republic surrendered Cyprus, the twin dominion, to the Turks. The situation appeared so gloomy that in the following year the Venetian government despatched Giacomo Foscarini as special commissioner (*provveditore generale*) to Crete with instructions to take whatever measures he thought fit for the safety of the island and for the reform of abuses.

Foscarini indeed found its administration and defences in disarray, with the population depressed and demoralized. At a time of acute danger the fief-holders, both Latin and Greek, were deliberately shirking their military and public duties. Many of the former seemed to have forgotten their Venetian ancestry. They tended to speak only Greek, to adopt Greek manners and to drift into the Orthodox Church. Others, through the sale or division of their properties, had become impoverished and lived like peasants. Blatant corruption in the government had enormously swelled the number of persons entitled to privileges and exemptions, with the result that the unprivileged, particularly among the class of free countrymen, were weighed down with burdens. Sphakia, where a local insurrection had recently been cruelly stamped out by the *provveditore* Marino Cavalli, was racked by blood feuds between quarrelling Greek magnates.

The commissioner used his dictatorial powers to great advantage. In four years of hard work he purged the administration, abolished privileges, restored the finances and completely reorganized the system of defence. The fief-holders were once more obliged to render regular military service, forts and harbours were strengthened and, in addition to the professional garrisons, a local militia was formed in which even the Sphakiots, now pacified, were induced to participate. His general policy in dealing with the native Cretans was to avoid severity and to secure voluntary co-operation. He took steps, however, to repress disaffection among the Orthodox clergy and to curtail the freedoms of the Jews of Candia, whom he accused of corrupting their Christian neighbours.[39]

His reforms, though salutary, were only temporarily effective. Ten years later another commissioner, Giulio Garzoni, was reporting that the same abuses had crept back and that he had been obliged to do the work over again. Like his predecessor, he earned a great reputation for justice and common sense. At all events their efforts helped the regime to survive comfortably until 1645. If we may trust Venetian statistics, seven decades of peace and comparative prosperity raised the population, which had previously been on the wane, from 219,000 in Foscarini's time to 287,000 on the eve of the war of Candia. Cultural activity too had never been more lively.

299

But the main relief came from the relaxation of Turkish pressure and the exhaustion of the combatants on both sides (Spain, Venice and the Ottoman Empire) after the epic struggles of the mid-sixteenth century. The Turks were repulsed from Malta in 1656 and defeated at Lepanto (Naupaktos) in 1571, while their occupation of Cyprus in 1573 was the last blow struck in the period of Ottoman aggression connected with the reign of Suleiman the Magnificent. The status quo in the Eastern Mediterranean was thereafter maintained because any further Turkish maritime advance was firmly blocked and the Western powers were too weak and divided to attempt to recover lost territories. Also internal changes in Ottoman society, partly resulting from too rapid an expansion, discouraged serious confrontation. Crete therefore survived in its isolated position. But in 1631 Venice suffered heavily from the plague. At the same time its commerce was declining steeply as Mediterranean sea borne trade passed into English and Dutch hands and the Thirty Years War blighted the whole economic scene. Finally provocations by Maltese and other Christian corsairs stung the Turks into retaliation, which was inevitably directed against Crete.

That the so-called War of Candia should have lasted for twentyfive years is the measure of inadequacies on both sides. The Venetian navy, caught at a moment of weakness, failed to prevent the Turkish army from landing. It took Canea at once and Rethimnon in the following year. By 1648 it had overrun the whole of the island with the exception of Candia itself. When the siege began, however, the Turkish guns made no impression on the immensely strong fortifications. Accordingly the invaders settled down to living off the land, with disastrous results to its economy. Nevertheless they treated the inhabitants mercifully and agreed, as the Venetians had never done, to the appointment of a full complement of Orthodox bishops. Consequently the Cretans showed no inclination to thwart them by engaging in fruitless guerrilla warfare. But in the 1650s the Venetians rallied. Their fleet succeeded in reinforcing Candia and even penetrated into the sea of Marmora. Thus the war was prolonged for another eleven years.

In 1666 the Grand Vizier, Achmet Köprülü, personally took command of the besiegers and the fight became a duel between him and the last and most heroic defender of Candia, Francesco Morosini. After three years the Venetians were heartened by the arrival of a large French force of fifty ships and eight thousand men under the Dukes of Navailles and Beaufort, but their intervention came too late to be effective. When Beaufort was killed the French withdrew and Morosini had no choice but to arrange a capitulation. Under its terms the Republic was allowed to retain only the three coastal forts of Suda, Spinalonga and Grabusa, which were not given up until 1715. By then its presence in Crete had lasted for half a millennium, from the era of the Crusades to that of the full-bottomed wig.

One epilogue leads to another, but it would be wrong to end without a mention of Venice's inspiring reaction to the loss of Crete. After the repulse of the Ottoman attack on Vienna in 1683, Austria, Poland and Venice entered into a Holy League against the Turks, and in fulfilment of its engagements under the pact Venice delivered a massive onslaught on the Turkish positions in the Morea. With Morosini in command and strengthened by a strong contingent of German mercenaries under Count Königsmarck, the Republic's forces methodically reduced all the famous fortresses which had so often changed hands since the first arrival of the Franks. In the following years they fell one by one—Modon, Coron, Kalamata, Nauplia, Patras, Corinth and Monemvasia. The liberation of the Peloponnese led to the siege of Athens, during which the Parthenon, still intact as a mosque but containing the defenders' powder magazine, was blown up by an accurately aimed shell from Königsmarck's batteries. Although Morosini was checked at Negroponte, the Morea passed to Venice in 1699 by the peace of Karlowitz. It was a brilliant feat of arms, and the determination with which it was accomplished contrasted pointedly with the indecision of previous military leaders. The surprised Moreots found themselves once again briefly subject to a Latin power. But unless continuously sustained by allies, eighteenth-century Venice could not muster the strength to retain what it had taken, and within twenty years the Turks were back in possession. A hundred years later the Greeks won their freedom by their own exertions.

NOTE ON SOURCES

This book is derived from both contemporary and modern sources. The original mediaeval sources consulted include works in the Greek, Latin, French, Italian and Aragonese languages, while the second category comprises a long succession of historians active from the seventeenth century until the present day.

As explained in the Introduction to the book, its first two chapters, entitled 'The Death of Ancient Hellas' and 'Hellas Re-hellenized', are devoted to a summary, indispensable for the general reader, of events and changes, demographic and otherwise, in Greece between the decline of the Classical world of the Roman Empire and the Frankish occupation of the country in the early thirteenth century.

For the first part of this long period I have drawn on the relevant passages in late Classical and early Byzantine writers such as Plutarch, Dio Chrysostom and Pausanias (first and second centuries), Ammianus Marcellinus (fourth century), Zosimus (fifth century) and Procopius, Agathias and Menander (sixth century). The best general descriptions of that age, including valuable references to Greece, are provided by J.B. Bury's *History of the Later Roman Empire* and A.H.M. Jones's *The Later Roman Empire*.

For the subsequent 'Dark Age' of the Slav colonization of Greece the evidence is fragmentary and I have therefore relied chiefly on those secondary sources which sum up and evaluate the material derived from contemporary writings. Particularly useful in that respect are G. Ostrogorsky's *History of the Byzantine State*, A. Bon's *Le Peloponnèse Byzantin jusqu'en 1204* and D. Obolensky's *The Byzantine Commonwealth*, but much profitable information can also be extracted from earlier historians, e.g. G. Finlay, F. Gregorovius and, again, J.B. Bury. Byzantine sources are not very informative for this period, but occasional gleams of light are thrown on an otherwise obscure scene by documents such as the Miracles of St Demetrios of Thessalonica preserved in the *Acta Sanctorum* and in the *Chronicle of Monemvasia*.

For the ensuing period, the re-colonization of Greece by Byzantium, the original literary evidence is much more abundant. In this connection I should mention the *Tactica* of the Emperor Leo VI; the *De*

Administrando Imperio of the Emperor Constantine VII Porphyrogenitus and the latter's biography of Basil II which forms part of the chronicle known as *Theophanes Continuatus*; the eye-witness account by John Kameniates of the Saracen sack of Thessalonica; the *Alexiad* of Anna Komnena; the twelfth-century dialogue known as the *Sufferings of Timarion*; the *Itinerary* of the Judaeo-Spanish rabbi Benjamin of Tudela and the letters of Michael Choniates, the last Greek Metropolitan of Athens before the Latin conquest. The two invasions of Greece in the twelfth century by the Normans of Sicily are described in considerable detail by Niketas Choniates, John Kinnamos and the Metropolitan Eustathios of Thessalonica.

So much for the two introductory chapters. For the Frankish period proper the source material is vast and diverse. It has been minutely explored by scholars during the last two centuries, but the results of their researches are largely published in numerous specialist periodicals. To list them in an authoritative bibliography would be a gigantic task and exceed the purposes of the present book.

Most of the basic documentary material is, or was, contained in the Papal, Venetian and Neapolitan archives.

The richest collection of all, that of the Angevin Kingdom of Naples, was totally destroyed during the last World War without ever having been fully and systematically published. Important collections of documents are also to be found in the archives of Florence, Palermo and Barcelona. Apart from the existing archives, the main basic writings are as follows:

Greek

(i) The Greek *Chronicle of the Morea*, the fourteenth century chronicle in verse which is the primary source for the history of the Principality of Achaia and, by extension, of the whole of Frankish Greece. Its authorship and relation to the parallel Chronicles in French, Aragonese and Italian are discussed in Chapter III.

(ii) For the thirteenth century, the histories of Niketas Choniates, George Akropolites and George Pachymeres.

(iii) For the fourteenth century, those of the Emperor John Cantacuzenos and Nikephoros Gregoras.

(iv) For the fifteenth century, a Pleiad of historians—Dukas, Phrantzes (or Sphrantzes), Chalkokondyles and Kritoboulos—tell the story of the collapse of Frankish Greece under pressure from the Ottoman Turks. Their writings are complemented by those of the Emperor Manuel II Palaeologos, of the philosopher-statesman George Gemistos Plethon and of the satirist Mazaris.

Latin

(i) The French, Aragonese and Italian versions of the *Chronicle of the Morea*.

(ii) For the early years of the Frankish Conquest, Geoffroy de Villehardouin's *La Conquête de Constantinople*, *L'Histoire de l'Empereur Henri de Constantinople* by Henri de Valenciennes, the *Chronicle* of Aubri des Trois Fontaines and the *Assizes of Romania*, or *Liber Consuetudinum Imperii Romaniae* (the Law Code of Frankish Greece).

(iii) Marino Sanudo Torsello. This Venetian, a cousin of the Duke of Naxos, frequented the courts of both the Archipelago and Achaia. He wrote, in the late thirteenth and early fourteenth century, a useful history of the Kingdom of Romania and another work, the *Secreta Fidelium Crucis*, warning the western world against the Turkish danger.

(iv) Ramon Muntaner, who held high command in the Catalan Grand Company, wrote a history of its exploits in the Levant (much later, in 1623, Don Francisco de Moncada, Marques de Aytona, published an account of the expedition entitled *Expedicion de los Catalanes y Aragoneses contra Turcos y Griegos*.)

(v) Cyriacus of Ancona, the Italian antiquary, travelled through Greece in the fifteenth century, shortly before the Turkish conquest, and left an interesting though fragmentary account of his journeys.

Modern Works

The pioneer historian of the Latin states in the Levant is Du Cange, who published his *Histoire de l'Empire de Constantinople sous les Empereurs Francais* as long ago as 1659, but it was not until the nineteenth century that the subject again began to attract the serious notice of scholars. It was first tackled on a grand scale by another Frenchman, J.A. Buchon (1791–1846), who not only published the findings of his researches but edited a variety of original texts and translations. He also planned a general history, of which only one volume appeared before his death. Even more encyclopaedic was the work of his German contemporary Carl Hopf (1832–73), whose massive history of mediaeval Greece was largely based on a painstaking study of the Venetian and Neapolitan archives. At about the same time J.P. Fallmerayer promulgated his theory that the mediaeval Greek subjects of the Franks were not Greeks at all. Subsequently several eminent nineteenth-century historians presented the material first worked over by Buchon and Hopf in an equally comprehensive but more easily digestible form. Thus G. Finlay (1799–1875) devoted to the mediaeval period three volumes of his *History of Greece from the*

Conquest by the Romans to the Present Time. The period was also well covered by the relevant volumes of the general histories compiled by the Greek G. Paparregopoulos and the German G.F. Hertzberg, while in 1889 there appeared the monumental *History of the City of Athens in the Middle Ages* by F. Gregorovius. Finally, in the first decade of the twentieth century, the threads were drawn together by two outstanding work published in Great Britain, Sir R. Rodd's *The Princes of Achaia and the Chronicles of Morea*, and William Miller's *The Latins in the Levant; a History of Frankish Greece*.

The rapid development of Byzantine studies during the present century has naturally led to a greater understanding of the Frankish period. Perhaps the most significant contributions have been those of G. Ostrogorsky, Steven Runciman, D. Obolensky, K.M. Setton and D.M. Nicol. Among works dealing solely or largely with the Latin states, those of A. Bon, J. Longnon, K.M. Setton, P.W. Topping, F. Thiriet and D. Zakynthinos are indispensable. Bon's masterly study *La Morée Franque* is especially important; indeed developments in the Peloponnese seem to have on the whole enjoyed more thorough treatment than those in northern Greece.

Basic bibliographies of original sources and of modern works are attached hereto. References to CSHB are to the series Corpus Scriptorum Historiae Byzantinae.

APPENDIX: LISTS OF RULERS AND GENEALOGIES

1. *Byzantine Emperors* (from 395)

395–408	Arcadius
408–450	Theodosius II
450–457	Marcian
457–474	Leo I
474	Leo II
474–491	Zeno
(475–476	Basiliscus)
491–518	Anastasius I
518–527	Justin I
527–565	Justinian I
565–578	Justin II
578–582	Tiberius I
582–602	Maurice
602–610	Phokas
610–641	Heraclius
641	Constantine III
	Heraclonas
641–668	Constans II
668–685	Constantine IV
685–695	Justinian II
695–698	Leontius
698–705	Tiberius II
705–711	Justinian II
711–713	Philippicus
713–715	Anastasius II
715–717	Theodosius III
717–741	Leo III
741–775	Constantine V
775–780	Leo IV
780–797	Constantine VI
797–802	Irene
802–811	Nikephoros I
811	Stavrakios
811–813	Michael I
813–820	Leo V
820–829	Michael II

829–842	Theophilos
842–867	Michael III
867–886	Basil I
886–912	Leo VI
912–913	Alexander
913–959	Constantine VII
920–944	Romanos I
	Lekapenos
959–963	Romanos II
963–969	Nikephoros II
	Phokas
969–976	John I Tzimiskes
976–1025	Basil II
1025–1028	Constantine VIII
1028–1034	Romanos III
	Argyros
1034–1041	Michael IV
1041–1042	Michael V
1042	Zoe and Theodora
1042–1055	Constantine IX
1055–1056	Theodora
1056–1057	Michael VI
1057–1059	Isaac I
	Komnenos
1059–1067	Constantine X
	Dukas
1068–1071	Romanos IV
	Diogenes
1071–1078	Michael VII
	Dukas
1078–1081	Nikephoros III
	Botaneiates
1081–1118	Alexios I Komnenos
1118–1143	John II Komnenos
1143–1180	Manuel I Komnenos
1180–1183	Alexios II
	Komnenos
1183–1185	Andronikos I
	Komnenos

1185–1195	Isaac II Angelos	1210–1228(?)	Geoffroy I de Villehardouin
1195–1203	Alexios III Angelos	1228?–1246	Geoffroy II de Villehardouin
1203–1204	Isaac II and Alexios IV Angeloi	1246–1278	Guillaume II de Villehardouin
1204	Alexios V Mourtzouphlos	1278–1285	Charles I of Anjou
1204–1222	Theodore I Laskaris	1285–1289	Charles II of Anjou
1222–1254	John III Vatatzes	1289–1307	Isabelle de Villehardouin
1254–1258	Theodore II Laskaris		m (i) Florent de Hainaut
1258–1261	John IV Laskaris		(1289–1297)
1259–1282	Michael VIII Palaeologos		(ii) Philip of Savoy (1301–1307)
1282–1328	Andronikos II Palaeologos	1307–1313	Philip I of Tarentum
1328–1341	Andronikos III Palaeologos	1313–1318	Mahaut of Hainaut
1341–1391	John V Palaeologos		m Louis de Bourgogne (1313–1316)
1347–1354	John VI Cantacuzenos	1318–1333	John of Gravina
1376–1379	Andronikos IV Palaeologos	1333–1364	Robert of Tarentum and Catherine de Valois (to 1346)
1390	John VII Palaeologos	1363–1370	Marie de Bourbon
1391–1425	Manuel II Palaeologos	1370–1373	Philip II of Tarentum
1425–1448	John VIII Palaeologos	1373–1381	Jeanne I, Queen of Naples
1449–1453	Constantine XI Palaeologos	1381–1383	Jacques des Baux
		1383–1386	Charles III, King of Naples

2. Latin Emperors

1204–1205	Baldwin I of Flanders
1206–1216	Henry of Flanders
1217	Peter of Courtenay
1217–1219	Yolande
1221–1261	Baldwin II
1231–1237	John de Brienne

Navarrese Company occupy the Principality from 1380. Other claimants during the period are Louis de Clermont, Duc de Bourbon (1387–1388) and Amadeo of Savoy (1387–1391).

1396–1402	Pierre de St Superan
1402–1404	Maria Zaccaria, Regent
1404–1439	Centurione Zaccaria

3. Princes of Achaia

1205	Guillaume I de Champlitte

4. Despots of Epiros

1204–1215	Michael I Dukas

1215–1230	Theodore	c 1316	Andronikos Asen
	(1224–1230	1321	John Cantacuzenos
	Emperor		(appointed, did
	of Thessalonica)		not proceed)
1230–1237	Manuel	1348	Manuel Cantacuzenos
1237–1271	Michael II	1380	Matthew
1271–1296	Nikephoros I		Cantacuzenos
1296–1318	Thomas	1383	Theodore I
1318–1323	Nicolas Orsini		Palaeologos
1323–1335	John Orsini	1407–1443	Theodore II
1335–1340	Nikephoros II		Palaeologos

5. *Governors and Despots of Mistra*

		1428–1449	Constantine
			Palaeologos
		1430–1460	Thomas Palaeologos
		1449–1460	Demetrios
c 1286	a Cantacuzene		Palaeologos

6. The Villehardouins

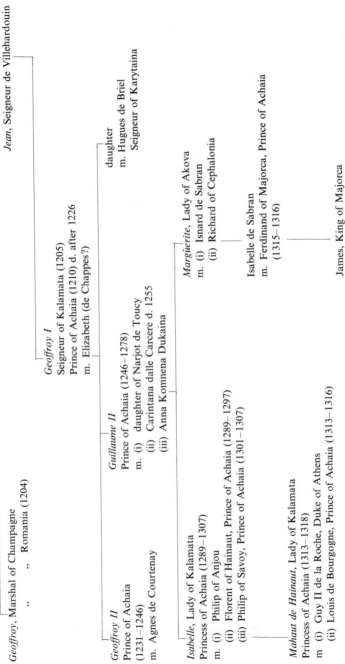

Jean, Seigneur de Villehardouin

Geoffroy, Marshal of Champagne
" " " Romania (1204)

Geoffroy I
Seigneur of Kalamata (1205)
Prince of Achaia (1210) d. after 1226
m. Elizabeth (de Chappes?)

daughter
m. Hugues de Briel
Seigneur of Karytaina

Geoffroy II
Prince of Achaia
(1231–1246)
m. Agnes de Courtenay

Guillaume II
Prince of Achaia (1246–1278)
m. (i) daughter of Narjot de Toucy
   (ii) Carintana dalle Carcere d. 1255
   (iii) Anna Komnena Dukaina

Margüerite, Lady of Akova
m. (i) Isnard de Sabran
   (ii) Richard of Cephalonia

Isabelle de Sabran
m. Ferdinand of Majorca, Prince of Achaia
(1315–1316)

Isabelle, Lady of Kalamata
Princess of Achaia (1289–1307)
m. (i) Philip of Anjou
   (ii) Florent of Hainaut, Prince of Achaia (1289–1297)
   (iii) Philip of Savoy, Prince of Achaia (1301–1307)

Mahaut de Hainaut, Lady of Kalamata
Princess of Achaia (1313–1318)
m. (i) Guy II de la Roche, Duke of Athens
   (ii) Louis de Bourgogne, Prince of Achaia (1313–1316)

James, King of Majorca

7. The Dukes of Athens (*La Roche*)

Othon, Seigneur of La Roche-sur-Ognon (1130–1170)

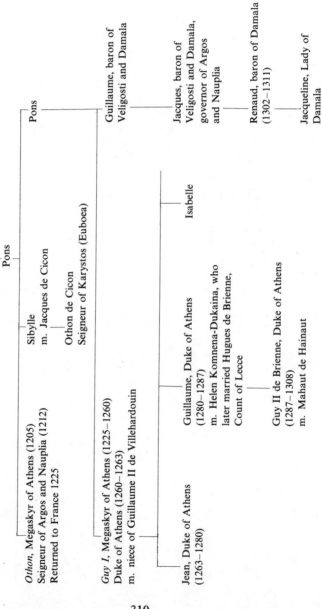

Pons

Othon, Megaskyr of Athens (1205)
Seigneur of Argos and Nauplia (1212)
Returned to France 1225

Sibylle
m. Jacques de Cicon

Othon de Cicon
Seigneur of Karystos (Euboea)

Pons

Guillaume, baron of
Veligosti and Damala

Guy I, Megaskyr of Athens (1225–1260)
Duke of Athens (1260–1263)
m. niece of Guillaume II de Villehardouin

Jean, Duke of Athens
(1263–1280)

Guillaume, Duke of Athens
(1280–1287)
m. Helen Komnena-Dukaina, who
later married Hugues de Brienne,
Count of Lecce

Isabelle

Jacques, baron of
Veligosti and Damala,
governor of Argos
and Nauplia

Guy II de Brienne, Duke of Athens
(1287–1308)
m. Mahaut de Hainaut

Renaud, baron of Damala
(1302–1311)

Jacqueline, Lady of
Damala
m. Martino Zaccaria

8. The St Omers of Thebes

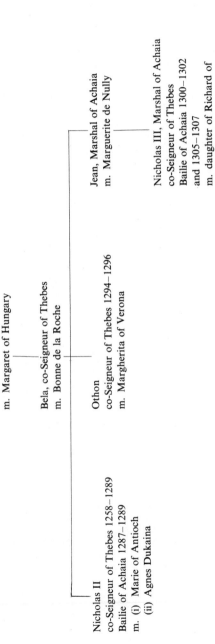

Nicholas I, in Boeotia from 1204
m. Margaret of Hungary

Bela, co-Seigneur of Thebes
m. Bonne de la Roche

Nicholas II
co-Seigneur of Thebes 1258–1289
Bailie of Achaia 1287–1289
m. (i) Marie of Antioch
   (ii) Agnes Dukaina

Othon
co-Seigneur of Thebes 1294–1296
m. Margherita of Verona

Jean, Marshal of Achaia
m. Marguerite de Nully

Nicholas III, Marshal of Achaia
co-Seigneur of Thebes
Bailie of Achaia 1300–1302
and 1305–1307
m. daughter of Richard of
   Cephalonia

9. The Acciaiuoli

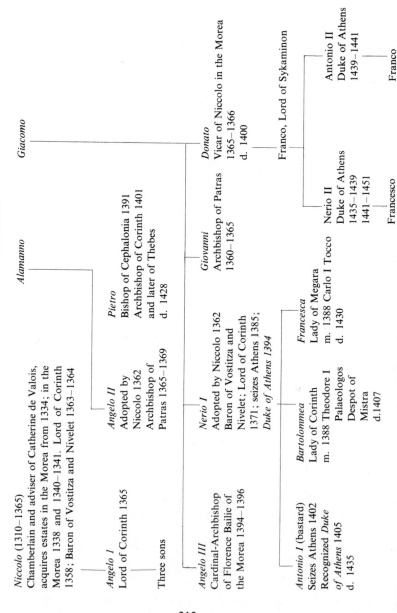

Niccolo (1310–1365)
Chamberlain and adviser of Catherine de Valois,
acquires estates in the Morea from 1334; in the
Morea 1338 and 1340–1341. Lord of Corinth
1358; Baron of Vostitza and Nivelet 1363–1364

Alamanno

Giacomo

Angelo I
Lord of Corinth 1365

Three sons

Pietro
Bishop of Cephalonia 1391
Archbishop of Corinth 1401
and later of Thebes
d. 1428

Angelo II
Adopted by
Niccolo 1362
Archbishop of
Patras 1365–1369

Donato
Vicar of Niccolo in the Morea
1365–1366
d. 1400

Angelo III
Cardinal-Archbishop
of Florence Bailie of
the Morea 1394–1396

Nerio I
Adopted by Niccolo 1362
Baron of Vostitza and
Nivelet; Lord of Corinth
1371; seizes Athens 1385;
Duke of Athens 1394

Giovanni
Archbishop of Patras
1360–1365

Franco, Lord of Sykaminon

Antonio I (bastard)
Seizes Athens 1402
Recognized *Duke
of Athens* 1405
d. 1435

Bartolommea
Lady of Corinth
m. 1388 Theodore I
Palaeologos
Despot of
Mistra
d.1407

Francesca
Lady of Megara
m. 1388 Carlo I Tocco
d. 1430

Nerio II
Duke of Athens
1435–1439
1441–1451

Antonio II
Duke of Athens
1439–1441

Francesco

Franco

10. The Orsini of Cephalonia and Epiros

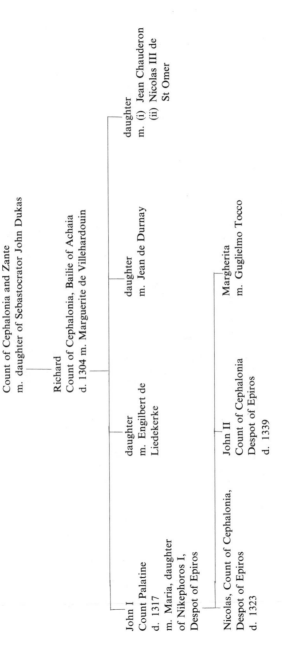

Matthew
Count of Cephalonia and Zante
m. daughter of Sebastocrator John Dukas

Richard
Count of Cephalonia, Bailie of Achaia
d. 1304 m. Marguerite de Villehardouin

John I
Count Palatine
d. 1317
m. Maria, daughter
of Nikephoros I,
Despot of Epiros

Nicolas, Count of Cephalonia,
Despot of Epiros
d. 1323

John II
Count of Cephalonia
Despot of Epiros
d. 1339

Margherita
m. Guglielmo Tocco

daughter
m. Engilbert de
Liedekerke

daughter
m. Jean de Durnay

daughter
m. (i) Jean Chauderon
   (ii) Nicolas III de
        St Omer

11. *The Tocchi, Counts of Cephalonia*

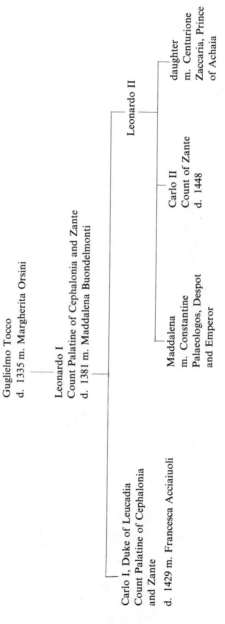

Guglielmo Tocco
d. 1335 m. Margherita Orsini

Leonardo I
Count Palatine of Cephalonia and Zante
d. 1381 m. Maddalena Buondelmonti

Carlo I, Duke of Leucadia
Count Palatine of Cephalonia
and Zante

d. 1429 m. Francesca Acciaiuoli

Maddalena
m. Constantine
Palaeologos, Despot
and Emperor

Carlo II
Count of Zante
d. 1448

Leonardo II

daughter
m. Centurione
Zaccaria, Prince
of Achaia

NOTES

NOTES TO INTRODUCTION

1. P. Leigh-Fermor, *Mani* (London, 1958) pp 294–5.
2. R. Rodd, *The Englishman in Greece* (Oxford, 1950) p 7.

NOTES TO CHAPTER I

1. Bury I. 13.
2. A.J. Toynbee, *A Study of History* (Oxford, 1934), Vol III, pp 77–8.
3. Frazer, *Studies in Greek Scenery*, pp 1–159 passim, especially pp 24–5, 43–4.
4. Pausanias Book X, Ch 34.
5. Zosimus I. 29.
6. Thompson xlix. 61–72.
7. Ibid. pp 67–9.
8. Zosimus IV. 8; V. 5.
9. Gregorovius p 38.
10. Zosimus V. 7; Bury I. 68–9.
11. For Athenais see F. Gregorovius, *Geschichte einer byzantinischen Kaiserin* (Dresden, 1927).
12. For a clear and concise account of the Slav penetration of Greece see Vlasto pp 5–12. Also Obolensky pp 64–97.
13. For the exact location of Justinian's birthplace see Browning p 97.
14. For Chilbud, see Procopius, *Histories* IV. 263–5; Obolensky p 70; Bury II. 20–2. One would like to know more about this commander, who did his best to defend the Danube frontier while Belisarius was scoring his spectacular successes against the Vandals in Africa.
15. Procopius, *The Buildings*, pp 219–315.
16. John of Ephesus pp 432–3.
17. It is not only plausible but reasonable to assume that during the Slav in-

vasions the Greek population should have regrouped along the coasts, particularly in the Peloponnese. On the other hand, there is little or no evidence for Slav settlement in the south-east of the peninsula. On the west coast, it is probable that the mediaeval town of Arkadia (on the site of the ancient Kyparissia) was refounded by refugees from the Arkadian plateau (Zakynthinos II. 151–3).
18. Repeated attempts by the Slavs, with or without Avar help, to take Thessalonica were repulsed in the late sixth and throughout the seventh centuries (Vlasto p 5 and note 8).
19. It was about that time that Isidore of Seville, the great Spanish scholar and ecclesiastic, recorded baldly that the Slavs had 'taken Greece from the Romans' (Sclavi Graeciam Romanis tulerunt). See Isidore, *Chronicon* (Migne, *Patrologia Latina* (Paris 1844–55) 83, col 1056). That was no doubt the opinion held by educated people in the Mediterranean world.
20. 'Vita S Willibaldi', *Monumenta Germaniae Historica Script* XV. 1, p 93. Bury II. 453 note 1.
21. Constantine Porphyrogenitus, *De Thematibus*, p 91. It would take a whole volume to analyse the vast literature that has accumulated around the question of to what extent the Greek population of Hellas was displaced by Slavs. G. Ostrogorsky's summing up (*History of the Byzantine State*, p 85) surely gets the balance right. His footnote 3 on that page contains a valuable list of authorities.
22. Nikephoros I restored and repo-

pulated both Patras and Lacedaemon, the ancient Sparta. To the former he brought back its inhabitants who had fled to Greek Calabria (Zakynthinos II. 161–2). They were joined during the ninth century by refugees from Sicily, which was being gradually conquered by the Arabs.

23. The Greek *Chronicle of Monemvasia* (c. A.D. 900) describes the Peloponnesian Slavs as 'subjects neither to the emperor of the Romans nor to anyone else' (Charanis pp 147–8). In other words, the situation had not greatly changed since Isidore wrote in the seventh century.

24. Bury II. 338; Obolensky p 81. It was inevitable that such people should drift into the Byzantine orbit.

25. Bury II. 525.

26. According to the eleventh-century chronicler Michael Glykas (CSHB ed I. Bekker, 1836).

27. The survival of place names of Slavonic origin proves merely that at some time in the past the locality was occupied by Slavs. It does not prove that its present inhabitants are necessarily of Slav descent. Shifts of population have continuously occured in Greece down to modern times. Today one village with an impeccably Greek name may well be populated exclusively by the descendants of Albanian immigrants, while another with an obviously Slav or Albanian name is inhabited by Greeks expelled from Asia Minor in 1922. But some significance must be attached to the fact that Slavonic place names are, in general, vastly outnumbered by the non-Slavonic. For the Peloponnese see Zakynthinos II. 164–5. From Thessaly southwards to Attica and the Corinthian Gulf, Slavonic names are relatively rare, but they are more numerous on the western side of the Pindus range (Vlasto p 8).

NOTES TO CHAPTER II

1. On the Arabs in Crete see Chapter XIV, p 274.

2. Constantine Porphyrogenitus, *Life of Basil* pp 184–6. Finlay, *History of the Byzantine Empire* pp 232–3.

3. Runciman, *Byzantine Civilization* p 153.

4. A full summary of his account is given in Finlay, *History of the Byzantine Empire* pp 248–59.

5. Constantine Porphyrogenitus, *Life of Basil* p 227; Theophanes Continuatus pp 318–9.

6. Byzantium did not lack forceful and accomplished women, but those of whom we hear most were either empresses or members of families closely connected with the Imperial court. Highly educated women were also to be found among the higher bourgeoisie. The widow Danielis is unusual because she lived in a province recently rescued from barbarism, was extremely rich in her own right, managed her own estates and business affairs and lived anything but a retired life in the *gynaeceum*.

7. Theophanes Continuatus p 321. We know much about the widow Danielis, her affluence and the prosperity of that part of Greece where her properties were situated. We can however only guess, in view of the lack of evidence, to what extent similar social and economic conditions prevailed at the time in other productive districts such as Boeotia, Elis, Messenia and the Argolid. If there had been an all-round improvement, it is remarkable that it should have come about so quickly in the short half-century between the re-colonizing endeavours of Nikephoros I and Basil's youth, especially as Arab raids were so destructive during that period.

8. Finlay, *History of the Byzantine Empire*, p 299.

9. Runciman *Emperor Romanus Lecapenus*, p 84 and note 2; Obolensky p 152.

10. Runciman, *Byzantine Style and Civilization*, p 108.

11. Anna Komnena p 320.

12. Ibid. p 347.

13. Runciman, *History of the Crusades* I. 88.

14. Norwich, *The Kingdom in the Sun*; Chs 3,6,7,10 and 18, are particularly relevant.

15. Ibid. p 130, note 2.

16. Benjamin of Tudela p 10; Gregorovius pp 136–7. Benjamin estimated the number of Jews at Thebes at 2000, with 300 at Corinth, 200 at Negroponte (Chalkis) and 200 at Crissa on the Gulf of Corinth.

17. Text (with German translation), *Timarion* pp 41–186.

18. Ibid. pp 46–50.

19. Otto of Freising, 'De Gestis Friderici', (in *Monumenta Germanicae Historica* Vol XX. ch 20 English tr. by C.C. Mierow, New York 1953).

20. For *pronoia* see Ostrogorsky pp 329–30.

21. R.M. Dawkins, 'The Greek Language in the Byzantine Period', in *Byzantium*, Baynes and Moss (Oxford, 1948), p 252.

22. Gregorovius, p 144.

23. Ibid. p 138.

24. Ibid. p 147.

Notes to Chapter III

1. Niketas Choniates 391; *Cambridge Mediaeval History* IV. 2. 81.

2. S. Runciman, *The Eastern Schism*, *passim*.

3. Liutprand's observations and strictures on Byzantium are contained in two of his works, the *Antapodosis* and the *Legatio*, ed. I. Bekker (Hanover, 1915).

4. On Sgouros see A. Bon, *Le Péloponnèse Byzantin*, pp 173–4, 204–5.

5. Miller, *Latins in the Levant*, pp 32–3.

6. Aubri des Trois Fontaines pp 880–5.

7. The main sources, i.e. the Greek, French and Aragonese versions of *The Chronicle of the Morea* and the *Histoire de la Conquête de Constantinople* of Geoffroy de Villehardouin (the conqueror's uncle) are confused as regards the course and details of the Frankish conquest of the Peloponnese. For the sequence of events see Bon, *La Morée Franque*, pp 58–64.

8. Greek *Chronicle*, ed. Schmitt, lines 1770–85.

9. The general attitude of the archontic class is summed up in the Greek *Chronicle*, ed. Schmitt, line 2089 *et seq*. With certain notable exceptions these landowners, whose local power and prosperity were at their height at the time of the Latin conquest, saw every advantage in quickly coming to terms with the conquerors. That they hurried to do so is made quite plain by the Greek *Chronicle*, line 1641 *et seq* and by the French *Chronicle*, 106, pp 34–8.

10. Greek *Chronicle*, ed. Schmitt, lines 1760–3.

11. Bon, *Le Péleponnèse Byzantin*, p 68, note 2.

12. The story is given full treatment in the Greek *Chronicle*, ed. Schmitt, lines 2096–2434, and the French *Chronicle* 137–71, pp 49–60.

13. French *Chronicle*, 132, p 48.

14. The identity and character of the Tzakones have been defined in Zakynthinos II. 14–19 and in Bon, *Le Péloponnèse Byzantin*, pp 63–4, 71–4. Whether or not their name is a corruption of 'Lakonians', it seems clear that in the Middle Ages it designated the Greek inhabitants of the eastern flank of the Peloponnese from the Argolid southwards to Cape Malea, a territory into which there had been

little or no Slav penetration. They were a race of hardy and independent minded mountaineers and seafarers. For their dialect see R.M. Dawkins, 'The Greek Language in the Byzantine Period', in Baynes and Moss, *Byzantium*, Ch. IX, pp 251, 261 (Oxford, 1948).

15. The versions of the *Chronicle* fail to agree on the exact proportion of Greeks to Latins on the commission, but there is no doubt that the former were fully represented. See Bon, *La Morée Franque*, p 82, note 1.

16. On the various versions and texts of the *Chronicle* see Bon, *La Morée Franque*, pp 15–18. H.E. Lurier, in the introduction to his translation of the Greek *Chronicle*, pp 35–61, argues strongly that both the Greek and the French versions are derived from a lost French prototype composed between 1304 and 1314. He concludes from internal evidence and on linguistic grounds that the present French version is an abridgment of the prototype, while the Greek version 'was composed around the year 1388 by a Greek-speaking French scribe, who translated the original into Greek idiom for the benefit of Greek-speaking Franks'.

17. French *Chronicle*, Introduction, p 1.

18. For the original baronies and distribution of fiefs see Bon, *La Morée Franque*, pp 102–5.

19. French *Chronicle*, 130–1, pp 47–8; Miller, *Latins in the Levant* pp 52–3.

20. French *Chronicle*, 218, p 79. Many of the castles were of course of Byzantine and pre-Byzantine origin.

21. In view of the sheer numbers of fiefs distributed to Frankish barons and knights, it is hard to believe that many Greek archons did not in fact forfeit all or part of their lands. We must however accept that Villehardouin solved the problem with the least possible exemption of existing tenure. The existence of extensive estates belonging to the Byzantine Crown, or to absentee landlords, may have helped in that respect. We must admire the tenacity of the Moreot archons. They held their own with equal success under Frankish princes and Greek despots, and faded out only gradually under the Turks. See Ostrogorsky p 377 and note 1.

22. Bon, *La Morée Franque*, p 96.

23. It is true that under the Byzantine system the *paroikos*, though bound to the soil, was personally free, at least in theory. He could not be sold separately from the plot where he worked, nor removed from it to another plot. Therefore his condition may have been marginally more tolerable on the estate of a Greek archon than on that of a Frankish fief-holder (see Zakynthinos II. 201–2).

24. Miller, *Latins in the Levant*, p 55.

NOTES TO CHAPTER IV

1. From a commercial point of view Negroponte was excellently situated for Venetian merchants ro exploit the grain trade of Thessaly and the products of rich agricultural Boeotia.

2. Quoted in Gregorovius p 188.

3. Quoted in Miller, *Latins in the Levant*, p 68.

4. We have no names of Greek landowners in Attica. They certainly, however, existed in Boeotia (see N. Svoronos, 'Le Cadastre de Thebes', *Bulletin de Correspondance Hellenique* 83 (1959), pp 1–145) but were not the power to be reckoned with that they were in the principality.

5. Miller, *Latins in the Levant*, p 71, quoting Michael Choniates ii. 327.

6. Gregorovius p 227.

7. Bon, *La Morée Franque*, pp 75–6.

8. Aubri des Trois-Fontaines pp 938–9; Bon, *La Morée Franque*, p 79.

9. Sanudo Torsello pp 100–1.

10. Muntaner in Longnon, *L'Empire Latin*, pp 193–4.

11. Sanudo Torsello p 102.
12. Greek *Chronicle*, ed. Schmitt, lines 2901–65.
13. Ibid lines 2985–3042.
14. Ibid lines 3173–3331.
15. French *Chronicle* 242, p 88. 'Et puis que la pais fu faicte et complie li jone bachellier mennerent grant feste de joustes, de rompre lances a la quintaine, et de caroles.' (And now that peace was made and confirmed the young bachelors held a great feast of jousts and breaking of lances 'a la quintaine', and of carolling.)
16. French *Chronicle* 245, p 88. 'Et quant il fu a Paris, si ala tout droit au roy de France, et le salua, et li rois le recut moult honnereement quant il sot qu'il estoit le seignior d'Athenes et venoit de Romanie.' (And when he was at Paris, he went straight to the King of France and greeted him, and the King received him most honourably when he knew that he was the lord of Athens and came from Romania.)
17. Chaucer, *The Knight's Tale*, lines 1–2.
18. Greek *Chronicle*, ed. Schmitt, lines 3586–3607.
19. French *Chronicle* 299, p 109. 'Si commencerent archiers a traire et feroient et tenoient einsi les Alemans qui estoient de leurs gens comme celle dou seignior de Carintaine.' (Then the archers began to shoot, and thus they struck and held the Germans who were on their own side as well as those who fought for the lord of Karytaina.)
20. Greek *Chronicle*, ed. Schmitt, lines 4204–4323.
21. French *Chronicle* 325, p 121. 'Veez ci mon corps appareillié d'entrer en prison pour delivrer monseignor le prince. Et se il est pour raenchon de monnoye, se je deusse angaigier mon pays, je ne souffreroie que monseignor soit en prison.' (See, here is my body ready to go to prison in order to deliver my Lord the prince. And if it is a question of a money ransom, and even if I have

to commit my country, I will not allow my lord to stay in prison.)
22. Once in Byzantine hands, Monemvasia also developed a flourishing merchant navy. Its vessels traded with ports in Macedonia, Thrace, the Marmora and the Black Sea (see Zakynthinos II. 255). There was a colony of Monemvasiotes, engaged in the wine trade, at Candia in Crete.
23. Aragonese *Chronicle* 332–4.
24. Greek *Chronicle* ed. Schmitt, lines 4678–4850.
25. French *Chronicle* 344, p 133.
26. This campaign is described in the greatest detail in the Greek *Chronicle*, ed. Schmitt, lines 4885–5709. The space which the author devotes to it indicates that he regarded it as the highest point of military success which the Franks attained in Achaia, while in fact it was only a temporary reverse, though a serious one, for the Byzantines. In the concluding passage he remarks that some of the Turks were baptized and settled down in the Morea.
27. Greek *Chronicle*, ed. Schmitt, lines 6940–5.
28. See Runciman, *Sicilian Vespers*, pp 148–179.
29. Greek *Chronicle*, ed. Schmitt, lines 7215–26.
30. Miller, *Latins in the Levant*, pp 131–6.
31. Ibid. pp 136–41.
32. Nicol, *Last Centuries of Byzantium*, pp 70–1.
33. Greek *Chronicle*, ed. Schmitt, lines 7800–10.

NOTES TO CHAPTER V

1. Up to the death of Guillaume de Villehardouin the picture of Greece in the thirteenth century, and especially of the Morea, is reasonably clear. At any rate its main features are easily discernible. That is unfortunately not

the case in the period covered by the present chapter. As soon as the Angevins come on the scene the historian, whether he likes it or not, is involved in a tangle of dynastic ambitions and family intrigues. But unless the period is passed over altogether, some effort must be made to explore its shifting alliances and personal feuds, complicated as they are by the parts played by the Byzantine Emperor and by the Greek princes north of the isthmus of Corinth. The relations between the personalities and the territories in which they happened to be active at any particular moment are admittedly confusing, but given the circumstances of the time no apology can be offered for the unavoidable proliferation of personal and place names in the text. Perhaps the main interest of the period is the increasing intervention of Greeks in the internal running of Latin states and vice versa.

2. French *Chronicle* 501–4, pp 197–211.
3. Greek *Chronicle*, ed. Schmitt, lines 8110–8458.
4. Leigh Fermor, *Mani*, p 15.
5. Miller, *Latins in the Levant*, p 168.
6. Greek *Chronicle*, ed. Schmitt, lines 8080–5.
7. Bon, *La Morée Franque*, p 146.
8. French *Chronicle* 595, p 239.
9. Ibid. 605, p 242–3. The Greek *Chronicle*, lines 8709–10, described Philanthropenos as a 'great man of the palace, from one of the twelve families'. Presumably he was the Alexios Philanthropenos who campaigned against the Turks on the river Maeander in Asia Minor, rebelled under Andronikos II and was blinded in consequence (see Nicol, *The Last Centuries of Byzantium*, pp 131–2).
10. French *Chronicle* 606, p 243.
11. Ibid. 662–92, pp 264–75.
12. Ibid. 693–745, pp 275–96. Sgouromallis 'estoit preudomme et vaillant homme, et amoit trop les Latins'.

13. Ibid. 801–25, pp 318–26.
14. Ibid. 757–800, pp 300–18. The chronology of Roger's raid is uncertain. The Aragonese *Chronicle*, 483–503, places it after the death of Prince Florent. The French *Chronicle* stresses the chivalrous side of the episode while skating over the political implications brought out by Muntaner Ch 117. Roger's aggression was clearly a shock for the government of the principality.
15. Greek *Chronicle*, ed. Schmitt, lines 8480–9235.
16. Miller, *Latins in the Levant*, pp 192–4, after Muntaner Ch 244.
17. French *Chronicle* 831–40, pp 329–33.
18. Ibid. 855, p 338.
19. Bon, *La Morée Franque*, p 175.
20. French *Chronicle* 856–67, p 338–43; Miller, *Latins in the Levant*, pp 197–8.
21. French *Chronicle* 921–51, pp 363–73.
22. Ibid. 872–916, pp 345–361; Miller, *Latins in the Levant*, pp 199–201.
23. Ibid. 973–995, pp 381–9.
24. Ibid. 1007–1024, pp 393–9.

NOTES TO CHAPTER VI

1. Aragonese *Chronicle* 506
2. Rodd p 4.
3. Greek *Chronicle* ed. Schmitt, lines 8047–55.
4. Nicol, *The Last Centuries of Byzantium*, pp 233–6.
5. Following Ramon Muntaner, Setton, pp 3 and 14, puts the total strength of the Company at 6500–7000 men, allowing for losses and re-inforcements in the years 1303–11.
6. Miller, *Latins in the Levant*, pp 212–3.
7. Notably Pachymeres II. 393–652.
8. Moncada p 140.
9. Miller, *Latins in the Levant*, pp 216–9.
10. See Setton p 5 note 16, for a detailed list of sources dealing with the Catalans' movements up to their entry into Greece.
11. Muntaner pp 429–30; tr. Hakluyt Society II. 575–6.

12. Aragonese *Chronicle* 548–9, 551.
13. Moncada p 229.
14. Ibid. p 229.
15. Ibid. p 231.
16. Muntaner p 431, tr Hakluyt Society II. 577.
17. Quoted by Gregorovius pp 234–5.
18. The Catalans were certainly accompanied by many of their women from home, or elsewhere (see Muntaner ed. Lanz p 351, tr Hakluyt Society II, pp 485–6). See also Moncada p 28, 'Llevaban consigo hijos y mujeres' (They took children and women with them) and p 189, 'Ordenose que Ramon Muntaner . . llevase las mujeres, niñas y viejos por mas' (Ramon Muntaner was ordered to take the women, children and old men as well.) [on the way from the Marmora to Macedonia]. In other words they were organized as a community, and not only as an army, when they reached Athens.
19. Bon, *La Morée Franque*, pp 188–9.
20. Muntaner pp 472–3; Miller *Latins in the Levant*, pp 252–4.
21. Aragonese *Chronicle* 559.
22. Ibid. 560–623.
    Muntaner pp 478–9 and 484–5.
23. Bon, *La Morée Franque*, pp 193–5; Miller, *Latins in the Levant*, pp 257–8.
24. Bon, *La Morée Franque*, pp 204–6
25. Ibid. pp 206–7.
26. Greek *Chronicle* ed. Schmitt, lines 8086–92.
27. For the civil and ecclesiastical administration of the Catalan duchy, see Setton, VI. 74–97.
28. Setton pp 247–8.
29. Ibid. p 252, gives examples of this rule being broken, especially in upper-class marriages. The same prohibition was imposed by the Venetians in Crete, but in time it proved ineffective.
30. For Rendis, see Setton pp 166–73, and for Makris pp 168–9.
31. A more unusual Archbishop of Thebes was Simone Atumano, whom Pope Urban V appointed to the see in 1366. It appears that he was born at Constantinople of a Turkish father and a Greek mother and may have started his career in the Orthodox Church. Later he came to Italy and spent seventeen years as bishop of Gerace in Calabria, where the Greek language still lingered. He was an excellent scholar and translated Plutarch into Latin. But at Thebes he did not get on well with the Catalans and was accused of conniving at the capture of the city by the Navarrese. For his picturesque and well documented career see Setton pp 140–4. A contemporary Catalan prelate was Bishop Boyl of Megara (Setton pp 162–4), who could hardly have counted many Roman Catholic faithful in his little diocese.

Notes to Chapter VII

1. Talbot Rice pp 256–7.
2. Ibid. pp 255–6.
3. On Andronikos Asen, see Bon, *La Morée Franque*, pp 194 and 202 and Zakynthinos I. 70–71: French *Chronicle* pp 404–5: Aragonese *Chronicle* 641–54.
4. Bon, *La Morée Franque*, p 203.
5. See Nicol, *The Last Centuries of Byzantium*, Ch 11 passim, for the efforts of Andronikos III to restore and consolidate the Byzantine position in Northern Greece.
6. For the Moreot embassy to Cantacuzenos, see the latter's *Histories* III. 74–6; Zakynthinos I. 76; Bon, *La Morée Franque*, p 213.
7. Zakynthinos I. 101–2.
8. Ostrogorsky p 474.
9. Nicol, 'The Byzantine Family of Kantakouzenos', pp 122–9.
10. Bon, *La Morée Franque*, pp 213–4, lists the barons who supported the appeal.
11. Aragonese *Chronicle* 685–6; Bon, *La Morée Franque*, p 229.

12. Cantacuzenos, *Histories* III. 86–7; Miller, *Latins in the Levant*, p 282.
13. Zakynthinos I. 98–9.
14. Bon, *La Morée Franque*, p 242, and p 253, note 1.
15. Ibid. p 278; Zakynthinos l. 149 note 5.
16. Runciman, *Byzantine Style and Civilization*, pp 198–9.
17. Zakynthinos p 105; Bon, *La Morée Franque*, p 224.

Notes to Chapter viii

1. On the origins of the Acciaiuoli, see Gregorovius pp 390–3 and note p 934. Also Bon, *La Morée Franque*, pp 26, 209–11; Miller, *Latins in the Levant*, pp 270–3.
2. Bon, *La Morée Franque*, p 210, footnote 2.
3. Ibid. pp 216–19.
4. Ibid. pp 241–250.
5. Runciman, *A history of the Crusades*, III. 441–9.
6. The Lusignans were very short of money at the time. King Peter borrowed heavily from the Venetian capitalist Federico Corner, who in return received vast sugar plantations in Cyprus. See F.C. Lane, *Venice, A Maritime Republic* (Baltimore, 1973), pp 141–2. Corner was also active in Crete.
7. Aragonese *Chronicle* 705–13; Bon, *La Morée Franque*, p 252.
8. Aragonese *Chronicle* 714–22.
9. Bon, *La Morée Franque*, p 253.
10. Ibid. pp 253–4.
11. The Navarrese invasion of the Duchy of Athens effectively broke the power of the Catalans. Setton pp 125–148 discusses in detail the short but fatal Navarrese intervention and concludes (p 147) that the Catalans never regained possession of Thebes.
12. Bon, *La Morée Franque*, pp 254–6.
13. Nicol, *The Last Centuries of Byzantium*, p 293.
14. Miller, *Latins in the Levant*, p 277.

15. Setton pp 58–60.
16. Aragonese *Chronicle* 704; Bon, *La Morée Franque*, p 251.
17. Setton p 78.
18. Bon, *La Morée Franque*, p 262.
19. Setton p 187. In Catalan 'lo dit castell sia la pus richa joya qui al mont sia e tal que entre tots los Reys de cristians envides lo porien fer semblant'.
20. Ibid. p 174.
21. Ibid. p 186.
22. But, as Setton observes (p 99), after two generations the Catalans in Athens and Thebes had become hellenized (*criollos*). This Latin-American word is eminently applicable to all the Franks of Greece. Setton (p 243) estimates the total Catalan population of the city of Athens at only three thousand. Obviously many of these would have been absorbed. The Athenian Alphonsos who copied a manuscript there in the fifteenth century (Setton p 223) must have been a Catalan by descent. So perhaps was Frangos Catellanos, the painter–monk from Thebes who worked in the mid-sixteenth century on Mount Athos and at Meteora (see Byron pp 270–3).
23. Miller, *Latins in the Levant*, pp 334–7.
24. Bon, *La Morée Franque*, pp 263–4.
25. Ibid. p 268; Miller, *Latins in the Levant*, pp 340–2.
26. Bon, *La Morée Franque* p 269.
27. Miller, *Latins in the Levant*, pp 346–7; Gregorovius pp 471–2.
28. Miller, *Latins in the Levant*, pp 345–6.
29. Bon, *La Morée Franque*, p 271–2.
30. Ibid. p 270.
31. Gregorovius pp 468–70; Miller, *Latins in the Levant*, pp 353–6.
32. Zakynthinos I. 155–6.

Notes to Chapter ix

1. Zakynthinos I. 156–7.
2. Ibid. I. 158–60; Bon, *La Morée Franque*, pp 272–3.
3. Zakynthinos I. 160–1.

4. Ibid. I. 162.
5. Miller, *Latins in the Levant*, pp 359–62.
6. On the economic resources of the Morea, see Zakynthinos II. 245–53.
7. On Albanian immigration into the Morea, see Zakynthinos II. 29–36. Attica too was full of Albanian villages.
8. Bon, *La Morée Franque*, pp 283–4.
9. Zakynthinos I. 167–73.
10. For text see Mazaris pp 187–362. Ellissen's edition includes German translation and notes.
11. Mazaris has been tentatively identified with a Maximos Mazaris, monk and canonist, but out of character, surely, with the waspish satirist (see Zakynthinos II. 348–9).
12. Mazaris p 239.
13. The Emperor was writing to Euthymios, Patriarch of Constantinople (see Zakynthinos I. 174).
14. This work does not attempt to deal with the fascinating but complicated subject of Plethon's relations with, and influence on, the Italian humanists whom he impressed so greatly when he accompanied his sovereign to the Council of Florence. I confine myself to his activity at Mistra and the impulse he gave to the Greek intellectual revival.
15. Text, with German translation and notes, in Plethon pp 41–154.
16. Plethon's ideas on taxation may appear naive, but he may well have been appalled by the complexity of the Byzantine fiscal system as reintroduced into the Morea under the Despotate (see Zakynthinos II. 227–44).
17. Plethon p 78.
18. Zakynthinos I. pp 196–8.
19. Bon, *La Morée Franque*, pp 288–9.
20. Zakynthinos I. 199–201; Bon, *La Morée Franque*, p 291.
21. Zakynthinos I. 207–8; Bon, *La Morée Franque*, p 292.
22. Plethon's fiefs were both situated in rich agricultural districts. His fellow-scholar and future bishop, John Eugenikos, was granted the village of Petrina, also in Lakonia, and wrote a description of its rural delights. For Phanari and Brysis, see Zakynthinos II. 199–200, and for Petrina, p 213, note 4, and p 246.
23. Byron p 139. Talbot Rice pp 259–60.
24. Zakynthinos II. 315–6.

NOTES TO CHAPTER X

1. Nicol *The last Centuries of Byzantium*, pp 365–7, and p 387 note 13.
2. Miller, *Latins in the Levant*, pp 399–402; Gregorovius pp 493–4.
3. Miller, *Latins in the Levant*, pp 404–6.
4. So far as I am aware, no modern edition or English translation exists of the writings of Cyriacus. Nor have his fragmentary manuscripts ever been published in their entirety. For his travels see Cyriacus. Bon, *La Morée Franque*, p 32, note 3, list a number of partial studies. A lively account of his journeys in Greece is given by Miller, *The Latins in the Levant*, pp 417–25. Although he was chiefly interested in antiquities, he met nearly everyone of consequence in Greece on the eve of its absorption by the Ottomans. He also appreciated landscape as well as classical remains (see Zakynthinos I. 229).
5. Cyriacus 62–72.
6. Quoting Cyriacus of Ancona, Zakynthinos II. 229–30, draws attention to Constantine's efforts to raise Moreot morale by offering prizes for athletic contests, in the ancient Hellenic manner.
7. Miller *Latins in the Levant*, pp 410–11; Zakynthinos pp 230–2.
8. Zakynthinos I. 232–5.
9. Plethon p 43. The whole passage, in which he describes the defensive potential of the Morea, is of great interest.
10. Zakynthinos I. 235–6.

11. Ibid. I. 246.
12. Ibid. I. 247–55.
13. Miller, *Latins in the Levant*, pp 435–8.
14. By contrast with earlier periods of Moreot history, the final struggles with the Turks from 1452 to 1460 are described in full detail by the contemporary Greek historians Phrantzes, Chalkokondylas and Kritoboulos. Their accounts are followed closely in Zakynthinos I. 247–74. Zakynthinos explains the rift between Thomas and Demetrios as the result of conflicting political philosophies; the former was a Western sympathizer while Demetrios at heart preferred the Turks to the Latins. In addition, any well coordinated resistance to the Turks was frustrated by the selfish and factious behaviour of the Moreot archons.

NOTES TO CHAPTER XI

1. Miller, *Latins in the Levant*, pp 42–45.
2. On Sanudo's Cretan venture see Ch. XIV below, p 278.
3. Miller, *Latins in the Levant*, p 572.
4. Ibid. pp 573–5.
5. F. Braudel, *The Mediterranean* (London, 1972), Vol I, p 149.
6. Miller, *Latins in the Levant*, pp 576–8.
7. Ibid. pp 578–80.
8. Bon, *La Morée Franque*, pp 19–20.
9. Sanudo Torsello, 113–4; Miller, *Latins in the Levant*, p 581.
10. Miller, *Latins in the Levant*, pp 584–5.
11. Bon, *La Morée Franque*, pp 170–1.
12. Miller, *Latins in the Levant*, pp 248–50, 273–5; Nicol, *Last Centuries of Byzantium*, pp 183–7.
13. Miller, *Latins in the Levant*, p 250.
14. On the status of the protopapas, see Ch. XIV below, pp 294–5.
15. Miller, *Latins in the Levant*, pp 516–19, following Marmora, *Istoria di Corfu*, and Mustoxidi, *Delle Cose Corciresi*.
16. Miller, *Latins in the Levant*, pp 530–2.
17. Nicol, *Last Centuries of Byzantium* pp 367–8.

18. Miller, *Latins in the Levant*, pp 590–4.
19. Ibid. p 605.

NOTES TO CHAPTER XII

1. See Miller, *Latins in the Levant* XIV, passim.
2. According to Phrantzes (see Zakynthinos I. 270), it was Kladas who originally surrendered the castle of St George to the Sultan. Like other archons who had retained their lands under the Franks and subsequently under the Despot, he had counted on surviving under the Turks as well. For his revolt see Miller, *Latins in the Levant*, pp 489–90.
3. For the later history of the Crispi dukes, see Miller, *Latins in the Levant*, pp 611–36.
4. Joseph Nasi is described in Braudel p 816 as 'a sort of eastern Fugger'. See C. Roth, *The House of Nasi* and *The Duke of Naxos*.

NOTES TO CHAPTER XIII

1. Runciman's *The Eastern Schism* lays bare the roots of the antagonism between Latin West and Byzantine East. Chapters V, VI ('The Growth of Popular Animosity') and VII are particularly revealing.
2. Ostrogorsky p 377.
3. Ibid. p 377.
4. *The Chronicle of the Morea*, ed. J. Schmitt, Introduction p xxiii; see also pp xxxviii–xlvi.
5. Greek *Chronicle* ed. Schmitt, lines 3840–5.
6. *The Chronicle of the Morea*, ed. J. Schmitt, Introduction p xlii.
7. Belthandros and Chrysantza. Text (with German translation and commentary) in Analekten, and in E. Legrand, *Bibliothèque Grecque Vulgaire* (Paris, 1880), Vol I.
Lybistros and Rhodamne. See J.A. Lambert, *Le Roman de Libistros et Rhodamne* (Amsterdam, 1935).

For French translations of both romances see Gidel, *Etudes sur la littérature Grecque Moderne* (Paris, 1866). See also C. Diehl, *Figures Byzantines*, (Paris, 1908), second series.

8. See Bon, *La Morée Franque*, pp 535–6.
9. Ibid. pp 547–53; O. Lancaster, *Classical Landscape with Figures* (London, 1947), p 146.
10. Bon, *La Morée Franque*, pp 561–74.
11. On Isova and Zaraka, Ibid. pp 537–44 and pp 553–9 respectively.
12. Ibid. pp 608–29.
13. Ibid. pp 592–8.
14. Runciman, *The Fall of Constantinople*, p 8.
15. Talbot Rice p 254.
16. Runciman, *Byzantine Style and Civilization*, pp 194–5.
17. J.A. Symonds, *Renaissance in Italy* (London, 1902), 'Italian Literature', Part I, p 375.
18. Chaucer, *The Knightes Tale*, lines 2–3, 108–9, 117–26, 1641–2.
19. Shakespeare, *Midsummer Night's Dream*, Act IV, Scene 1.
20. Faust, Part II, Act 3, tr John Shawcross (London, 1959), pp 340, 355–6.
21. See Greek *Chronicle*, ed. J. Schmitt, Introduction, Section X, pp lviii–lxvi (Influence of the *Chronicle* on Goethe's *Faust*).

Notes to Chapter XIV

1. Two years later the Arabs began their conquest of Sicily, which took fifty years in all to complete. The exact date of their invasion of Crete is uncertain. It was due to two events unconnected with developments in the Byzantine world. The first was the migration of fifteen thousand Spanish Arabs to Alexandria as a result of internal troubles in Andalucia; the second was their migration to Crete after taking the wrong side in internal strife in Egypt. A preliminary raid was followed by an incursion by the whole body, but in relation to the total population of the island the Arabs were a small minority. Whatever knowledge we have of the conquest is derived from Theophanes Continuatus IV.

2. Choniates, p 843; L. de Monacis, *Chronicon* (Venice, 1758), p 153; Xanthoudides pp 4–7, (In Greek).

3. The size of the population of Crete in 1204 is a matter of guesswork. Stavrakis, *Statistics of Cretan Population* (Athens, 1890), put it at about half a million. He and other authorities assume that it declined sensibly during the Venetian occupation, the lowest level quoted being 160,000 (1573) and the highest 287, 165 (1644). See Zinkeisen IV. 709, 712 and 741, and Xanthoudides pp 189–90. By comparison it was 279, 165 in 1881 and 386,000 in 1928.

4. On the activities of St Nikon Metanoites (the Penitent), see G. Schlumberger, *Un Empereur Byzantin au dixième siècle* (Paris, 1890), p 96. The Saint died about 998.

5. The original archontic families were twelve in number. They believed that their ancestors had come to Crete in the late eleventh century but in some cases their origins might go back as far as Nikephoros Phokas (see Gerland, 'Histoire de la Noblesse Crétoise au Moyen Age', Vols X & XI. See also Xanthoudides pp 16–18.

6. Xanthoudides pp 11–15.
7. Ibid. pp 7–11, 15–16.
8. French *Chronicle* 106, pp 34–5.
9. The Venetians were themselves only too ready to flout Papal authority whenever it suited them. Hence the saying 'Semo Veneziani e poi Christiani'. (We are Venetians first and then Christians) They did not object to the practice of the Orthodox religion by their Cretan subjects, nor did they seek to persecute or proselytize (nor for that matter did the Franks in mainland

Greece). But they did keep a wary eye on the Orthodox Church as a possible focus of anti-Venetian disaffection.

In fact those desiring to be ordained did not have to travel further than Modon and Coron where, for reasons of administrative convenience, the Venetians had not suppressed the Orthodox bishoprics.

10. Xanthoudides pp 27–32.

11. Ibid. pp 21–23. The original remonstrance is preserved in the Venetian State archives; it was published by G. Cervellini, *Documento inedito Veneto-Cretense del Dugento* (Padua, 1906).

12. Xanthoudides pp 32–36.

13. L. de Monacis, *Chronicon*, (Venice, 1758), p 156; Xanthoudides pp 37–43.

14. See Thiriet p 131.

15. Xanthoudides pp 24–26.

16. This otherwise unknown Byzantine general is mentioned by both Laurentius and Cornelio. The latter (*Creta Sacra* II, 288) describes him as a 'dynast from Thrace'.

17. Xanthoudides pp 45–48.

18. On the Chortatzai, see Gerland, *Histoire de la Noblesse Crétoise*, passim.

19. Xanthoudides pp 49–55.

20. His family claimed descent from the Phokades, formerly an Imperial house in Byzantium (see Gerland, *Histoire de la Noblesse Crétoise*, pp 37, 50–56).

21. Xanthoudides pp 55–60.

22. Monemvasia was of course an important Byzantine fortress and trading centre, as well as the first stage on the export route of Cretan wine to the West.

23. Xanthoudides pp 64–71.

24. Ibid. pp 71–72.

25. See Noiret references under 'blé'.

26. On local production and foreign trade, see Xanthoudides pp 164–169, and numerous references in Noiret.

27. Laurentius came to Crete in 1388 and wrote his *Chronicle* about 1404. For the causes and course of the rebellion see Thiriet, pp 173–4 and 251–6 and detailed account in Xanthondides pp 81–110.

28. Dal Verme was edified, before he left Venice, by a pompous exhortation from his friend Petrarch, packed with classical allusions to the Minotaur, the Labyrinth etc. (Cornelivs Flaminius II. 332–3).

29. The Venieri were also lords of Kythera (see Ch. XI, p 224).

30. Sugar plantations were started in Cyprus in the late 1360s, over a century before it became part of the Venetian Empire, by Federico Corner, whose family had deep roots in Crete. He became vastly rich on the product of slave labour. The first planter in Crete seems to have been one Zanono, who in 1428 was granted a concession at Apokorona in the west of the island. See several references in Noiret, also R. Matton, *La Crète au cours des Siècles* (Athens, 1957), p 116. The industry remained profitable in the sixteenth century, though it was being slowly eclipsed by production in Madeira and the Americas.

31. Xanthoudides pp 133–142.

32. Ibid. pp 130–1.

33. Ibid. pp 154–162.

34. McNeill p 116. In the early fifteenth century Crete produced a learned Pope, Petros Philarges or Philargos, who occupied the Chair of St Peter from 7 July 1409 to 3 May 1410, under the name of Alexander V. Born in Candia, he was brought up by Minorite friars and later travelled for his education to Italy, England and France. He became successively Bishop of Novara, Brescia and Piacenza, Patriarch of Grado, Archbishop of Milan and Cardinal of the Twelve Apostles (F. Gregorovius, *Rome in the Middle Ages*, (London, 1908), tr. A. Hamilton, Vol. VI, Part 2, pp 606–12).

35. Xanthoudides pp 169–173.

36. Trypanis p xiv.

37. On popular Cretan literature, see Xanthoudides pp 173–183. On the Cretan literary movement as a whole, Byron pp 166–172 can hardly be bettered.

38. Byron pp 145–149, 163–166.

39. On Foscarini, see Zinkeisen IV. 629–723.

BIBLIOGRAPHY

1. ORIGINAL SOURCES

Agathias. *Histories*, ed. Niebuhr, CSHB; ed. R. Keydell (Berlin, 1967)
Akropolites, George. *History*, ed. A. Heisenberg (Leipzig, 1903)
Ammianus Marcellinus. *History*, ed. C.U. Clark (Berlin, 1910–15)
Assizes of Romania. Liber Consuetudinum Imperii Romaniae ed. G. Recoura, (Paris, 1930)
Benjamin of Tudela. *Itinerary*, ed. Asher (London, 1840) with English translation; with translation and notes by M.N. Adler (London, 1907)
Cantacuzenos, John. *Histories*, ed. L. Schopen CSHB (Bonn, 1828–32)
Chalkocondyles, Laonikos. *Historiarium Demonstrationes,* ed. I. Bekker, CSHB (Bonn, 1843); ed. E. Darko (Budapest, 1922–7)
Choniates, Michael. *Ta Sozomena*, ed. S.P. Lampros (Athens, 1879–80)
Choniates, Niketas. *Historia*, ed. I. Bekker, CSHB (Bonn, 1834)
Chronicon Breve ed. I. Bekker, CSHB (Bonn, 1834)
Chronicle of the Morea: Greek Version, ed. J. Schmitt (London, 1904)
——Greek Version, translated by Harold E. Lurier, with notes and introduction (Columbia University Press, New York, 1964)
——French Version, *Livre de la Conqueste de la Princée de l'Amorée*, ed. J. Longnon (Paris, 1911)
——Aragonese Version, *Libro de los Fechos et Conquistas del Principado de la Morea*, ed. A. Morel-Fatio (Geneva, 1885)
——Italian Version, *Cronaca di Morea*, ed. C. Hopf (Berlin, 1873)
Constantine VII Porphrogenitus. *De Administrando Imperio*, ed. G. Moravcsik (Washington, 1967), with English translation by R.J.H. Jenkins
——*De Ceremoniis*, ed. A. Vogal. *Le Livre des Cérémonies* (Paris, 1939–40), with French translation
——*De Thematibus*, ed. A. Pertusi (Vatican, 1952)
Cyriacus of Ancona. *Itinerarium*, ed. L. Mehus (Florence, 1742)
Dio Chrysostom. *Orations Teubner* (1915–19), Loeb Classical Library (London and New York, 1932)
Dukas. *Historia Byzantina*, ed. Bekker, CSHB (Bonn, 1834)
Eustathius, Metropolitan of Thessalonica. *De Thessalonica a Latinis Capta*, ed. I. Bekker, CSHB (Bonn, 1842). German translation by H. Hunger (Vienna, 1955)
Gregoras Nikephoros. *Letters*, ed. R. Guilland (Paris, 1927), with French translation
——*Roman History*, ed. Schopen and Bekker, CSHB (Bonn, 1829–55)
John of Ephesus. *The Third Part of the Ecclesiastical History of John, Bishop of Ephesus*, tr. R. Payne Smith (Oxford, 1860)
Kameniates, John. In CSHB (Bonn, 1838), after Theophanes Continuatus
Kinnamos, John. In CSHB (Bonn, 1836), ed. A. Meineke

Bibliography

Komnena, Anna. *The Alexiad*, tr. Elizabeth A.S. Dawes, (London, 1928)
Kritoboulos. *History of Mehmet the Conqueror*, tr. C.T. Riggs (Princeton, 1954)
Kydones, Demetrios. *Letters*, ed. G. Cammelli (Paris, 1930)
Laurentius de Monacis. *Chronicon de Rebus Venetis* (Venice, 1758)
Leo VI. *Tactica*, ed. R. Vari (Budapest, 1917–22)
Mazaris. *Sojourn in Hades*, ed. A. Ellissen, *Analekten der Mittel und Neugriechischen Literatur* (Leipzig, 1860)
Menander. Müller FHG iv 220–269
Muntaner, Ramon. *The Chronicle of Muntaner*, ed. K. Lanz (Stuttgart, 1844); tr. Lady Goodenough (Hakluyt Society, London, 1921)
Pachymeres, George. *Michael and Andronicus Palaeologus*, ed. I. Bekker, CSHB (Bonn, 1835)
Palaeologos, Manuel II. *Letters*, ed. E. Legrand (Paris, 1893).
——*De Vita Sua*, ed. H. Grégoire, *Byzantion XXIX-XXX* (1959–60), pp 447–475
Pausanias. *Description of Greece*, tr. J.G. Frazer (London, 1898)
Phrantzes (or Sphrantzes), George. *Chronicon Minus* and *Chronicon Maius*, ed. V. Grecu (Bucharest, 1966)
Plethon, George Gemistos. 'Addresses to Manuel II and Theodore Palaeologos', ed. A. Ellissen, *Analekten des Mittel und Neugriechischen Literatur* (Leipzig, 1860)
Plutarch. *Works*, Loeb Classical Library (London and New York, 1928)
Procopius. *Histories*, text and translation by H.B. Dewing, Loeb Classical Library (London, 1914–20). *The Secret History*, tr. G.A. Williamson (London, 1966). *The Buildings*, H.B. Dening (London, 1954)
Sanudo Torsello, Marino. *Istoria del Regno di Romania*, ed. C. Hopf, *Chroniques Gréco-Romanes inédites ou peu connues* (Berlin, 1873, reprint 1966), pp 99–170
Theophanes Continuatus, CHSB (Bonn, 1838)
Timarion, sufferings of, ed. A. Ellissen, *Analekten der Mittel und neugriechischen Literatur* (Leipzig, 1860)
Trois-Fontaines, Aubri des. *Monumenta Germaniae Historica*, Scriptores XXIII (1874)
Valenciennes, Henri de. *Histoire de l'Empereur Henri de Constantinople*, ed. J. Longnon, *Documents relatifs à l'histoire des Croisades* (Paris, 1948)
Villehardouin, Geoffroy de. *La Conquête de Constantinople*. Avec la continuation de Henri de Valenciennes, ed. E. Faral (Paris, 1938–9)
Zosimus. *History*, ed. L. Mendelssohn (Leipzig, 1887)

2. MODERN WORKS
Andrews, K. *Castles of Morea* (Princeton, 1953)
Bodnar, E.W. *Cyriacus of Ancona and Athens*, Collection Latomus XLIII, (Brussels, 1960)
Bon, A. *Le Peloponnèse Byzantin jusqu'en 1204* (Paris, 1951)
——*La Morée Franque* (Paris, 1969)
Browning, R. *Justinian and Theodora* (London, 1971)
Buchon, J.A. *Recherches et Materiaux pour servir à une histoire de la domination française* (Paris, 1840)
——*Recherches historiques sur la Principauté francaise de Morée* (Paris, 1845)

——*Nouvelles recherches historiques sur la Principauté francaise de Morée* (Paris, 1845)

——*Histoire des Conquêtes et de l'Etablissement des Français dans les états de l'ancienne Grece* (Paris, 1846)

Bury, J.B. *A History of the later Roman Empire* (London, 1889)

Byron, R. and Talbot Rice, D. *The Birth of Western Painting* (London, 1930)

Cambridge Mediaeval History, ed. J.M. Hussey (Cambridge, 1966), Vol. IV, esp. chapters VII, VIII & IX

Carmoly, E. *Don Joseph Nasev, Duc de Naxos* (Frankfurt, 1868)

Chambers, D.S. *The Imperial Age of Venice 1380–1580* (London, 1970)

Chapman, C. *Michel Paléologue, restaurateur de l'Empire byzantin* (Paris, 1926)

Charanis, P. *The Chronicle of Monemvasia and the Question of the Slavonic Settlements in Greece*, Dumbarton Oaks Papers V (Washington, 1950), 139–66

Cornelivs Flaminius. *Creta Sacra*, Vols I and II (Venice, 1755)

Diehl, C. *Figures Byzantines* I & II (Paris, 1906 and 1924)

Du Cange, C. de Fresne. *Histoire de l'Empire de Constantinople sous les Empereurs français* (Paris, 1657); ed. Buchon (Paris, 1826)

Fallmerayer, J.P. *Geschichte der Halbinsel Morea wàhrend des Mittelalters*

Finlay, G.A. *A History of Greece from its Conquest by the Romans to the Present Time*, ed. H.J. Tozer III, IV & V (Oxford, 1877).

——*History of the Byzantine Empire 716–1057* (London, Everyman, 1906)

Fotheringham J.K. *Marco Sanudo, Conqueror of the Archipelago* (Oxford, 1915)

Frazer, J.G. *Pausanias's Description of Greece*, translation and commentary (London, 1898).

——*Studies in Greek Scenery, Legend and History* (London, 1931)

Geanakoplos, D.J. *Emperor Michael Palaeologos and the West 1258–82. A Study in Byzantine-Latin Relations* (Cambridge, Mass. 1959).

——*Byzantine East and Latin West. Two Worlds of Christendom in the Middle Ages and Renaissance* (Oxford, 1966)

——*Greek Scholars in Venice* (Cambridge, Mass., 1962)

Gerland, E. *Geschichte des lateinischen Kaiserreiches von Konstantinopel* (Homburg, 1905), Vol II,

——*Neue Quellen zur Geschichte des lateinischen Erzbistums Patras* (Leipzig, 1903)

——'Histoire de la Noblesse Crétoise au Moyen Age,' *Revue de l'Orient Latin* (Paris, 1907), Vols X and XI

——'Kreta als Venezianische Kolonie; *Historisches Jahrbuch* (Munich, 1899), Vol XX, Fasc. 1

——*Das Archiv des Herzogs von Kreta* (Strassburg, 1899)

Gerola, G. *L'Arte Veneta a Creta* (Roma, 1908)

Gibbon, E. *The History of the Decline and Fall of the Roman Empire*, ed. J.B. Bury (London, 1900)

Gregorovius, F. *Geschichte der Stadt Athen im Mittelalter* (Dresden, 1927)

Guilland, R. *Essai sur Nicéphore Grégoras. L'Homme et l'Oeuvre* (Paris, 1926)

——*Correspondence de Nicéphore Grégoras* (Paris, 1927)

Hertzberg, G.F. *Geschichte Griechenlands seit dem Absterben des antiken Lebens-bis zur Gegenwart* II, III (Gotha, 1876–9)

Hopf, K. *Geschichte Griechenlands von Beginn des Mittelalters bis auf unsere zeit,*

Bibliography

in Ersch and Gruber, *Allgemeine Encyclopädie des Wissenschaften und Künste* (Leipzig, 1867–8)

——*Greco-Roman Chronicles* (Berlin, 1873)

Jones, A.H.M. *The Later Roman Empire AD 284–602* (Oxford, 1964)

Krumbacher, K. *Geschichte der byzantinischen Literatur von Justinian bis 3um Ende des oströmischen Reiches* (Munich, 1897)

Lambros, S. *Collection de Romans Grecs* (Paris, 1880)

Lane, J.C. *Venice, a Maritime Republic* (Beltimore, 1973)

Leigh Fermor P. Mani (London, 1958)

——*Roumeli* (London, 1966)

Longnon, J. *L'Empire latin de Constantinople et la Principaüté de Morée* (Paris, 1949)

——*Les Français d'outre-mer au moyen âge ; Essai sur l'expansion française dans le bassin de la Mediterranée* (Paris, 1929)

McNeill, W.H. *Venice, The Hinge of Europe* (Chicago and London, 1974)

Masai, F. *Plethon et le Platonisme de Mistra* (Paris, 1956)

Mayer, E. *Peloponnesiche Wanderungen* (Zurich, 1939)

——*Neue Peloponnesiche Wanderungen* (Berne, 1957)

Miller, W. *The Latins in the Levant. A History of Frankish Greece 1204–1566* (London, 1908)

——*Essays on the Latin Orient* (Cambridge, 1921)

Moncada, F. de. *Expedicion de los Catalanos y Aragoneses contra Turcos y Griegos*, Clasicos Castellanos (Madrid, 1941)

Nicol, D.M. *The Despotate of Epiros* (Oxford, 1957)

——*The Byzantine Family of Kantakouzenos*, Dumbarton Oaks Studies XI (Washington DC, 1968)

——*The Last Centuries of Byzantium* (London, 1972)

Noiret, H. *Documents inédits pour servir à l'histoire de la Domination venitienne en Crète* (Paris, 1892)

Norwich, J.J. *The Kingdom in the Sun, 1130–1194* (London, 1970)

——*Venice, the Rise to Empire* (London, 1977)

Obolensky, D. *The Byzantine Commonwealth; Eastern Europe 500–1453* (London, 1971)

Ostrogorsky, G. *History of the Byzantine State*, tr. Jean Hussey (Oxford, 1956)

Pashley, R. *Travels in Crete* I and II (London, 1837)

Pears, E. *The Destruction of the Greek Empire and the Story of the Capture of Constantinople by the Turks* (London, 1903)

Rodd, R. *The Princes of Achaia and the Chronicles of the Morea* (London, 1907)

Roth, C. *The House of Nasi* (Philadelphia, 1947)

—— *The Duke of Naxos* (Philadelphia, 1946)

Rubio y Lluch, A. *Diplomatari de l'Orient Catala 1301–1409* (Collection of documents for the history of the Catalan expedition to the Levant and of the Duchies of Athens and Neopatras), (Barcelona, 1947). Rubio's special studies and articles on the subject are too numerous to list

Runciman, S. *A History of the Crusades*, Vol III (Cambridge, 1954)

——*The Eastern Schism; A Study of the Papacy and the Eastern Churches during the XIth and XIIth Centuries*, (Oxford, 1955)

——*The Sicilian Vespers* (Cambridge, 1965)

——*The Fall of Constantinople, 1453* (Cambridge, 1965)

——*Byzantine Style and Civilization* (Penguin, 1975)
——*The Emperor Romanus Lecapenus amd his Reign* (Cambridge, 1929)
——*Byzantine Civilisation* (London, 1933)
Schlumberger, G. *Les Principautés franques du Levant* (Paris, 1877)
——*Expeditions des "Almugavares" ou routiers catalans en Orient de l'an 1302 à l'an 1311* (Paris, 1902)
Setton, K.M. *Catalan Domination of Athens, 1311–88* (Cambridge, Mass, 1948)
——*The Latins in Greece and the Aegean from the Fourth Crusade till the end of the Middle Ages*, Cambridge Mediaeval History IV, 1 (1966)
The Papacy in the Levant, 1204–1571, Vol I (Philadelphia, 1976)
Sherrard, P. *The Greek East and the Latin West; A Study in the Christian Tradition* (Oxford, 1959)
Talbot Rice, D. *Art of the Byzantine Era* (London, 1963)
Thiriet, F. *La Romanie Vénitienne aü Moyen Age* (Paris, 1959)
Thompson, H.A. 'Athenian Twilight AD 267–600', *Journal of Roman Studies* (London, 1959), vol xlix, pp 61–72
Topping P.W. *Feudal Institutions as revealed in the Assizes of Romania* (Philadelphia, 1949)
Trypanis, C.A. *Mediaeval and Modern Greek Poetry* (Oxford, 1951)
Vasiliev, A.A. *History of the Byzantine Empire, 324–1453* (Oxford, 1952)
Vlasto, A.P. *The Entry of the Slavs into Christendom* (Cambridge, 1970)
Xanthoudides, S. *The Venetian Domination in Crete* (Athens, 1939) in Greek
Zakynthinos, D.A. *Le Despotat Grec de Morée*, I (Paris, 1932); II (Athens, 1953)
Zinkeisen, J.W. *Geschichte des Osmanischen Reiches*, Vol IV (Gotha, 1856)

Index

Index

Index

Index

Index

Index

Mamonas, 43, 195
Mamonas, Paul, 185
Manolada, 145, 161, 232, 235
Manzikert, 31, 46
Marais, Vincent de, 125
Marathon, 5
Marcellinus, Ammianus, 302
Marcus Aurelius, Emperor, 5
Margounios, Maximos, 296
Maritza river, 83, 172
Marmora, 134, 136, 137, 300
Marzano, Thomas of, 154
Maure, Erard le, 162
Maurice, Emperor, 17, 20, 44
Mavrangoulos, Primikerios, 281
Mavropapas, George, 117
Mazaris, 198–200, 201–2, 303
Medici family, 209
Megalopolis, 6
Megara, 7, 89, 161, 178, 179, 183, 185, 186, 200
Megarid, 59, 78
Megaspelaion, 164
Mehmet I, Sultan, 196, 204, 207
Mehmet II, Sultan, 217, 219, 220, 222, 242, 246, 247–9
Melings, 19, 21, 62, 84, 87
Melissene, Maria, 206, 209, 210
Melissenoi family, 43, 60, 275, 280
Melissenos, Markos, 280; Michael, 279; Theodore, 279
Melos, 224, 229, 243
Menander, 302
Merbaka, 265
Mesarea, 289
Mesopotamia, 192
Messenia, 6, 43, 61–2, 85, 110, 111, 118, 129, 145, 155, 167, 168, 196, 204, 206, 222, 251, 265, 273
Messina, 105, 135, 144
Methone, 24–5, 44
Methone, Nicholas of, 44
Michael III, Emperor, 27
Michieli, Domenico, 292
Miguez, Joao, 254
Mikronas, George, 125; John, 125
Miller, W., viii, 58, 75, 110, 177, 209, 238, 305
Misito family, 162, 171
Mistra, 87, 94, 96, 109, 113, 115–16, 125, 145, 152–4, 160, 163, 170, 173, 176, 178, 182, 187, 191, 196, 197, 199, 200, 205–22 passim, 232, 248, 269, 272, 295
Mithridates, 4
Mnesibulus, 7–8
Mnesicles, 30
Mocenigo, admiral, 249
Modon, 24, 60–1, 67, 86, 109, 163, 172, 182, 190, 191, 193, 196, 206, 228, 247, 249, 250–1, 291, 301
Moesia, 10
Monacis, Laurentius de, 282, 284, 290
Monbel, Guillerme de, 124
Moncada, Francisco de, 136, 137, 141, 304; Matteo de, 171
Monemvasia, 18, 20, 24, 43, 44, 67, 68, 84, 87, 94, 96, 116, 117, 135, 152–3, 155, 163, 185, 191, 195, 205, 207, 212, 221, 222, 228, 232, 234, 247, 249, 250, 252, 287, 289, 301
Mongolia and Mongols, 83, 93, 192
Mons, Hugues de, 70
Montezuma, 135
Montferrat, Boniface de, 49, 55–63, 74, 79, 113, 274; Irene de, 126; Rainer de, 49; Simon de, 92
Montfort, Simon de, 92
Montona, Matteo de, 187

Morea, 61, 63, 65–6, 69, 72, 74, 76, 79, 82, 84–5, 89, 91, 94, 96, 98–9, 101, 103, 105, 107–24 passim, 127, 130, 133, 139, 142, 148, 152–3, 158, 160, 162–3, 166, 174, 181, 183–4, 186, 189, 190, 191, 192, 196, 202, 205, 207, 208, 211, 215–17, 219, 220, 222, 227, 232, 241, 242, 247, 251, 252, 255, 258, 263, 266, 267, 269, 287, 295, 301
Morlay, Guillaume de, 70
Morosini, Francesco, 300–1; Marino, 284
Moslems, 26, 35–6, 52, 56, 71, 76, 135, 144, 170, 185, 192, 220, 274, 275, 295
Mousouroi family, 275
Mousouros, Markos, 296
Mummius, 4
Muntaner, Ramon, 84, 121, 136, 138, 142, 144, 304
Murad I, Sultan, 172, 176, 183, 200, 241
Murad II, Sultan, 204, 208, 210, 215, 216
Mustafa, 204
Mycenae, vii, 71, 212, 218
Mykonos, 118, 142, 224, 244, 245
Mylopotamos, 285, 288
Myriokephalon, 46

Naples, Charles I of, 110–11; Charles II of, 111, 113, 116, 117, 120, 231, 239; Charles III of, 239, 240; Ferdinand of, 250; Joanna of, 167, 171, 173, 239; Ladislaus of, 240, Manfred of, 228; Robert of, 146, 148, 166
Nasi, Joseph, 254–5
Nauplia, 43, 57, 60–1, 65, 67, 68, 78, 81, 94, 107, 111, 143, 147, 163, 164, 182, 190, 196, 206, 217, 219, 244, 247, 249, 250, 252, 283, 293, 301
Naupaktos, 45, 60, 120, 173, 196, 247, 300
Navarino, 117, 145, 196, 205, 206, 222, 247, 249, 250
Navigajoso, 229
Naxos, 80, 117, 133, 142, 145, 168, 224, 227, 228, 231, 232, 243, 253–5, 278, 280, 304
Negroponte, 64, 78, 88, 103, 138, 147, 178, 180, 183, 187, 196–7, 211, 231, 243, 244, 247, 248–9, 250, 265, 295, 301
Nektarios, 296
Neopatras, 44, 81, 102, 111, 118, 126, 133, 139, 147, 148, 157, 185
Nero, Emperor, 4–5
Nicaea, 56, 58, 60, 71, 80, 82, 83, 84, 87, 91–4, 152, 207, 226, 227, 280, 281
Nicol, D.M., 305
Nikephoros I, Emperor, 21
Nikli, 28, 67, 70, 89, 95, 101, 113
Nikopolis, 4, 189, 190, 191, 214, 241, 268
Nivelet, Guy de, 70, 96; Jean de, 101
Nully, Jean de, 70, 95, 96; Marguerite de, 107–8
Nymphaeum, 283

Obolensky, D., 302, 305
Ochrida, 31
Odyssey, 260
Olympia, 6, 11, 97
Omorphi Boskopoulla, 297
Oraiokastron, 117
Orchomenos, 141
Oropos, 209
Orsini, family, 233; Anna, 157, 237; John I, 125, 234, 238; John II, 148, 157, 235–7; Marguerite, 237, 239; Matteo, 228, 233–4; Nicholas, 235–7; Nikephoros, 157–8, 237; Richard, 119, 234–5
Orsova, 189
Orvphas, Niketas, 24–5

338

Index

Index